"*Thomas F. Torrance and Evangelical Theology: A Critical Evaluation* is an important addition to the growing secondary literature on T. F. Torrance's theology. The editors and eleven additional scholars craft the definitive critical conversation between Torrance's Trinitarian perspective and evangelical theology across a spectrum of theology topics. Well-researched and written, the book is a must-read for anyone interested in Torrance's theology and evangelical thought."

Elmer M. Colyer,
professor of systematic theology,
University of Dubuque Theological Seminary

"Between theological rocks and hard places there is T. F. Torrance, who weaves the early Church Fathers, contemporary theologians, and a reverence for Scripture into a coherent, rigorous, and joyful theology. This is a delightful work in which evangelical scholars discuss T. F. Torrance for the sake of the church in fresh ways, always seeking application and transformation. This is theology as doxology at its best."

Julie Canlis,
author of *Calvin's Ladder* and *Theology of the Ordinary*

"Full of complexity, challenge, and the embodied love of God in Christ, these thoughtful, discursive essays are a testament to Torrance and his own desire to bear witness to our Incarnate Lord and to share witness across perspectives, disciplines, and eras. In a day when theological fellowship in unity and difference is hard won, this volume succeeds not by setting up straw men or ideas, wearing down the opposition, or building unstable bridges. Rather, it plates a multicourse feast, harmonizing distinctly acquired theological tastes in new ways that invite some serious chewing and savoring. Enjoy!"

Cherith Fee Nordling,
sessional professor of theology, Regent College

T0366981

"This wide-ranging volume reinforces the view that Torrance is the most important English language theologian of the twentieth century. Central to each chapter in this impressive work are Torrance's evangelical views of Christology, the Trinity, and atonement, and how those doctrines invariably mean good news for all when rightly understood."

Paul D. Molnar,
professor of systematic theology,
St. John's University, New York

"Thomas F. Torrance is arguably one of the most important Anglophone theologians of the twentieth century. His work covers an astonishing range of issues and engages an astounding range of sources and conversation partners (including patristic, Reformation, and modern theology along with modern philosophy and advances in the natural sciences), and it has been formative and foundational for many theologians. His work has, however, been criticized and rejected by some evangelicals, and it has been ignored by many others. This volume offers a set of mature reflections that are appreciative but not uncritical. It will serve both the growing guild of Torrance specialists and the broader evangelical theological community."

Thomas H. McCall,
Timothy C. and Julie M. Tennent Professor of Theology,
Asbury Theological Seminary

THOMAS F. TORRANCE *and* EVANGELICAL THEOLOGY

A Critical Analysis

STUDIES IN HISTORICAL & SYSTEMATIC THEOLOGY

S H S T

THOMAS F. TORRANCE *and* EVANGELICAL THEOLOGY

A *Critical Analysis*

Edited by **MYK HABETS** *and* **R. LUCAS STAMPS**

STUDIES IN HISTORICAL AND SYSTEMATIC THEOLOGY

LEXHAM
ACADEMIC

Thomas F. Torrance and Evangelical Theology: A Critical Analysis
Studies in Historical & Systematic Theology

Lexham Academic, an imprint of Lexham Press
1313 Commercial St., Bellingham, WA 98225
LexhamPress.com

Print ISBN 9781683596936
Digital ISBN 9781683596943
Library of Congress Control Number 2022951703

Lexham Editorial: Todd Hains, Allisyn Ma, Katrina Smith, Jessi Strong, Mandi Newell
Cover Design: Joshua Hunt, Brittany Schrock
Typesetting: Abigail Stocker

CONTENTS

DEDICATION

—

I dedicate this volume to the members of the Thomas F. Torrance Theological Fellowship. The Fellowship is not a society or exclusive club; it is a fellowship. In the true spirit of the name, I have found a warm, receptive, and stimulating group of colleagues, friends, and dialogue partners. Members of the fellowship meet on equal footing and quickly become friends. From time spent on the shores of Loch Tay to late nights in hotel lobbies during ETS and AAR, members of the fellowship have listened to my ideas, sharpened my theology, and provided models of what evangelical academics should be. Thank you. May your tribe increase.

Myk Habets,
Doctor Serviens Ecclesiae
Auckland, New Zealand

I dedicate this book to two men whose name I share: Robert Stamps. To my cousin, Robert Julian Stamps, who was the first bearer of the name to publish on the rich theology of T. F. Torrance. His 2007 volume, *The Sacrament of the Word Made Flesh: The Eucharistic Theology of Thomas F. Torrance*, remains a significant contribution to the field of Torrance studies. And to my father, Robert Eugene Stamps, whose untimely death during the production of this volume casts a dark shadow over its completion, but not without a ray of light. To my knowledge, he never read any Torrance (other than what he read in the footnotes of my published work), but he, along with my mother, was the first to teach me the biblical truths that I find so compelling in Torrance— most notably, the unconditional love of God through the vicarious work of Jesus Christ. My father was embarrassingly proud of everything that I accomplished academically, and, I can't imagine, if I may be so bold, that that fatherly affection has ended in the supernal realms.

Robert Lucas Stamps
Shawnee, Oklahoma

LIST OF CONTRIBUTORS

—

Marc Cortez, PhD, is professor of Theology at Wheaton College. His teaching and writing focus primarily on the nature of the human person and how Jesus informs our understanding of humanity. He is the author of several books in theological anthropology including *Christological Anthropology in Historical Perspective, ReSourcing Theological Anthropology: A Constructive Account of Humanity in the Light of Christ,* and *Theological Anthropology: A Guide for the Perplexed.*

Marty Folsom, PhD, is executive director, Pacific Association for Theological Studies, and Contingent Faculty, Seattle Pacific University, Seattle University, Northwest University, The Seattle School for Theology & Psychology, Trinity Lutheran, and Shiloh University. He is the author of the Face to Face series (Eugene, OR: Wipf & Stock, 2013-2016), and the multivolume *Karl Barth's Church Dogmatics for Everyone* (Grand Rapids: Zondervan Academic).

Myk Habets, PhD, MRSNZ, is senior lecturer in theology and head of the School of Theology at Laidlaw College and has leading researcher status with AUT. He is co-vice president of the Thomas F. Torrance Theological Fellowship, Associate Editor of *Participatio: The Journal of the Thomas Torrance Theological Fellowship,* and past Co-editor of *Journal of Theological Interpretation* (Penn State University Press). He publishes work on constructive systematic theology. His recent work includes editing with Paul Molnar the *T&T Clark Handbook of Thomas F. Torrance* (London: Bloomsbury T&T Clark, 2020), and "Theological Theological Interpretation of Scripture," *IJST* 23 (2021): 235-58. Myk is associate pastor of Albany Baptist Church.

Ross Hastings, PhD, is the Sangwoo Youtong Chee Professor of Theology at Regent College in Vancouver. He earned a PhD in both theology and chemistry. He has recently published *The Resurrection of Jesus Christ* (Baker Academic) and *Theological Ethics* (Zondervan Academic).

Stavan Narendra John, is a PhD candidate at the Oxford Centre for Mission Studies, Middlesex University, and is a faculty-in-training in the Department of Theology and History at the South Asia Institute of Advanced Christian Studies, Bangalore, India. His doctoral thesis focuses on Thomas F. Torrance's theology of the ascension. His theological interests lie in the areas of Christology, ecclesiology, systematic theology, and evangelical theology.

Peter K. W. McGhee, PhD, is senior lecturer and deputy head of the Department of Management at AUT University Business, Economics and Law School. His expertise and research interests lie in business ethics, workplace spirituality, sustainability, and critical management studies; his recent work focuses on ethical leadership, human quality treatment at work, educating for sustainability, and the theology of work. Peter is widely published in a range of esteemed business, ethics, and sustainability journals including "Faith & Organizational Ethics," in E. Pio and R. Kilpatrick, ed., *Reimagining Faith and Management: The Impact of Faith in the Workplace* (Abingdon: Routledge, 2021), 77–89; and with P. Grant, "Hedonic Versus (True) Eudaimonic Well-Being in Organizations," in D. Satinder, ed., *The Palgrave Handbook of Workplace Well-Being* (Cham, Switzerland: Springer, 2021), 925–43.

Andrew T. B. McGowan, PhD, is director of the Rutherford Centre for Reformed Theology and Professor of Theology in the University of the Highlands and Islands. He is vice chairman of the World Reformed Fellowship and serves as chairman of its Theological Commission. He is president of the Scottish Evangelical Theology Society and is a member of the Tyndale Fellowship. His publications include *The Divine Inspiration of Scripture* (London: Apollos, 2007).

Thomas A. Noble, PhD, is research professor of theology at Nazarene Theological Seminary in Kansas City, Missouri, and a senior research fellow at Nazarene Theological College, Manchester. His publications include *Tyndale House and Fellowship: The First Sixty Years* (2006) and *Holy Trinity: Holy People: The Theology of Christian Perfecting* (2013). He has coedited several books including the second edition of the *IVP New Dictionary of Theology* and chairs the Christian Doctrine study group of the Tyndale Fellowship.

Jenny Richards, LLB, is lecturer in law at the College of Business Government and Law at Flinders University in South Australia, and Barrister and Solicitor at Old Port Chambers, Port Adelaide. She works predominantly in criminal law, social work law, and legal theory. She is currently writing a PhD dissertation on holistic criminal justice responses to violence against Christian women using the theology of T. F. Torrance and J. B. Torrance.

Fred Sanders, PhD, is professor of theology in the Torrey Honors College at Biola University. He writes mainly on the doctrine of the Trinity. He is the author of *The Deep Things of God: How the Trinity Changes Everything*, The *Triune God* in the New Studies in Dogmatics series, and *Fountain of Salvation: Trinity and Soteriology.*

R. Lucas Stamps, PhD, is chair of the Hobbs School of Theology and Ministry and professor of biblical and theological studies at Oklahoma Baptist University in Shawnee, Oklahoma. He is the author of the forthcoming *Thy Will Be Done: A Dogmatic Defense of Two Wills Christology*, which examines, in part, the Christology of T. F. Torrance. He also serves on the board of directors for the Center for Baptist Renewal.

Jerome Van Kuiken, PhD, is professor of Christian thought and dean of the School of Ministry and Christian Thought at Oklahoma Wesleyan University. He is a member of the executive committee of the Thomas F. Torrance Theological Fellowship and an associate editor of *Participatio: The Journal of the Thomas Torrance Theological Fellowship*. His recent work includes co-editing *Methodist Christology: From the Wesleys to the Twenty-first Century* (Nashville: Wesley's Foundery, 2020) and contributing to the *T&T Clark Handbook of Thomas F. Torrance* (London: Bloomsbury T&T Clark, 2020).

Jonathan Warren P. (Pagán), PhD, is an Anglican priest serving at Resurrection Anglican Church in Austin, Texas. He is the author of *Giles Firmin and the Transatlantic Puritan Tradition: Polity, Piety, and Polemic* (Leiden: Brill, 2019) as well as, most recently, an essay tracing the reception of the book of Job in early modern Europe.

Christopher Woznicki, PhD, is adjunct assistant professor in theology at Fuller Theological Seminary. He works for Young Life in Los Angeles as a ministerial staff trainer. His research has been published in *Journal of Reformed Theology, Philosophia Christi*, and *Scottish Bulletin of Evangelical Theology*. Chris is author of *T. F. Torrance's Christological Anthropology: Discerning Humanity in Christ* (Routledge, 2022).

Geordie Ziegler, PhD, is an ordained presbyterian (PCUSA) minister, and holds a PhD in theology from the University of Aberdeen, Scotland, and an MDiv from Regent College in Vancouver, B.C. He is the author of *Trinitarian Grace and Participation: An Entry into the Theology of T. F. Torrance* (Fortress, 2017).

FOREWORD

—

After relating one of the startling stories about the zealous exploits of Francis of Assisi, his biographer Bonaventure remarked that some things the saint did were "easier admired than imitated." The theology of T. F. Torrance poses a similar question to evangelical theologians today: To what extent is he to be merely admired, and to what extent ought he to be imitated?

Readers picking up a book like this one are probably already fully aware that T. F. Torrance is a deeply admirable theological figure. Torrance's most characteristic work looms up out of its late twentieth-century context in a striking manner, unique in several ways. From his earliest works he wrote from a strong commitment to a kind of realism about how theological language actually refers to divine realities. He requisitioned all sorts of resources from the philosophy of science to describe how this was the case. Even when his account of the implications of those resources seemed a bit idiosyncratic to most of his readers, it was impossible to deny that he worked from an unusually high level of confidence that theology could speak the truth. When Torrance described the central doctrinal affirmations of Christian faith, he wrote exactly like somebody who has a steady vision of something real and solid, an object of inquiry that was giving off definite impressions that its student was recording on paper.

As a result of working out of this realism, Torrance had a lot to say about the great, objective Christian doctrines. With few exceptions, what he had to say took the form of expansive commentary on authoritative texts from the tradition. Above all, there was the Nicene Creed, to which he returned time after time, never quite repeating himself but always demonstrating the Creed's fruitfulness as a renewable source of insight into the realities of God and salvation. Compared with what other theologians were producing during these same decades, Torrance's work seems uniquely focused on creedal exposition. But nearly all his work was driven by exposition, whether it was "depth exegesis" of Scripture or the tracing of trajectories through theological histories. In service to this vision of how theology ought to be done, Torrance even developed a distinctive writing style. A stereotypical page of T. F. Torrance theology is easily recognizable: it alternates between authoritative block quotations, analytically precise conceptual paraphrase, long strings of Greek in its own font, and an incantatory descriptive pattern, circling around central ideas. He believed in a Polanyian epistemology of indwelling the tradition, and it was that style of cognitive indwelling that found its way into a corresponding literary style of production. In an academic theological culture that tends to reward novelty and critique, Torrance set himself to retrieval and commentary. Paradoxically, this made his work novel, gave him a steady stream of new things to say, and positioned him to make critical interventions into the direction of modern theology. In retrieving the emphases of important figures from the Christian theological tradition, we can say Torrance knew his ABCs: Athanasius, Barth, and Calvin. But this trio of major influences is just the most prominent subset of a vast cast of characters.

And this is probably the hinge point where those who admire his theology are also bound to take the next step to imitating him in some regard. T. F. Torrance's habit of writing constructive theology by means of retrieval meant that in all his work he was constantly pointing readers to larger figures behind him. There is simply no way of construing his main claims without coming to terms with the tradition of these other figures. He made himself a kind of gateway into the great resources of Christian doctrine. You read a few pages of Torrance and come away with ideas from Irenaeus, Nazianzus, Epiphanius, and more.

Of course each of these figures is famously inflected in a Torrantian way. Appreciative readers of Torrance quickly learn that when they turn excitedly to his sources they are likely to discover that Torrance has described those sources in some characteristic ways. Critical thinkers quickly learn to distinguish between Athanasius simpliciter and Athanasius kata Torrance; between what can responsibly be affirmed about the history of theology itself, and what can be said about Torrance's creative reading of it. The adjustment is simple enough, and the result is enriching. We now have not only the classic texts, but Torrance's creative reading of them as well. What expands and deepens in the meantime is the theological insight into the doctrinal foundation of Christian faith. And that deepening of the Christian frame of mind was always the goal of T. F. Torrance's instruction.

The theology of T. F. Torrance is, in other words, an ideal dialogue partner for the kind of evangelical theology that is serious about the central matters of the Christian faith. This collection of essays strikes an excellent balance between broad-minded exploration of theological horizons and the particular urgencies of evangelical commitment. The result is a helpfully focused examination of the extent to which T. F. Torrance is to be admired, and the extent to which he is to be imitated by contemporary evangelical theology. The relative proportions of these answers vary from doctrine to doctrine, and are subject to the judgments of the relevant experts in these pages. But broadly speaking, the book showcases how his theological legacy calls for both admiration and imitation.

Fred Sanders
Torrey Honors College, Biola University

INTRODUCTION

—

TORRANCE AND EVANGELICAL THEOLOGY IN CONVERSATION

Myk Habets and R. Lucas Stamps

Thomas Forsyth Torrance (1913-2007) was arguably the most important English language theologian of the twentieth century.[1] Born in Chengdu, China, to missionary parents, Torrance would become one of the most important figures in the Church of Scotland, publishing voluminously, especially from his longtime professoriate at New College, University of Edinburgh. Torrance's theology represents a creative fusion of theological influences both ancient and modern and both Eastern and Western. Torrance drew upon a wide range of sources from Athanasius to Karl Barth (with whom he completed postgraduate studies at Basel), and from John Calvin to Michael Polanyi. Recent years have witnessed a growing interest in the theology of Torrance but his exposure in the evangelical world remains relatively subdued. This book aims to bring Torrance into closer conversation with evangelical theology on a range of important theological loci. This introduction sets the stage for the discussion by briefly considering the broad theological commitments of both dialogue partners: evangelical theology and Torrance himself.

---

1. See Brian Hebblethwaite, "Review of T. F. Torrance: An Intellectual Biography," *Scottish Journal of Theology* 53 (2000): 239-40, and Myk Habets, *Theology in Transposition: A Constructive Appraisal of T. F. Torrance* (Minneapolis: Fortress Press Academic, 2013), 3-22.

EVANGELICAL THEOLOGY

As to evangelicalism, many wonder whether the term has outlived its useful-ness. In a North American context, "evangelical" is widely seen as a political identifier, not a set of theological distinctives. Matters are further compli-cated—better: enriched!—by the fact that evangelicalism is now a global phenomenon and not limited to the Anglo-American contexts in which it originally developed.[2] As an added complication, one could argue that the term may not even be exclusively Protestant, with some Roman Catholics adopting the descriptor as well.[3] Despite these legitimate qualifications, it is our contention that the term "evangelical" still captures something theo-logically significant and, therefore, should not be rejected. Evangelicalism has a rich heritage and an enduring power to capture a distinctive theolog-ical agenda.

The history of evangelicalism is well-documented, and this is not the place to rehearse every detail.[4] Suffice it to say, evangelicalism's theological roots branch out in several directions. Its taproot, we might say, is the six-teenth-century Protestant Reformation, but it has been nourished as well by the influence of pietism, Puritanism, the modern missions movement, and especially the Great Awakenings of the eighteenth and nineteenth centuries. The current trajectories of evangelicalism have also been definitively shaped by the so-called neo-evangelical movement in the post–World War II era (led by Carl Henry and Billy Graham, among others) that sought to distance evan-gelicalism from a more culturally quietistic and adversarial fundamentalism (see chapter 4). The movement has now gone global, with some arguing that the center of gravity is no longer in the West but in the majority world.[5]

It is by now a well-worn path to summarize the theological commitments of evangelicalism along the lines of the famous quadrilateral suggested by

---

2. Philip Jenkins, *The Next Christendom: The Coming of Global Christianity*, 3rd ed. (Oxford: Oxford University Press, 2011).

3. For example, see Edward T. Oakes, S. J., *Infinity Dwindled to Infancy: A Catholic and Evangelical Christology* (Grand Rapids: Eerdmans, 2011).

4. For an entryway into the voluminous literature on this topic, see Andrew Atherstone and David Ceri Jones, eds., *The Routledge Research Companion to the History of Evangelicalism* (London: Routledge, 2019). See also the volumes in IVP's History of Evangelicalism Series, edited by David W. Bebbington and Mark A. Noll.

5. In addition to Jenkins, see also Soong-Chan Rah, *The Next Evangelicalism: Freeing the Church from Western Cultural Captivity* (Downers Grove, IL: InterVarsity, 2009).

evangelical Baptist historian, David Bebbington. Bebbington suggests that four characteristics have especially marked the evangelical movement: "*conversionism*, the belief that lives need to be changed; *activism*, the expression of the gospel in effort; *biblicism*, a particular regard for the Bible; and what may be called *crucicentrism*, a stress on the sacrifice of Christ on the cross. Together they form a quadrilateral of priorities that is the basis of Evangelicalism."[6] This list of emphases is far from exhaustive, and evangelical theologians and historians may want to supplement it.[7] Still, it remains a helpful rubric, at least as a starting point, for understanding the unique cocktail of doctrines that have shaped the evangelical movement. Evangelicalism takes its name from the *evangel*—the gospel, the good news. So, we might say that evangelicals are gospel people: those who emphasize the good news of salvation (understood in Protestant terms), the necessity of personal conversion that it demands, and the life of holiness and mission that flow from it. The authors in this volume represent the wide geographical spread of evangelicalism—ranging from New Zealand to India, and Britain to North America—but each is committed to these broad theological parameters. There are diverse views represented here, to be sure. The authors do not agree on every doctrinal point nor even on every disputed issue in the interpretation and appropriation of Torrance's work. But for each there is a general identification with the global evangelical movement as stated.

THE THEOLOGY OF TORRANCE

This volume offers an evangelical engagement with some of the major themes in the theology of Torrance. The book aims not so much to provide a comprehensive introduction to Torrance's thought as to explore some of the promises and perils of his impressive theological project from the perspective of evangelical theology (addressed directly in chapter 1). Most of the standard *loci communes* (common places) of Christian systematic theology are addressed, as are other important aspects of Torrance's methodology and historiography. This introduction certainly cannot adequately capture the whole of Torrance's rich and multi-layered theological program, but a few

---

6. David W. Bebbington, *Evangelicalism in Modern Britain: A History from the 1730s to the 1980s* (London: Routledge, 1989), 2–3.

7. For a recent assessment of the evangelical movement, see Thomas S. Kidd, *Who Is an Evangelical? The History of a Movement in Crisis* (New Haven: Yale University Press, 2019).

distinctive and interrelated themes may highlight the important ways his theology interfaces with evangelicalism. No claim is made that these are the most important or the central motifs in Torrance's theology. Indeed, they are somewhat arbitrarily chosen but are, we believe, representative of Torrance's significance for evangelical engagement. Perhaps these will whet the appetite of the reader to explore more in the chapters that follow. While Torrance obviously did not explicitly work within the categories of Bebbington's quadrilateral, it may be helpful to use this rubric as an organizing principle as we bring our dialogue partners into conversation.

CONVERSIONISM

While critical of forms of holiness and pietistic altar calls and crisis moments of faith, Torrance's theology can be seen to be in sympathy with the evangelical emphasis on conversionism, if by that term is meant, not a focus on technique (Charles Finney et al.) but the need for a personal response to the gospel. In Torrance's hands, conversion is first of all realized by the incarnate Son and only then is it a reality in the life of the believer. Torrance thus emphasizes something called "the vicarious humanity of Christ."

One of the richest themes in Torrance's theology is his understanding of Christ's vicarious humanity and ministry. Christology was a central theme for Torrance's theology. A certain Christocentrism marks all that Torrance touches, from the doctrine of the Trinity to the divinization of humanity in the eschaton (*theosis*, addressed in chapter 11). And at the heart of Torrance's Christology is a tight connection between the person and the work of Christ, that is, between the incarnation and atonement. These two are really one doctrine in Torrance's thought. Building on Calvin's emphasis on "the whole course" of Christ's obedience, Torrance stresses that Christ began his work of atonement (that is, reconciliation) from the moment he was conceived in the womb of the Virgin Mary. Humanity is saved not only by Christ's passive obedience (his suffering and death) but also by his active obedience (his whole life of obedience). For Torrance, this means that every step in Christ's journey is vicarious. Torrance ascribes to Christ a vicarious faith, a vicarious obedience, and even a *vicarious repentance* (not in terms of any personal sin but in terms of his identification with sinners, especially expressed in his baptism). And under all these aspects of Christ's work stands his vicarious humanity itself. Self-consciously building on patristic and Eastern influences, Torrance emphasizes the saving significance of the incarnation (see chapter 9). By taking a concrete human nature into personal union with himself, the eternal Son already effects the reconciliation between God and man. There are universal implications of this doctrine that remain a matter of debate, but the richness of this theme provides fertile ground for evangelical consideration.

ACTIVISM

Dogmatics was not merely a theoretical exercise for Torrance. Rather, dogmatics is the bringing of the human person under the full control of the Triune God in order to be drawn up into worship, out into ministry, and deep into acts of Christian witness. Torrance's Christianity is an active one, which models, in many ways, the evangelical activism Bebbington identified in his historical work. For Torrance, this means the rejection of all invented dualisms that would justify an inactive faith. Torrance calls such dualisms *the Latin heresy*.

Related to the notion of Christ's vicarious humanity is the critique that Torrance levels against what he calls the "Latin heresy." For Torrance, the Western Christian tradition, especially under Augustine's influence, has held to a gospel of *extrinsicism*, where Christ's humanity is seen as something external to God's own life and where Christ himself is seen as something external to the humanity that he came to save. In this understanding, the incarnation is merely a prerequisite to the atonement, rather than constitutive of it. And Christ's work is seen in transactional (especially forensic) rather than participatory terms. Torrance sees in the Greek Fathers a more thorough integration of incarnation and atonement that avoids this so-called heresy. Torrance's historical generalizations are certainly open to critique, but his theological insights on these matters are nonetheless worthy of evangelical consideration. When the Latin heresy is avoided, so too are those theologies that would argue for an activism based upon a works-based righteousness (Pelagianism), or those that argue for an inactive form of quietism. Both fall short of an evangelical theology. The addition of essays on work (chapter 13), justice and domestic violence (chapter 12), and personal relationships (chapters 7 and 11) is ample evidence of this.

CRUCICENTRISM

The emphasis on the cross of Christ is often thought to be missing in Torrance, but that is a mistake. Torrance does bring incarnation and atonement together, but not at the expense of the cross. An important theme in Torrance's theology of atonement is *the fallen flesh of Christ*. One implication of the Latin heresy, for Torrance, is a tendency in Western theology to deny Christ's participation in our concrete humanity in all of its fallenness and misery. Following Edward Irving and Karl Barth, Torrance maintains that Christ assumed a fallen human nature (though he differs with Irving especially in some important ways). Christ himself is sinless, but he assumes humanity in its fallen state in order to heal it and bend it back to God from within. This is perhaps the most controversial aspect of Torrance's theology from an evangelical perspective, and much ink has been spilled trying to position it biblically, historically, and theologically. One of the leading voices in these debates, Jerome van Kuiken, weighs in on the issue in chapter 10 of this book. The cross is the climax of the work of Christ; it is the most intense moment of the incarnation and is the supreme example of his vicarious ministry. At the cross, Torrance argues, Christ meets and triumphs over sin, evil, and death. This is confirmed in the resurrection and sealed at Pentecost.

BIBLICISM

All his life Torrance held Holy Scripture in high regard as the Word of God. His personal devotional life consisted of reading the Bible daily and reading through the entire Bible annually. Hundreds of sermons by Torrance survive, all displaying what today we might call an expositional style, centered on a single text of Scripture applied to the congregation. Torrance was insistent that the way to hear the voice of God was through Scripture, and he devoted his life to its dogmatic exposition. At times Torrance followed the path of his mentor Karl Barth and found himself off-side with certain evangelical sensitivities regarding the nature of Scripture (see chapter 3); but he was often equally off-side with liberals who thought him too conservative, too biblicist, and too evangelical.

Again, these themes are selective, and while they are not the terms Torrance would likely have chosen, they are representative of key aspects of his thought. Torrance's theology is deeply grounded in Scripture and tradition, but he often synthesizes those source materials in creative and

controversial ways, as the essays in this book demonstrate. Rather than pre-
view each of the book's chapters, we invite readers to peruse the table of
contents and begin wherever they feel most provoked! However, Thomas
Noble's opening biographical essay would be an obvious choice to begin with,
since it sketches Torrance's life from the unique perspective of his interaction with evangelicalism. It is our hope and prayer that these essays would
send readers back to Torrance's own works, where they will find plenty to
challenge and confront but also much to comfort and cheer. To that end, we
close with these stirring words of evangelical hope from Torrance himself:

> God loves you so utterly and completely that he has given himself
> for you in Jesus Christ his beloved Son, and has thereby pledged his
> very being as God for your salvation. In Jesus Christ God has actual-
> ised his unconditional love for you in your human nature in such a
> once for all way, that he cannot go back upon it without undoing the
> Incarnation and the Cross and thereby denying himself. Jesus Christ
> died for you precisely because you are sinful and utterly unworthy
> of him, and has thereby already made you his own before and apart
> from your ever believing in him. He has bound you to himself by his
> love in a way that he will never let you go, for even if you refuse him
> and damn yourself in hell, his love will never cease. Therefore, repent
> and believe in Jesus Christ as your Lord and Saviour.[8]

---

8. Thomas F. Torrance, *The Mediation of Christ* (Edinburgh: T&T Clark, 1992), 94. The notion
of God's love continuing even for those in hell could imply a kind of universalism, which many
evangelicals would want to reject. At the least, it implies a universal atonement, which Torrance
explicitly affirmed. One need not follow Torrance on either account in order to appreciate the
overall thrust of his homiletical flourish in this evocative passage.

1

—

THOMAS F. TORRANCE AND
THE EVANGELICAL TRADITION

Thomas A. Noble

Thomas F. Torrance was born into a missionary family in Chengdu in the Sichuan province of western China on August 30, 1913. His first visit to Scotland was in 1920–1921 when his parents, Thomas and Annie Torrance, were on furlough, and he returned to Scotland with his family in 1927 to live there for the majority of his life. A biographical sketch of his early life beginning with his heritage from his missionary parents and their evangelical faith will therefore give us a key insight into T. F. Torrance's relation to the evangelical tradition and to evangelical theology. His years as professor of Christian dogmatics at New College, Edinburgh and his final decades as a leading theologian can then be seen against the background of the developments in the evangelical tradition in the late twentieth century.

EVANGELICAL MISSIONS

Kenneth Scott Latourette called the nineteenth century "the great century" of missionary expansion. What is particularly relevant here is to note that the advance of foreign missions throughout the century was rooted in the eighteenth-century Evangelical Revival. Methodist missions began as early as 1786 with the blessing of John Wesley when Thomas Coke and three other missionaries landed in Antigua in the Leeward Islands. William Carey founded the Baptist Missionary Society in 1792 and left for Calcutta the next year. The London Missionary Society, formed in 1795, was supported mainly by Nonconformists. The Church Missionary Society was founded in 1799, led by the evangelical Members of Parliament, Henry Thornton and William

Wilberforce, and was supported by Charles Simeon, vicar of Holy Trinity and Fellow of King's College, Cambridge. Simeon's curate, Henry Martyn, went to India as the first Anglican missionary in 1806.

Thomas Chalmers, the leader of the Evangelical party in the Church of Scotland, eventually persuaded the General Assembly to support foreign missions, and their first missionary, Alexander Duff, arrived in India in 1830. When Chalmers led the evangelicals out of the national church to form the Free Church of Scotland at the Disruption in 1843, all the church's missionaries except one became missionaries of the Free Church. They quite clearly identified with the evangelical tradition. In the middle of the nineteenth century, a new passion for foreign missions was stimulated by the fame of David Livingstone and led to the faith missions, the first of which was Hudson Taylor's China Inland Mission, founded in 1865.

Twenty years later, there were new developments with numbers of young university graduates volunteering for missionary service for the first time. Something of a sensation was caused by the commitment of the Cambridge Seven, led by the cricketer, C. T. Studd, who sailed for China with the China Inland Mission in 1885. This followed a mission to Cambridge University led by the American evangelist, D. L. Moody, at the invitation of the Cambridge Intercollegiate Christian Union (CICCU). Studd's brother, J. E. Kynaston Studd, who had been president of CICCU, undertook a speaking tour of American colleges at the invitation of Moody. As a result of that, the Student Volunteer Movement was launched. Led by Robert Wilder and J. R. Mott, it adopted the famous watchword, "The evangelization of the world in this generation." The Student Volunteer Missionary Union was formed in the United Kingdom in 1892 at a conference in which three of the four Scottish universities were represented. The World Student Christian Federation was formed in 1895.[1]

AN EVANGELICAL FAMILY

It was the same year, 1895, that Thomas Torrance went to China with the China Inland Mission (CIM), arriving in January 1896. He was clearly part of that generation of evangelical students who took the watchword as their

---

1. See Oliver Barclay and Robert Horn, *From Cambridge to the World* (Leicester: IVP, 2002); see also David W. Bebbington, *Evangelicalism in Modern Britain: A History from the 1730s to the 1980s* (London: Unwin Hyman, 1989).

guide and consecrated their lives to the evangelization of the world. Although his family belonged to the established Church of Scotland (the Auld Kirk), which had no missionaries, he was converted through a Free Church minister and with his conversion came a call to the mission field. He prepared for missions at Hulme Cliff College in Derbyshire (later Cliff College, the Methodist college for evangelists). Two cousins whose branches of the Torrance family belonged to the Free Kirk, served as missionaries, one as a doctor at Tiberias in Palestine and one in India. After language study in Shanghai, Thomas Torrance was placed by the CIM in Chengdu in the province of Sichuan in western China.

The same evangelical commitment is seen in the English missionary who became his wife, Annie Elizabeth Sharpe. The youngest son of their family, David W. Torrance, writes this in his memoirs, "My mother was also converted in her teen years and, with her conversion felt the call to mission and evangelism. Soon she felt the call to Overseas Missions and to China. She studied at Redcliffe College, Chelsea and then in the CIM Mission's Training Home at Grove Park, London."[2] In 1910, Thomas Torrance resigned from the CIM and returned to Scotland in time for the World Missionary Conference in Edinburgh. This was inspired by the Student Volunteer Movement and chaired by one of its leaders, J. R. Mott. Torrance returned to China the following year as a superintendent of the American Bible Society based once again in Chengdu, later adding to that further work as a superintendent of the British and Foreign Bible Society. In 1911, he married Annie Sharpe. David Torrance recalls:

> In his new post Father was his own master and had the freedom to be the pioneer missionary that he was. He worked tirelessly preaching and, with his Chinese colporteur helpers, distributing Bibles and portions of Scripture. He wrote many of his own Gospel tracts and never, as my mother used to say, lost an opportunity to preach the Gospel.

Until the end of his life he was a passionate evangelist. He carried gospel tracts in his pocket and where possible he never lost an opportunity to witness to Christ.[3]

---

2. David W. Torrance, *The Reluctant Minister* (Haddington: Handsel Press, 2015), 6.

3. D. W. Torrance, *The Reluctant Minister*, 3 and 5.

Six children were born to the missionary couple. The eldest, Mary, was born in Shanghai, where missionary wives and children had gone because of the unrest following the revolt of Sun Yat-Sen against the Chinese imperial government. Thomas Forsyth Torrance was born back in Chengdu, followed by two more girls, Grace and Margaret, and two boys, James and David, over the next decade.[4]

The family had a fully evangelical devotional life. The children took part in family prayers and also prayed individually with one of their parents. They were taught to read through the Bible each year by reading three chapters every day and five on a Sunday. David Torrance recalled the way in which they were nurtured in their faith by their parents:

> They always emphasized that the Christian life involved a personal relationship with a living Lord. Mother often spoke of the person of the Lord Jesus as someone who was living and alive, someone whom we can meet and know personally and who wanted day by day to speak to us and calls us to obey him. The Christian faith was not just something to be understood intellectually. It is something living and alive and something which the youngest child can relate to and something which relates to our everyday living. For this personal emphasis I have always been deeply grateful to my parents.[5]

He also emphasized the role which the Bible played in their evangelical Christian upbringing: "My parents also stressed the importance of listening to and knowing God's Word." He explains:

> Mother also encouraged me and the others of the family always to pray each time we opened the Bible before reading. We were encouraged to ask the Lord to speak personally to us. She said, which I never forget, that when we grew up we would find that many people would deny that the Bible was God's Word or would say many wrong things about it and deny its inspiration, but if we heard God speaking to us through the Bible and through the passage which we were reading, then we would know that the Bible is God's Word and we would never

---

4. Alister E. McGrath, *T. F. Torrance: An Intellectual Biography* (Edinburgh: T&T Clark, 1999), 12–13. See McGrath for many of the biographical details in this chapter.

5. D. W. Torrance, *The Reluctant Minister*, 7.

doubt it. I, and I think others of the family, were never given any theory about Scripture or its inspiration. We were simply told that it was God's Word and that God spoke to us through it.[6]

T. F. Torrance himself recounted the strong belief in God with which he was imbued from his earliest days: "Moreover, as long as I can recall my religious outlook was essentially biblical and evangelical, and indeed evangelistic." He recalled the habit of daily Bible reading and his father's memorization of Psalms and Romans: "Family prayers led by my father on his knees and the evangelical hymns he taught us nourished our spiritual understanding and growth in faith. I can still repeat in Chinese, 'Jesus loves me, this I know; for the Bible tells me so.' " He was deeply conscious of the task to which his parents had been called by God to preach the gospel and win people to Christ: "This orientation to mission was built into the fabric of my mind, and has never faded—by its essential nature Christian theology has always had for me an evangelistic thrust."[7]

In 1927, missionary families were leaving China because of the unrest and civil war. The Torrances returned to Scotland, finding a home in Bellshill in North Lanarkshire, east of Glasgow and not far from Shotts where Thomas Torrance had grown up. But Thomas Torrance felt that his work in China was not finished. Together, he and his wife made the decision that he would return to Chengdu for the standard missionary term of seven years while she brought up the family alone. This was the kind of commitment evidenced again and again by evangelical missionaries. The ringing words of C. T. Studd inspired that whole generation: "If Jesus Christ be God and died for me, then no sacrifice can be too great for me to make for him."[8]

Their son, Thomas F. Torrance, was fourteen when the family went to live in Bellshill, and he enrolled in Bellshill Academy. Instead of attending the parish church of the Church of Scotland, Annie Torrance took her six children to the Baptist Church, where she could be sure of an evangelical

---

6. D. W. Torrance, *The Reluctant Minister*, 9.

7. Thomas F. Torrance, *"Itinerarium mentis in Deum,"* 1, quoted in McGrath, *T. F. Torrance*, 13.

8. No good critical biography of Studd has ever been written, but see Norman Grubb, *C. T. Studd: Cricketer and Pioneer* (Fort Washington, PA: CLC, 2008), originally published in 1933, and the article on Studd in the *Biographical Dictionary of Evangelicals*, ed. Timothy Larsen (Downers Grove, IL: InterVarsity Press, 2015), 648–49.

ministry. It was at a prayer meeting there that she requested prayer for her husband in China, and later she learned that at that very moment communist soldiers who were hunting for him had searched every house in a village except the one where he was.[9]

It is quite clear that T. F. Torrance was brought up in a deeply evangelical family. His parents lived with a personal faith in Christ, were committed to the Great Commission, lived a life of prayer, and shaped their lives according to the Scriptures which they believed to be the inspired Word of God. All six children were brought up to share in that living active faith, and their eldest son, Thomas F. Torrance, committed himself from childhood to evangelism and to missions.

THE EVANGELICAL STUDENT

In 1931, when her eldest son began his studies at the University of Edinburgh, Annie Torrance moved her family to the city. He specialized in classics and philosophy in his studies for the master of arts (MA) degree, a requirement for beginning theological studies in the divinity faculty for the more advanced degree of bachelor of divinity (BD). Two years previously, in 1929, the United Free Church (already a union of the majority in the Free Church with the United Presbyterians) had united with the established church to form, once again, one national church of Scotland. New College, the U. F. theological college in Edinburgh, united with the faculty of divinity in the university, and the combined faculty inhabited the New College building perched dramatically on the castle rock overlooking Princes Street. The evangelical tradition of the United Free Church was well represented, therefore, in Torrance's teachers.

That tradition had gone through some difficult years in the late nineteenth century over the issue of higher criticism, but in the early twentieth century, its dominant theologians took a clearly evangelical position (though no longer that of traditional Calvinism) but rejected the obscurantism that completely denied the validity of historical and literary criticism of the Bible. The outstanding theologians in the Scottish evangelical tradition at the turn of the century were James Orr, James Denney of Glasgow, and the Congregationalist, P. T. Forsyth, who were all deeply committed to a theology

---

9. D. W. Torrance, *The Reluctant Minister*, 8.

focused on "Christ crucified."[10] It is important to understand however, that while they remained in the Reformed tradition, broadly in the tradition of Calvin, they did not fully espouse the theology of the Westminster Confession. That remained the official confession of faith in the Scottish Presbyterian churches, but ministers were allowed to hold reservations on matters not entering into "the substance of the faith." By the last decades of the nineteenth century, the influence of John McLeod Campbell and others meant that none of these leading theologians held, for example, to the Federal Calvinist doctrine of particular redemption or limited atonement—that Christ did not die for all, but only for the elect. And while they held to the inspiration and authority of the Scriptures, they did not subscribe to the doctrine defended by the American Calvinist tradition of nineteenth-century Princeton—that the Scriptures were inerrant.[11]

This great generation of Scottish theologians had however passed away before Torrance's time. Orr had died in 1913, Denney in 1918, and Forsyth in 1921, but at New College, H. R. Mackintosh was professor of Christian dogmatics, and Daniel Lamont was professor of apologetics and pastoral theology. T. F. Torrance was to be deeply influenced by them both—Mackintosh as a theologian, and Lamont for his interest in the relationship between theology and science. Like Denney and Forsyth, Mackintosh had been influenced while a student in Germany by the dominant school of Ritschlian liberalism, but like them, he had returned in his mature years to evangelical theology.[12]

---

10. See James Orr, *Revelation and Inspiration* (London: Duckworth, 1910). On Orr, see Glen G. Scorgie, *A Call for Continuity: The Theological Contribution of James Orr* (Vancouver: Regent College Publishing, 2004), also Andrew T. B. McGowan, "James Orr," in *British Evangelical Theologians of the Twentieth Century*, ed. Thomas A. Noble and Jason S. Sexton (London: Apollos, 2022), 11–32; on Denney, see James M. Gordon, *James Denney (1856–1917): An Intellectual and Contextual Biography* (Milton Keynes: Paternoster, 2006), also Thomas V. Findlay, "James Denney," in *British Evangelical Theologians of the Twentieth Century*, 33–50; on Forsyth, see Trevor A. Hart, ed., *Justice the True and Only Mercy: Essays on the Life and Theology of Peter Taylor Forsyth* (Edinburgh: T&T Clark, 1995); also Trevor Hart, "Peter Taylor Forsyth," in *British Evangelical Theologians of the Twentieth Century*, 51–70.

11. For Orr's position on the inspiration of Scripture and its difference from the American tradition of Hodge and Warfield, see Andrew T. B. McGowan, *The Divine Spiration of Scripture: Challenging Evangelical Perspectives* (Leicester: Apollos, 2007).

12. For a fuller examination of Torrance's relation to the Scottish Reformed tradition, see David Fergusson, "Thomas F. Torrance as a Scottish Theologian," in *T&T Clark Handbook of Thomas F. Torrance*, ed. Paul D. Molnar and Myk Habets (London: Bloomsbury T&T Clark, 2020), 37–50.

T. F. Torrance was also active in the Edinburgh University Evangelical Association. There had been developments in the evangelical student world since his parents had been part of the generation who had volunteered for missionary service in the 1880s and 1890s. As we have seen, the Student Volunteer Movement had become an international force, and its leader, J. R. Mott, had chaired the Edinburgh Missionary Conference of 1910.[13] There the interdenominational outlook which had always characterized the evangelical movement developed into the full-blown ecumenical movement. But in the course of that, some compromises were made. In 1913, the Student Volunteer Movement, now known in the United Kingdom as the Student Christian Movement (SCM), dropped their declaration of faith specifically in the deity of Christ, arguing that doubters should be allowed to become members in order to help their movement to faith. In 1910, CICCU, the original root of the Student Volunteer Movement, disaffiliated, followed by the London Inter-Hospital Christian Union (LIHCU) in 1912. In 1918, led by Godfrey Buxton of CICCU and Noel Palmer of OUBU (Oxford University Bible Union), those two unions, along with LIHCU cooperated in an InterVarsity Conference, which became an annual event.[14] By 1928, when the InterVarsity Fellowship was formed, there were fourteen more Christian unions affiliated, including those in the four Scottish universities, and by the time T. F. Torrance graduated with his MA in 1934, another eleven had joined. Howard Guinness, a former president of what was now LIFCU (London Inter-Faculty Christian Union), toured the universities of the English-speaking world, leading eventually to the spread of InterVarsity to the United States and to the formation of the IFES (International Fellowship of Evangelical Students) in Boston in 1947.[15]

As a student, T. F. Torrance was involved in this whole development. In 1933, theological students active in the InterVarsity Fellowship in several universities formed the Theological Students' Prayer Fellowship (TSPF),

13. See C. Howard Hopkins, *John R. Mott, 1865–1955* (Grand Rapids: Eerdmans, 1979).

14. So called because it met on the evening of the Oxford and Cambridge InterVarsity rugby match!

15. For a fuller account of the development of the InterVarsity Fellowship, see Thomas A. Noble, *Tyndale House and Fellowship: The First Sixty Years* (Leicester: InterVarsity Press, 2006), 19–27, and Douglas Johnson, *Contending for the Faith: A History of the Evangelical Movement in the Universities and College* (Leicester: IVP, 1979). InterVarsity spread from Canada to the United States largely through the work of the Australian, Stacey Woods. See A. Donald MacLeod, *C. Stacey Woods and the Evangelical Rediscovery of the University* (Downers Grove, IL: InterVarsity Press Academic, 2007).

and Torrance served as secretary of that during the academic year 1934–35.[16] One of the clear lines of division between InterVarsity and the SCM was the authority of the Bible. In an autobiographical memoir written years later, Torrance recalled:

> So far as my view of Holy Scripture was concerned, I had been brought up to believe in its verbal inspiration, but my mother had taught me to have an objective and not a subjective understanding of the Word of God. This did not lessen but rather deepened my sense of the divine authority and verbal inspiration of the Bible which mediated to us the Gospel of salvation. She taught us to adopt a Christ-centred approach to the Holy Scriptures, for Christ was the Word of God made flesh. In him Word and Person are one, and it is therefore in terms of the living personal Word of God incarnate in Christ that we are to hear God addressing us in the Bible.[17]

Torrance clearly shared the evangelical view of the inspiration and authority of the Bible at a time when that had become a clear dividing line. Not only was there a division between the evangelical position and that of those still influenced by Ritschlian liberalism, but there was a division within the evangelical movement between liberal and conservative evangelicals, and Torrance was clearly numbered amongst the conservatives.

To clarify the theological options as they appeared to British students in the 1920s and 1930s, we can broadly characterize four typical positions.[18] Outright theological liberalism still survived, compromising on the deity of Christ, rejecting the long-established doctrine of the atonement, and tending to dismiss the doctrine of the Trinity. Adolf von Harnack's doctrines still attracted some: the fatherhood of God, the infinite value of the human soul, and the kingdom of God, understood as advancing social reform. But this optimistic liberal theology had been severely weakened by the catastrophe of the First World War. Evangelicalism had split into two streams. Liberal Evangelicalism, so-called from a book title of 1923, was orthodox in its subscription to the creeds and genuinely concerned with evangelism but tended

---

16. Noble, *Tyndale House and Fellowship*, 28

17. T. F. Torrance, *"Itinerarium mentis in Deum,"* 9, quoted in McGrath, *T. F. Torrance*, 25.

18. This is a necessary simplification: for a detailed account, see Bebbington, *Evangelicalism*, 181–228.

to hold loosely the full inspiration and authority of Scripture. It thought of inspiration more subjectively as the Spirit speaking to us through Scripture so that particular texts *became* the Word of God to the believer at specific moments. Not all of canonical Scripture was objectively the Word of God, and so some passages of Scripture could be discounted. Conservative Evangelicalism, so-called only to differentiate from liberal Evangelicalism, held to the long-established doctrine that canonical Scripture as a whole was the inspired, authoritative Word of God but fully understood that it had to be interpreted, and it accepted the validity of higher biblical criticism, although not the conclusions reached by many biblical scholars.

It is important to see that the position of conservative evangelicals was not the same as the fourth group, the fundamentalists who had appeared in the United States. The original pamphlets from which they were named, *The Fundamentals*, were published in Chicago between 1910 and 1915, but their authors were not fundamentalists in the later meaning of the term. They included James Orr of Glasgow, B. B. Warfield of Princeton, and Handley Moule, the bishop of Durham, and they mainly represented the quite different position of conservative evangelicalism. But the fundamentalists of the 1920s took a more hard-and-fast position on the inerrancy of Scripture, rejecting biblical criticism. Fundamentalism was a grassroots movement among Christian believers rather than professional theologians, and it was motivated by a rejection of Darwinian evolution (which evangelical theologians such as Orr and Warfield accepted)[19] and, in many cases, the adoption of extreme views on eschatology, such as the new theory of dispensationalism or at least premillennialism.[20]

The position known in the 1930s as conservative evangelicalism, affirming the verbal inspiration of canonical Scripture as a whole but not adopting a view of inerrancy which ruled out biblical criticism, was clearly the position of the InterVarsity Fellowship, shared by T. F. Torrance. It was the moderate position adopted by the leading figures of British evangelicalism,

---

19. See David N. Livingstone, *Darwin's Forgotten Defenders: The Encounter between Evangelical Theology and Evolutionary Thought* (Grand Rapids and Edinburgh: Eerdmans and Scottish Academic Press, 1987). See W. M. Capper and D. Johnson, *Arthur Rendle Short: Surgeon and Christian* (London: The Inter-Varity Fellowship, 1954).

20. On the difference between evangelicalism and fundamentalism, see George M. Marsden, *Understanding Fundamentalism and Evangelicalism* (Grand Rapids: Eerdmans, 1991).

including the Anglicans John Stuart Holden, J. Russell Howden, and Harold Earnshaw-Smith, the Baptist Graham Scroggie, and the Bristol surgeon, A. Rendle Short, a leading member of the Christian Brethren.[21] These were all senior advisers of the InterVarsity Fellowship. Torrance's first publication was an IVF publication, *The Modern Theological Debate*, three addresses given at the TSPU conference in Bewdley in Worcestershire over a New Year conference from December 30, 1940, to January 2, 1941.[22] By that time, however, he had already encountered the strong determination of the leaders of the IVF not to cooperate with the Student Christian Movement, which in their minds represented a more liberal evangelicalism, if indeed it was still evangelical at all. As a postgraduate student resident at Oriel College, Oxford, in 1940, while completing his Basel doctoral thesis, Torrance joined the Oxford Inter-Collegiate Union (OICCU) and was invited to conduct a mission to the university. But when the Oxford SCM invited him to be their president, the invitation to conduct the OICCU mission was withdrawn by the leaders of the IVF in London.[23]

THE INFLUENCE OF KARL BARTH

Over the next twenty years, Torrance and the evangelical movement represented by InterVarsity Fellowship moved apart, and it is important to assess how this came about. In a nutshell it was a developing disagreement over the theology of Karl Barth. Torrance tells us how he first encountered the theology of Barth:

> After I entered New College my dear mother wisely gave me a copy of Barth's *Credo* to help me. Hence I found myself in conflict not only with the rationalistic liberalism of some of my teachers, but with the rather rationalistic and fundamentalistic way of interpreting the Bible being advocated in InterVarsity Fellowship circles together with

---

21. See Bebbington, *Evangelicalism*, 222 and David F. Wright, "Soundings in the Doctrine of Scripture in British Evangelicalism in the First Half of the Twentieth Century," *Tyndale Bulletin* 31 (1980): 87–106, also Mark A. Noll, *Between Faith and Criticism: Evangelicals, Scholarship and the Bible* (Leicester: Apollos, 1986), 78–80.

22. See Noble, *Tyndale House and Fellowship*, 33, and McGrath, *T. F. Torrance*, 250.

23. Thomas F. Torrance, "My Parish Ministry: Alyth, 1940–43," in *Gospel, Church, and Ministry: Thomas F. Torrance Collected Studies I*, ed. Jock Stein (Eugene, OR: Pickwick, 2012), 26.

a rather deterministic Calvinism which was then mistakenly being imported into the thinking of the Christian Unions.[24]

It should be noted that Torrance is referring here to debates going on within the InterVarsity Christian Unions. Not surprisingly, the evangelical students in the Christian Unions, while united on the deity of Christ, the centrality of the cross, the authority of the Bible, and the call to mission and evangelism, had varied views on other matters. There were paedobaptists and credobaptists, Calvinists and Arminians, there were debates on sanctification, and some were influenced by the millenarianism which was more popular in America. So also, while they agreed on the authority of the Bible, there were different ways of understanding that. Undoubtedly some students in the InterVarsity Christian Unions tended toward the more fundamentalist position.[25] But the new continental phenomenon of dialectical theology or the theology of the Word, represented particularly by the Swiss theologian, Karl Barth, was beyond the horizons of many. Mrs. Annie Torrance was evidently better informed.

Her son also encountered the theology of Barth through his beloved teacher, H. R. Mackintosh, the professor of Christian dogmatics. As a student in Germany, Mackintosh had studied at Marburg under the liberal theologian, Wilhelm Herrmann, and he had translated into English a volume of Ritschl and Schleiermacher's *The Christian Faith*. But Mackintosh was aware of the new school of German theology that was deeply critical of theological liberalism. Torrance records that in the printed versions of his lectures handed out to the class in 1935–36, Mackintosh asked his students to delete sections, and it seemed to Torrance that "he was shedding the last vestiges of Ritschlianism from his thought, and that this process of transition could actually be discerned within his lectures."[26] John McConnachie, minister of St. John's Church, Dundee, was the main advocate of Barth's theology in Scotland. His first major study of Barth was published in 1926, and in the 1930s, several

---

24. T. F. Torrance, "*Itinerarium mentis in Deum*," 9, quoted in McGrath, *T. F. Torrance*, 25.

25. James Barr's later ill-informed attack on fundamentalists in InterVarsity in *Fundamentalism* (1977) was clearly a reaction against such fundamentalist students who no doubt were present in the Christian Unions. But Barr (a student at New College in the late 1940s and Torrance's colleague there in the 1950s) seriously misrepresented the position of the leaders of the IVF and also attacked Torrance in the same book.

26. McGrath, *T. F. Torrance*, 33.

works of Barth were published in English, including *The Word of God and the Word of Man* and *Credo*. The second edition of Barth's *Römerbrief*, translated by E. C. Hoskyns, was published in 1933. That same year F. W. Camfield published *Revelation and the Holy Spirit: An Essay in Barthian Theology*.

Torrance won the Blackie Fellowship in 1936, allowing him to visit the Holy Land, and he spent six adventurous months in the Middle East, much of which was then under British control or influence following the defeat of the Ottoman Empire in the First World War.[27] It was while he was in Damascus that he learned of the death of H. R. Mackintosh. This deprived him of Mackintosh's teaching in his final year at New College, 1936–37, but Mackintosh's Croall Lectures were published posthumously as *Types of Modern Theology, Schleiermacher to Barth*. Here he gave his exposition of Barth's theology. He was succeeded as professor of Christian dogmatics by G. T. Thomson, who had translated the first half-volume of the *Church Dogmatics*.

Torrance completed his studies for the BD degree in 1937, graduating with first-class honors and was licensed as a minister by the Presbytery of Edinburgh. His vision of his future had now been modified, and he had a new vision of serving the mission of the church through theological teaching and writing. He was awarded the Aitken Fellowship, allowing him to pursue research at the university of his choice, and he chose to go to Basel to study with Karl Barth. After language study in Berlin and a visit to Marburg, Torrance attended Barth's lectures four times a week in Basel—lectures later published as *Church Dogmatics* II/1. He also participated in Barth's weekly seminar attended by around fifty students and was selected to enter the *Sozietät*, a smaller, more select group who met in Barth's home. Barth refused to allow such a young student to write his doctoral dissertation on theology as a science, and Torrance chose instead to further his growing interest in the Greek Fathers by writing on the doctrine of grace in the Apostolic Fathers.[28]

That project was interrupted when Torrance acceded to an urgent request from John Baillie, the Professor of Divinity in New College, to fill a vacancy teaching theology at Auburn Theological Seminary in the State of New York during the academic year 1938–39. But at the beginning of the Second World War, Torrance decided that he had to return to Britain. He was ordained and

---

27. See McGrath, *T. F. Torrance*, 39–42, for an account of his adventures.

28. For Torrance's education from 1927 to 1938, see McGrath, *T. F. Torrance*, 19–46.

inducted into parish ministry in 1940, and he served for two years as a chaplain with the British Army in North Africa and Italy from 1943 to 1945. Having continued his research and writing through these busy years, he returned to Basel briefly in 1946 to take the oral exam to complete his doctorate. He continued to serve in parish ministry until he was appointed Professor of Ecclesiastical History at New College in 1950. As a parish minister, he had not been inactive theologically. He founded the Scottish Church Theology Society in 1945 and the *Scottish Journal of Theology* in 1948. Despite the opposition of John Baillie, the professor of divinity at Edinburgh, principal of New College, and dean of the faculty of divinity, he transferred to the chair of Christian dogmatics in succession to G. T. Thomson in 1952 and that same year founded the Society for the Study of Theology. Over the next two decades, he was to supervise the English translation of Barth's *Church Dogmatics* and became the leading advocate of Barth's theology in the English-speaking world. But even by the time of his appointment to New College in 1950, some changes had taken place in the theological stance of British evangelicalism, at least as represented by the InterVarsity Fellowship.

DEVELOPMENTS IN BRITISH INTERVARSITY

We have already noted the variety of views on theological matters among the students active in the InterVarsity Christian Unions, but we now need to take note of the development in the theological positions held by the senior leaders of the IVF. During the 1930s, there already had been some changes in the theological stance, largely due to the influence of its driving force, the General Secretary, Dr. Douglas Johnson. As a medical student who also took classes in theology, Johnson had been secretary of the InterVarsity Conference since 1924 and was the organizing secretary of the InterVarsity Fellowship (IVF) in 1928. When he finished his second hospital appointment in 1932, he decided in consultation with Professor Rendle Short to change course, and instead of going abroad as a medical missionary, he devoted himself to the development of the work of IVF among students.[29] A key step in the changing theological complexion of IVF was his invitation to Dr. D. Martyn Lloyd-Jones to address the IVF annual conference at Swanwick in 1935.

---

29. See Noble, *Tyndale House and Fellowship*, 28.

Lloyd-Jones had abandoned a potentially brilliant medical career to become the pastor of a mission hall in a working-class area of Port Talbot in his native Wales.[30] Such was the impact of his preaching throughout Wales that Dr. Campbell Morgan of Westminster Chapel in London, one of the leading Congregationalist churches in the country, invited him to become his assistant and successor. Lloyd-Jones was a Welsh Calvinistic Methodist who had first become convinced of the Calvinist doctrine of predestination at the age of seventeen and who dated his evangelical conversion to a later deep conviction of sin. He had no formal theological education but followed the advice of a fellow minister in Wales to study the doctrine of the atonement and was deeply influenced by P. T. Forsyth and James Denney. In 1932, in the library of Knox College, Toronto, he came across the writings of B. B. Warfield of Princeton and came to view Warfield, who had died in 1921, as "undoubtedly the greatest theologian of the past seventy years in the English-speaking world."[31] Owing primarily to Lloyd-Jones's influence, this representative of the old Princeton school of Calvinism, hitherto of little significance for British evangelicals, was to have considerable influence on their theology.

Douglas Johnson had to persuade Lloyd-Jones to become involved in the InterVarsity Fellowship. He found much English evangelicalism shallow and subjectivist and, as a Welsh Nonconformist, mistrusted the dominance of Anglicans. Johnson persuaded him that the Anglican evangelicals were moderate Calvinists in the tradition of Charles Simeon.[32] He became President of IVF for three consecutive years during the Second World War (1939-1942) and, in 1947, became the first President of the IFES, the International Fellowship of Evangelical Students. During the war, T. F. Torrance's younger brother James ran the youth group for Lloyd-Jones at Westminster Chapel while he was stationed in London with the Royal Air Force (RAF) and spent a number of weekends in the Lloyd-Jones's home.[33] The evangelical movement has always included a variety of traditions working together despite their differences.

---

30. This paragraph is based on Noble, *Tyndale House and Fellowship*, 67–70.

31. Iain H. Murray, *D. Martyn Lloyd-Jones: The First Forty Years 1899-1939* (Edinburgh: Banner of Truth, 1982), 285–86. See also David Ceri Jones, "Martyn Lloyd-Jones," in *British Evangelical Theologians of the Twentieth Century*, 133–154.

32. For Simeon as the key figure in the evangelical tradition in Cambridge leading eventually to the establishment of CICCU and for his pivotal role in establishing the evangelical tradition in the Church of England, see Barclay and Horn, *From Cambridge to the World*.

33. Letter from James B. Torrance to the author, August 17, 1998.

The different traditions, Anglicans in the Simeon tradition, Welsh Calvinistic Methodists, Wesleyan Methodists, Baptists, Christian Brethren, and Scottish and Irish Presbyterians, worked together through IVF in evangelism and for the defense of the gospel. Throughout the 1930s and 1940s, the leaders of IVF were aware that theological liberalism dominated the university divinity faculties and the theological colleges and that a long-term strategy had to be adopted to counter that. A number in IVF circles were aware that the promising young theologian, T. F. Torrance, could be a key person in a recovery of evangelical theology.

In 1938, at the request of the Theological Students' Prayer Union, led by John Wenham, the IVF had set up a Biblical Research Committee to republish works of evangelical theology and to look for new works to publish. A fellow student of Wenham's at Cambridge, Geoffrey W. Bromiley, wrote to the committee in December 1940 from Edinburgh giving a report of a theological conference held in Edinburgh by T. F. Torrance.[34] The committee invited Torrance (unsuccessfully) to join them. Two years later, in 1942, Bromiley (who had started research at New College, Edinburgh) suggested "study circles" in Old Testament, New Testament, and dogmatics. Among the twenty-one dogmaticians who might be part of the third group, he included G. T. Thomson, Daniel Lamont of New College, and T. F. Torrance. Bromiley's suggestions led a few years later to the formation of the Tyndale Fellowship.

That was part of a remarkably daring venture at the end of the war. Under the chairmanship of F. F. Bruce, the IVF Biblical Research Committee established a biblical research library in Cambridge, calling it Tyndale House. Bruce was a Scot who belonged to the Christian Brethren and was a classicist who moved into biblical studies, eventually becoming the Rylands Professor of Biblical Criticism at Manchester. The Hebrew scholar, W. J. Martin of the University of Liverpool, was also one of the founding fathers of the House. Both these men stood in the tradition of the believing critics, and the establishment of Tyndale House to further biblical criticism illustrated that, no matter what fundamentalist opinions might be represented by some enthusiastic young students in the IVF Christian Unions, conservative evangelicals might reach conservative conclusions on matters of biblical criticism, but

---

34. See Noble, *Tyndale House and Fellowship*, 45–46.

they were certainly not fundamentalists.[35] The assistant General Secretary of IVF, Dr. Oliver Barclay (who later succeeded Douglas Johnson), was a zoologist who ensured that they did not embrace the obscurantist position of the fundamentalists on scientific matters.

It is significant that both the Christian Brethren tradition and the evangelical Anglican tradition were deeply committed to the authority of Scripture and to expository biblical preaching but were not really interested in systematic or dogmatic theology. The evangelical Anglican tradition produced its most prominent and influential representative in the person of John Stott, who succeeded Harold Earnshaw-Smith as rector of All Souls, Langham Place in London in 1950.[36] Two years later, Stott conducted a memorable CICCU mission to the University of Cambridge, and the addresses developed in succeeding missions to universities around the English-speaking world eventually became the basis of his best-selling and influential book, *Basic Christianity*.[37] Given the strength of the evangelical Anglicans and those in the Christian Brethren tradition in the leadership of the InterVarsity Fellowship, it was understandable that Tyndale House was devoted exclusively to biblical research and not to theological research. Indeed, among some, there was something of a suspicion of theology! That was not true, however, of Lloyd-Jones. While he had never taken a theological degree, he was deeply committed to expository preaching and to biblical theology, but in his mind, that was largely influenced by the Calvinist tradition, including the theology of B. B. Warfield. The influence of Warfield was also strong in the thinking of a young Anglican student converted at Oxford during the war, James Packer, who developed a passionate interest in the theology of the English Puritans.[38]

Through Lloyd-Jones and Packer, some developments in one branch of American evangelicalism began to influence the British scene. The old

35. See F. F. Bruce, "The Tyndale Fellowship for Biblical Research," *Evangelical Quarterly* 19 (1947): 52–61, reprinted in Noble, *Tyndale House and Fellowship*, 314–25.

36. See Timothy Dudley-Smith's two-volume biography, *John Stott: The Making of a Leader* and *John Stott: A Global Ministry* (Leicester: IVP, 1999 and 2001); also Roger Steer, *Inside Story: The Life of John Stott* (Leicester: IVP, 2009); and Alister Chapman, *Godly Ambition: John Stott and the Evangelical Movement* (Oxford: Oxford University Press, 2012). See also Ian M. Randall, "John R. W. Stott," in *British Evangelical Theologians of the Twentieth Century*, 155–75.

37. John Stott, *Basic Christianity* (London: IVP, 1958).

38. See Alister McGrath, *J.I. Packer: A Biography* (Grand Rapids: Baker, 1997); also Don J. Payne, "James I. Packer," in *British Evangelical Theologians of the Twentieth Century*, 176–96.

Princeton tradition of Charles Hodge, A. A. Hodge, and of B. B. Warfield had lost its hold on Princeton in 1929, and led by Gresham Machen, those loyal to it had founded Westminster Theological Seminary in Philadelphia. In line with the position of the Hodges and Warfield, biblical criticism was acceptable so that the seminary was not strictly speaking fundamentalist, but very conservative positions were taken on the authorship and dates of the biblical books. The seminary was deeply committed to the theology of the Westminster Confession, embodying the tradition of Federal Calvinism with its commitment to predestination and the doctrine of limited atonement, that Christ died only for the elect. As a Welsh Calvinistic Methodist, Lloyd-Jones found that tradition very attractive so that, whereas the evangelical Anglicans and the Christian Brethren scholars like Bruce did not share an enthusiasm for Westminster Calvinism, the influence of Lloyd-Jones and Packer gave that school of theology an influence in InterVarsity circles in the early 1950s which had not been typical of British evangelicalism as a whole.

Westminster Calvinism was particularly opposed to the theology of Barth. Cornelius Van Til, who left Princeton with Machen and became professor of apologetics and systematic theology at Westminster, published an attack on Barth in 1946 entitled, *The New Modernism*. The label "neoorthodox" compared Barth and some others unfavorably with the "orthodoxy" of the Calvinist theologians of the post-Reformation era, but for Van Til, Barth was not orthodox at all; he represented a new variety of modernism. Van Til followed with another attack some years later provocatively entitled *Christianity and Barthianism* (1962).

THE PARTING OF THE WAYS

Given the sensitivity, indeed the fear and suspicion, among many evangelicals of liberalism, a fear justified by the corrosive effect on the faith of many promising young theology students in previous decades, the accusation that Barth was a wolf in sheep's clothing was damaging. It is worth bearing in mind, too, that InterVarsity had its origins in the way the Student Christian Movement had slipped from its original evangelical theology. In reaction, and because of the influence of Warfield and Van Til on Lloyd-Jones and others, the traditional Federal Calvinism with its predestinarian accent on the covenants and the decrees of God gained some strength, not in British evangelicalism as a whole, but in university circles associated with InterVarsity.

Not all were convinced, of course, and it seemed to some that some open discussion should take place on whether evangelicals should examine carefully whether Barth was friend or foe. Geoffrey Bromiley proposed to the Tyndale Fellowship committee that they should devote their conference in July 1950 to "Modern Trends in Theology in the Light of Holy Scripture." Cornelius Van Til and G. C. Berkouwer accepted an invitation, and T. F. Torrance was invited to come with a colleague of his choice to state his position on Barthianism. Lloyd-Jones was to chair the debate. Some decade later, Bromiley reflected:

> Why did I want a discussion on Barth? I did not want us to become Barthians (something Barth himself disliked!). But Barth, for all our disagreements on some of his reconstructions, would be a valuable ally. For he had a fair grasp of the Trinity, the Incarnation, the virgin birth, the atonement, the resurrection, the authority and power of scripture, and the church's primary mission. Did we really do any good by treating him as a foe, as Van Til had done?[39]

In the end the debate did not take place.

T. F. Torrance himself was not actively involved in InterVarsity activities after his lectures to the Theological Students' Prayer Union published by IVF in 1941. But during the late 1940s, his two younger brothers, James and David, were.[40] They were both about a decade younger, James being born in 1923 and David in 1924. Both served in the forces during the war: James in the RAF and David in the British army in the Far East. Immediately after that, both were mature students, active in the Edinburgh University Christian Union and more widely in InterVarsity.

In his memoirs, David Torrance recounts their involvement in student missions and in evangelism through IVF conferences.[41] Both were also active in evangelism among students and in student missions in various parishes in Scotland. They both prayed with James Barr, among others, at the time of Barr's conversion. James Torrance was president of Edinburgh Christian Union during 1946–1947 and David during 1947–1948. As the Christian Union

---

39. Letter to the author, June 8, 2004, quoted in Noble, *Tyndale House and Fellowship*, 64.

40. For this paragraph, see D. W. Torrance, *The Reluctant Minister*, 80–93.

41. See chapter 5 of D. W. Torrance, *The Reluctant Minister*.

president, David Torrance took the lead in dropping the words "infallible" and "inspired" from the Edinburgh Christian Union basis of faith, leaving only the statement, "The Bible is the Word of God." This led to an interview with the IVF General Secretary, Dr. Douglas Johnson, at which David Torrance presented his view that all Scripture was inspired but that Christ was primarily the Word of God. The same issue came up again during the next academic year when he served on the UK Student Executive Committee.

By this time, David Torrance had graduated with his honors degree in philosophy and had started BD studies at New College, studying under his older brother T. F. Torrance as professor of church history and then as professor of Christian dogmatics in his final year. During that year, the university chaplain started to prepare for an evangelistic mission to the students of the university, and both the SCM and the IVF Christian Union agreed to help and began to meet weekly for prayer. Since this was contrary to the longstanding IVF policy in place since the split with the SCM not to cooperate with other groups, a message was delivered from Douglas Johnson to discontinue the prayer meeting or be disaffiliated. The majority of the Edinburgh committee refused to comply, and the Christian Union split. Even though he was following a longstanding policy, Johnson's action seems rather abrupt, but to the InterVarsity national leaders, the Edinburgh Union was seen to be deeply influenced by Barthianism.[42]

That same year, 1953, James Torrance participated in the annual conference of the Tyndale Fellowship held in Tyndale House, Cambridge. It had been decided to devote the conference to "The Plan of Salvation," by which was meant the five points of traditional Federal Calvinist doctrine often remembered by the mnemonic TULIP—Total depravity, Unconditional election, Limited atonement, Irresistible grace, and the Perseverance of the saints. This did not indicate that the Tyndale Fellowship as a whole was committed to these doctrines, but it was agreed that they should be debated and "the Doctor," Martyn Lloyd-Jones, was asked to chair. James Torrance was given the topic unconditional election, but a debate rose over the doctrine of limited atonement or particular redemption, a doctrine of strict Calvinism which had

---

42. In his letter to the author on June 8, 2004, Geoffrey Bromiley recalled being present at a confrontation over the disaffiliation between T. F. Torrance and Douglas Johnson; see Noble, *Tyndale House and Fellowship*, 78.

been dropped by most evangelicals even in Scotland two generations earlier. The Torrances' missionary parents, along with the missionary volunteers of their generation, affirmed the doctrine of the universal church that Christ died for all. When James Torrance rejected the doctrine of limited atonement and argued that Christ died for all, he was supported by some, including the veteran missionary, A. M. Stibbs, who lectured at Oak Hill College. John Murray, a Scot who had followed Machen in leaving Princeton and was professor of systematic theology at Westminster Seminary, tried to defend the doctrine exegetically but lost the argument. James Packer, however, asserted the logical necessity of the doctrine for a systematic understanding.[43]

James Torrance was rather shaken by the whole experience of what seemed to him to be aggressive opposition, and his old friend, Martyn Lloyd-Jones, tried to encourage him. But after that, he was no longer involved in InterVarsity and was a strong opponent of scholastic Federal Calvinism for the rest of his life.[44] This episode presumably contributed to T. F. Torrance's criticism of rationalistic, fundamentalistic, and deterministic tendencies in InterVarsity. Even those who were not Calvinists saw the authority of the Bible as the crucial issue. That went along with a strong emphasis on the intellectual strength of the Christian faith and on the life of the mind, and Torrance, with his strong emphasis on the rationality of the Christian faith, could not have agreed more. But when the defense of the Bible became the focus, it was too easy to slip into an apologetic that first assumed or tried to prove the inspiration, authority, and historical reliability of the Bible as a necessary prelude to faith in Christ rather than a corollary. Torrance took the view that the authority of the Bible was an implication of faith in Christ, but that was now being dismissed as Barthianism. But in fact, while the Reformed influence remained strong in

---

43. See the fuller account of the debate in Noble, *Tyndale House and Fellowship*, 74–77, based on the letter from James Torrance, August 17, 1998, and a letter from Peter Cook (who took the Calvinist position), December 11, 1998.

44. He did attend a Tyndale Fellowship study group at Durham in 1979 on the theology of Calvin, rejoicing in R. T. Kendall's argument that Calvin himself taught that Christ died for all. See R. T. Kendall, *Calvin and English Calvinism to 1649* (Oxford: Oxford University Press, 1979). The author recalls a sparkling verbal duel there with a professor from Westminster Seminary in which James Torrance accused him of putting election before grace instead of grace before election.

British InterVarsity, evangelical Christianity grew and became increasingly varied in the succeeding decades.[45]

THE SUCCEEDING DECADES

In this brief sketch, we have traced T. F. Torrance's upbringing in an evangelical missionary family and looked at his developing theological understanding during the years of his education and early ministry. He was to serve as professor of Christian dogmatics at New College, Edinburgh from 1952 until his retirement in 1979, writing his major contributions to Trinitarian theology after that. His final publications, his lectures on incarnation and atonement, edited by his nephew Robert Walker, came at the very end of his long life.[46] We cannot examine here all those succeeding decades in detail. But we can attempt to set his theological work against a brief synopsis of the developments in evangelicalism.

In the 1950s, while T. F. Torrance was a young professor at New College, most evangelicals in the United Kingdom united to support the Billy Graham crusades centered at Haringey in London in 1954 and at Glasgow's Kelvin Hall in 1955. These had a considerable national impact. Graham was invited to Scotland by the Tell Scotland organization, which was supported by conservative and liberal evangelicals. James Packer wrote an evangelical manifesto defending Billy Graham and InterVarsity Fellowship against the charge of fundamentalism.[47] But T. F. Torrance was also a leading supporter of Billy Graham's evangelism.[48] In the 1960s, when Bultmann's existentialism and demythologization were in theological fashion, Torrance attacked both, and he defended historic Christianity against the superficial attack of John

---

45. InterVarsity Fellowship in the United Kingdom adopted the new designation UCCF (Universities and Colleges Christian Fellowship) in the 1970s.

46. Thomas F. Torrance, *Incarnation: The Person and Life of Christ*, ed. Robert T. Walker (Downers Grove, IL and Milton Keynes: IVP and Paternoster, 2008); and Thomas F. Torrance, *Atonement: The Person and Work of Christ*, ed. Robert T. Walker (Downers Grove, IL and Milton Keynes: IVP and Paternoster, 2009).

47. James I. Packer, *"Fundamentalism" and the Word of God* (London: IVF, 1958). The quotation marks in the title are significant. Packer was not defending fundamentalism; he was arguing that evangelicals were not "fundamentalists."

48. The lifelong mutual appreciation between the two men was evident decades later at Torrance's funeral in the tribute sent by Graham.

Robinson, the bishop of Woolwich, in his best-selling book, *Honest to God*, published by SCM Press in 1963.[49]

At the same time as he supported the evangelist Billy Graham, Torrance was active in the ecumenical movement.[50] It should not be forgotten that this originated in the Edinburgh Conference of 1910, initiated by the Student Volunteer Movement, which had influenced his parents. He responded to the preparatory volumes written to prepare for the initiating conference of the World Council of Churches in 1948[51] and participated in the conversations between representatives of the Church of Scotland and the Church of England from 1949 to 1951. A series of works in the 1950s were on issues of ecclesiology raised by the ecumenical movement. His association with the Orthodox Church was to lead later in his career to the conversation between the Orthodox Church and the World Alliance of Reformed Churches to try to reach a common mind on the doctrine of the Trinity. By contrast, many evangelicals were suspicious of the ecumenical movement, but Torrance was an evangelical who (like Lesslie Newbigin) kept alive the ecumenical perspective of the original Student Volunteer Movement without in any way compromising on the Trinitarian heart of the Christian faith.[52] He was a much bigger figure than a sectarian evangelicalism could contain.

In the second half of the twentieth century, evangelical Christianity grew in the United Kingdom, the United States, and around the world. A split appeared among British evangelicals when Lloyd-Jones seemed to call for evangelicals to leave the Church of England at a meeting of the Evangelical Alliance in 1966, but he was countered by the chairman, John Stott. In the Church of Scotland, William Still began his ministry at Gilcomston South Church in Aberdeen in 1950, adopting, like both Lloyd-Jones and Stott, the expository preaching of the Reformed tradition. By the last decades of the century, well over a hundred parish ministers attended prayer conferences he chaired and were sympathetic to traditional Calvinist theology. Others identified themselves as evangelical without belonging to that particular

---

49. He had already rejected Robinson's universalism in "Universalism or Election?" *SJT* 2 (1949): 310–18.

50. See McGrath, *T. F. Torrance*, 94–102.

51. See *SJT* 2 (1949): 241–70.

52. See Donald LeRoy Stults, "Lesslie Newbigin," in *British Evangelical Theologians of the Twentieth Century*, 220–39.

tradition. Torrance saw himself as belonging to a different Reformed tradition within Scottish theology. However, after friends of William Still set up
a research center in Edinburgh, Rutherford House, he was happy to participate in the Edinburgh Conference on Dogmatics, which they organized.[53] Like
Lloyd-Jones, Still was opposed to Billy Graham's mass evangelism, whereas
Stott, like Torrance, was a strong Graham supporter. While there were those,
therefore, who did not regard Torrance as an evangelical, that can only be
seen as the result of a very narrow definition of the word by one tradition
within the broad coalition.

The evangelical movement grew strongly within the Church of England
and was strongest in Baptist churches. The National Evangelical Anglican
Congress at Keele in 1967 marked the emergence of evangelicals under Stott's
leadership as a major and influential tradition within the national church. A
decade later, largely as a result of the work of Anthony Thiselton, the conference in Nottingham marked an increased understanding that the simple
insistence on the Bible's authority had to be refined by a more sophisticated
understanding of hermeneutics. Evangelicals also recovered their former
commitment to social action with the establishment of the TEAR Fund (The
Evangelical Alliance Relief agency) in 1968. The 1960s also saw the development of the charismatic movement across the denominations.[54] By the end
of the century, there were perceived to be three traditions within growing
Anglican evangelicalism: conservative, charismatic, and open evangelicals.[55]
The strength of the Anglican evangelical tradition across the globe became
evident with the emergence of the Global Anglican Future Conference
(GAFCON), held initially in Jerusalem in 2008.

The international dimension of evangelical Christianity had become evident forty years earlier in the development of the Lausanne Movement. This
began with the International Congress on World Evangelization initiated by

---

53. See Thomas F. Torrance, *Scottish Theology: From John Knox to John McLeod Campbell*
(Edinburgh: T&T Clark, 1996). See also Thomas F. Torrance, "The Atonement: The Singularity
of Christ and the Finality of the Cross: The Atonement and the Moral Order," in *Universalism
and the Doctrine of Hell*, ed. Nigel de S. Cameron (Exeter: Paternoster, 1982; repr. Grand Rapids:
Baker, 1993), 225–56. The theologian and Barth scholar Bruce McCormack was later a frequent
participant in the Edinburgh conferences.

54. Torrance's former student, Tom Smail, became a leading figure in the charismatic movement before developing a more critical appreciation as a theologian.

55. See *Anvil* 20 (2003) for a useful series of articles on these three branches of the Anglican
evangelical tradition.

Billy Graham in 1974. John Stott emerged as the theologian of the movement, and at a significant conference at Manila in 1989, social action was seen to be as much a part of Christian mission as evangelism.[56] Through his Langham Partnership, Stott took a particular interest in the theological education of the ministry in the new churches of the global East and South. Sometime in the 1970s, a global shift took place in the Christian demography: the majority of Christians in the world now lived outside Europe and North America, mostly in evangelical churches.

There was some resistance from American evangelicals at the Manila conference to the new emphasis on social action, indicating that their tradition had been much more deeply affected by the fundamentalist reaction against the social gospel early in the twentieth century. American evangelicals also split over the issue of the inerrancy of the Bible following the publication of Harold Lindsell's *Battle for the Bible* in 1976,[57] a division that was not replicated in the United Kingdom. American evangelicals also became more deeply involved in politics through their opposition to the new legal rights of abortion, and the moral majority gravitated toward a more right-wing political stance. This was not so in British or continental European evangelicalism nor in the rest of the world.

EVANGELICAL THEOLOGY

Of more relevance to the relationship of T. F. Torrance to the evangelical tradition are the theological developments, but the most promising developments among those recognized as evangelicals were in biblical studies and philosophical theology rather than in dogmatic or systematic theology. The InterVarsity investment in biblical studies, particularly through Tyndale House, encouraged a whole generation of biblical scholars, and this extended to the United States through the Institute for Biblical Research (IBR). Many significant scholars could be mentioned, but it will be enough here to mention the names of James Dunn, N. T. Wright, and Richard Bauckham. Dunn grew up in the Church of Scotland and graduated in theology at Glasgow. He came from the evangelical tradition, becoming a Methodist in England, but

---

56. [47] See Robert A. Hunt, "The History of the Lausanne Movement, 1974–2011," *International Bulletin of Missionary Research* 35 (2011): 81–84.

57. Harold Lindsell, *The Battle for the Bible* (Grand Rapids: Zondervan, 1976).

the conclusions he reached on critical issues gradually separated him from the evangelical mainstream. Toward the end of Torrance's life, N. T. Wright's scholarship withstood the continued historical skepticism and established a strong case for the historical trustworthiness of the portrayal of Jesus in the New Testament.[58] Larry Hurtado, Richard Bauckham, and others established a strong case that the notion of a gradual growth through the first century of belief in the divinity of Christ, which had dominated twentieth-century scholarship, was implausible.[59] On the contrary, the evidence was strong that right from his resurrection, Jesus had been worshiped and included within the identity of the one God of Israel.[60]

In the post-war decades, evangelicals were also working in philosophy and apologetics. Carl F. H. Henry was influential in moving American evangelicals away from fundamentalism[61] and involved, as the first editor of *Christianity Today*, in the founding of various new institutions such as the Evangelical Theological Society. The authority of the Bible was at the front and center of his defense of evangelical theology, a position put forward in *Revelation and the Bible*, and elaborated in a six-volume defense of his position, *God, Revelation, and Authority*.[62] He was one of the signatories of the *Chicago Declaration on Inerrancy* in 1978. But while Henry represented a strong tradition within American evangelicalism, others saw his position as rationalism and preferred the approach of theologians such as Bernard Ramm, who moved from an evidentialist apologetics to a kind of presuppositional apologetics, and eventually he embraced the theology of Barth.[63]

---

58. See particularly N. T. Wright, *The New Testament and the People of God*, vol. 1 of *Christian Origins and the Question of God* (Minneapolis: Fortress, 1992); and *Jesus and the Victory of God*, vol. 2 of *Christian Origins and the Question of God* (Minneapolis: Fortress, 1996).

59. This group was facetiously referred to as the EHCC (the Early High Christology Club).

60. Larry Hurtado, *One God, One Lord: Early Christian Devotion and Ancient Christian Monotheism* (Minneapolis: Augsburg Fortress, 1988); and *Lord Jesus Christ: Devotion to Jesus in Earliest Christianity* (Grand Rapids: Eerdmans, 2003). See also Richard Bauckham, *God Crucified: Monotheism and Christology in the New Testament* (Carlisle: Paternoster, 1998); and *Jesus and the God of Israel* (Milton Keynes: Paternoster, 2008).

61. See Carl F. H. Henry, *The Uneasy Conscience of Modern Fundamentalism* (Grand Rapids: Eerdmans, 1947).

62. Carl F. H. Henry, ed., *Revelation and the Bible* (Grand Rapids: Baker, 1958); and *God, Revelation, and Authority*, 6 vols. (Waco: Word, 1976–1983).

63. See Bernard Ramm, *After Fundamentalism: The Future of Evangelical Theology* (San Francisco: Harper & Row, 1983).

In the next generation, evangelicals who were professional philosophers—Alvin Plantinga, Nicholas Wolterstorff, William Lane Craig, and others—reestablished the case for theism, turning the tide against the long dominant atheism. The history of missions and missiology flourished with the writings of Lesslie Newbigin,[64] Andrew Walls, and David Bosch. Christopher Wright of the Langham Partnership published a one-volume biblical theology entitled *The Mission of God* in 2006.

It was not that evangelical attempts at systematic theology were missing. Donald Bloesch, who characterized himself as a progressive Evangelical, published the first volume of a two-volume systematics, *Essentials of Evangelical Theology*, in 1978.[65] The English Methodist, Geoffrey Wainwright of Duke Divinity School, published *Doxology* in 1980,[66] although his involvement with the ecumenical movement (like Torrance) would still have led to mistrust among many evangelicals. Thomas Oden, another Methodist, received more widespread acceptance among evangelicals following his conversion from various liberal causes to what he called "paleo-orthodoxy." The first volume of his three-volume systematics was published in 1987,[67] and eventually, all three volumes were published in one book, *Classic Christianity*, in 2009. Oden was more of a historical theologian. He eschewed originality in theology, and his systematics were more of a compendium of classic sources, deliberately more from the Christian fathers, fewer from medieval and Reformation theologians, and least of all from the modern era. The Baptist theologian, Stanley Grenz, produced a series of major works on theology and ethics, completing two books on the Trinity before his untimely death in 2004.[68] Other more

---

64. Like Torrance and Wainwright, Newbigin would have been suspected by the more conservative as too close to ecumenism.

65. Donald M. Bloesch, *Essentials of Evangelical Theology*, vols. 1 and 2 (San Francisco: Harper & Row, 1978 and 1984).

66. Geoffrey Wainwright, *Doxology* (New York: Oxford University Press, 1980).

67. Thomas Oden, *The Living God* (Nashville: Abingdon, 1987). For assessment, see Kenneth J. Collins, "Paleo-orthodoxy and the Diminishment of Theological Method: A Critical Examination of the Theological Method of Thomas C. Oden," *Wesleyan Theological Journal* 54 (2019): 72–99.

68. Stanley J. Grenz, *The Social God and the Relational Self: A Trinitarian Theology of the Imago Dei* (Louisville: Westminster John Knox, 2001), and *Rediscovering the Triune God: The Trinity in Contemporary Theology* (Minneapolis: Fortress Press, 2004).

conservative systematic theologies published during Torrance's lifetime include those by Millard Erickson[69] and Wayne Grudem.[70]

In the United Kingdom, Colin Gunton had a significant influence, which was critical, like Torrance, of the continuing compromises of liberal theology, and he consciously stood in the tradition of P. T. Forsyth and championed the work of Barth with critical appreciation. He stood in the Reformed tradition while not identifying with conservative evangelicalism. But if Forsyth and Denney were evangelical theologians, then so too was Gunton. He published several works on the doctrine of the Trinity, but his sudden and early death robbed us of an intended comprehensive work of dogmatics.[71] John Webster was perhaps viewed with more appreciation by the more conservative, but he too wrote a number of books sympathetic to Barth. Alister McGrath identified as an evangelical, and in 2001 he published *Christian Theology: An Introduction*. This excellent introductory textbook was used throughout the world, but it was written by essentially a historical theologian. His biography of Torrance helped many conservative evangelicals to understand the brilliance and profundity of Torrance's theology.

TORRANCE AS AN EVANGELICAL THEOLOGIAN

While all of these were notable contributions, none of these scholars attained the front rank in systematic theology in the same way as evangelical biblical scholars such as N. T. Wright and philosophical theologians such as Alvin Plantinga did in their fields. But as the decades passed and the evangelical tradition diversified and became global, the early suspicion of Barthianism came to seem rather small-minded to many. While some evangelicals remain somewhat wary of Barth or those who are seen to appreciate him, a more balanced long-term view could see Barth, in Bromiley's words, as an ally rather than a foe. What is more, the fuller development of Torrance's theology in

---

69. Millard J. Erickson, *Christian Theology* (Grand Rapids: Baker, 1983).

70. Wayne Grudem, *Systematic Theology: An Introduction to Biblical Doctrine* (Leicester: Zondervan, 1994). As the subtitle suggests, this is more an attempt to lay out "biblical doctrine" systematically.

71. See Colin E. Gunton, *The Promise of Trinitarian Theology* (Edinburgh: T&T Clark, 1991; 2nd ed. 1997); *The Triune Creator: A Historical and Systematic Study* (Grand Rapids: Eerdmans, 1998); and *Father, Son and Holy Spirit: Toward A Fully Trinitarian Theology* (London: T&T Clark, 2003). For a vivid picture of Gunton, the man and the theologian, see John E. Colwell, "Colin E. Gunton," in *British Evangelical Theologians of the Twentieth Century*, 240–59.

his major works on the Trinity published after his official retirement make it clear that Torrance cannot be dismissed as merely a Barthian.[72] He differed from Barth on several matters as he also differed from Calvin, but such was his respect for these two doctors of the global church that he seldom criticized them openly.[73] The one theologian with whom he seemed to have no disagreements at all was Athanasius, and that brings us to see why Torrance's theology can provide a vital strength for evangelical theology today.

It is clear that Torrance's thought has a range and depth that much evangelical theology lacks.[74] Whereas evangelical theology tends to trace its roots back to the Reformation, particularly to Luther or Calvin, Torrance's adherence to Calvin's Reformed tradition is deepened by his insistence that we need to go back beyond the Reformers to the fathers for whom Calvin himself had such profound respect.[75] In Torrance's later decades, many evangelicals gained a new interest in the fathers, a few even leaving evangelicalism for Eastern Orthodoxy. Thomas Oden quoted the fathers copiously in his systematics and edited the multivolume *Ancient Christian Commentary on Scripture*. But a study of *The Trinitarian Faith*, Torrance's major work of theology marking the sixteen-hundredth anniversary of the reformulation of the Nicene Creed at the Council of Constantinople, demonstrates that the fathers rather than Barth or Calvin are the deep source of his theology.

The Anglican evangelical theologian, Gerald Bray, notes that the creeds are the Christian hermeneutic for the interpretation of Holy Scripture,[76]

---

72. See Thomas F. Torrance, *The Trinitarian Faith: The Evangelical Theology of the Ancient Catholic Church* (Edinburgh: T&T Clark, 1988); *Trinitarian Perspectives: Toward Doctrinal Agreement* (Edinburgh: T&T Clark, 1994); and *The Christian Doctrine of God: One Being Three Persons* (Edinburgh: T&T Clark, 1996). See also Paul D. Molnar, "Thomas F. Torrance and Karl Barth," in *T & T Clark Handbook of Thomas F. Torrance*, ed. Paul D. Molnar and Myk Habets (London: Bloomsbury T&T Clark, 2020), 67–84.

73. See McGrath, *T. F. Torrance*, 175–94, on Torrance's distinctive view of Natural Theology; see also Molnar, "Thomas F. Torrance and Karl Barth," in *T & T Clark Handbook of Thomas F. Torrance*.

74. The most comprehensive and accessible introduction to Torrance's theology is Elmer M. Colyer, *How to Read T. F. Torrance: Understanding His Trinitarian and Scientific Theology* (Eugene, OR: Wipf and Stock, 2007). But a good place to begin is the excellent introduction by Torrance's nephew and former student, Robert T. Walker, "Thomas F. Torrance," in *British Evangelical Theologians of the Twentieth Century*, 197–219.

75. See Anthony N. S. Lane, *John Calvin: Student of the Church Fathers* (Grand Rapids: Baker, 1999).

76. Gerald L. Bray, "Scripture and Confession: Doctrine as Hermeneutic," in *A Pathway into the Holy Scripture*, ed. Philip E. Satterthwaite and David F. Wright (Grand Rapids: Eerdmans,

and in that light, Torrance's one-volume work, *The Trinitarian Faith*, is a significant work indeed. It provides not only evangelicals but the whole catholic church with a one-volume work of theology based on his understanding of the fathers, whose theology is formulated in the Nicene Creed. It is not merely a work of historical theology but his twentieth-century interpretation of the orthodox fathers, whose theology formulated the central Christian doctrines of Christ and the Trinity.[77] His later work, *The Christian Doctrine of God: One Being Three Persons*, evidences a depth and balance which neither falls into the virtual Tritheism of some social Trinitarians nor places an emphasis on the divine unity which fails to be fully Trinitarian.[78] And for Torrance, this is not in any way irrelevant speculation far removed from the preaching of the gospel. This is the very grammar of faith. He refers to the economic Trinity as the "evangelical Trinity," indicating that God reveals himself as Father, Son, and Holy Spirit in the preaching of the gospel. By the Spirit we are united in the Son and so come to worship the Father.[79]

But Torrance's love of the Nicene fathers does not lessen his love for the Reformers, particularly for Calvin. While he rejects the later development of scholastic Federal Calvinism and clearly does not endorse Calvin's doctrine of predestination, he strongly defends Calvin's overall perspective and genius.[80] He remains truly evangelical in his focus on the death and resurrection of Christ, although he deepens the traditional Anselmic and evangelical understanding of the cross by integrating the doctrine of the atonement with the depths of the patristic understanding of the incarnation.[81] He did

---

1994), 221–36.

77. See Jason R. Radcliff, *Thomas F. Torrance and the Church Fathers: A Reformed, Evangelical and Ecumenical Reconstruction of the Patristic Tradition* (Eugene, OR: Pickwick, 2014); and *Thomas F. Torrance and the Orthodox-Reformed Theological Dialogue* (Eugene, OR: Pickwick, 2018).

78. See Paul D. Molnar, *Thomas F. Torrance: Theologian of the Trinity* (Farnham: Ashgate, 2009). See also the critical appreciation in Christopher R. J. Holmes, "Thomas F. Torrance and the Trinity," in *T&T Clark Handbook of Thomas F. Torrance*, 161–72.

79. See Dick O. Eugenio, *Communion with the Triune God: The Trinitarian Soteriology of T. F. Torrance*, Princeton Theological Monograph Series (Eugene, OR: Pickwick, 2014).

80. See Thomas F. Torrance, *Calvin's Doctrine of Man* (London: Lutterworth Press, 1949), and *Calvin's New Testament Commentaries—A New Translation*, ed. Thomas F. Torrance and David W. Torrance, 12 vols. (Grand Rapids: Eerdmans, 1972).

81. See *Incarnation* and *Atonement*, both edited by Robert T. Walker. See also Thomas A. Noble, "Incarnation and Atonement," in *T&T Clark Handbook of Thomas F. Torrance*, 173–88. Torrance also championed the integration of incarnation and atonement and the understanding of "satisfaction" in the theology of John McLeod Campbell.

not share the scholastic approach to Scripture favored by some traditions of Reformed theology, but his commitment to the inspiration and authority of Scripture in the work of theology was clear.[82] His examination of theological method in comparison with the methodology of the natural sciences drawing upon the thought of Michael Polanyi also provides a profound basis for evangelicals who still wrestle with the influence of fundamentalism in this area.[83] The breadth of his vision and the depth of his understanding give evangelicals a voice heard with respect in other branches of the Christian church, such as Eastern Orthodoxy, and provide a basis for serious conversation among all who are true to biblical, Nicene theology.[84] In short, an evangelical Christianity which is not monolithic, but embraces several different traditions, has in T. F. Torrance a theologian of the first rank. In Torrance, the suspicious sectarianism which has characterized some evangelicalism is left behind, and the catholicity of evangelicals such as Wesley or Simeon is recaptured.[85]

As a final note, Torrance's visits back to China late in his life speak volumes about his commitment to evangelical Christianity. In 1984 at the age of seventy, Torrance took the renewed opportunity to travel within China to find his way by bus up into the remote hill country where his father had planted churches in order to find the fellowship of Christians he had last seen decades before at age fourteen.[86] He returned ten years later at the age of eighty with money to rebuild church buildings and finance theological education for pastors. Nothing could more vividly illustrate his lifelong commitment to mission, to the preaching of the gospel, and to evangelical faith in Christ.

---

82. See Bruce Ritchie, *T. F. Torrance in Recollection and Reappraisal* (Eugene, OR: Pickwick, 2021) for a critical appraisal of Torrance by an evangelical fellow-student of the author.

83. See McGrath, *T. F. Torrance*, 195–236 on "Theology and the Natural Sciences." See also Thomas F. Torrance, ed., *Belief in Science and Christian Life: The Relevance of Michael Polanyi's Thought for Christian Faith and Life* (Edinburgh: Handsel Press, 1980).

84. Highly significant here is the book arising out of his conversations with the Orthodox Church, *Trinitarian Perspectives: Toward Doctrinal Agreement* (Edinburgh: T&T Clark, 1994).

85. See John Wesley, Sermon 39, "The Catholic Spirit," in *The Works of John Wesley*, vol. 2 (Nashville: Asbury Press, 1985), 79–95.

86. See McGrath, *T. F. Torrance*, 237–41.

2

—

TORRANCE, THE TACIT DIMENSION, AND THE CHURCH FATHERS

Jonathan Warren P. (Pagán)

INTRODUCTION

It would be impossible within the confines of an essay to account for the immense project of patristic retrieval in Torrance's massive oeuvre. A full account of his indebtedness to the fathers is only now just being articulated.[1] The scope of this brief essay will be limited to those dimensions of Torrance's thought that are most relevant to my perspective and work as an Anglican parish priest. For me, it is above all in Torrance's theological method that the fruitfulness of his meditation upon the thought of the fathers is most evident. This method depends explicitly upon both an *epistemic realism* concerning divine revelation and the *scientific ordering* of theological knowledge, which in turn hinges upon the tacit dimension of knowledge, or the fact that "we know more than we can tell."[2] Torrance's scientific theology requires participation in the ongoing worship of the church in word and sacrament in order for theological concepts to remain epistemically realistic, that is, well-founded in the gracious, revelatory self-giving of God in Jesus Christ. Detached from the tacit dimension of theology, which is given in worship,

---

1. Jason Radcliffe's *T. F. Torrance and the Church Fathers* (Eugene, OR: Pickwick, 2015) is the first dedicated monograph to begin to reckon with this lifelong preoccupation of Torrance's, and Myk Habets's *Theosis in the Theology of Thomas F. Torrance* (Farnham: Ashgate, 2009), has also dealt at some length with Torrance's retrieval of Athanasius and Cyril. The more recent edited volume *T. F. Torrance and Eastern Orthodoxy*, ed. Matthew Baker and Todd Speidell (Eugene, OR: Wipf & Stock, 2015) deals with his patristic integration at some length.

2. Elmer M. Colyer, *How to Read T. F. Torrance* (Eugene, OR: Wipf & Stock, 2007), 335.

theological thinking becomes mythological, which is to say, merely projectionist.[3] Theological thinking that participates in the reality of God requires evangelical and doxological participation, which forms the tacit dimension of our knowledge of God.[4] Torrance would judge much of contemporary academic theology to be projectionist precisely because of its detachment from the ongoing life of the church.

In this essay, I will be focusing on three facets of Torrance's theology in which the patristic connection between doctrine and doxological participation is evidenced: 1) Torrance's reliance on the *homoousion* of Nicaea I and Constantinople I, which implicitly rejects the Hellenistic distinction between the *kosmos noetos* (intelligible world) and the *kosmos aisthetos* (sensible world)—the impermeable boundary between the divine and created orders; 2) his reliance on the Athanasian-Cyrillian axis of patristic thought about the nature of the incarnation, which insists upon a Christology that stresses the coinherence of "the being of God in his in acts" and the "acts of God are in his being";[5] and 3) his understanding of the σκοπός (*skopos*) or goal of Scripture being Christ, which drives his assessment that the Old Testament is the "pre-history of the incarnation" and his vision of theological exegesis. In my judgment, there is almost no insight of Torrance's more relevant to contemporary academic theology than the need for a restored connection with the worshiping church. Outside of the evangelical and doxological dimension of theology imparted and experienced in the context of the synaxis (that is, the worshiping assembly), academic theology morphs into a reflection of the priorities imparted from other forms of tacit knowledge and derived from sources extrinsic to God in Christ.

Torrance was not a patrologist, and his retrieval of the fathers was selective and guided by his social location and aims as a Reformed churchman and professor of dogmatics. For this reason, he has been accused of reading his

---

3. Torrance, *The Trinitarian Faith* (Edinburgh: T&T Clark, 1987), 47.

4. Colyer writes, "Because theology is concerned with a redemptive self-communication by the living God, theological inquiry requires evangelical and doxological participation, if it is to reflect the redemptive character of God and God's activity in the biblical witness. Of course, this is what makes theology rather different than natural science, since theological inquiry deals with the living God who comes to us in *Self*-revelation that demands a participation with characteristics different than what is found in natural science. Torrance often asserts that we cannot know God behind God's back or apart from God's purposes for our lives," Elmer M. Colyer, *The Nature of Doctrine in T. F. Torrance's Theology* (Eugene, OR: Wipf & Stock, 2001), 61.

5. Thomas F. Torrance, *Theology in Reconstruction* (London: SCM Press, 1965), 265.

own Barthian-Calvinian synthesis back into patristic theology. Torrance was aware of his selectivity, and understanding his aims in his project of retrieval is critical to grasping how he uses the fathers and conceptualizes the patristic consensus. He did not intend to repristinate the church fathers as a whole, as if such a thing were possible, but to engage the fathers as privileged peers in the interpretation of Scripture. Thus, as Jason Radcliff has argued, "While truly returning to the Greek Fathers on their own terms Torrance was, at his core, an evangelical and Reformed theologian and churchman, and he approached the Fathers from this perspective."[6] This perspective inevitably inflected his reading and appropriation of the fathers, and over the course of this essay we will have occasion to discuss some of the limitations of his retrieval project for contemporary Reformed catholicity.

THE TACIT DIMENSION AND THE HOMOOUSIOS

Central to Torrance's theological vision is the conviction that God is really given and known in Jesus Christ. Through the election of Israel and his self-revelation in and through that nation, the images and themes that emerge in Israel's history become the types through which Christ may be understood. Israel is, as Torrance liked to stress, the "womb" of the incarnation.[7] Israel is therefore ever ancient, ever new in its relationship to Christ. Christ may only be understood as the culmination and climax of all that God revealed of himself in Israel and as an absolutely new fact introduced into history by God's entry into it. The glory of God flashes forth in the face of Jesus Christ in such a way that all that God is and all that he wills for humanity is known in and through Christ.

As he puts it in *The Trinitarian Faith*, "The ὁμοούσιος τῷ Πατρί (*homoousios tō Patri*) was revolutionary and decisive: it expressed the fact that what God is 'toward us' and 'in the midst of us' in and through the Word made flesh, he really is in himself; that he is in the internal relations of his transcendent being the very same Father, Son, and Holy Spirit that he is in his revealing and saving activity in time and space toward mankind."[8] There is thus an unprecedented and momentous upsurge in the capacity of humanity

---

6. Radcliff, *Torrance and the Church Fathers*, 50.

7. For example, see Thomas F. Torrance, *God and Rationality* (Eugene, OR: Wipf & Stock, 1997), 149.

8. Torrance, *Trinitarian Faith*, 130

to know God in Jesus Christ and to use ordinary human language drawn from the creation to describe God's character and nature. The *homoousion*, as the doctrinal expression of this ontological shift, "stands, not for the projection of the human into the divine, but for the projection of the divine into the human, and as such is the rock upon which all mythology is shattered."[9]

Among the various schools of Platonism, a distinction between the *kosmos aisthetos* and the *kosmos noetos* was axiomatic, a distinction between the world experienced in sense perception and the spiritual world known only by the mind in abstracting from things known empirically.[10] This distinction, Torrance argues, introduces a dualism into the creator-creation relationship that makes genuine knowledge of God impossible. Torrance argues that early Christian theologians such as Justin Martyr, Irenaeus, and Athenagoras all insisted upon the ontological realism of God's incarnation in Christ for this reason. Only if God makes himself known *within* the *kosmos aisthetos*, by inhabiting the experiential order from the inside, can there be real epistemic connection established between human beings and God: a real overcoming of the dualism between an unknowable creator and the created order through the mediator in whom divine and human are mingled together, yet without confusion.

The incarnation obliterates this axiomatic Platonic distinction by insisting that God has indeed become part of his creation and has therefore mediated a knowledge of himself through the person of Jesus Christ. The emphasis that Torrance places upon God's self-revelation and saving activity in the person of Christ leads him to insist upon the indissolubility of the person and work of Christ. The incarnation is atoning, and the atonement is incarnational. Any attempt to separate these two elements that converge in Christ results in a tragic dualism in which God is not really imparted in Christ. Not only does Christ do his atoning work vicariously, but he assumes humanity on our behalf vicariously as well. As I will discuss more in the section below, the redemptive weight accorded to the humanity of Christ leads Torrance to place Athanasius as the central figure in the patristic age. Torrance is

---

9. Torrance, *Trinitarian Faith*, 71.

10. See Thomas F. Torrance, *Theology in Reconciliation* (Grand Rapids: Eerdmans, 1996), 224, 240; "Theological Realism," in *The Philosophical Frontiers of Theology*, ed. Brian Hebblethwaite and Stewart Sutherland (Cambridge: Cambridge University Press, 1982), 171; and, *Christian Theology and Scientific Culture* (Oxford: Oxford University Press, 1981), 88.

especially drawn to Athanasius's development of a theological conceptuality capable of accommodating the newness of the divine self-revelation in Christ. The *homoousion* is the great achievement of Athanasius, because of the way in which it enables him to conceptualize the theandric and thus mediatorial personhood of Christ. It was Athanasius who enabled the church to

> develop an organic structure in theological understanding of God through discerning the coordination between the concrete pattern taken by the divine condescension in the Incarnation of the Son, and the inherent order of Trinitarian relations in the Godhead, linking them together through the pattern of God's interaction with us described in terms of *from* (or to) *the Father, through the Son, and in the Spirit.*[11]

When the Platonic distinction between the empirical and spiritual realms was reintroduced, especially in the Alexandrian context by Origen, it produced Arianism, which Torrance regards as a reversion to the conviction that God is, in essence, unknowable, and therefore that Jesus is a mere messenger, along the same lines as an angel, who does not really reveal God's nature and essence. When a distinction is posited between the creator and the created that does not account for the real knowledge of God proffered in the incarnation, then there is always posited with it some reserve, some differentiation between who God is in himself and who God is for us in Jesus Christ. But Torrance argues, with the early church, that "we cannot go behind the incarnation, for there is in fact no God behind the back of Jesus Christ, and no God apart from his own self-revelation."[12] One of Torrance's favorite aphorisms is that "God is really like Jesus."[13] Torrance was in agreement with the archbishop of Canterbury Michael Ramsey, another mid-twentieth-century theologian engaged in a project of Nicene retrieval, who repeated in many different contexts that "God is Christlike and in him is no unchristlikeness at all."[14]

---

11. Torrance, *Theology in Reconciliation*, 251.

12. Thomas F. Torrance, "Apprehension of God the Father," in *Speaking of the Christian God*, ed. Alvin Kimel Jr. (Grand Rapids: Eerdmans, 1992), 136.

13. Thomas F. Torrance, *Preaching Christ Today* (Grand Rapids: Eerdmans, 1994), 55–56; and Thomas F. Torrance, *Trinitarian Perspectives* (Edinburgh: T&T Clark, 2000), 86.

14. Arthur M. Ramsey, *God, Christ, and the World: A Study in Contemporary Theology* (London: SCM Press, 1969), 98.

Torrance naturally expressed proper modesty about the measure of the knowledge of the divine nature and the Trinitarian relations revealed in Christ, as well as the capacity of our words to name those realities. "To know God in this way [that is, through the incarnation] does not mean that we can know *what* the being of God is," Torrance writes, "but it does mean that we are given knowledge of God that is directly and objectively grounded in his eternal being." The purchase that the incarnation gives us is the confidence that what we know of God in Jesus Christ *is* the divine identity, that we will not discover more of God that contradicts what we know of him in Jesus Christ. It is thus not a comprehensive knowledge of God that is given, but it is, Torrance insists, an ontological knowledge. It is a knowledge that becomes well-founded through a disciplined process of refinement and attunement to the divine reality of which it is the expression in the human mind.

The knowledge of God in Christ, Torrance argues, is a knowledge ascetically won. The knowledge of God in Christ comes, in other words, only to the mind that has become attuned to "discerning the body" (1 Cor 11:29) through the practice of piety. Only by disciplining the mind and imagination are the concepts derived from ordinary language sanitized under the pressure of God's presence so as to be annexed by him in a genuine impartation of revelatory knowledge. Following Irenaeus, Torrance argues that holiness of life, prayer, fasting, and constant meditation upon the Scriptures (in the context of the *koinonia* of the gathered church and the witness of the historic doctors of the church) are all essential elements to apprehending the revelation of God.[15] A theologian who has not disciplined the mind through ascesis is a theologian in name only, because he or she lacks the necessary incipient theology that is the foundation of doctrinal formulation at a level of abstraction.[16]

The tacit dimension of theology formed through evangelical and doxological participation explains how ascesis and doctrine are related to one another. The problem of the knowledge of God is not simply a problem of the immensity of the object of knowledge, but the fact that we are not reconciled to God. Thus, "transformation and reconciliation of the mind" are

---

15. Torrance, *Trinitarian Faith*, 33, citing *Adversus Haereses*, 1.1.15; 2:40–45.

16. Thomas F. Torrance, *The Christian Doctrine of God: One Being Three Persons* (Edinburgh: T&T Clark, 1996), 89.

more important in the process of doctrinal formulation than is the academic habitus.[17] It is in evangelical or doxological participation and ascesis that we are transformed by the renewing of our minds so that we are made capable of being imprinted with the knowledge of God. The tacit dimension forms us, therefore, both in being reconciled to God so that we have the capacity to know him, and in really imparting that knowledge to us. As Torrance puts it in *The Christian Doctrine of God,*

> A child by the age of five has learned, we are told, an astonishing amount about the physical world to which he or she has become spontaneously and intuitively adapted—far more than the child could ever understand if he or she turned out to be the most brilliant of physicists. Likewise, I believe we learn far more about God as Father, Son and Holy Spirit, into whose Name we have been baptised, within the family and fellowship and living tradition of the Church than we can ever say: it becomes built into the structure of our souls and minds, and we know much more than we can ever tell. This is what happens evangelically and personally to us within the membership of the Church, the Body of Christ in the world, when through the transforming power of his Word and Spirit our minds become inwardly and intuitively adapted to know the living God. We become spiritually and intellectually implicated in patterns of divine order that are beyond our powers fully to articulate in explicit terms, but we are aware of being apprehended by divine Truth as it is in Jesus which steadily presses for increasing realisation in our understanding, articulation and confession of faith. That is how Christian theology gains its initial impetus, and is then reinforced through constant reading and study of the Bible within the community of the faithful.[18]

Formation in the tacit dimension of theology is not a sufficient condition of doctrinal formulation, but it is a necessary one, so that Evagrius's oft-repeated but rarely understood maxim is true as a necessary condition of theological reasoning: "If you pray, you are a theologian, and a theologian is one

---

17. Thomas F. Torrance, *Atonement: The Person and Work of Christ,* ed. Robert T. Walker (Downers Grove, IL and Milton Keynes: IVP and Paternoster, 2009), 437–47.

18. Torrance, *The Christian Doctrine of God,* 89.

who prays."[19] All true theology, as Hans Urs von Balthasar pointed out, is *betende und kneide Theologie*, "praying and kneeling theology."[20] Torrance writes that "to know God and be holy, to know God and worship, to know God and be committed to him in consecration, love and obedience, go inseparably together."[21] It is critical reflection on what is given in this evangelical or doxological strata of theological reasoning that facilitates the process of doctrinal clarification. Doctrinal reflection is a process that resembles a spiral based upon increasing insight that emerges from rumination on the same material in public worship and private devotions. Taking the example of Athanasius, Torrance demonstrates that the *homoousion* emerges from his reading of Scripture and then becomes the lens through which he reads Scripture. This is a form of circularity, Torrance argues, but not a vicious circularity[22] because it indicates that words do not create the structures of reality but rather serve and express those realities as they are increasingly comprehended in their complexity and manifold strata.

Therefore, Torrance argues, theology is a disciplined science, analogous to other sciences, because it is bound in its manner of knowing to the object of its knowledge. Torrance argues that this a theme articulated in Irenaeus's discussion of the *regula fidei*, or the canon of truth, as "assertions of belief that are organized from beyond themselves by their common ground in the apostolic deposit of faith and ultimately by the self-revelation of God in Jesus Christ."[23] It can also be discerned in Hilary's assertion that "God cannot be apprehended except through Himself."[24] Since the fullness of the revelation of God is given in Christ, there is no possibility of an autonomous natural theology. All theology that is "in accordance with the nature (κατὰ φύσιν) of the reality investigated," is theology that is disciplined by the knowledge of God as it really is in Christ.[25]

---

19. Evagrius, *The Praktikos & Chapters on Prayer*, trans. John Bamberger (Kalamazoo: Cistercian Publications, 1981), 65.

20. See Aidan Nichols, *The Shape of Catholic Theology* (Edinburgh: T&T Clark, 1991), 26.

21. Thomas F. Torrance, *The Mediation of Christ* (Grand Rapids: Eerdmans, 1994), 26.

22. Thomas F. Torrance, *Space, Time, and Resurrection* (Edinburgh: T&T Clark, 1976), 15.

23. Torrance, *Trinitarian Faith*, 34.

24. Torrance, *Trinitarian Faith*, 21.

25. Torrance, *Trinitarian Faith*, 51.

If God can only be known through God—that is, God as he is known in Jesus Christ—then we do not approach doctrinal formulation primarily by resourcing knowledge brought from other intellectual foundations and attempt to interpret God under the aspect of those sources. Speaking of God with epistemic realism requires that we be united with God through the humanity of Christ, so that our speech may be characterized by *theosebeia* (godliness) and *eusebeia* (piety).[26] This is a correlate of the *homoousion*—that natural theology is a theology that approaches the "Father of lights" (Jas 1:16–17) from a grounding in the union with Christ, rather than by reasoning autonomously about God from the attributes revealed in creation. Athanasius's axiom that it is more accurate and devout to approach God as Father through the Son "than to approach him through his works by tracing them back to him as their uncreated source" is critical for Torrance.[27] As Athanasius pointed out, there was a time when God was not creator, but never a time when the Son was not a son, and therefore never a time when the Father was not Father. The Son incarnate in Christ reveals what is most true about the eternal life of God.

Even though we can only speak about God in ordinary human language (and the language of the Scriptures is ordinary human language), God annexes that language to imprint us with knowledge of himself in the synaxis and in the rigorous study of Scripture, which makes possible its disciplined purification. Since God really gives himself in Jesus Christ, and since Jesus is really present by the Holy Spirit in word and sacrament, the gathered people of God become the central and indispensable way that God reveals himself and objectifies himself. "Theological thinking," Torrance writes, "is *theo*-logical, thinking not just from our own centres, but from a centre in God, from a divine ground. It is essentially *theo*-nomous thinking. It pivots upon the fact that God has made Himself known and continues to make Himself known, that He objectifies Himself for us, so that our knowledge is a fulfilled meeting with objective reality."[28]

That God really gives himself in Jesus Christ is the lynchpin to the cogency and coherence of dogmatic theology, which repairs the damaged

---

26. Torrance, *Trinitarian Faith*, 38.

27. Torrance, *Trinitarian Faith*, 49.

28. Thomas F. Torrance, *Theological Science*, 2nd ed. (Edinburgh: T&T Clark, 1996), 29.

relationship that exists between language and ontology.[29] Words themselves do not possess the power to signify but only insofar as they are cleansed through the process of reconciliation in the body to Christ, which occurs in the ascetical economy of the Christian life centered upon the synaxis. As Torrance writes, "The application of our ordinary language to speech about God involves a fundamental shift in its meaning. We cannot but use language taken from our common experience in this world when we make theological statements, but even so it is the subject that must be allowed to determine the meaning."[30]

This is important because there is nothing magical or hallowed about particular words, even the words of Scripture. The *homoousion*, Torrance argues, "was gained through hard exegetical activity," even though it is a not a biblical term. "It is by no means a speculative construction, an interpretation put upon the facts by the fathers of Nicaea; rather it is a truth that was forced upon the understanding of the Church as it allowed the biblical witness to imprint its own patterns upon its mind."[31] Thus the *homoousion* emerged as the privileged, but by no means exclusive, word to describe the identity of the shared *ousia* of Father and Son when this confession was threatened by Arianism. It was a term whose meaning developed over time from its original association with the form of monarchianism advocated by Paul of Samosata to the proper expression which identifies the shared *ousia* of Father, Son, and Holy Spirit.[32] This previous use does not become a barrier to its updated use at Nicaea. As Jason Radcliff argues, "Terms remain open to being re-defined and changed on the basis of the realities they signify. ... This means that knowledge of new realities forced new terms to be used and old terms to be reused with different meanings in order to make them appropriate to the realities to which they refer."[33]

Theological language is, as Torrance frames it, "functional and not analytical language,"[34] which comes to signify under the pressure of divine

---

29. Torrance, *Theology in Reconstruction*, 18.

30. Torrance, *Theology in Reconstruction*, 30.

31. Torrance, *Theology in Reconstruction*, 40.

32. Torrance, *Trinitarian Faith*, 72, 77, 116, 121, 125, 128, 194, 206, 217, 221, 226, 237, 246, 310, 315, 319, 321, 327, 334.

33. Radcliff, *Torrance and the Church Fathers*, 80.

34. Torrance, *Theology in Reconciliation*, 242.

self-disclosure in the church's penetrative union with Christ. Citing Athanasius and Basil the Great, Torrance argues that theological reasoning proceeds through the words used, which point away from themselves to the genuine knowledge of God, rather than out of or from the ordinary referent of the words. The latter is mythological reasoning rather than true theology:

> The plain fact is, as Basil insisted, that if the Son were only a creature, mankind would be without any revelation of God whatsoever. In that case the Church would be left with no more than some kind of human self-understanding projected into God from a centre in itself and passed off as "revelation." As Athanasius frequently pointed out, that was the kind of "revelation" heretics trafficked in, something they devised (Κατ'ἐπίνοιαν) in accordance with their subjective fantasies, rather than something which they received from beyond themselves and thought out (κατὰ διάνοιαν) in accordance with the objective truth of God. If it is not God himself in his own being that we have to do in revelation, then it is not with *theologia* (θεολογία) but *mythologia* (μυθολογία), not with theology but mythology, that we are concerned. Moreover, if Christ is detached from God, then he himself is no longer central to the substance of the Gospel, but is only a transient variable representation of God, a detached symbolic image and no more. And inevitably, as Arius claimed, there would be "many words" and even "myriads" of conceptions of God.[35]

The *homoousion*, to summarize what we have said so far, was a theological term that emerged through critical reflection, not from a source within itself but from the revelation of God in Jesus Christ. It is the church united to Christ by the Spirit that is capable of discerning the depths of God revealed in Christ. The church confesses the *homoousion* of Son and Spirit with the Father as the Spirit intensifies the work of Christ in the doxological participation of the church in the atoning work of Christ. Thus, this taxis of evangelical participation in the reality of God in worship and critical reflection upon the deposit imparted in word and sacrament was the indispensable foundation of speaking with godliness and piety for the early church, and it is central to Torrance's project of retrieval.

---

35. Torrance, *Trinitarian Faith*, 134.

TORRANCE AND THE ATHANASIAN-CYRILLIAN
AXIS IN CHRISTOLOGY

As we have already mentioned, at the heart of Torrance's retrieval project is the figure of Athanasius. Rev. Fr. George Dragas recalls that the first time he met Torrance in his office, he noticed two artifacts: an icon of St. Athanasius and a picture of John Calvin. When asked about Athanasius, Torrance replied, "*Always* follow the example of Athanasius."[36] Athanasius becomes the yardstick by which other patristic figures are measured. Rather than demarcating a golden era in patristic theology, as Jason Radcliff argues, Athanasius serves as an exemplar thinker, embodying the patristic consensus for Torrance. Irenaeus is a worthy progenitor; Hilary is a worthy peer; Cyril is a worthy successor. Between the two extreme tendencies in Christology represented by Alexandria and Antioch, Torrance sees a "middle stream" that leads from "Irenaeus to Athanasius to Cyril."[37]

Famously, the Cappadocians, particularly Basil and Gregory of Nyssa, are compared unfavorably with Athanasius by Torrance, a judgment that created a barrier in his dialogues with the Eastern Orthodox.[38] Gregory the Theologian is affirmed insofar as he agrees with Athanasius. Torrance understands Cyril of Alexandria as the rightful heir of Athanasius, being the figure who most consistently worked the *homoousion* through to its logical conclusions in Christology. The vicarious humanity of Christ in its redemptive dimensions that the mature Torrance commits himself to probably owes more to Cyril than to Athanasius in its concrete formulations.

The sorting that Torrance engages in throughout his patrological research is indicative of his broader predilection for typology, and he has

---

36. George Dragas, quoted in Jason Radcliff, *Thomas F. Torrance and the Orthodox-Reformed Theological Dialogue* (Eugene, OR: Pickwick, 2018), 14.

37. Torrance, *Theology in Reconciliation*, 229.

38. George Dragas is critical of Torrance's polarization of the "Athanasian-Cyrillian axis" and the "Orthodox Cappadocian deviation" as concerns the *taxis* in the procession of the persons in the Trinity. Matthew Baker and George Dragas, "Interview with Protopresbyter George Dion. Dragas regarding T. F. Torrance," in *T. F. Torrance and Eastern Orthodoxy*, 14. Torrance claimed that both Athanasius and Cyril refused any subordinationism in the Trinity, whereas the Cappadocians, and in particular Basil and Gregory of Nyssa introduced the idea of *arche* into the divine life as a principal of generation associated with the person of the Father, rather than the shared *ousia* substance of the Trinity. Torrance writes, "The *Mone Arche* ... is identical with the trinity, the *Monas* with the *Trias* ... and it is precisely in the *Trias* that we know God to be *Monas*. ... The *Monarchia* or the *Monas* is essentially and intrinsically Trinitarian in the inner relations of God's eternal *Ousia*," Torrance, *Christian Doctrine of God*, 183.

been rightly criticized for sloppiness in this regard. Torrance tends to sort patristic thought into streams, with an evangelical stream emerging from the Athanasius-Cyril axis in Christology; the Cappadocian stream which leads to a Byzantine form of dualism, represented by the neo-Palamism of Vladimir Lossky and the resourcing of the essence/energies distinction in the God-creation interaction; and the Western stream beginning with Augustine that leads to a distinctively Latin form of dualism that Torrance often referred to as the "Latin heresy." The Latin heresy, in which the work of Christ becomes separated from his person, turning the atonement into a forensic, transactional exchange between Christ and God on behalf of humanity, has been widely disputed and is probably the most contested aspect of his research in patristics.[39] For our purposes, it should be said in Torrance's defense that he is willing to resource both the Byzantine and Western streams insofar as they support the Athanasius-Cyril axis, as he does in borrowing from Leontius of Byzantium the *anhypostasia* and the *enhypostasia* of Christ's humanity, discussed below. However, his project of patristic retrieval is decidedly centered on the fourth and fifth centuries and, in particular, on the *Nicenum*.

Torrance focuses on Athanasius and Cyril because he believes that in them the dualism that posits an unbridgeable chasm between God and creation has been healed. In Christ God enters human experience in such a way that he can be fully representative of God and fully representative of the whole of humanity at the same time. In the incarnation, Torrance writes, "God and man are so related in Jesus Christ, that *Jesus exists as man only so far as he exists as God,* and yet as God he also has an existence as flesh or *sarx.*"[40]

Following several patristic precedents and through a profound meditation on and exegesis of the book of Hebrews (especially 5:7), Torrance insists that the flesh that Christ assumes is fallen flesh—the *sarx* that Paul says is in rebellion against God (Gal 5:17-25). Living fallen human existence as God, Christ through "loud cries and tears" wrestles with our fallen humanity and bends it back into obedience and submission to God. "In his incarnation Christ not only took upon himself our physical existence from God, but in taking it into himself he at the same time healed it, sanctified it, and changed

---

39. On Augustine's continuity with Nicaea, see Lewis Ayres, *Augustine and the Trinity* (Cambridge: Cambridge University Press, 2010).

40. T. F. Torrance, *Incarnation: The Person and Life of Christ,* ed. Robert T. Walker (Downers Grove, IL: InterVarsity Press, 2008, 67.

it, bending our will back to agreement with the divine will, and bringing our human mind back into agreement with the divine mind—and so in the innermost being of the incarnate Son, throughout the whole course of his life, Jesus Christ converted the mind and will of estranged humanity back to the Father. That was the great *palingennesia*, the renewing and sanctifying of humanity before God."[41] The *homoousion* does not mean merely that the revelation of God comes to us in Christ. Rather, it means that Christ faithfully lives out the human vocation in obedience to God and thus brings humanity back to God. As Torrance puts it in his dogmatic theology lectures at Edinburgh,

> The New Testament teaches … that though Jesus Christ assumed our fallen human existence, our fallen flesh under the dominion of sin and under the judgment of the law of God, he was yet without sin. He was wholly and perfectly obedient to God the Father. In the Hebrew idiom the Word became event in a way that corresponds faithfully to the Word, and therefore the Word made flesh is God's truth. He is the faithful and the true, the perfect amen to God in the flesh. Although the Son enters into the resistance and hostility of our flesh against God, he does not resist God but throughout the whole course of his life is obedient and true and faithful. "I am the truth," Jesus said and that applies not only to his bringing the truth of God to mankind but to his whole human life as truth done into the flesh, as truth enacted in the midst of our untruth, as truth fulfilled from within man and from the side of man, truth issuing out of human life in obedient response to the truth of God.[42]

Thus, Jesus's humanity is vicarious, assumed for our sake, because the unassumed is the unhealed. And in itself, his vicarious humanity is redemptive. All that Christ does in the flesh is atonement, including the cross, the resurrection, and the ascension, and the atonement is continued in the work of the Holy Spirit, who is *homoousios* with the Father and the Son, uniting the church to the person of the mediator. The wondrous "atoning exchange" that happens when Christ is made ours through the Holy Spirit, wherein

---

41. Torrance, *Atonement*, 70.

42. Torrance, *Incarnation*, 64.

his humanity becomes ours is in fact "the atonement operating within the ontological depths of human being."[43] The Greek fathers of the church did not hesitate to call this renewal and transformation of our humanity θεοσίς or θεοποιεσίς, that is, deification. Torrance was initially uneasy with this word because of his Reformed commitments, but by the mid-1960s he was regularly using it, at least as qualified by scare quotes.[44]

Christ's humanity is humanity in its ontological depths, and it exhibits or "bodies forth" what humanity was intended to be in its creation. This is because, as Torrance writes, "in the strict sense God only is Person, for he is in himself the fullness of personal Being—he is personalising Person."[45] Christ is the "icon" of the invisible God (Col 1:15), living humanly as God. Thus, in the hypostatic union, Christ's humanity becomes personalizing or humanizing as well. In developing this theme, Torrance is explicitly following the lead of Cyril of Alexandria, for whom the humanity of Christ, through its incorporation into the Word, deifies our humanity as we ingest him in the Eucharist and are "clothed with him" in the whole ascetical economy of the Christian life.[46]

Christ's humanity becomes the archetype of restored humanity, just as Adam was the archetype for fallen humanity (Rom 5:12-17). Thus, all of humanity is caught up into, incorporated into, and represented by Christ's humanity in his incarnation: "To hold that some people are not included in his incarnate and redeeming activity is to cut at the very root of his reality as the Creator incarnate in space and time, as he in whom all things in the universe, visible and invisible, were created, hold together and are reconciled by the blood of his cross (Col. 1:15-20)."[47] His human personhood is not "an empty mask of the divine Person,"[48] nor is it merely a gracious union and adoption into Sonship with an already existent individual. By insisting that Christ is the "personalizing person," God living humanly, Torrance is explicitly

---

43. Torrance, *Trinitarian Faith*, 189.

44. Matthew Baker, "The Correspondence between T. F. Torrance and Georges Florovsky (1950–1973)," in *T. F. Torrance and Eastern Orthodoxy*, 292.

45. Thomas F. Torrance, "The Goodness and Dignity of Man," *Modern Theology* 4 (1988): 318.

46. John McGuckin, *Saint Cyril of Alexandria* (Leiden: Brill, 1994), 187, 197.

47. Thomas F. Torrance, "The Atonement. The Singularity of Christ and the Finality of the Cross: The Atonement and the Moral Order," in *Universalism and the Doctrine of Hell*, ed. Nigel M. de S. Cameron (Exeter: Paternoster, 1992), 245.

48. Torrance, *Mediation of Christ*, 67.

guarding against both monophysitism on the one hand and Nestorianism on
the other. Here, Torrance expressly follows the conciliar reading of Cyril in
Chalcedon, rather than his later miaphysite followers. The humanity of Christ
is not absorbed into the Word so that it becomes a mere shell or avatar of the
Word, but Jesus's humanity is nonetheless unique and paradigmatic. It is the
humanity to which all other instantiations of humanity must be conformed
by grace precisely because of its "natural" union with the Word.

The theandric existence of Christ means that he is at once the creative
source and the true secret of our humanity, "because in him our humanity
is lodged, because all mankind consists in him," and therefore "he is the
only one who can really represent all men and women from the innermost
center and depth of human being."[49] As the source and summit of all that is
most human, all of humanity is caught up into his gracious work of renewal
and regeneration by the Holy Spirit. In the resurrection, this hominization
reaches its crescendo. It is the "actualization of human reality, the humanizing in Jesus of dehumanized man, the establishing of the fact that man
is."[50] In Christ's resurrection humanity is given a permanence and a solid-
ity that puts to rest the futility, the wreckage, the anti-creation of this age.
So, "the resurrection of Jesus Christ and of human nature in him is therefore the foundation and source of a profound and radically new Christian
humanism," an incarnational humanism which looks to Christ as the meaning and purpose and orientation of human beings.[51] Christ's representation
and incorporation of humanity is essentially a corporate reality—something
that applies to humanity as a whole, but something to which human persons
must add their "amen." This grace can be refused, as Torrance makes clear,
but because Christ's hominization of humanity is so complete, "if anyone
goes to hell they go to hell, only because, inconceivably, they refuse the positive act of the divine acceptance of them, and refuse to acknowledge that
God has taken their rejection of him upon himself."[52]

Christ is at once the singular representative and paradigmatic exemplar of humanity, and a particular human being, a pious Israelite sharing
the hopes of his people. He is not a generic human being, humanity in the

---

49. Torrance, *Atonement*, 126.

50. Thomas F. Torrance, Space, Time and Resurrection (Edinburgh: T&T Clark, 1998), 79.

51. Torrance, *Atonement*, 239.

52. Torrance, *Atonement*, 157.

abstract (if such a thing were possible), sanitized of all cultural and biological characteristics, but a tangible human person. He is the Messiah, the culmination of the hopes of Israel. He is the suffering servant of Israel, elect from that nation, just as that nation was elect among the nations to incarnate the redemptive movement of God to reconcile the nations to himself. Precisely as this tangible human person, he is the paradigm and the representative of all humanity. As Torrance writes in his first work *Theological Science,*

> In the incarnation the eternal Son assumed human nature into oneness with himself but in that assumption Jesus Christ is not only real man but a man. He is at once the One and the Many, for in Jesus the Creator become man, all human nature has been assumed. The point for our consideration here is the fact that it is in this union of the human hypostasis or person and the divine Hypostasis or Persons that Jesus Christ is the personalising Person whose saving power is brought to bear directly upon us. In him the incarnate Son and Word of God, Creator and creature, divine and human nature, are united in one Person, so that in Jesus our human being is radically personalised and indeed humanised, and as such is brought into intimate union with God and into the Communion of the Holy Trinity.[53]

The doctrinal architecture that makes possible this critical distinction is his borrowing of the patristic predication of the *anhypostasia* and the *enhypostasia* of Christ's humanity. This distinction is traceable, though not in the exact formulation in which it was later taught, to Cyril of Alexandria. It flowers in the writings of Severus of Antioch, Leontius of Byzantium, and John of Damascus.[54] The *anhypostasia* refers to the fact that Christ's humanity has no personal subsistence outside the Word of God. In other words, God did not adopt an already existing human being as his Son, but rather created humanity afresh for his own personal indwelling from the Virgin Mary. Indeed, that is the significance of the virginal conception and virgin birth, as Torrance makes clear. Christ is therefore *sui generis,* not identifiable with any other human being.

---

53. Torrance, *Theological Science*, 161.

54. Man Kei Ho, *A Critical Study on T. F. Torrance's Theology of the Incarnation* (Bern: Peter Lang, 2008), 91.

The hypostatic union is a unique union, a *natural* union, not a *gracious* union, between God the Son and the man Jesus Christ. The divine *ousia* in the hypostasis of the Son is mingled together with humanity, but not confused. No other human being can claim personally to be the Messiah or the redeemer of humanity. All other human beings united to Christ by grace are derivatively "personalized" by Christ but are not themselves Christ: "his full and complete human nature was united to God in a unique way (hypostatically in one person) as our human nature is not, and never will be."[55] In that sense Christ can be representative of all humanity, rather than just a particular subset of humanity, such as ethnic Jews or men only. As Torrance puts it, "Because he was God's Son become man he could both incarnate God for us, and represent us before God, this one man on behalf of all men and women."[56]

The *enhypostasia* affirms that the humanity that Christ assumed was not independent of a particular incarnation as a specific person. The Word "subsists," or is enhypostatic, in a particular person. Although apart from the incarnation there was no person called Jesus, since the human nature of Jesus was the humanity assumed by the Word, Jesus was not a generic or abstract human being, but rather a real flesh-and-blood person who could faithfully obey the covenant entered into between Yahweh and Israel, who could be the "servant" of Isaiah's songs who summed up or concentrated Israel in himself. Christ fulfills the covenant with Israel and in so doing fulfills God's purposes for humanity and makes it possible for humanity as a whole to participate in those purposes.

For the fathers of the church, the personalization and humanization of persons united with Christ did not occur automatically or reflexively but rather through participation in the rhythms of the church. The ascetical economy of fasting, almsgiving, and prayer, together with the gathered worship of the church expressed in word and sacrament are the chief means of grace that Christ uses to incorporate his body into himself. The fathers profess a "sacramental realism" in which the divine humanity of Christ stabilizes or divinizes the humanity of the church so that it is conformed to his image. Both Hilary and Cyril use the undisputed fact that the Spirit divinizes humanity through the body of Christ present in the Eucharist in order to

---

55. Torrance, *Incarnation*, 230.

56. Torrance, *Incarnation*, 153.

condemn Arian and Nestorian opponents for refusing to confess the divinity of Christ and the hypostatic union.[57]

Torrance, likely because of Barth's influence on his theology, can sometimes speak as though the incorporation of all humanity in Christ means that all human beings are automatically or involuntarily transformed by Christ. He is in fact happy to admit something like this. In his description of baptism he insists that it is not our "faith and decision to accept him as our savior" that is signified, but rather "what Christ has done on our behalf when he incorporated himself into our humanity and acted in our place and in our name before God."[58] However, at other points Torrance makes clear that it is piety and worship through which Christ unites and transforms persons into his humanity. Because of his engagement with the fathers, Torrance places a much greater emphasis upon sacramental participation and sacramental realism than do many of his Reformed peers.[59] Unquestionably, the sacraments are real participations in Christ's risen and ascended humanity which fortify and sustain his people. It is through sacramental participation that there is a real engrafting into Christ and a maintaining of that union with him through the Eucharist. In his dogmatic lectures Torrance writes,

> Between the times, faith and hope are confirmed and nourished by the two sacraments of the Word made flesh, baptism and holy communion, which are essentially signs belonging to the fullness of time, that is to say, filled with the complete incarnate presence of the Son of God, who gives himself to us in forgiveness and reconciliation through the cross and the resurrection. That is communicated in baptism, on the one hand, in a once and for all sense, and here the wholeness of Christ and the completeness of our salvation are particularly enshrined. In baptism we have to do with the new creation, the perfect body of Christ into which we become incorporated. In holy communion, on the other hand, we have to do with the continuance of that new creation and its breaking in as enduring event in conditions of time, with the church

---

57. Hilary, *The Trinity*, trans. Stephen McKenna (Washington, D.C.: Catholic University of America Press, 1954), 8.13, page 265; Cyril of Alexandria, *Third Letter of Cyril to Nestorius* 7, in John McGuckin, *St Cyril of Alexandria*, 270–1.

58. Torrance, *Atonement*, 192.

59. George Hunsinger is a highly notable exception. *The Eucharist and Ecumenism: Let Us Keep the Feast* (Cambridge: Cambridge University Press, 2008).

as the bodying forth in this fallen world of communion with Christ. … Unquestionably, therefore, the two sacraments are given to us to enshrine the double consciousness of the New Testament eschatological faith and hope, to enable us to hold in the grasp of our faith and hope the *parousia* as both a real presence here and now and yet as an advent presence still to come. At the same time both sacraments make it quite clear that the kingdom of God is amongst us not in word only with suspended action, not in Spirit only, but in deed and in power, as real act in time, as word-deed enacted in our flesh and blood and inserted into history.[60]

The highlighting of the proleptic and eschatological presence of Christ in the sacraments and Torrance's insistence that the saving flesh of Christ is given to the church in its participation in these rites emerges from his resourcing of Athanasian-Cyrillian Christology and sacramentology. These foci, especially in his later work, distinguish him from other Reformed persons of the era and constitute a movement toward a Reformed catholicity rooted in the confession of the ancient church.

ATONEMENT AND THE CHURCH FATHERS

The final aspect of Torrance's thought that I want to highlight in this essay that reflects his indebtedness to the patristic age is Torrance's pioneering work on the atonement. As a work of contemporary dogmatics, his research into the atonement is significant for its development of an intentionally theological exegesis of Scripture that is open to the insights of the early church. Torrance admits the validity and necessity of historical-critical modalities to contextualize and unearth the diverse strata of the texts of the Bible, but he is skeptical that these insights in themselves can do justice to the character of the Bible, and in particular the Old Testament, as Christian Scripture.[61] The early church's confession emerged from a pattern of exegesis which understood the *scopus* or key to understanding the Scripture to be Christ.

---

60. Torrance, *Atonement*, 413–14.

61. Torrance writes that although historical-critical studies are necessary, "the theologian knows that he cannot get very far *theologically* with historico-critical and historico-analytical methods, which can be of help to him only at comparatively superficial and formal levels of thought," Torrance, *Space, Time, and Resurrection*, 12.

By centering interpretation upon Christ, the Old Testament became, for the early church, the "pre-history of the incarnation,"[62] and Israel the "womb for the incarnation, the appropriate matrix of thought, speech and life for the definitive reception of revelation in Christ."[63] The Old Testament, Torrance argues, "is the revelation of the *verbum incarnandum;* the New Testament is the revelation of the *verbum incarnatum:* the center of gravity in both is the Incarnation itself, to which the Old Testament is stretched out in expectation, and the New Testament looks back in fulfillment."[64] Without Israel, there would have been no conceptual apparatus with which to understand Christ's redemptive work. However, through the unfolding narrative of God's prepa-ratory work in Israel, thematic elements emerge which converge upon and find their proper configuration in Christ. Among these structures, Torrance includes "the Word and Name of God, revelation, mercy, truth, holiness, mes-siah, prophet, priest, covenant, sacrifice, forgiveness, reconciliation, redemp-tion, atonement, etc., and those basic patterns of worship found in Israel's ancient liturgy or in the psalms."[65] These elements must be understood not on their own terms, but insofar as they find their center in Christ. Nonetheless, one cannot have Christ without Israel: "Jesus Christ, not Israel, constitutes the reality and substance of God's self-revelation, but Jesus Christ in Israel and not apart from Israel, so that Israel the servant of the Lord is neverthe-less included by God for ever within his elected way of mediating knowledge of himself to the world."[66] Torrance is guided in his typological reading of Scripture by the patterns of promise and fulfillment and shadow and reality developed in the patristic period.[67]

Torrance sees redemption expressed in three different ways or under three different aspects in the Old Testament represented by three Hebrew terms, and these strands are powerfully taken up into the person and work of Christ. Torrance identifies these three aspects as *padah* redemption, *kipper*

---

62. Torrance, *Incarnation,* 38.

63. Colyer, *The Nature of Doctrine in T. F. Torrance's Theology,* 137.

64. Thomas F. Torrance, "Israel and the Incarnation," *Interpretation* 10 (1956): 306.

65. Colyer, *The Nature of Doctrine,* 137.

66. Torrance, *Mediation of Christ,* 22–23.

67. He explicitly names the motif of shadow to reality in *Theological Science:* "the shadowy prefigurements of redemption under the old covenant have now given way to the final truth of redemption through the sacrifice of Christ in the new covenant." Torrance, *Theological Science,* 172.

or *kopher* redemption, and *go'el* redemption. *Padah* highlights the dramatic aspect of God's redeeming work, because it focuses attention on the judgment of God and deliverance of his people from out of the hands of an alien power. It is not only deliverance from oppression, but from the "bondage of guilt and out of the thraldom of sin," and therefore it is always accompanied by sacrifice, which is somehow involved in the liberatory release.[68] The *kipper* or *kopher* aspect of redemption focuses on the ritual aspect of redemption, on the covering over or the blotting out of sin that happens through the sacrifice: "as atonement it involves judgment upon the wrong either directly or vicariously through the offering of an equivalent, of life for life, and through this expiation of the wrong, atonement involves reinstatement to favour and restoration to holiness before God."[69] *Go'el* redemption focuses attention on the ontological aspect of redemption, as it is rooted in the sure purpose of God to save, his steadfastness and his loving-kindness to his people. It is through this purpose that God takes Israel's cause upon himself and stands as their vindicator and advocate, analogously to the role of the kinsman-redeemer, as in the case of Naomi and Ruth. These three elements must be held together in the atonement or there is distortion introduced. Torrance is especially concerned that *padah* and *go'el* conceptions of redemption be wedded to the *kipper* aspect. Elevation of the *kipper* element above the other two is what produced, he thinks, the Latin heresy, which consists of "construing salvation in wholly forensic and external categories, and results in an instrumental conception of the humanity of Christ"[70] rather than seeing that "in the very act of assuming our flesh the Word sanctified and hallowed it."[71]

Each of these three strands of redemption finds culmination and convergence in the work of Christ in his prophetic, priestly, and kingly offices, although these offices do not neatly map onto the concepts advanced through the Hebrew terms. The ideas or motifs rather than the terms themselves are drawn into service to inflect the meaning of each of these offices. These patterns, Torrance argues, were identified early in the life of the church, and his project of patristic retrieval involves a recapitulation of these themes

---

68. Torrance, *Atonement*, 30.

69. Torrance, *Atonement*, 35.

70. Torrance, *Atonement*, 54.

71. Torrance, *Incarnation*, 63.

from the writings of the fathers. Torrance believes that especially the Greek fathers held together these three aspects of redemption drawn from the text of Scripture in their conceptions of Christ and, in so doing, developed both the *homoousion* and the vicarious humanity of Christ.

In *Divine Meaning*, Torrance expressly identifies this threefold pattern of understanding the atonement of Christ with the sermons on *pascha* by Melito of Sardis.[72] For Melito, the "incarnation is … intrinsically atoning, and the atonement is essentially incarnational, for the saving act and the divine-human being of the Saviour are inseparable. As Saviour, Christ embodies the act and the fact of our salvation in his own person."[73] Melito develops this theme through rumination upon God's mighty act of deliverance of Israel from Egypt and linking this to the atoning sacrifice of Jesus, connections which are internalized by the church in the ongoing celebration of Easter as *pascha*, the new deliverance of God's people from a greater oppression to sin, death, and the devil. In this description of redemption, the dramatic aspect is highlighted, particularly in the comparison of God's deliverance of Israel from "the house of bondage and the power of death" with "what has actually taken place in Christ who came from heaven to become man in order to take our desperate condition upon himself, to be judged in our place, and to ransom us from the power of evil through his own blood, thereby destroying the power of death over us, and thus through his own death and resurrection to be the Pascha of our salvation."[74]

As already indicated in the preceding quote, the dramatic aspect is bound together in Melito's preaching with the ritual aspect. Christ is at once the dramatic victory, in the unity of his being-in-his-acts and his acts-in-his-being, over sin, death, and the devil, and the covering and sacrifice for sin that is ransoming the church from the "service of the world, delivering us from slavery to liberty, from darkness to light, and thereby constituting us a new priesthood and a special people belonging to himself forever."[75] Lastly, by highlighting the incarnational character of the atonement and the atoning character of the incarnation, Melito expresses the ontological dimension

---

72. Torrance, "Dramatic Proclamation of the Gospel: Melito of Sardis, *Homily on the Passion*," in *Divine Meaning: Studies in Patristic Hermeneutics* (Edinburgh: T&T Clark, 1995), 75–92

73. Torrance, *Divine Meaning*, 84.

74. Torrance, *Divine Meaning*, 84.

75. Torrance, *Divine Meaning*, 86.

of the atonement, ensuring at once that the ritual and dramatic dimension are not dissevered from Christ's person and that they are not permitted to fracture into a merely transactional exchange between humanity in God. Through Christ's atoning action humanity itself is changed by being taken up into an intimate relationship with God in the person of the Word.

Torrance highlights in *Divine Meaning* that the context of Melito's theological exposition is preaching, and therefore it is in the synaxis that these connections between the various strata of redemption become internalized by the people of God. Worship of Christ by the gathered body in word and sacrament is the context in which it becomes possible to link his atoning action with the Passover and to see each of these three aspects of redemption converging upon and taken up into Christ.[76] In his work on atonement, then, Torrance remains focused on the tacit dimension of theology, highlighting the emergence of doctrinal formulation from doxological and evangelical participation in the reality of Christ. Here as well as in the other areas we have discussed in the essay, Torrance remains committed to epistemic realism and evangelical theology, grounded in the gift of God's self-disclosure in Christ which is received in the gathered worship of the church and in its piety.

CONCLUSION

This essay has focused on the way in which Torrance's project of patristic retrieval aids both his attempt to overcome the dualisms between creator and creature and between the person and work of Christ that have emerged in various theological traditions, including his own Reformed tradition, and his insistence on the close connection between the experience of God in worship and the capacity to speak of God truthfully. In my experience in the academy, the gathered church was always problematic. Either the gathered church was embarrassing to academic theologians, a perennial source of bigotry, ignorance, odious political opinions, and apathy about social evils, or it was a laboratory in which newly minted patterns of constructive or correlational theology could be pioneered from the pulpit or in the church's common life. Torrance is refreshing because he offers a different paradigm that sees academic theology as a process of disciplined clarification in humility of what the church confesses in its worship. This pattern of thinking theologically

---

76. Torrance, "Dramatic Proclamation of the Gospel," 80–1.

from the church rather than to the church is to me the most fruitful aspect of Torrance's patristic retrieval project. In this way theology is the hand-maiden of the church, knowing that it is in the assembly, rather than in the cunning and craft of those privileged to think about the faith, that Jesus is most fully present.

3

—

TORRANCE AND THE DOCTRINE OF SCRIPTURE

Andrew T. B. McGowan

INTRODUCTION

I have been asked to engage with Torrance's doctrine of Scripture from the perspective of evangelical theology. This is a somewhat difficult subject, since Torrance never completed a study on the doctrine of Scripture. It means that his views on the origins, nature, and authority of Scripture must be culled from his books and other writings, which inevitably involves a degree of interpretation. It is, nevertheless, a very important subject, given that one's view of Scripture often helps to determine the main lines of one's theology. It is also a controversial subject, not least in understanding Torrance's place within British evangelicalism. His view of Scripture was regarded as some-what different from that of other evangelicals, and this means that, in some evangelical circles, Torrance has always been viewed with a degree of sus-picion. This suspicion is compounded by the fact that Torrance sometimes used language to describe Scripture which seemed to place him squarely within traditional evangelical theology, while on other occasions he used quite different language and seemed some distance away. We shall explore some of these tensions in what follows.

One point I must make at the beginning is that Torrance loved Scripture and was steeped in Scripture. Brought up in a missionary family in China, he was taught to read several chapters of Scripture every day, a practice he maintained throughout his whole life. As he said himself, "It has been my custom since I was a child to read through the Bible once or twice a year."[1] This scriptural commitment is apparent in all his theological writings. Even when he does not specifically quote Scripture, those who have a knowledge of the King James Version of the Bible can identify the influences. In all his work, we see the deep influence of a life lived studying the Scriptures.

Perhaps the most revealing statement that Torrance makes in respect of Scripture is from an unpublished manuscript which is quoted by Alister McGrath:[2]

> So far as my view of Holy Scripture was concerned, I had been brought up to believe in its verbal inspiration, but my mother had taught me to have an objective and not a subjective understanding of the Word of God. This did not lessen but rather deepened my sense of the divine authority and verbal inspiration of the Bible which mediated to us the Gospel of salvation. She taught us to adopt a Christ-centred approach to the Holy Scriptures, for Christ was the Word of God made flesh. In him Word and Person are one, and it is therefore in terms of the living personal Word of God incarnate in Christ that we are to hear God addressing us in the Bible. My epistemological realism did not detract from that fact, but it did lead me to object to a crudely fundamentalist and objectivist understanding of the Scriptures and to mechanistic and rationalistic concepts and propositions in theology, as it had done in my understanding of the laws of nature brought to light and given human formalisation in human science. I could not think of the book of nature or of the Bible, albeit in different ways, as a transcription, far less a codification, of the mind of God, so that for one to think scientifically or theologically was necessarily to think God's thoughts after him. That would be to impose upon nature rigid logico-deterministic patterns and to project on to God the kind of logico-causal relations which appeared to obtain in this world. A deeper, more dynamic and personal, yet objective way, was needed in relating God to nature and in relating the Word of God to the Holy Scriptures. That is what I hoped to find in the Faculty of Divinity, which indeed

---

1. Thomas F. Torrance, *Preaching Christ Today* (Carberry: Handsel Press, 1994), 10.

2. The manuscript is entitled *"Itinerarium mentis in Deum*: T. F. Torrance - My Theological Development,"* and is held in the T. F. Torrance archive at Princeton Theological Seminary.

H.R. Mackintosh and Karl Barth helped me to do. After I entered New College my dear mother wisely gave me a copy of Barth's *Credo* to help me. Hence I found myself in conflict not only with the rationalistic liberalism of some of my teachers, but with the rather rationalistic and fundamentalistic way of interpreting the Bible being advocated in Inter-Varsity Fellowship circles together with a rather deterministic Calvinism which was then mistakenly being imported into the thinking of the Christian Unions.[3]

It is clear from this quotation that Torrance's developed doctrine of Scripture was influenced by three key factors. First, his understanding of God and revelation; second, his christological method; and third, the influence of Karl Barth. We will explore these three factors as a way of entering into dialogue with Torrance's view of the doctrine of Scripture.

GOD AND REVELATION

Torrance's theological program is driven by the view that it is not possible for human beings to know God unless God chooses to reveal himself. For Torrance, Scripture can only be understood in the context of that revelation. As John Webster puts it: "The doctrine of scripture is a function of the doctrine of God and of God's inner and outer intelligibility in his communicative and reconciling presence to creatures."[4]

This emphasis on the self-revelation of the triune God as the fundamental starting point for theology was brought home to me in a very striking way. When I was a student of divinity at the University of Aberdeen, the pattern was to study the philosophy of religion and the arguments for the existence of God in the first year and then to begin the study of dogmatics the following year. This pattern goes back to medieval times and reflects a view that says we must first establish the existence of God before going on to say anything about God. When James B. Torrance arrived in Aberdeen as professor of systematic theology during my final year, one of the first changes he made was to reverse that order. He insisted that we must not begin with an attempt to prove the existence of God but rather begin with divine revelation. Thus,

3. Alister E. McGrath, *T. F. Torrance: An Intellectual Biography* (Edinburgh: T&T Clark, 1999), 25.

4. John Webster, "T. F. Torrance on Scripture," *Scottish Journal of Theology* 65 (2012): 42–43.

dogmatics was given priority and not just any dogmatics but a dogmatics centered on the God who reveals himself as Father, Son, and Holy Spirit. The message was clear: it is only out of this Trinitarian self-revelation, particularly in the incarnation of Jesus Christ, that we can know anything about God.

In his introduction to *Space, Time and Resurrection*, T. F. Torrance explains the relationship between this self-revelation and the Scriptures. He begins by speaking about the "community of reciprocity" that God established between his people and himself. He then writes, "As the new decisive form which that community of reciprocity has taken with the incarnation of God's Word in Jesus Christ, the Christian Church is essentially and necessarily bound up with the unique self-revelation of God in Jesus Christ which, in communicable form, is handed on to us in the apostolic Scriptures of the New Testament."[5] This relationship between God, revelation, the incarnation, the church, and Scripture is the nexus that has to be opened up in order to understand Torrance's doctrine of Scripture.

Torrance places his understanding of revelation and Scripture over against those whose presuppositions led to a "fatal deistic disjunction between God and the world which does not allow for any real Word of God to cross the gulf between God and the creature or therefore to permit man in space and time any real knowledge of God as he is in himself."[6] He has in mind those whose understanding of the universe as a closed causal continuum leaves no place for miracles or the supernatural. This is part of his consistent critique of the older liberal theology, which he believed was tied to the Newtonian worldview and failed to understand the implications the significant developments in science through Einstein and others could have on theology.

As Torrance goes on, however, he develops a view which is more problematic for other evangelicals. The problem is that Torrance's theological approach to the doctrine of Scripture appears to involve a separation of the scriptural writings from the reality to which Scripture points. He insists that the interpreter does not deal simply with the written words or statements in Scripture "but looks through them at the objective centre of reference

---

5. Thomas F. Torrance, *Space, Time and Resurrection* (Edinburgh: Handsel Press, 1976), 2.

6. Torrance, *Space, Time and Resurrection*, 2.

beyond."[7] Elsewhere he elaborates on this distinction between the Scriptures and the "reality beyond":

> It must be stressed that the theologian handles the New Testament by reflecting on its reports in the light of the reality which they claim to indicate, and tries to understand that reality in its own right, independent of the reports, by letting his mind fall under the power of its intrinsic significance. Only in that way will he be in any position to offer a judgement as to the adequacy of those reports, that is, as to how far they succeed in indicating and how far they fall short of the reality they intend. But since he interprets the reports not by subjecting the reality they indicate to the reports but by subjecting the reports to the reality they intend, he takes into account the fact that the reports do inevitably fall short of what they indicate, for they bear witness to what is other than and beyond themselves and which is true, if it is true, apart from them.[8]

Torrance offers this approach by way of contrast to what he saw as the common approach of contemporary New Testament scholars (with Bultmann as the chief perpetrator) who sought to interpret Scripture by the literary and structural tools of twentieth-century scholarship, instead of allowing the Word of God to speak through the Scriptures. In this critique, Torrance would have the support of most evangelicals. It is when he says that Scriptures point to a reality beyond themselves, which is then to be used as the interpretive tool to judge the adequacy or otherwise of the scriptural writings, that a difficulty emerges.

To put this another way, Torrance is arguing that, since the Scriptures point to the self-revealing God who in Christ has made himself known, it is the self-revealing God who will judge the adequacy or otherwise of the scriptural writings. The problem is the means by which this is achieved. How does God judge the adequacy of the Scriptures, and how is this communicated to us? More worrying, if Torrance's grasp of the reality to which Scripture points is mistaken, how can this be addressed and corrected? By making the

---

7. Thomas F. Torrance, *Reality and Evangelical Theology* (Philadelphia: The Westminster Press, 1982), 102.

8. Torrance, *Space, Time and Resurrection*, 5–6.

reality the final authority, without explaining how that reality can be understood apart from Scripture, Torrance can make theological statements that lie beyond the text itself.

Torrance's concern was that the interpretation of Scripture did not focus solely on the text but on the reality beyond, in the self-revelation of God in Jesus Christ. The importance of this theme to Torrance is underlined by Webster in his article on Torrance's doctrine of Scripture.[9] In describing Torrance's view of Scripture as a sign or sacrament, Webster notes that "the interpreter must not be arrested by the merely phenomenal, but instead press through the text to the Word of which it is the ambassador."[10] In several places in his writings, Torrance speaks of this "looking through" the Scriptures to the reality beyond, not least in his Trinitarian works.[11]

In practice, this notion of "looking through" the Scriptures to the reality beyond enables Torrance to make doctrinal assertions from his own understanding of the self-revealing God without feeling any need to establish his position by exegetical argument from the Scriptures themselves. In this we observe what happens when a reality beyond Scripture can achieve theologically what is not clearly taught in the Scriptures themselves. We might well ask if this is fundamentally different from the liberal theologian who says the Scriptures teach that God is love and then works out an entire theology from that starting point, thereby undermining the teaching of the Bible on judgment and hell.

When Torrance attempts to explain precisely how the reality beyond the text is discovered and how it can be verified and established, he speaks of the "intuitive insights" that guide the theologian in his theological inquiry and argues that these insights are "controlled by the intrinsic significance of God's self-revelation."[12] Then there comes a striking statement:

> How those insights arise in his mind he is unable to say beyond that it takes place under the generative power of the Word and Spirit of God himself. As a matter of fact, how ideas are related to the realities we

---

9. Webster, "T. F. Torrance on Scripture," 34–63.

10. Webster, "T. F. Torrance on Scripture," 49.

11. Thomas F. Torrance, *The Christian Doctrine of God: One Being Three Persons* (Edinburgh: T&T Clark, 1996), 37.

12. Torrance, *Space, Time and Resurrection*, 10–11.

experience and apprehend cannot be specified in any area of human knowledge, let alone the knowledge of faith, for this is a relation of an ontological kind which by its very nature eludes, and therefore vanishes in the face of, analytical explicitation and formalization; yet it is in and through that very relation alone that we can attain genuine knowledge of the realities concerned.[13]

We are being asked to accept that the theologian's grasp of the reality behind Scripture that determines our dogmatic theology takes the form of intuitive insights, which cannot be explained, except that they come to fruition as the theologian meditates on the inner reality of God's self-revelation by word and Spirit.

The same position is spelled out in relation to biblical interpretation, such as in his book, *The Hermeneutics of John Calvin*:

> In summing up, we may say that the positive task of the interpreter is to handle the written text in such a way that it is allowed to be *perspicuous* or self-revealing, i.e. to react to it in much the same manner that he reacts to living speech (*sermo*) in which he allows the intentions of the speaker to show through his actual words, and does not let his intention stop short at the words themselves and thus obscure the meaning (*sententiam*) they are intended to convey. Interpretation will thus involve any operation which clears away the unrealities or ambiguities that distort the understanding of a text, whether they may be in the reader or in the writer.[14]

Colyer recognizes that Torrance's view could be challenged as giving more weight to the realities beyond than to the text of Scripture itself, but he defends Torrance: "There is an appropriate circularity to this theological activity in which exegesis and interpretation of Holy Scripture proceed with, and are guided by, a theological understanding of the truths and realities they mediate. Yet at the same time the theological understanding of those truths is itself controlled by the ongoing exegesis and interpretation of the

---

13. Torrance, *Space, Time and Resurrection*, 11.

14. Thomas F. Torrance, *The Hermeneutics of John Calvin* (Edinburgh: Scottish Academic Press, 1988), 111.

biblical texts."[15] Indeed, Colyer sees the advantages in Torrance's position: "Furthermore, in Torrance's mind, this 'inevitably has the effect of allotting to the Scriptures a subsidiary status' to the realities they intend. This is why Torrance is willing to grant the difficulties and even contradictions in the New Testament accounts of the resurrection, for example, and yet not be terribly concerned by them."[16]

For many evangelicals this approach is deeply problematic. If the realities beyond are the controlling interpretive grid through which we read the Scriptures and if, therefore, it does not matter if there are mistakes or contradictions in Scripture, then surely this involves an undermining of God's written word?

Now it is possible that the safeguards Torrance puts in place are adequate to prevent a distortion of the plain meaning of Scripture by the theologian looking beyond. In an analysis of Torrance's understanding of the theological interpretation of Scripture, Myk Habets argues that the dual controls of word and Spirit provide this safeguard.[17] Even Habets admits, however, that "unfortunately, Torrance does not fully develop the constitutive role of the Holy Spirit in his depth exegesis. Without this corresponding work of the Spirit Torrance's depth exegesis is somewhat distorted and undeveloped."[18]

One underlying difficulty is that, in arguing his case, Torrance only offers three possible approaches to Scripture. First, the liberal biblical scholars who interpret the text according to their own modern historico-critical analysis, in which a false epistemology is imported and the empirical and the theoretical are divided. Second, the fundamentalist who is an unthinking rationalist and literalist, who does not see beyond the text but reduces the scriptural text to a set of propositions that must then be arranged in a certain order so as to determine doctrine. Third, his own position. One must protest that it is possible to have a high evangelical view of Scripture, which is neither liberal, fundamentalist, nor Torrancian, in which the text

---

15. Elmer M. Colyer, *How to Read T. F. Torrance: Understanding his Trinitarian and Scientific Theology* (Downers Grove, IL: InterVarsity Press, 2001), 358-9.

16. Colyer, *How to Read T. F. Torrance*, 358-9.

17. Myk Habets, "Theological Interpretation of Scripture in Sermonic Mode: The Case of T. F. Torrance," in *Ears That Hear: Explorations in Theological Interpretation of the Bible*, ed. Joel B. Green and Tim J. Meadowcroft (Sheffield: Sheffield Phoenix Press, 2013), 43-69.

18. Habets, "Theological Interpretation of Scripture," 53.

is taken seriously and in which the reality to which the text points is found in the text and not beyond the text. That is to say, it is possible to have sympathy with Torrance's intention, namely to insist that authority lies with the self-revealing God of Scripture and not with a book, but it is not necessary to give Scripture a "subsidiary status"[19] in order to achieve this. We must instead speak of the authority of God as he speaks by his Spirit through the Scriptures.

CHRISTOLOGICAL METHOD

Having noted the centrality of revelation in Torrance's thought, we must go on to note that the revelation central to his thinking is the revelation which comes in and through Christ. He speaks about Jesus as the truth to which Scripture directs us, saying,

> This means that our interpretation and understanding of the Bible cannot be established or defended simply by appealing to biblical texts or passages or even biblical concepts, but only through listening to the truths they signify or attest and allowing our minds to be objectively determined by them. That is to say, biblical statements are to be treated, not as containing or embodying the Truth of God in themselves, but as pointing, under the leading of the Spirit of Truth, to Jesus Christ himself who is the Truth.[20]

Colyer puts this another way by focusing on inter-Trinitarian relationships, arguing that we must investigate realities in terms of their onto-relations, "for they are what they are by virtue of the relations in which they are embedded." Thus, he can argue, "The goal of theology, according to Torrance, is to investigate and bring to coherent articulation the essential interrelations embodied in our knowledge of God through Jesus Christ in the Holy Spirit." [21] Thus, to understand Christ we must view him, first, in his relations with the covenant people and, second, in his relations within the Trinity.

The basic argument here is that God reveals God. To put it another way, when the Second Person of the Trinity takes flesh and becomes incarnate, he

---

19. Torrance, *Space, Time and Resurrection*, 12.

20. Thomas F. Torrance, *Reality and Evangelical Theology* (Philadelphia: The Westminster Press, 1982), 119.

21. Colyer, *How to Read T. F. Torrance*, 56.

is the revelation of God. When people looked at the face of Jesus, they were looking into the face of God. As Jesus is recorded saying in John 14:9, "Anyone who has seen me has seen the Father" (NIV). Christ, then, is the primary and complete revelation of God; therefore, Scripture must be understood in relation to that revelation. In John Webster's article on Torrance's doctrine of Scripture we read, "His primary interests in the matter of scripture were in its mediating relation to the divine Word, and in the epistemological and hermeneutical questions which arise when giving a theological account of the several divine and human acts which compose the economy of revelation."[22]

This focus on the self-revelation of God in Christ leads Torrance to state: "By its very nature the self-revelation of this God summons us to acknowledge the absolute priority of God's Word over all the media of its communication and reception, and over all understanding and interpretation of its Truth."[23] Once again, it is possible to agree wholeheartedly with Torrance that the revelation of God in Christ is fundamental to all of our thinking, but the barrier he appears to erect between Christ as the Word of God and the "media of its communication," which must surely include Scripture as the written word of God, gives us pause for thought.

As part of his christological approach to the doctrine of Scripture and his insistence that Christ himself, the Second Person of the Trinity, is the true Word of God, Torrance goes back to Nicaea to show its significance for Scripture. He quotes Johann Reuchlin, who wrote toward the end of the Middle Ages and sought to demonstrate that a proper understanding of the Nicene doctrine of the *homoousion* is vital for a proper doctrine of Scripture. As Torrance writes, Reuchlin "argued that since Jesus Christ is the Word of God as well as the Son of God, we must think of the Word of Jesus which we hear in the Gospel as the incarnate Word of God that is consubstantial with God or of the same substance as God."[24] Torrance approves of Reuchlin's argument and demonstrates the impact it had on the Reformers who, he says, viewed Scripture as "the inspired medium through which we hear the very Word of God." Torrance also highlights the Reformation emphasis on the

---

22. Webster, "T. F. Torrance on Scripture," 34–63.

23. Torrance, *Reality and Evangelical Theology*, 13.

24. Torrance, *Preaching Christ Today*, 14–15.

"objectivity of the Word of God and of the authority of the Holy Scriptures."[25] Torrance concludes, "If in the Bible people have to do with a Word that is consubstantial with God, then they read and interpret the Holy Scriptures in quite a different kind of way as the Word of God addressing them directly in and through them."[26]

One problem with Torrance's christological approach to the doctrine of Scripture is that it somewhat undermines a historical account of God's revelation. As the writer to the Hebrews says in 1:1–3, "In the past God spoke to our ancestors through the prophets at many times and in various ways, but in these last days he has spoken to us by his Son, whom he appointed heir of all things, and through whom also he made the universe" (NIV). In other words, God spoke to Adam, to Abraham, to Moses, and to the prophets, all before the incarnation of Christ. Yet, as Robert Walker notes in his editor's introduction to T. F. Torrance's lectures on the incarnation, Torrance's view was "we can know nothing of God other than what he makes known to us in time in Christ."[27] At a deeper, theological level, John Morrison argues that Torrance's failure to root his doctrine of revelation in a historical, covenantal relationship undermines Torrance's own argument and is in danger of dragging him back into the very dualism he seeks to reject. Morrison seeks to rectify the problem, not by opposing Torrance's view but by seeking to strengthen Torrance's core argument.[28]

Even as we seek to put the best possible construction on what Torrance says, there remains the suspicion that his christological approach to the doctrine of Scripture (and to every other doctrine) can be used to undermine the value of the God-breathed text itself. Combined with what we saw earlier regarding the intuitive insights with which the theologian interprets the biblical witness, insights which cannot be explained, we have a serious difficulty. Perhaps it can be best illustrated by considering an issue recently debated in the Church of Scotland. T. F. Torrance's brother, David W. Torrance,

---

25. Torrance, *Preaching Christ Today*, 14–15.

26. Torrance, *Preaching Christ Today*, 15.

27. Robert T. Walker, "Editor's Introduction," in Thomas F. Torrance, *Incarnation: The Person and Life of Christ*, ed. Robert T. Walker (Downers Grove, IL and Milton Keynes: IVP and Paternoster, 2008), xl.

28. John D. Morrison, *Knowledge of the Self-revealing God in the thought of Thomas Forsyth Torrance* (Eugene, OR: Wipf & Stock, 2005), 285–352.

argued strongly that same-sex marriage was not biblically acceptable. Yet T. F. Torrance's son, Iain R. Torrance, argued, in his capacity as convener of the Church of Scotland's Theological Forum, that there was no theological impediment to same-sex marriage. If pressed, both would probably articulate the same doctrine of Scripture as T. F. Torrance, yet they came to radically different conclusions. Could it be that in the older generation (T. F., J. B., and D. W.) there was more emphasis on the text of Scripture, whereas in the next generation there is more emphasis on the intuitive insights? In other words, is there a fundamental weakness in the doctrine of Scripture, as articulated by T. F. Torrance, whereby it is subject to interpretive insights which can go against the very text of Scripture itself?

Torrance resists the idea that Scripture is a revelation of God but insists that it is a witness to Christ, who is himself the revelation of God. That is to say, Scripture can only be considered to be revelation in a secondary sense and not in a primary sense. This is how he expressed it: "Moreover, the way in which the theologian handles the Scriptures, by directing his attention along the line of their witnessing to the self-revealing and reconciling God, inevitably has the effect of allotting to the Scriptures a subsidiary status in the face of what he apprehends *through* them, for what really concerns him, to use Pauline language, is the heavenly treasure and not the earthen vessels (2 Cor. 4:7)."[29]

Torrance argued that many Christians sought to disconnect Scripture from that to which it testified, namely, Jesus Christ, the living Word of God. He argued that to view Scripture as a stand-alone revelation from God that could be understood grammatically and historically, using normal human hermeneutical tools, was deeply inadequate. He believed that the absence of an ontological understanding of its relationship to the self-revealing God emptied Scripture of its power and risked having two separate and largely unconnected ways of establishing truth. That is to say, Scripture on its own, without seeing it in its relation to the one who brought it into existence, becomes an empty text. For this reason, we must always regard Scripture as revelation in a secondary sense and not in a primary sense. Robert Walker, in his editorial introduction to Torrance's lectures on the atonement, puts it even more bluntly. He says that the "basic text of the New Testament is

---

29. Torrance, *Space, Time and Resurrection*, 12.

the obedient humanity of Jesus Christ" and that "the New Testament is the inspired secondary text."[30]

Donald Bloesch rejects the notion that a distinction must be made between revelation and Scripture. He insists that Scripture can be both revelation and the bearer of revelation:

> The Bible is both the revelation and the means and bearer of revelation. It is revelation cast in written form and the original witness to revelation. It is a component of revelation and a vehicle of revelation. It objectively contains revelation in the sense that its witness is based on revelation, but it becomes revelation for us only in the moment of decision, in the awakening to faith. Scripture is not simply a pointer to revelation (as Torrance sometimes describes it) but a carrier of revelation. Scripture is the mediate source of revelation, but only Jesus Christ is the original or eternal source.[31]

In other words, it is possible to take seriously Torrance's view that Scripture is the means by which God reveals his Son without denying that Scripture is itself a revelation from God.

THE INFLUENCE OF BARTH

Torrance's theology was largely formed through the influence of two of the most important of his early teachers in theology. In the quotation with which we began, Torrance expresses his appreciation of what he learned from Mackintosh and Barth, as opposed to some of his teachers who were influenced by the old liberal theology.

The influence of Barth in particular is one of the areas where evangelicals have been critical of Torrance's view of theology. His view of Scripture has sometimes been dismissed simply as Barthian without any serious engagement with what he actually wrote and with no attempt to set his doctrine of Scripture in the context of his principal theological concerns. Due to the writings of Cornelius Van Til and others, Barth's doctrine was regarded as

---

30. Robert T. Walker, "Editor's Introduction," in Thomas F. Torrance, *Atonement: The Person and Work of Christ*, ed. Robert T. Walker (Downers Grove, IL: InterVarsity Press, 2009), lvii.

31. Donald G. Bloesch, *Holy Scripture: Revelation, Inspiration and Interpretation* (Downers Grove, IL: InterVarsity Press, 1994), 63.

a significant departure from evangelicalism and Torrance was then tarred with precisely the same brush.

Following G. C. Berkouwer, who protested against the prevailing evangelical treatment of Barth,[32] there has emerged within evangelicalism a more positive view of Barth's theology,[33] although some remain critical.[34] The most significant evangelical attempt in recent years to reevaluate and to reappropriate the theology of Torrance has been the movement known as Evangelical Calvinism, led by Myk Habets and Bobby Grow.[35]

Nevertheless, it is undoubtedly the case that Barth had a huge influence on Torrance's thinking and in his developed theology. Indeed, following the earlier work of Mackintosh, Torrance became a key figure in Barth reception and in the discussion of Barth's theology, not least through his editorial oversight of the translation of Barth's *Church Dogmatics* into English and his co-founding with J. K. S. Reid of the *Scottish Journal of Theology*, which became a focal point for discussions of Barth's theology. At the same time, we must note that Torrance did not consider himself to be a Barthian. Some years ago, on behalf of Rutherford House, I chaired a discussion of Torrance's book on Scottish theology.[36] We had invited Professor Donald Macleod of the Free Church College to give a review of the book with Torrance then replying. When Macleod had finished, Torrance stood up and almost the first thing he said was, "You have called me a Barthian. I am not a Barthian, I am an Athanasian!"

Many evangelicals routinely say that Torrance did not believe Scripture was the Word of God but only bore witness to Christ, the true Word of God. Paul Molnar is right to say that this involves an unfortunate misunderstanding: "Torrance does not believe that Scripture is not the Word of God as some have suggested. Rather, for Torrance, Scripture is not the Word of God *as*

---

32. Gerrit C. Berkouwer, *The Triumph of Grace in the Theology of Karl Barth* (London: Paternoster, 1956).

33. See, for example, Philip P. Thorne, ed., *Evangelicalism and Karl Barth* (Allison Park, PA: Pickwick, 1995).

34. See, for example, David Gibson and Daniel Strange, eds., *Engaging with Barth* (Nottingham: Apollos, 2008).

35. Myk Habets and Bobby Grow, eds., *Evangelical Calvinism: Essays Resourcing the Continuing Reformation of the Church* (Eugene, OR: Wipf & Stock, 2012); Myk Habets and Bobby Grow, eds., *Evangelical Calvinism Volume 2: Dogmatics and Devotion* (Eugene, OR: Wipf & Stock, 2017).

36. Thomas F. Torrance, *Scottish Theology: from John Knox to John McLeod Campbell* (Edinburgh: T&T Clark, 1996).

Jesus is. Scripture is thus holy because that is the historical witness the triune God uses to continue to reveal himself to us. But the authority and significance of Scripture reside not in themselves but only as they point to Jesus Christ, the Word made flesh and 'cohere in him.' "[37] We should note, however, that even as serious and sympathetic a writer as Alister McGrath can write, "Torrance follows the general Barthian approach of regarding the Bible as a witness to revelation, which may become the Word of God."[38]

Torrance does not seek to diminish Scripture, but rather he believes he is giving Scripture a vital place in the life of the believer and the life of the church without giving it the place which can only be held by Christ. Hence, he writes, "Our theological statements are true in so far as they are faithful responses to the self-communication of the Truth of God in the way in which He reveals Himself in and through the witness of the Holy Scripture, in the historical life of the Church, for it is there in the Holy Scripture that we actually hear God's Word."[39]

As we have seen, Torrance's view of Scripture stands in marked contrast to the doctrine of Scripture as expressed by other evangelicals. Torrance argued that many evangelicals regarded the Scriptures as a collection of propositions which can be taken and put together to form doctrinal statements, probably referring to Charles Hodge.[40] For Torrance, to view Scripture in propositional terms and then to use logic to assemble doctrines is to misunderstand the nature of Scripture. He writes:

> The Scriptures of the Old and New Testaments rightly evoke from us profound respect and veneration not because of what they are in themselves but because of the divine revelation mediated in and through them. That is why we speak of them as "Holy" Scriptures. Since God's self-revelation in and through the Bible must be experienced and cognized in the reality it is apart from the words and statements of the Bible, something would appear to have gone wrong if we become too obsessed with the Bible, as so often happens in the

---

37. Paul D. Molnar, *Thomas F. Torrance: Theologian of the Trinity* (Farnham: Ashgate, 2009), 330.

38. McGrath, *T. F. Torrance*, 135.

39. Thomas F. Torrance, *Theological Science* (London: Oxford University Press, 1969), 191.

40. Charles Hodge, *Systematic Theology*, vol. 1 (London: James Clarke & Co Ltd., 1960), 1–2.

stress that is laid upon its inspiration when our attention is directed to the Bible itself instead of to what it is intended to bear witness.[41]

He goes on to spell out his meaning: "Ontological priority and authoritative primacy must be given to divine revelation and not to the Bible. It is the subordination of the Bible to that revelation and the semantic service it fulfills in mediating that revelation to us that gives the Bible its singular status in our respect and its decisive authority in our knowledge of God."[42]

We see Torrance's concern about rationalism and fundamentalism in his objection to the way in which Scripture is understood and used in the old Princeton tradition. Despite Torrance's affirmation of verbal inspiration in the quotation with which we began, he attacks the old Princetonian expression of that doctrine. The best example of this critique is found in his review of B. B. Warfield's *The Inspiration and Authority of the Bible*.[43] In the review, Torrance expresses great admiration for Warfield and his massive contribution to theology, calling him "a giant in the history of Reformed theology." However, when he turns to Warfield's understanding of the verbal inspiration of Scripture, he registers "profound disagreement." Torrance writes, "It is clear that his whole doctrine of revelation and inspiration is bound up with a philosophical doctrine of predestination, in which Biblical eschatology is ousted for an un-Biblical notion of rational causation."[44] He rejects any notion of a two natures doctrine of Scripture (divinity and humanity) as recent writers like Pete Enns have proposed.[45] Torrance writes, "The basic error that lurks in the scholastic idea of verbal inspiration is that it amounts to an incarnation of the Holy Spirit. It is only strictly Christological theology which can obviate that heresy, but Dr Warfield's theory of inspiration neglects the Christological basis of the doctrine of Scripture, and fails therefore to take the measure both of the mystery of revelation and the depth of sin in the human mind."[46]

---

41. Torrance, *Reality and Evangelical Theology*, 95–96.

42. Torrance, *Reality and Evangelical Theology*, 96–97.

43. Thomas F. Torrance, "Review of B. B. Warfield, *The Inspiration and Authority of Scripture*," in *Scottish Journal of Theology* 7 (1954): 104–8.

44. Torrance, "Review of Warfield," 106.

45. Peter Enns, *Inspiration and Incarnation: Evangelicals and the Problem of the Old Testament*, 2nd ed. (Grand Rapids: Baker Academic, 2015).

46. Torrance, "Review of Warfield," 107.

Torrance elsewhere speaks of the inflexible nature of fundamentalism and writes, "The practical and the epistemological effect of a fundamentalism of this kind is to give an infallible Bible and a set of rigid evangelical beliefs primacy over God's self-revelation which is mediated to us through the Bible. This effect is only reinforced by the regular fundamentalist identification of biblical statements about the truth with the truth to which they refer."[47] Elsewhere he writes, "Faith and certainty do not rest on biblical authority as such, far less on ecclesiastical authority, but on the solid truth that underlies all the teaching of the Holy Scriptures. Christian theology arises properly out of a compulsive thinking and speaking face to face with the God revealed to us through the Holy Scriptures, for its real content is not the signifying truths of the Scriptures but the Truth of God revealed in and through them."[48]

This opposition to what he regarded as a rationalistic theology, which was insufficiently theological, was one of the points at which he came into conflict with fellow evangelicals. It ultimately led to the division of evangelicals in the University of Edinburgh and the disaffiliation of the Edinburgh Christian Union (CU) from the InterVarsity Fellowship (IVF). Densil Morgan helpfully spells out the three areas of division among evangelicals in the post-war years.

The first division was on the matter of the authority of Scripture in relation to critical scholarship. Morgan highlights as examples the difference between F. F. Bruce on the one hand and J. I. Packer on the other. Morgan notes Bruce's view that the members of the incipient Tyndale Fellowship "should not be beholden to a scholastic doctrine of biblical inerrancy," and he comments, "It was clear that his vision of evangelicalism should be compatible with critical scholarship." Others followed J. I. Packer, who did advocate a position of biblical inerrancy.[49]

The second division concerned Karl Barth. Most of the leaders of the InterVarsity Fellowship movement supported the critique of Barth as found in the writings of Cornelius Van Til. Others, such as Torrance and Geoffrey Bromiley, believed that Barth was more of an ally than an enemy. Morgan tells how Bromiley tried to persuade the IVF leaders to organize a conference to

---

47. Torrance, *Reality and Evangelical Theology*, 17.
48. Torrance, *Reality and Evangelical Theology*, 135.
49. D. Densil Morgan, *Barth Reception in Britain* (London: T&T Clark, 2010), 248–49.

discuss Barth's theology, suggesting that they invite Torrance, Cornelius Van Til, and G. C. Berkouwer. This conference never took place.[50] The majority of conservative evangelicals within the movement continued to hold that Barth was an enemy of orthodox biblical Christianity, and many of them identified Torrance's view with that of Barth.

The third division was on the matter of ecumenical cooperation, and it was this debate which led to the division within the Christian Union in Edinburgh University. In his autobiography, David Torrance tells the story:

> The problem of co-operation with the SCM and with those with whom we may not fully agree evangelically arose some three years later and split apart the Edinburgh Christian Union. I was near the end of my final year in New College: Reid, the chaplain to Edinburgh University planned an all university mission the following year. Both Edinburgh CU and SCM agreed to support him in the planning and conduct of the mission. In preparation for the mission members of CU and SCM were meeting weekly for prayer. Mark Wilson, a student in Glasgow, was at that time the IVF Scottish student representative. Quite unexpectedly Mark appeared at the beginning of one of our weekly meetings and asked to speak. He had been sent by Douglas Johnson and his colleagues to instruct us to cease forthwith our joint prayer meetings with SCM. If we did not we would be disaffiliated from IVF.

The meeting erupted! The committee with the support of the majority refused to comply. The result was that the Edinburgh CU was disaffiliated. The Christian Union split, which was very sad. The majority continued as the CU. A smaller group continued as IVF.[51]

It is clear, however, that disagreements over biblical authority and the significance of Karl Barth provided the backdrop which set the scene for the split. Thomas Noble, in his history of Tyndale House and Fellowship, notes the division on doctrinal grounds between those who shared the views of J. I. Packer on the one hand and those who shared the views of Torrance on the other hand, not least in relation to Calvinism and the doctrine of limited atonement. It is in this context that Noble describes the split in the Edinburgh

---

50. Morgan, *Barth Reception in Britain*, 249.

51. David W. Torrance, *The Reluctant Minister* (Edinburgh: Handsel Press, 2015), chapter 5.

Christian Union, an indication that the split was not simply about cooperating with the SCM on a mission to the university.[52] Having discussed this matter with Noble recently, he believes that there was much misunderstanding on both sides, and the language used was capable of a variety of interpretations. Whatever the truth of this analysis, it remains a fact that Torrance's doctrine of Scripture served (and serves) as a barrier for many evangelicals to an understanding of his overall theological position.

CONCLUSION

As we conclude it is important to emphasize that we have great sympathy with Torrance's desire to have the self-revelation of God in Christ at the center of all our thinking and theologizing. But some of Torrance's statements remain troubling from an evangelical perspective.

Perhaps the best way to express our reservations regarding Torrance's doctrine of Scripture is to say that it does not pay sufficient attention to what the Scriptures say of themselves. Torrance holds that Scripture is part of the media through which we come to know Christ, or that Scripture is a witness to Christ. But in 2 Timothy 3:16 we learn that "all Scripture is God-breathed" (NIV). This clearly implies not only that Scripture is of divine origin (with which Torrance would agree) but that it is the word of God written, as the *Westminster Confession of Faith* affirms.[53] Then in 2 Peter 1:21, we are told that Scripture did not originate with human beings but rather the writers of Scripture "spoke from God as they were carried along by the Holy Spirit." Most evangelicals would take this to mean that God acted in order to communicate with human beings through the Scripture writers in such a way that their words could be accepted as having come from the Holy Spirit.

We indicated at the beginning that one of the problems in writing about Torrance's doctrine of Scripture is that he never wrote a sustained monograph on the subject. Even when we gather all of what he did say, this major weakness remains, namely that Torrance does not engage exegetically with the verses mentioned above or with the many other references where Scripture describes and defines itself. Even while stating that Torrance's

---

52. Thomas A. Noble, *Tyndale House and Fellowship: The First Sixty Years* (Leicester: InterVarsity Press, 2006), 77–78.

53. See *Westminster Confession of Faith* 1.2.

writings on Scripture "constitute one of the most impressive accounts of the field in the last half century," Webster notes that there is a "lack of extended exegesis."[54] The anxiety which Torrance's view of Scripture occasioned to other evangelicals in the debates within the Christian Union at Edinburgh University have not been securely laid to rest even after so many thousands of words have poured from Torrance's pen.

---

54. Webster, "T. F. Torrance on Scripture," 34.

4

—

REVELATION, RATIONALISM, AND AN EVANGELICAL IMPASSE[1]*

Myk Habets

One area in which the theology of Thomas F. Torrance challenges certain forms of evangelicalism is epistemology and a doctrine of revelation associated with it. A considerable amount of evangelicalism, especially in its North American manifestations, is still wedded to forms of modernity and the rationalism it espouses. By going back to a debate between Carl Henry and Thomas Torrance, new insights can be gleaned for contemporary evangelical theology. Henry represents a persistent stream of North American evangelicalism, while Torrance, in turn, represents a more open orthodoxy from which evangelicals could learn. Of course, it is not all one way. Torrance's theology also can be adjusted in light of Henry's counter-critique. In contrast to Henry's foundationalism, Torrance's theology operates from a critical-realist basis, a natural ally to his doctrine of revelation and the mediation of Christ. Given the enduring polarity around the doctrine of revelation and a Christian epistemology, bringing Henry and Torrance into direct dialogue will be informative for how contemporary evangelicals might be able to critically receive this aspect of Torrance's work with renewed appreciation.

---

1. *This is an adapted version of an essay which originally appeared as "Beyond Henry's Nominalism and Evangelical Foundationalism: Thomas Torrance's Theological Realism," in *Gospel, Truth and Interpretation: Evangelical Identity in Aotearoa New Zealand*, Archer Studies in Pacific Christianity, ed. Tim Meadowcroft and Myk Habets (Auckland: Archer Press, 2011), 205-40. Used with permission.

ONE HISTORY, TWO DIRECTIONS

Carl Henry's and Thomas Torrance's careers share many similarities, yet they could not have chartered more different courses in theology had they tried. Both men were born in 1913 and lived into their nineties. Both were theology professors: Henry at Fuller Theological Seminary, which he helped to establish; Torrance at the University of Edinburgh. Both were prolific authors: Henry's magnum opus being the six-volume *God, Revelation and Authority;*[2] Torrance's magnum opus being *The Christian Doctrine of God* (and *The Trinitarian Faith*).[3] Both were also editors of influential theological journals: Henry of the popular *Christianity Today*[4] and Torrance of the *Scottish Journal of Theology*. Both were international speakers and first-order systematic theologians. Finally, both were guardians of what they considered orthodoxy: Henry of the evangelical heritage, which developed out of fundamentalism,[5] and Torrance of an orthodoxy developed in line with the great tradition.

While clearly of the same mind regarding a range of theological beliefs, Henry and Torrance did not share the same epistemic commitments. Thus, their theological methods were drastically different, resulting in what can only be considered radically differing theologies. Having met on several occasions, they disagreed considerably, and this spilled over into their respective *oeuvres*. What follows is a focused reflection on what may be considered the heart of their theological disagreement: Henry's nominalism versus Torrance's realism.

CARL HENRY VS. THOMAS TORRANCE

In *God, Revelation and Authority*, Henry sought to establish the foundations of an apologetic theology, an evangelical response to modernity on modernity's terms, with the aim of establishing the intellectual coherence and academic

---

2. Carl F. H. Henry, *God, Revelation and Authority*, 6 Vols. (Waco: Word, 1976–1983).

3. Thomas F. Torrance, *The Christian Doctrine of God: One Being Three Persons* (Edinburgh: T&T Clark, 1996); *The Trinitarian Faith: The Evangelical Theology of the Ancient Catholic Church*, 2nd ed., (Edinburgh: T&T Clark, 1995).

4. While *Christianity Today* has become a popular, lay-driven magazine, it started out as a theological magazine–journal in opposition to *The Christian Century*.

5. In Grenz's estimation, Henry remained a fundamentalist in many respects. Stanley J. Grenz, *Renewing the Center: Evangelical Theology in a Post-Theological Era* (Grand Rapids: Baker, 2000), 87.

credibility of a Christian "world-life view," as Henry termed it. In volume 1, *God Who Speaks and Shows*, he sets forth the nature of theology, and in volumes 2, 3, and 4, he comments at length upon fifteen foundational theses on divine revelation. Volumes 5 and 6, *God Who Stands and Stays*, develop a classically orthodox approach to the doctrine of God. The ordering of the work is important; Henry privileges treating method before theology proper; Scripture is epistemologically prior to God in his theology. To be clear, it was Henry's express conviction that the foundation for correct theology can only be found in the divine revelation of God as deposited in the Holy Scriptures. Henry defines revelation as:

> that activity of the supernatural God whereby he communicates information essential for man's present and future destiny. In revelation God, whose thoughts are not our thoughts, shares his mind; he communicates not only the truth about himself and his intentions, but also that concerning man's present plight and future prospects.[6]

Revelation is thus objective and available to unaided human reason. So insistent was Henry on this point that he rejected all attempts by the so-called neo-orthodox of his day (read here Barth, Bultmann, and Brunner especially) to establish a relational and participatory theology whereby only those united to Christ and enlivened by the Spirit could know God. Henry wrote, "If a person must first be a Christian believer in order to grasp the truth of revelation, then meaning is subjective and incommunicable"; and further, "the new birth is not prerequisite to a knowledge of the truth of God."[7]

According to Henry, the Bible is almost entirely propositional in content; thus, God communicates to convey truths in propositional sentences.[8] The purpose of theology is to take such sentences and form doctrines or propositions from them. In this regard, we might note the affinities of Wayne Grudem's approach to systematic theology with that of Henry when Grudem defines theology as "any study that answers the question: 'What does the whole Bible teach us today?' about any given topic."[9] John Franke calls this the

---

6. Henry, *God, Revelation and Authority*, 3:457.

7. Henry, *God, Revelation and Authority*, 1:229.

8. Henry, *God, Revelation and Authority*, 1:181–409.

9. Wayne Grudem, *Systematic Theology: An Introduction to Biblical Doctrine* (Grand Rapids: Zondervan, 1994), 21. Grudem's definition is insufficient and deficient in that it ignores the

"concordance conception of theology," which has characterized evangelical theology in general to the extent that it has assumed the methodology of post-Reformation Protestant scholasticism.[10]

In a programmatic passage, Henry sets forth his "basic epistemological axiom" as follows:

> *Divine revelation is the source of all truth, the truth of Christianity included; reason is the instrument for recognizing it; Scripture is its verifying principle; logical consistency is a negative test for truth and coherence a subordinate test. The task of Christian theology is to exhibit the content of biblical revelation as an orderly whole.*[11]

One may inquire about the relationship between Scripture and general revelation, given the epistemological axiom above. Henry states that:

> The scriptural revelation takes epistemological priority over general revelation, not because general revelation is obscure or because man as sinner cannot know it, but because Scripture as an inspired literary document republishes the content of general revelation objectively, over against man's sinful reductive dilutions and misconstructions of it.[12]

It was Henry's conviction that general revelation was sufficient for the independent use of reason for a knowledge of God. He thus believed that special revelation was an objective given. In a 1964 work, *Frontiers in Modern Theology*, Henry, in Grenz's words, "charted an agenda that proved to be an apt summary of his entire theological program."[13]

If Christianity is to win intellectual respectability in the modern world, the reality of the transcendent God must indeed be proclaimed by the

---

interplay in all knowing between tradition, reason, and experience, not to mention culture or community. See Graham McFarlane, *A Model for Evangelical Theology: Integrating Scripture, Tradition, Reason, Experience, and Community* (Grand Rapids: Baker Academic, 2020).

10. See John R. Franke, *The Character of Theology: An Introduction to Its Nature, Task, and Purpose* (Grand Rapids: Baker, 2005), especially 88–89.

11. Henry, *God, Revelation and Authority*, 1:215 (italics in the original). This is not to deny that the triune God is Christianity's basic ontological axiom. Henry, *God, Revelation and Authority*, 1:219.

12. Henry, *God, Revelation and Authority*, 1:223.

13. Grenz, *Renewing the Center*, 92.

theologians—and proclaimed on the basis of man's rational competence to know the transempirical realm.[14]

This is not to say that Henry was an advocate of natural theology; he wasn't. Henry was a biblicist who rigorously upheld the inerrancy and infallibility of Scripture.[15] Thus, correct thinking about God can only be found through Scripture, for here alone, one finds the authoritative word of God in objective form. While Henry does allow that revelation is personal, simply because God and humans are personal, his theology amounts to a rejection of personal revelation in favor of an absolute propositional revelation. This is asserted in his Thesis Ten: "God's revelation is rational communication conveyed in intelligible ideas and meaningful words, that is, in conceptual-verbal form."[16] Henry clarifies that he is opposed to all definitions of revelation, which are expressed as God's "*self*-revelation, or *cosmic* revelation, or *historical* revelation, in express contrast to a divine disclosure of truths and information."[17] Henry cites Karl Barth and Thomas Torrance as two such champions of the dialectical and existential (read as nonevangelical) theology he is opposed to.

Focusing specifically upon Torrance's doctrine of the knowledge of God mainly drawn from Torrance's 1969 work *Theological Science*,[18] Henry devotes an entire chapter of *God, Revelation and Authority* to rebut Torrance's position.[19] In Henry's estimation, Torrance's formulation of what he terms "theologic" is evangelically inadequate and an example of the "unstable neo-Protestant formulation of man's knowledge of God."[20] What, exactly, Henry takes exception to is Torrance's attempt to relate human logic to the logic of God in a nonformal way.

---

14. Carl F. H. Henry, *Frontiers in Modern Theology a Critique of Current Theological Trends* (Chicago: Moody, 1964), 154–55, cited in Grenz, *Renewing the Center*, 92.

15. For his defense of inerrancy, infallibility, and inspiration see Henry, *God, Revelation and Authority*, 4:103–219. Henry did not, as many other fundamentalist evangelicals have done, make inerrancy a badge of evangelical orthodoxy. See Carl F. H. Henry, "Reaction and Realignment," *Christianity Today* 20 (July 2, 1976): 30.

16. Henry, *God, Revelation and Authority*, 3:248.

17. Henry, *God, Revelation and Authority*, 3:248.

18. Thomas F. Torrance, *Theological Science* (London: Oxford University Press, 1969).

19. Chapter 14: "The Logos and Human Logic," in Henry, *God, Revelation and Authority*, 3:216–29.

20. Henry, *God, Revelation and Authority*, 3:216.

Acknowledging that Torrance rises above the neo-orthodox (a pejorative and inaccurate term in itself) antithesis of propositional and personal revelation by locating revelation in Jesus Christ, himself the truth and the one who manifests the truth, Henry then accuses Torrance of "unjustifiably converting the fact that God objectifies himself for us and meets us in Jesus Christ into an eclipse of general revelation, a devaluation of the prophetic revelation, and a cognitive deflation of all Logos-revelation."[21] Henry takes umbrage at the idea that outside of Jesus there is no knowledge of God.[22] In the first instance, Henry appeals to the Old Testament (then to nature, history, and the conscience) as evidence that God has spoken in propositional form through prophets, kings, priests, and directly in divine manifestations. Henry considers these to be defeating arguments against Torrance's insistence that there is no knowledge of God outside of Christ. But this is to misunderstand Torrance's position that Jesus Christ is epistemologically determinative. Thus, there is no knowledge of God outside of Jesus Christ, given Christian theology as a science is posterior to an actual encounter with a real event.[23]

Henry agrees with Torrance that humanity after the fall is estranged from God and thus cannot think rightly about God, truth, or reality. However, that does not mean, argues Henry, that we must attribute this to an epistemic deficiency in humanity whereby only through regeneration and repentance may one know God.[24] Henry then levels his charge against Torrance:

> Torrance here overstates the deformity of human reason in relation
> to divine revelation; he disregards the general revelation that pene-
> trates man's reason and conscience with the knowledge of God which
> confronts him consciously with light and truth and knowledge and
> in relation to which he is culpable. The change in logical structure
> which a revelation is held to require, it develops, is nothing less than

---

21. Henry, God, Revelation and Authority, 3:217.

22. This is the fourth of Torrance's five points as to what characterizes theological science, Torrance, Theological Science, 137; and Torrance, Christian Doctrine of God, 1.

23. For a constructive account in line with Torrance's theology see Habets, "Crossing the Epistemological Impasse: Thinking out of a Centre in God and Not out of a Centre in Ourselves," in Evangelical Calvinism, Vol. 2: Dogmatics and Devotion, ed. Bobby Grow and Myk Habets (Eugene, OR: Pickwick, 2017), 17–29.

24. Henry, God, Revelation and Authority, 3:218. See Torrance, Theological Science, 147.

a rejection of the law of contradiction and if that be the case—so we shall argue, against Torrance—nonsense can be regarded as divine truth.[25]

Henry was not one to lack rhetorical flourish or force a point!

Interpreting Torrance accurately, Henry shows that according to Torrance, only Jesus, who is the Logos, can know the truth through human concepts and statements because Christ is the God-man. For all other people, our statements point away from ourselves to some objective truth, but Christ is the truth incarnate; thus, his statements do not point away from himself but to himself. Torrance can thus say, "Theological knowledge and theological statements participate sacramentally in the mystery of Christ as the Truth."[26] As such, revelation is, for Torrance, *uniquely* personal and *propositional to Christ, and mediated to others to the extent* they participate in Christ.[27] It is therefore faith (revelation) in Christ and not a philosophy that forms the conceptual bridge between God and humanity.

What Henry is pushing back on is Torrance's dialogical/dialectical theological method. According to Henry, truth and statements of the truth correspond so that the truth is objectively known despite the condition—fallen or otherwise, Christian or not—of the subject. Henry's correspondence theory of the truth (similar to Wittgenstein's "picture language")[28] comes up squarely against Torrance's realistic theory of the truth. In Henry's estimation, all such dialectical/dialogical reasoning must end up "either saying nothing or of stating gibberish."[29]

Henry appears to misunderstand Torrance's claim that only those united to Christ genuinely know Christ. Torrance, it seems to me, does not insist that there is no general revelation, simply that general revelation does not provide enough information for the unredeemed person to come to a saving

---

25. Henry, *God, Revelation and Authority*, 3:218.

26. Torrance, *Theological Science*, 150, cited by Henry, *God, Revelation and Authority*, 3:219.

27. Torrance, *Theological Science*, 42, 148, cited by Henry, *God, Revelation and Authority*, 3:219.

28. See David Munchin, *Is Theology a Science? The Nature of the Scientific Enterprise in the Scientific Theology of Thomas Forsyth Torrance and the Anarchic Epistemology of Paul Feyerabend* (Leiden: Brill, 2011), 205–9, for a description of various correspondence theories of truth, including that of Torrance.

29. Henry, *God, Revelation and Authority*, 3:221.

knowledge of God.[30] Henry appears to adopt something of a Thomistic theology of conversion whereby reason acts as a genuine and natural *preambula fidei*, the means by which one is led to faith. Any other view, Henry avers, amounts to fideism—the blind leap of faith, with Søren Kierkegaard mistakenly being the poster child of such a theology. In short, what Henry would seem to take exception to in this part of his argument is Torrance's Reformed doctrine of election, whereby faith itself is a gift imparted to the believer. In relation to the work and role of human reason, Henry is a semi-Pelagian as opposed to Torrance's Reformational *sola gratia* and *sola fidei* commitments. In Henry's best estimation, "the insistence on a logical gulf between human conceptions and God as the object of religious knowledge is erosive of knowledge and cannot escape a reduction to scepticism."[31] And finally, "We are therefore back to the emphasis that the laws of logic belong to the *imago Dei*, and have ontological import."[32]

Henry is particularly critical of what he sees as the illogical presuppositions of Torrance's intuitive theology. Torrance rejects the form of propositional revelation espoused by Henry in favor of a personal knowing. Reality is known by faith through an existential encounter with the ultimate reality—Jesus Christ, the incarnate Word (Logos). Henry believes this amounts to mysticism, something he is not disposed to favorably.[33]

Henry sees the critical mistake of Torrance's epistemology, derived in part from Kierkegaard but more from Michael Polanyi, to lie in his seeming rejection of any objective revelational knowledge. From Kierkegaard, Torrance is committed to the idea that the truth of God is communicated through personal relations, not, as Henry would have it, objectively and even dispassionately.[34] However, Torrance holds that theology that accepts the

---

30. See Alister E. McGrath, *The Open Secret: A New Vision for Natural Theology* (Oxford: Blackwell, 2008); Paul D. Molnar, *Thomas F. Torrance: Theologian of the Trinity* (Farnham: Ashgate, 2009), 93–99; and Habets, *Theology in Transposition: A Constructive Appraisal of T. F. Torrance* (Minneapolis: Fortress Press Academic, 2013), 63–89.

31. Henry, *God, Revelation and Authority*, 3:229.

32. Henry, *God, Revelation and Authority*, 3:229.

33. On mysticism see Myk Habets, "T. F. Torrance: Mystical Theologian *Sui Generis*," *Princeton Theological Review* 14 (2008): 91–104. Also see the brief discussion in Titus Chung, *Thomas Torrance's Mediations and Revelation* (Farnham: Ashgate, 2011), 127–29.

34. For an interesting insight into how Torrance articulated some of these convictions in response to a liberal Christian methodology see the account of his job interview for Princeton University in I. John Hesselink, "A Pilgrimage in the School of Christ—An Interview with

absolute primacy of its proper object of inquiry can be considered rational and scientific—hence objective. Torrance understands Kierkegaard's "truth as Subjectivity" as, in fact, theological objectivity and realism, the subject's proper relation to the object.

Henry appears to misread Torrance (and Polanyi) also at this point and interprets the notion of personal knowledge, which acknowledges the necessity for responsible commitment—Polanyi's term for personal knowledge—in terms of subjectivism. This is especially so when personal knowledge is applied to religious knowing and is virtually equated with biblical faith.

Utilizing as he does Polanyi's epistemology, Torrance would no doubt react to this criticism that Henry, and other critics, are perhaps looking to an impersonal procedure that operates along detached and mechanical lines and ultimately must appeal to the concept of autonomous reason. This autonomous reason is then directed at an external authority, in this religious case, the Holy Scriptures, and a system of propositional truth is worked out in a purely impersonal but logical way. It is this program that Torrance is particularly concerned to eradicate.

This use of Polanyi further explains Torrance's form of realism in his theological method. This commitment to critical realism constitutes one of Torrance's main reasons for drawing on the work of Polanyi. In Polanyi, Torrance finds a philosophical ally and one who has illustrated Torrance's point in the natural sciences as Torrance is seeking to do in Christian theology.

Not only is Polanyi appealed to, but also the theological method of Athanasius, Anselm of Canterbury, John Calvin, and not least, Karl Barth. Throughout his reading of the tradition, Torrance develops what he calls a *kata physic* form of theological methodology that is as applicable to the sciences as it is to the humanities, specifically to systematic theology. An overview of Torrance's theology illustrates his methodology, and an examination of his use of Scripture highlights the fundamental differences between the fundamentalist orientation of Henry's—and popular evangelicalism's—theological methodology and biblical hermeneutics.

T. F. Torrance," in *Reformed Review* 38 (1984): 54–55; and Alister E. McGrath, *T. F. Torrance: An Intellectual Biography* (Edinburgh: T&T Clark, 1999), 57–58.

As can be gleaned from this brief survey of Henry's critique of Torrance's theological method, Henry's theology may be characterized as rationalist, foundationalist, and nominalist, at least to some extent. As Grenz observed, Gordon H. Clark, Henry's professor of philosophy when he was a young student at Wheaton College, was perhaps the single most important intellectual influence on Henry's thought, giving it its rationalist-oriented worldview.[35] Not all would agree with this assessment, though. "Put simply, if the term 'foundationalist' is to be applied to Henry's theological outlook, his sounds more like that of a soft than a hard foundationalist,"[36] writes Mavis Leung. Chad Brand agrees when he writes:

> Is Henry a foundationalist? If one means by "foundationalist," the search for Cartesian certainty through the discovery of indubitable and noninferential truth claims arrived at through reason or reflection, then the answer is a resounding, "no.". . . It might be correct, on the other hand, to call Henry a scriptural foundationalist.[37]

And further,

> In regards to Scripture, Henry is certainly a firm, biblical foundationalist; in regards to the outworking of the theological implications of biblical asseverations, it appears that Henry is a soft foundationalist, one who is willing to admit that all our claims to understanding are subject to the eternal bar of God's judgment.[38]

It will pay us to consider Torrance's theological methodology directly before forming some critical conclusions.

THOMAS TORRANCE VS. CARL HENRY

In 1981 Torrance presented the Payton Lectures at Fuller Theological Seminary (subsequently published as *Reality and Evangelical Theology*), wherein he was "concerned to establish a realist basis in evangelical theology in contrast

---

35. Grenz, *Renewing the Center*, 90.

36. Mavis M. Leung, "With What Is Evangelicalism to Penetrate the World? A Study of Carl Henry's Envisioned Evangelicalism," *Trinity Journal* 27NS (2006): 240.

37. Chad O. Brand, "Is Carl Henry a Modernist? Rationalism and Foundationalism in Post-War Evangelical Theology," *Trinity Journal* 20NS (1999): 18.

38. Brand, "Is Carl Henry a Modernist?" 19.

with the nominalism that prevails so widely among so-called 'evangelicals.' "[39] While at Fuller Theological Seminary, Torrance singled out Carl Henry as one such evangelical doyen. In answer to a student's question on the extent of the atonement Torrance replied:

> You see there is nowhere in the Christian faith, there is no such thing as partial representation, as partial substitution. It's a total act and therefore the total being comes under the death and resurrection of Christ and therefore under the judgement of the cross. So that you, whether you are good or evil—Christ died for you. Now for you with your good as well as your evil comes under the judgment of the cross. Now that applies to the whole of creation. That applies to this creation that God made to be good, but which has become estranged from him. So, there you have to take seriously, dead seriously, the fact that the Creator became creature made atonement for the whole creation, consecrated the whole creation for God, not part of it. Now this is very important, you see.
>
> Carl Henry, for example, in a discussion with me on this very issue, would not agree that Christ died for all of him. There is still an integrity in his reason that doesn't come under the judgement of the cross, you see. So, I said to him, Carl Henry do you believe in a partial substitution, and therefore there is something in your reason Carl Henry, that hasn't really come under the judgement of the cross of Christ. And that's why you are a rationalist.
>
> So you see that is the point; and this is where the Gospel comes at its hardest. It's a good man, a righteous man, a man who is rich in goodness, it's as impossible for him to be saved as it is a camel to go through the eye of a needle. And yet that's possible for God, you see. And so the more we cling to our rationality, the more we cling to our goodness, the more difficult it is for us to have salvation.[40]

Torrance is accurate in his assessment of Henry and popular evangelicalism. According to Henry, the fall affects the will and not the mind: "Man wills,"

---

39. Torrance, "A Pilgrimage in the School of Christ," 60.

40. Thomas F. Torrance, "The Ground and Grammar of Theology," lectures given at Fuller Theological Seminary, 1981, Lecture 6, Q & A, 20.54–22.42. Transcribed from the audio available at http://www.gci.org/audio/torrance.

writes Henry, "not to know God in truth, and makes religious reflection serviceable to moral revolt. But he is still capable of intellectually analyzing rational evidence for the truth-value of assertions about God."[41]

Echoing the same critique, Donald Bloesch rightly observed that Carl Henry and other evangelicals provided a "transcendence in ontology but not in epistemology, for they are confident that human reason can lay hold of the truth of divine revelation apart from special grace."[42] He then outlines a four-stage taxonomy of how contemporary Christianity has sought to respond to the challenges of modernity. Henry is allocated to stage one, a theology of restoration, which Bloesch characterizes as a return to the rationalistic idealism of the early Enlightenment: "In this approach we arrive at truth by beginning with universal principles and then proceeding to deduce particular conclusions."[43]

Like Torrance and Bloesch, John Webster makes a trenchant and enlightened case for the need for reason itself to be sanctified and converted if it is to be of use in thinking theologically. "Christian theology is an aspect of reason's sanctification. ... Good Christian theology can only happen if it is rooted in the reconciliation of reason by the sanctifying presence of God."[44] This is a central point that Henry misses, even rejects. According to Henry, reason is a natural faculty seemingly unaffected by the fall, and as such, reason is not involved in the drama of God's saving work. As Webster notes of this approach, "Consequently, 'natural' reason has been regarded as 'transcendent' reason,"[45] and Webster argues, "Holy reason is eschatological reason."[46] Torrance accepts the basic orientation of Webster's claims with his dialectical/dialogical method in theology.[47]

---

41. Henry, *God, Revelation and Authority*, 1:226–27. Henry locates the *imago Dei* in the cognitive capacity of humanity and does not see this as inoperative after the fall. See Henry, *God, Revelation and Authority*, 1:394, 405; 2:136.

42. Donald G. Bloesch, *A Theology of Word and Spirit: Authority and Method in Theology* (Downers Grove, IL: InterVarsity Press, 1992), 252.

43. Bloesch, *A Theology of Word and Spirit*, 253. Bloesch identifies the influence of Gordon Clark on Henry, along with the influence of Descartes and Leibniz.

44. John Webster, *Holiness* (Grand Rapids: Eerdmans, 2003), 10.

45. Webster, *Holiness*, 10.

46. Webster, *Holiness*, 12.

47. See Thomas F. Torrance, "The Reconciliation of Mind: A Theological Meditation upon the Teaching of St Paul," in *Atonement: The Person and Work of Christ*, 437–47, where Torrance writes: "This applies not lest to 'evangelical Christianity' today, which on the whole still seems

Torrance directly accuses Henry of being a nominalist in his insistence that revelation is propositional and not also personal. He then provides an example: "This paper is white" is not the truth but is a statement about the truth. However, according to Henry, "This paper is white" is truth itself. Torrance is thus a metaphysical realist against Henry's nominalism, presumably because Torrance thinks Henry rejects universals. Torrance then draws a comparison with the law when he says, "I thought lawyers would have seen through this much clearly [sic] and more early [sic]." Juridical law is based upon actual law and is utterly consistent. By actual law Torrance appears to mean natural law, the reality that juridical law is meant to codify and conform to. A clue is thus found in juridical law—law testifies to actual law, which imposes itself upon us. Therefore it may be that Torrance's little book on juridical law may say more about his hermeneutics and method than has been previously thought.[48]

In Tom McCall's estimation, Torrance is a modest foundationalist.[49] While this, in McCall's opinion, is better than Ronald Thiemann's coherentism, it is not without its problems. He writes, "Torrance's epistemological foundationalism will likely continue to draw criticism from his detractors ... but the general position seems to be a stable one. If there is a problem with his theology of revelation it will appear when he relates his doctrine of revelation to Scripture."[50] McCall's theory was spot on, and Henry was one such detractor to make this point.

CRITICAL REALISM

For Torrance, the truth can be known and apprehended by the human person, and this knowledge represents a genuine disclosure of that which is real. Christian theology and natural science operate with an understanding of

---

to work with what may be called an 'unbaptised reason,' for it does not seem to have thought through sufficiently the transformation of human reason in the light of the Word made flesh in Jesus Christ. Hence the *mind* of the church and the *mind* of society are not inwardly formed by the gospel—they remain basically unevangelised"(438).

48. Thomas F. Torrance, *Juridical Law and Physical Law: Toward a Realist Foundation for Human Law* (Eugene, OR: Wipf & Stock, 1997). In this work it is legal positivism Torrance is reacting to with his realist epistemology.

49. Thomas C. McCall, "Ronald Thiemann, Thomas Torrance and Epistemological Doctrines of Revelation," *IJST* 6 no. 2 (2004): 164–65.

50. McCall, "Ronald Thiemann, Thomas Torrance," 165.

knowledge that has its "ontological foundations in objective reality." Torrance develops his critical realism in two directions: first, from natural science, especially from the works of John Philoponus, Clerk Maxwell, Albert Einstein, and Michael Polanyi; and second, from theology, especially from the works of Athanasius, Anselm, and Barth. Torrance argues that theology and the sciences share a common commitment to a realist epistemology (given an ordered universe), with each responding appropriately to their respective objects of study (*kata physin*).[51] Each of these disciplines recognizes

> the impossibility of separating out the way in which knowledge arises from the actual knowledge that it attains. Thus in theology the canons of inquiry that are discerned in the process of knowing are not sep-arable from the body of actual knowledge out of which they arise. In the nature of the case a true and adequate account of theological epis-temology cannot be gained apart from substantial exposition of the content of the knowledge of God, and of the knowledge of man and the world as creatures of God. ... This means that all through theolog-ical inquiry we must operate with an *open* epistemology in which we allow the way of our knowing to be clarified and modified *pari passu* with advance in deeper and fuller knowledge of the object, and that we will be unable to set forth an account of that way of knowing in advance but only by looking back from what has been established as knowledge.[52]

Torrance has exceptionally high regard for the work of Einstein and often returns to his scientific insights as illustrations of a realist epistemology in practice. From Einstein's scientific realism, Torrance sees great application for theology through the means of a "critical realism." Accepting the legiti-mate status of epistemic realism, what is the nature of the correspondence between reality and our understanding of it? The question of correspondence theories of truth is of great importance to our discussion.[53]

---

51. Alister McGrath, characterizes Torrance's method as "scientific realism," in *Reality: A Scientific Theology*, vol. 2 (London: T&T Clark, 2002), 130. The alternative to scientific realism would be constructive empiricism, whereby theories are empirically adequate but may not necessarily correspond to reality.

52. Torrance, *Theological Science*, 10.

53. See the discussion of Torrance's Christocentric analogy in regard to a "created correspon-dence" in Roland Spjuth, *Creation, Contingency and Divine Presence: In the Theologies of Thomas F.*

Torrance is a realist, not a positivist. He does not advocate scientific positivism, which argues for a direct correspondence between concepts and experience. He made this clear when he wrote:

> The fundamental difficulty with abstractive and positivist science ... is that it operates with a logical bridge between concepts and experience, both at the start and the finish, that is, in the derivation of concepts from the universe as we experience it and in the verificatory procedures relating concepts back to experience. ... This is not only a difficulty, but an impossibility, for this is not and cannot be any logical bridge between ideas and existence. There is indeed a deep and wonderful correlation between concepts and experience, and science operates with that correlation everywhere, but since there is no logical bridge the scientist does not work with rules for inductive procedures, and cannot finally verify his claims to have discovered the structures of reality by logical means.[54]

Torrance also rejects naïve realism in which there is a direct correspondence between knowledge and reality.[55] What Torrance does advocate is critical realism.[56] Perhaps one of the best known advocates of critical realism in biblical theology today is N. T. Wright. In his 1992 work, he defines critical realism as:

> A way of describing the process of "knowing" that acknowledges the *reality of the thing known, as something other than the knower* (hence "realism"), while also fully acknowledging that the only access we have to this reality lies along the spiralling path of *appropriate dialogue or conversation between the knower and the thing known* (hence "critical"). This path leads to critical reflection on the products of our enquiry into "reality," so that our assertions about "reality" acknowledge their

---

Torrance and Eberhard Jüngel (Lund: Lund University Press, 1995), 47–57.

54. Thomas F. Torrance, *Reality and Scientific Theology* (Edinburgh: Scottish Academic Press, 1985), 76.

55. See Spjuth, *Creation, Contingency and Divine Presence*, 94–101. With a phrase borrowed from Nancy Murphy, Spjuth characterizes Torrance's critical realism as "chastened modern" (98).

56. See Paul M. Achtemeier, "The Truth of Tradition: Critical Realism in the Thought of Alasdair MacIntyre and T. F. Torrance," *Scottish Journal of Theology* 47 (1996): 355–74; John D. Morrison, "Heidegger, Correspondence Truth and the Realist Theology of Thomas Forsyth Torrance," *Evangelical Quarterly* 69 (1997): 139–55; Morrison, *Knowledge of the Self-Revealing God.*

own provisionality. Knowledge, in other words, although in principle concerning reality is independent of the knower, is never itself independent of the knower.[57]

Unless Torrance is misunderstood, realism involves at least three elements, identified by Andrew Moore as ontological (realism vs. idealism), epistemological (realism vs. empiricism), and semantic (realism vs. linguistic idealism).[58] While interconnected, these three elements are distinct, and confusion often results in insufficiently distinguishing between them in a person's work. As David Munchin has observed, "The debate concerning realism becomes therefore a matter of epistemic degrees."[59] Torrance asserts,

> Belief is not something that is freely chosen or arbitrary, that is, without evidential grounds, for that would be highly subjective, a mere fancy. Nor is it something hypothetical or conditional, for then it would not be genuine, since we would entertain it, as it were, with our fingers crossed. Rather does belief arise in us, as we have seen, because it is thrust upon us by the nature of the reality with which we are in experiential contact. It arises as we allow our minds to fall under the compelling power of an intelligible structure or order inherent in the nature of things which we cannot rationally or in good conscience resist. That is to say, belief has to be understood strictly within the context of rational submission to the claims of reality upon us and of obligation towards the truth laid upon us by truth itself.[60]

This leads us to ask about the relationship between Scripture and theology within Torrance's scientific theology.

---

57. Nicholas T. Wright, *The New Testament and the People of God* (London: SPCK, 1992), 35. (Italics in original.)

58. Andrew Moore, *Realism and Christian Faith: God, Grammar and Meaning* (Cambridge: Cambridge University Press, 2003), 1.

59. Munchin, *Is Theology a Science?* 190.

60. Thomas F. Torrance, *Belief in Science and in Christian Life: The Relevance of Michael Polanyi's Thought for Christian Faith and Life* (Edinburgh: Handsel Press, 1980), 13.

SCRIPTURE AND DOGMATICS

There is an inseparable relation between Scripture and dogmatics for Torrance, which may be explained by three interrelated movements. First, dogmatics explains Scripture, and Scripture explains Christ. Second, Christ explains Scripture. Third, dogmatics is only rightly conducted when Christ is rightly known.[61] Consequently, Scripture stands in the middle between Christ and dogmatics, as the mediator of Christ, but it needs illumination itself from both ends, from Christ, and from dogmatics. The result is that Christ the Word is known both through and in the written word, which means the written word has unique and normative authority in our knowledge of him.

There is a *theological* reason for Torrance's method. For Torrance, revelation is always divine self-disclosure in which God communicates *himself* to his creatures. This self-revelation was made decisively through the incarnation. Scripture thus plays a secondary (but indispensable) role in the self-revelation of God through Christ. In Torrance's theology, revelation determines both Scripture and the *depositum fide*. The *depositum fide* is a gracious work of God in which knowledge of God through Christ is made possible in a personal and participatory way in the knower.

While Scripture is an imperfect and inadequate text, when it is appropriated by God's complete, final, and Holy Word (Jesus Christ), it is made to serve his reconciling revelation and infallible communication of his absolute truth. Thus, one of Torrance's central tasks is explicating the relationship between the Word incarnate and the written word. In a sermon on Matthew 18:1–22, "Christ in the Midst of His Church," Torrance narrates the relationship between Christ and Scripture by means of a meditation on "Christ in us." Christ lodges permanently within us by means of his word, but they are more than merely human words; they are "creative words," "personal words," "life-giving words" that create personal communion and presence; they "germinate in the human heart and create room for Christ there."[62] Christ and Holy Scripture are in such an intimate union that Torrance can say:

---

61. These relations are articulated in Robert T. Walker, "Editor's Foreword," in Thomas F. Torrance, *Incarnation: The Person and Life of Christ*, ed. Robert T. Walker (Milton Keynes: Paternoster, 2008), xxvi.

62. Thomas F. Torrance, "Christ in the Midst of His Church," in *When Christ Comes and Comes Again* (London: Hodder & Stoughton, 1957), 110.

It is as we allow the Word of the Gospel to saturate our minds and imaginations, to penetrate into our memories, and to master all our thinking, that Christ is born within us, that all that He is and has done becomes, as it were, imprinted upon us within, and becomes so truly and permanently the very centre of our being that we are transformed into His image and likeness, and even partake of His nature.[63]

Here the goal of Scripture is clearly stated,[64] related as it is to the Word incarnate. We also begin to see how the christological analogy and the Chalcedonian formula are integral to Torrance's understanding of the relation between the written word and the living Word.[65]

BETWEEN REALISM AND IDEALISM

Torrance's use of Scripture avoids fundamentalist and Roman Catholic foundationalism on the one hand and, on the other hand, a liberal and neo-Protestant idealism. Torrance considers both approaches to be mistaken.[66] In relation to many evangelicals, Christian dogmas or doctrines are not to be read directly off the pages of Scripture in a propositional way: "The assumption that the Scriptures are impregnated with universal, changeless divine truths which can be read off the sentential sequences of the inspired text, provided that it is properly or authoritatively interpreted."[67] Commitments of this sort result in a position where faith is placed in Scripture directly rather than in that to which Scripture bears witness—God's being and actions. To

---

63. Torrance, "Christ in the Midst of His Church," 110.

64. For more on the ultimate goal of salvation see Myk Habets, *Theosis in the Theology of Thomas Torrance* (Surrey: Ashgate, 2009), and *Heaven: An Inkling of What's to Come* (Eugene, OR: Cascade, 2018).

65. For his articulation of this point see Thomas F. Torrance, *Atonement: The Person and Work of Christ*, ed. Robert T. Walker (Downers Grove, IL: InterVarsity Press, 2009), 333–40.

66. Torrance deals with both fundamentalism and liberalism on many occasions. See for instance: Thomas F. Torrance, *God and Rationality* (London: Oxford University Press, 1971), 36; *Space, Time and Resurrection*, 1–26; and *Reality and Evangelical Theology* (Downers Grove, IL: InterVarsity Press, 1999), 52–83. Barth avoided both positions as well, but in Hunsinger's words he labeled the two extremes "literalism" and "expressivism." See George Hunsinger, "Beyond Literalism and Expressivism: Karl Barth's Hermeneutical Realism," in *Disruptive Grace: Studies in the Theology of Karl Barth* (Grand Rapids: Eerdmans, 2000), 210–25. In his own work John Webster labels both poles as "objectification" and "spiritualisation" respectively, and argues that both are pneumatologically deficient. See Webster, *Holy Scripture*, 33–36.

67. Torrance, *Space, Time and Resurrection*, 7–8. Similar ideas are expressed in Torrance, *Reality and Evangelical Theology*, see especially page 17.

mistake the text of Scripture for the truths they seek to reveal is to adopt some form of nominalism or extreme realism.[68] According to Torrance,

> In a scientific theology, on the contrary, we are concerned not with thinking thoughts, far less with thinking statements themselves, but with thinking realities through thoughts and statements, and with developing an understanding of God from his self-revelation mediated to us by the Holy Scriptures in the Church, in which the connections we think are objectively and ontologically controlled by the intrinsic connections of God's *self*-communication as Father, Son and Holy Spirit.[69]

The second position Torrance distances himself from is that of liberalism or neo-Protestantism, in which Christian dogmas or doctrines are reached by simple empirical observations of uninterpreted facts—that is, existentially.[70] This form of neo-Protestantism is considered the by-product of the scientific world of Newton. This was a radically dualist conception of science that carried over into theology, exemplified, as Torrance notes, by Johann Wilhelm Hermann's distinction between *Geschichte* and *Historie*.[71]

DEPTH EXEGESIS

In distancing himself from both fundamentalist forms of evangelicalism and liberalism, Torrance argues that the theologian is seeking to penetrate the depths of meaning that Scripture is witness to. Thus a genuinely theological reading of Scripture is attempted. The theologian "operates with the whole apostolic tradition in its stratified depth to allow himself to be directed from

---

68. As background to Torrance's discussion on truthfulness and the truth, see Thomas F. Torrance, "Truth and Authority: Theses on Truth," *Irish Theological Quarterly* 39 (1972): 215–42, especially thesis 5. Torrance's commitment to critical realism is also at play here.

69. Torrance, *Space, Time and Resurrection*, 8. (Italics in original.)

70. Torrance believes contemporary existentialists have distorted the referring function of language so that people are thrown back upon themselves to supply meaning, something already seen in the late medieval times. Torrance concludes that modern exegesis has much in common with the allegorical exegesis of the Augustinian tradition and that "as we look back upon allegorical exegesis with a little pathetic ridicule, so they in the days ahead will look back upon modern existentialist exegesis with the same sort of pathetic ridicule because it was oblique and rejected the *intentio recta*," Torrance, "Truth and Authority," 221, see also 219.

71. Torrance, *Space, Time and Resurrection*, 8–9; and *Preaching Christ Today* (Grand Rapids: Eerdmans, 1994), 42–43.

all sides to the objective realities under the creative impact of which all the apostolic tradition incorporated in the New Testament took its rise and shape in the primitive church."[72] Throughout this process, the theologian is under the influence of the self-revelation of God in Jesus Christ and the Holy Spirit through Scripture and beyond. This process involves spiraling upward from one level to another as successive layers of meaning and order are uncovered. This is the essence of Torrance's depth exegesis, realist hermeneutics, and theological interpretation of Scripture.[73]

Torrance is highly indebted to Barth's doctrine of Scripture, especially his 1930 work on Anselm, *Fides Quaerens Intellectum*, which Torrance considers to be the turning point in Barth's theological method.[74] Scripture contains a word of God in rational form. This word is not an end in itself but is accompanied by the living Word of God in the *event* of revelation.[75] Due to this event true knowledge of the Object of our study is also true knowledge of the Subject—God himself. This involves penetrating its inner rationality: the practice of depth exegesis.[76] Elsewhere Torrance refers to depth exegesis as a "cross-level movement of thought" in which we understand the text

---

72. Torrance, *Space, Time and Resurrection*, 10.

73. See Habets, "Theological Interpretation of Scripture in Sermonic Mode: The Case of T. F. Torrance," in *Ears that Hear: Explorations in Theological Interpretation of the Bible*, ed. Joel Green and Tim Meadowcroft (Sheffield: Sheffield Phoenix Press, 2013), 43–69, and "Theological Theological Interpretation of Scripture," *IJST* 23 no. 2 (2021): 235–58.

74. Thomas F. Torrance, *Karl Barth: An Introduction to His Early Theology, 1910–1931* (Edinburgh: T&T Clark, 2000), 183.

75. See the articulation of this in Karl Barth, *Church Dogmatics* (Edinburgh: T&T Clark, 1956–1975), I/1, 113. According to a Barthian exposition of revelation as event which Torrance subscribes to, "the term revelation refers *not to the objective self-manifestation alone, but equally to the act of faith in which it is heard and received and obeyed*," Trevor Hart, *Regarding Karl Barth: Toward a Reading of His Theology* (Downers Grove, IL: InterVarsity Press, 1999), 30 (italics in original). See Christina Baxter, "The Nature and Place of Scripture in the Church Dogmatics," in *Theology Beyond Christendom: Essays on the Centenary of the Birth of Karl Barth*, ed. John Thompson (Allison Park, PA: Pickwick, 1986), 35. In a sermon Torrance explains this event when he says, "That is how God always speaks to us, not directly out of the blue, as it were, nor simply through the witness of others. It is when both these come together, the vertical Word of God from above, and the horizontal witness of others, that we know God and hear His Word personally and directly for ourselves," Torrance, "The Lamb of God," in *When Christ Comes and Comes Again*, 56.

76. The term "depth exegesis" is taken from William Manson. See Torrance, *God and Rationality*, 110; and Thomas F. Torrance, "Introduction," in William Manson, *Jesus and the Christian* (London: James Clarke & Co, 1967), 9–14. The idea, however, is directly attributed by Torrance to the Greek fathers. See Thomas F. Torrance, "Introduction: Biblical Hermeneutics and General Hermeneutics," in *Divine Meaning: Studies in Patristic Hermeneutics* (Edinburgh: T&T Clark, 1995), 5.

and the *realities* to which it bears witness.[77] It is also a bi-polarity (dialectic) between the words and the Word, the worldly form of revelation and its divine content that renders Scripture a *witness* to the self-revelation of God.[78] Torrance traces his method of depth exegesis back to the Athanasian difference between *lalia* and *Logos*, according to which the *lalia* or human words are to be interpreted in terms of the *Logos*.[79] On other occasions, Torrance refers to this method as a "stereoscopic" reading of Scripture in which the *scope* of the Bible means its sacramental frame of reference, so that we must look not only at the text of Scripture but through it to the reality it signifies. When theologically interpreted, Jesus Christ becomes the *skopos* of the Bible.[80] Torrance is explicit at this point:

> Strictly speaking Christ himself is the scope of the Scriptures, so that it is only through focusing constantly upon him, dwelling in his Word and assimilating his Mind, that the interpreter can discern the real meaning of the Scriptures. What is required then is a theological interpretation of the Scriptures under the direction of their ostensive reference to God's self-revelation in Jesus Christ and within the general perspective of faith.[81]

Accordingly, the function of theological understanding or *intelligere* is the act of reading (*legere*) the text embedded within (*intus*) the object. Torrance remarks:

> God reveals himself to us by his Word in the Holy Scriptures, but our task in reading the outward text is to get at its inner meaning and basis, to read it at the deeper level of the solid truth on which the text rests. By a special act of the understanding that goes beyond mere reading, we penetrate into the objective *ratio* of the Word which enlightens and informs us.[82]

---

77. Torrance, *Reality and Evangelical Theology*, 99.

78. T. F. Torrance, *Karl Barth: Biblical and Evangelical Theologian* (Edinburgh: T&T Clark, 1990), 111–12.

79. See Torrance, *Space, Time and Resurrection*, 5, 167.

80. This is articulated in Torrance, *Reality and Evangelical Theology*, 100–107; *Space, Time and Resurrection*, 166–69; and *Theology in Reconstruction* (Grand Rapids: Eerdmans, 1965), 88–89.

81. Torrance, *Reality and Evangelical Theology*, 107.

82. Torrance, *Karl Barth: An Introduction to His Early Theology*, 186.

Ratio carries within it a threefold sense: first, it refers to the means we employ (noetic *ratio*); second, the end of our quest (ontic *ratio*); but ultimately, third, to the transcendent rationality of God behind all this (*ratio veritatis* or *ratio* of God). "*Ratio* is used then in a dimension of depth," writes Torrance, "of the ultimate Truth, the *ratio* of God himself; of the words and acts of God in Revelation, the *ratio* proper to the object of faith; and of man's knowledge of the object, the knowing *ratio* which corresponds to the *ratio* of the object."[83]

This final *ratio veritatis* is identical with God's being; it is the Divine Word consubstantial with the Father. Theological activity is derived from and is determined by the activity of God himself in his Word, for it is that Word (Christ) communicated through Holy Scripture which is the real object of our knowledge. When our statements are simply and formally identical with statements of the text of Scripture in which Christ speaks his word to us, they are directly authoritative. Any other theological statements have a derived and thus lesser authority status and are constantly open to revision in light of the Word of God. Consider Kevin Vanhoozer's distinction between the magisterial authority of Holy Scripture and the ministerial authority of churchly interpretations.[84] But theology is not content merely to recite or repeat biblical texts but instead seeks to make statements about the truth revealed in the inner text and so must seek conformity to the truth at a deeper level beyond formal conformity to the external text. "Hence, scientific theological activity begins where straightforward biblical quotations end, precisely because it is the task of theology to penetrate to the solid truth upon which biblical statements rest."[85] Torrance's method of depth exegesis or realist hermeneutics thus involves taking the biblical text and seeking to discern the inner, deeper structures of reality or truth inherent in it. It never leaves behind the text for another, for this is *Holy* Scripture.[86] But it never rests content on the mere *ipsissima vox* ("the very words or gist of Scripture").

Torrance is insistent that the voice of God must be heard through Scripture alone—*sola scriptura*, but not *nuda scriptura*. In a sermon on Christ the redeemer,

---

83. Torrance, *Karl Barth: An Introduction to His Early Theology*, 187.

84. Kevin Vanhoozer, "Interpreting Scripture Between the Rock of Biblical Studies and the Hard Place of Systematic Theology: The State of the Evangelical (Dis)union" (Renewing the Evangelical Mission Conference, Gordon-Conwell Theological Seminary, October 13–15, 2009).

85. Torrance, *Karl Barth: An Introduction to His Early Theology*, 188.

86. For a recent account of what it means to call Scripture "holy" see Webster, *Holy Scripture*.

Torrance asserts that "we cannot see Jesus just by piecing together pictur-
esque historical detail about Him,"[87] clearly a rejection of the historical-critical method as an end in itself in biblical exegesis. Instead, "Jesus must be
transfigured before our very eyes."[88] This is accomplished through his cross
and resurrection, by means of which he now stands at the door of the church
and knocks, and his voice is heard inside the church, "speaking to us out of
the pages of the Bible."[89] Torrance speaks of this as a miracle:

> We cannot see Jesus, for He has withdrawn Himself from our sight;
> and we will not see Him face to face until He comes again—but we *can
> hear* His *voice* speaking to us in the midst of the Church on earth. That
> is the perpetual miracle of the Bible, for it is the inspired instrument
> through which the voice of Christ is still to be heard. ... The Church
> is, in fact, the Community of the Voice of God.[90]

Theology is an inherently rational discipline for the precise reason that
faith itself is inherently rational. In revelation, God himself is being communicated so that in the Word, we are confronted with an Object that is
also Subject, with one who is both person and message. "Hence, Christian
Theology cannot tolerate the idea that faith is not rational in its own right
and that it is the task of theology to give it rational interpretation through
employing conceptual forms drawn from elsewhere."[91] From this premise,
Torrance concludes that the real issue is *ratio*, in both senses of the word—
rationality and method—which defines a scientific theology or dogmatics.
Scientific theology or dogmatics is thus different from biblical theology,
which remains content with the linguistic and phenomenological exegesis
of the Scriptures. Theology must press on to inquire into the relation between
biblical thought and speech and their source in the truth and being of God.
It is the specific task of theology to inquire into what we have to say based
on the biblical revelation and articulate its relation to the object so that our
knowledge may be established as true. Torrance goes even further in suggesting that unless this happens, "we have not engaged upon genuine exegesis,

---

87. Torrance, "When Christ Comes to the Church," 26.
88. Torrance, "When Christ Comes to the Church," 26.
89. Torrance, "When Christ Comes to the Church," 27.
90. Torrance, "When Christ Comes to the Church," 27.
91. Torrance, *Karl Barth: An Introduction to His Early Theology*, 182.

for then we are setting aside the all-important relation between the external text and the inner meaning and objective basis upon which it rests."[92] We may conclude from this that Torrance would only consider *theological* interpretation of Scripture as ultimately worthy of the epithet "Christian exegesis."

Torrance is trying to clarify how an exegesis of Scripture by a believer is different from that of the unbeliever. One could rephrase this somewhat to show that Torrance pointed out the necessary ecclesial commitments and contexts for a correct reading of Scripture. According to Torrance, "the decisive point in interpretation is not reached until there is inquiry into the reality signified. True interpretation arises where perception of the meaning of the letter of Holy Scripture and understanding of the reality it indicates are one."[93] This form of argument is another application of one of Torrance's fundamental commitments in theological science: the *kata physic* nature of scientific inquiry in which the object dictates the method of inquiry under study.[94] "It belongs to the rationality of theology that the reason should operate only with objects of faith, for faith is the specific mode of rationality which is demanded of the reason when it is directed to the knowledge of God."[95]

According to Polanyi, things are only understood by indwelling them, not merely by observing them.[96] Hence, when Torrance applies this philosophy of science or epistemology to theological method, he concludes that we only know the truth through indwelling the word, both written and incarnate.[97] In this light, evangelical exegesis should not be the mere study of a text but a way of life in which God, through Christ, and by the Holy Spirit, leads us into deeper communion with himself through the written word.[98] The ends

---

92. Torrance, *Karl Barth: An Introduction to His Early Theology*, 189. This is followed by a clarification: "No exegesis that is content only with noetic rationality can be regarded as properly scientific, for scientific activity must penetrate through noetic rationality into the ontic rationality of its basis and so lay bare its inner necessity."

93. Torrance, *Karl Barth: An Introduction to His Early Theology*, 189.

94. Or alternatively: the nature of the object prescribes the mode of rationality proper to its investigation. See a potted summary of this position in Torrance, "Truth and Authority," 223-24.

95. Torrance, *Karl Barth: An Introduction to His Early Theology*, 192.

96. Michael Polanyi, "Science and Man's Place in the Universe," in *Science as a Cultural Force*, ed. H. Woolf (Baltimore: Johns Hopkins Press, 1964), 54-76; and Michael Polanyi, *The Tacit Dimension* (London: Routledge and Kegan Paul, 1967), 21.

97. Webster, *Holy Scripture*, 68-106, presents a similar view.

98. Though not identical, see the sort of participatory exegesis recommended by Matthew Levering, *Participatory Biblical Exegesis: A Theology of Biblical Interpretation* (Notre Dame: University of Notre Dame Press, 2008).

of exegesis are thus kept squarely at the forefront of Torrance's theological interpretation of Scripture.[99]

INSPIRATION AND REVELATION

Torrance's doctrine of Scripture regards revelation as dynamic because it is initiated by Christ and enabled by the Holy Spirit. This means Scripture is not, strictly speaking, revelation but a vehicle for revelation or a medium through which God's revelation in Christ and by the Spirit can be given. Donald Bloesch is one of many contemporary evangelicals who follow this line of reasoning carefully. Bloesch maintains that "the Bible in and of itself is not the Word of God—divine revelation—but it is translucent to this revelation by virtue of the Spirit of God working within it and within the mind of the reader and hearer."[100] Scripture is a human medium of the divine Word and as such cannot be, according to Torrance, simply mistaken for God's living eternal Word, who is Jesus Christ. All human speech must have a reservation about it until God reveals all. Torrance brings out this eschatological character of revelation in his early work *Theological Science*:

> While God has made His Word audible and apprehensible with our human speech and thought, refusing to be limited by their inadequacy in making Himself known to us, He nevertheless refuses to be understood merely from within the conceptual framework of our natural thought and language but demands of that framework a logical reconstruction in accordance with His Word. Hence a theology faithful to what God has revealed and done in Jesus Christ must involve a powerful element of apocalyptic, that is epistemologically speaking, an

---

99. It is Webster's contention that "the referential or signifying function of Scripture is ... a primary element in Torrance's understanding of biblical interpretation." John Webster, "T. F. Torrance on Scripture" (keynote address at annual meeting of Thomas F. Torrance Theological Fellowship, Montreal, November 6, 2009), 12.

100. Donald G. Bloesch, *Holy Scripture: Revelation, Inspiration, and Interpretation* (Downers Grove, IL: InterVarsity Press, 1994), 27. Bloesch's use of "translucent" is reminiscent of Torrance's language of Scripture as a "transparent medium" through which "the divine Light shines from the face of Jesus Christ into our hearts." Torrance, *Space, Time and Resurrection*, 12, and *Theology in Reconstruction*, 257. In addition to Bloesch, see other contemporary evangelical theologians who share the same basic convictions, especially: Grenz, *Renewing the Center*; and Alister E. McGrath, *A Passion for Truth: The Intellectual Coherence of Evangelicalism* (Leicester: Apollos, 1996), 53–118; and *The Genesis of Doctrine: A Study in the Foundation of Doctrinal Criticism* (Grand Rapids: Eerdmans, 1990).

eschatological suspension of logical form in order to keep our thought ever open to what is radically new.[101]

The relation between God's self-revelation and Scripture is fundamentally asymmetrical.[102] Scripture points to, and is the divinely chosen medium for, the revelation of God's eternal Word. I want to affirm that it would be closer to the truth to say Holy Scripture *is* revelation but must not be misunderstood as the *end* of revelation or as authoritative as Christ the Word.

Torrance develops this realist hermeneutic more fully in a discussion on the referring relation of language. If statements are adequate to the object, asks Torrance, how can we distinguish the object from statements about it? If language and statements are to perform their denotative function adequately, directing us to reality/truth beyond themselves in such a way that there takes place a disclosure of reality/truth, then, Torrance concludes, they must have a measure of inadequacy in order to be differentiated from that to which they refer.[103] "The Scriptures of the Old and New Testaments rightly evoke from us profound respect and veneration not because of what they are in themselves but because of the divine revelation mediated in and through them. This is why we speak of them as 'Holy' Scriptures."[104] Barth's formulation of the dynamic between God's revelation in Christ and in Scripture proposed his famous threefold distinction of the word: the living Word, the written word, and the proclaimed word. Barth understands that it becomes revelation proper only when the written or proclaimed word is united with the revealed Word. Torrance, in line with Barth, considers the written word to point to God's revelation. Yet, for Torrance, revelation cannot be detached from the Bible, for in space and time, this is how God has "uniquely and sovereignly coordinated the biblical word with his eternal Word, and adapted the written form and contents of the Bible to his Word, in such a way that the living Voice of God is made to resound through the Bible to all who have ears to hear."[105]

---

101. Torrance, *Theological Science*, 279–80.

102. Torrance, *Reality and Evangelical Theology*, 96.

103. See the discussion in Torrance, "Truth and Authority," 229–31, especially 231.

104. Torrance, *Reality and Evangelical Theology*, 95. In a footnote Torrance then directs the reader to Barth's *Church Dogmatics* I/2, ch. 3 on "Holy Scripture," 457–537.

105. Torrance, *Karl Barth: Biblical and Evangelical Theologian*, 88.

CRITICAL CONCLUSIONS

As I conclude, clearly I am favorably disposed to the theological methodology of Torrance, as opposed to that of Henry. Henry's theological method falls foul of what Kevin Vanhoozer has dramatically termed "epic classicism," or what Lindbeck termed "cognitive-propositional" approach.[106] It is also clear where I disagree with Henry and where I might want to push back on his fundamentalist-leaning ideas, which are also prevalent in sectors of contemporary evangelicalism. However, before Carl Henry is dismissed as some fundamentalist fossil of an embarrassing history, there are aspects of his critique and his perspective that are important to note and which most evangelicals will appreciate.

It can appear that Torrance sees Scripture as less than revelation and that it only *becomes* revelation through personal communion with Christ by the Spirit. Indeed, if that is the case, evangelicals would want to push back with Henry and say that our response to revelation does not make it revelation but rather makes it *revelatory* and personally affective. We must say, then, that Scripture *is* divine revelation regardless of whether one is in union with Christ. In the words of Tom McCall, "Perhaps what Torrance needs is a strong dose of his own epistemological medicine. The trajectory of his thought might well result in belief in Scripture as the written revelation standing in a direct but subordinate relation to the self-revelation of God in Jesus Christ."[107] If this were the case, then Torrance would be able to affirm, with Henry, that Scripture *is* revelation, without this being a denial that ultimate or final revelation is found in Jesus Christ alone. Scripture is revelation as far as it is a divinely given witness to the God revealed in Jesus Christ by the Spirit.

I conclude with the words Marguerite Shuster used to finish her short article on Torrance's theological method: "What is truth? The True Man said, 'I am the truth.' True men, responding in the faith of God's grace, can start nowhere else than to proclaim, 'Indeed, *he* is the truth.' "[108]

---

106. Kevin J. Vanhoozer, *The Drama of Doctrine: A Canonical Linguistic Approach to Christian Theology* (Louisville: Westminster John Knox, 2005), 83.

107. McCall, "Ronald Thiemann, Thomas Torrance," 167.

108. Marguerite Shuster, "'What Is Truth?' An Exploration of Thomas F. Torrance's Epistemology," *Studio Biblica Et Theologia* 3 (1973): 56.

5

—

THEOLOGY AND SCIENCE IN TORRANCE

W. Ross Hastings

INTRODUCTION

"Magisterial and highly original,"[1] is P. Mark Achtemeier's assessment of the contribution of Thomas F. Torrance to the dialogue between theology and science. It still rings true, even as science has continued to advance. Naturally, the fact that Torrance was awarded the Templeton Foundation Prize for Progress in Religion in 1978 justifies this judgment. Accolades from others abound. Alister McGrath, impressed by the scientific acumen of Torrance,[2] referred to his work in this area as "serious, informed and important ... quite simply, of landmark significance."[3] It is my opinion that if one has not come to terms with Torrance's theology as it was affected by science, and the discipline of science as it has been elucidated by Torrance's theology, one will not have an adequate grasp of either of these magisterial realms of knowledge.

---

1. P. Mark Achtemeier, "Natural Science and Christian Faith in the Thought of T. F. Torrance," in *The Promise of Trinitarian Theology: Theologians in Dialogue with T. F. Torrance*, ed. Elmer M. Colyer (Lanham, MD: Rowman & Littlefield, 2001), 269.

2. Elmer Colyer records the fact that Torrance's early interest in theology and science was stimulated by the influence of his wife's cousin, the eminent physicist and radio astronomer, Sir Bernard Lovell (1913-2012). Torrance felt that before he could even talk to Lovell about the relations between science and theology, he needed to learn much more about science and so spent twenty years studying science, especially physics and the philosophy of science. This contributed to Torrance's acumen and reputation as a theologian of science. Elmer Colyer, *How To Read T. F. Torrance: Understanding His Trinitarian and Scientific Theology* (Downers Grove, IL: InterVarsity Press, 2001), 40-41.

3. Alister E. McGrath, *T. F. Torrance: An Intellectual Biography* (Edinburgh: T&T Clark, 1999), xii.

Myk Habets, in his fine summation, has commented that "Torrance's academic career was almost entirely absorbed by concerns over methodology. ... [It was] a clearing of the epistemological ground for a starting point in theological discourse."[4] This search for an explicitly Christian epistemology took him in the direction of interaction with the natural sciences to the extent that he articulated theology as indeed the science of theology, as is reflected in his 1969 work *Theological Science*.[5]

As Elmer Colyer has indicated, "The linking of the two terms, scientific and theological, has created significant misunderstanding (and misgiving) about Torrance's theological and methodological vision for many." Once it is clarified that this did not imply a "preconceived idea of *science as a universally applicable method* (*scientia universalis*) ... with presuppositions and/or procedures to which all (*scientia speciales*), including theology, must conform if they are to be scientific," fears of practitioners in both science and theology are allayed. Rather, "each science has to be developed *kata physin*, in strict conformity to the nature of the object"[6] being studied, including theology, which because of the nature of its object has its own particular requirements and procedures. More will be said to clarify the concerns for both vocations. Suffice it to say that Torrance acknowledges both the irreducible distinctiveness of science (and the various sciences and their different hierarchical levels of knowledge) and theology, *and* their formal similarities and mutually enriching nature, with respect to both epistemology and ontology.

In short, Torrance's writing in this integrative field, more than that of any other scholar, has influenced my own conviction that the relationship between theology and science is *not* one of conflict, or even nonoverlapping magisteria ("independence," according to Stephen Jay Gould), nor yet mere dialogue or bridge-building. It may, from the perspective of protagonists in both fields, still require much integration.[7] Torrance, however, based on the interwoven history of ideas, considered their relation to be one of profound

---

4. Myk Habets, *Theology in Transposition: A Constructive Appraisal of T. F. Torrance* (Minneapolis: Fortress, 2013), 21.

5. T. F. Torrance, *Theological Science* (London: Oxford University Press, 1969).

6. Elmer M. Colyer, "A Scientific Theological Method," in *The Promise of Trinitarian Theology*, 206–7.

7. The terms "conflict," "independence," "dialogue," and "integration" reflect Ian Barbour's typology for the various ways in which theology and science are related. See Ian Barbour, *Religion in an Age of Science: The Gifford Lectures, 1989–1991*, vol. 1 (San Francisco: Harper, 1990), chapter 1.

mutuality. In light of inferences made,[8] I audaciously offer the term coinherence as a way to describe how Torrance viewed the being and functioning of these disciplines. In a manner analogous to the persons of the Holy Trinity, theology and science have their own irreducible identity as disciplines and yet have profound mutuality such that each is in the other and animates and enriches the other.

The Christian theologian's counter to the warfare model, or the polarization between science and theology in modernity, is to insist that these great traditions of thought have, as Torrance himself insisted, "deep mutual relations, and increasingly cry out for each other" and are the richer for the reality of the other. That there is "hidden traffic between theological and scientific ideas of the most far-reaching significance for both theology and science."[9] Torrance was above all convinced that "both result from *a posteriori* reflection on an independent reality which they attempt to describe in their respective manners."[10] This is to say that a postcritical, "faith seeking understanding" epistemology,[11] or a *motivated* belief system (as John Polkinghorne puts it), pertains to both. Which is to say that critical realism applies to both. Achtemeier astutely develops the theme of this mutuality regarding both the

---

8. The relationship between coinherence (or perichoresis) in the incarnation, then by extension to persons of the Trinity, and then on to concepts in science (modern particle theory and quantum theory), as well as the relationship between the disciplines, is implicit in Thomas F. Torrance, *The Ground and Grammar of Theology* (Charlottesville: University of Virginia Press, 1980), 174–78. It is most interesting that the physicist Jim Neidhardt who writes the introduction to *The Christian Frame* approvingly notices the coinherent approach in Torrance's theology and makes the connection explicit with respect to the coinherence of the disciplines of theology and science. W. Jim Neidhardt, "Introduction," in Thomas F. Torrance, *The Christian Frame of Mind: Reason, Order and Openness in Theology and Natural Science* (Handsel, 1980; repr. Eugene, OR: Wipf & Stock, 1989), xl.

9. Thomas F. Torrance, *Reality and Scientific Theology: Theology and Science at the Frontiers of Knowledge* (Edinburgh: Scottish Academic Press, 1985), x.

10. Alister E. McGrath, *Science and Religion: An Introduction*, 2nd ed. (Malden, MA: Wiley-Blackwell, 2010), 226.

11. The influence of chemist and philosopher of science Michael Polanyi on Torrance's pursuit of a Christian epistemology was significant. The fiduciary component of human knowledge was one of the emphases in Polanyi. Over against logical positivism, he argued for a "post-critical philosophy" which he believed to be consistent with the great tradition since Augustine who stated, "Unless you believe, ye shall not understand" (cited in *Personal Knowledge*, 266). From the Enlightenment and John Locke's introduction of the dualism of knowledge and faith, what had been joined together was put asunder. As Polanyi wrote, "All belief was reduced to the status of subjectivity: to that of an imperfection by which knowledge fell short of universality," *Personal Knowledge: Towards a Post-Critical Philosophy* (Chicago: University of Chicago Press, 1974), 266. This Augustinian-Anselmian-Barthian epistemology shaped Torrance profoundly.

history and future prospects of each discipline in three primary areas: epistemology, common material interests (ontology), and histories of development. I will, due to space limitations, shape this essay around only the first two aspects of this mutuality.

CHRISTOLOGICAL FOUNDATIONS

Before considering each of these categories, I wish to draw attention to what I perceive to be, at the most fundamental level, what inspired Torrance to speak confidently of correspondences in knowing and being in the theology/science interface: his Christology. Torrance's search was for a specifically Christian epistemology, which for Torrance meant "one that took seriously the starting point for all knowledge of God in Christology, mediated by the Word written through the Holy Spirit."[12] But in light of the nature of the living Word as the triune God's agent in creation, this search took Torrance in the direction of interaction with the natural sciences. The starting point, which Torrance discovered to be in common for the study of creation and the study of God, was what drew Christ and the sciences together. This starting point was "a commitment to a realistic view of the world and then the adoption of a methodology in conformity with the nature of the object under study,"[13] which, as noted above, Torrance called a *kata physin* form of scientific inquiry. What Torrance saw in the work of James Clerk Maxwell (who discovered the properties of an electromagnetic field of force, a paradigm shift which led to the birth of modern physics) and Einstein (who built on Maxwell's work and expressed the general and special theory of relativity, doing so in a manner that supremely illustrated the scientific method of *kata physin*) contributed to the conceptual basis of Torrance's own theological methodology rooted in the revelation of Jesus Christ. Torrance saw in Einstein's scientific realism an important resource and resonance for doing theology. Against all dualism, Torrance believed that knowledge should be gained in all realms by the same basic methodology.

This epistemological correspondence between theology and science relates to the fact that all reality is just that, reality. And whether divine or creational reality, it is empirically discoverable through revelation, in the

---

12. Habets, *Theology in Transposition*, 21.
13. Habets, *Theology in Transposition*, 21.

case of divine, the revelation of the Word made flesh, by the Spirit, made to the church, and in the case of creational reality, the gracious gift of an intelligible universe. This was a correspondence that Torrance found paradigmatically in the incarnation. He was comfortable making this move on the grounds that Christ is Lord over all realms, but also because he observed that this was the method by which the church had discovered the identity of the person of Christ (see 1 John 1:1 "That which was from the beginning, which we have heard, which we have seen with our eyes, which we have looked at and our hands have touched—this we proclaim concerning the Word of life" NIV). It was also the method by which the church had crafted the doctrine of the Trinity based on the revelation of the incarnate Son by the Spirit.

Thus, rather than rehashing excellent and systematic accounts concerning Torrance in this science/theology area, I wish to emphasize the person and work of Christ. One of the greatest challenges for the ordinary Christian wrestling with the theology/science interface is christological: how to put together the Jesus of history with the cosmic Christ. How do we integrate Jesus of Nazareth—the Jesus of reconciliation and redemption—with the cosmic Christ, who was the agent within the Trinity for creation *ex nihilo*, has been the divine agent (along with the Spirit) in the providential (not deterministic) evolution of the universe and of life on earth, and is perpetually the sustainer of all things? Placing a christological rubric over the work of T. F. Torrance will, I hope, prove fruitful. I believe it is faithful especially to the importance of the incarnation and the high priesthood and kingship of Christ in his whole theological corpus.[14] Reflecting on Christ in this way also keeps the whole exercise doxological, a sentiment true to the mood or tone of the rich christological passages of the New Testament (specifically passages on creation, which usually pull together creation and redemption: John 1:1–18; Heb 1:2–3; Col 1:13–20).

Torrance's christological emphasis has, of course, been noticed by most scholars of his work in this area. For example, Alister McGrath, writing about the early influences on Torrance's work on the natural sciences and theology

---

14. Torrance's theology is aptly summed up by Gerrit Scott Dawson and other scholars in conference on the theology of T. F., J. B., and D. W. Torrance, as *Discovering the Incarnate Saviour*. See Gerrit Scott Dawson, ed., *An Introduction to Torrance Theology: Discovering the Incarnate Saviour* (London: T&T Clark, 2007). Similarly, Myk Habets in *Theology in Transposition* expresses the christocentricity of Torrance's theology throughout (2).

(such as that of Daniel Lamont's *Christ and the World of Thought* in his student days at New College in Edinburgh), draws attention to an evangelistic tone that resounded in his lectures on science and theology. "Torrance," says McGrath, "concluded his lectures with what seems remarkably like an altar call." It is the identity of Jesus Christ which was at stake in these appeals.[15]

Though Torrance moved beyond Barth in that he *engaged* the natural sciences,[16] he did not, as McGrath emphasizes, leave behind Barth's central affirmation that "the distinctive nature of theology is determined by its object, which is defined as God revealed in Jesus Christ." In fact, McGrath adds, "Torrance invokes the theological principle of the *homoousion* in making the point that this epistemological insight is ontologically determined. God already is in himself what he is in his historical self-revelation in Christ. Epistemology is thus correlated with ontology."[17] McGrath indicates that Torrance stressed this point from 1938 onward. Even in his Auburn Lectures, he states that "the *ordo cognoscendi* is only possible on account of the *ordo essendi*."[18] As we consider the two aspects of Torrance's discussion of the history of ideas with respect to scientific theology and science and their christological foundations—that is, the epistemological and the ontological—McGrath's comment will be proved true.

KNOWING: EPISTEMOLOGY— CHRIST THE LOGOS OF GOD

Torrance's theological method is most remarkable for its consistency throughout his career and in all his varied publications. In contrast with the apophaticism of the Eastern Orthodox tradition, he built his epistemological foundation on a scientific method. Instead of a purely phenomenalist

---

15. McGrath, *T. F. Torrance*, 204, citing Torrance, "Science and Theology" (lectures at Auburn Theological Seminary, 1938–1939), 61.

16. Barth treated theology and science as noninteractive disciplines in a manner that has resonance with Stephen Jay Gould's nonoverlapping magisteria viewpoint, although differently motivated and conceived. Torrance found in the theology of Barth the construction of a unitary approach to reality, an approach he found also in Einstein. Barth was not aware of this but apparently seemed pleased about it when Torrance informed him of this. See Thomas F. Torrance, *Transformation and Convergence in the Frame of Knowledge: Explorations in the Interrelations of Scientific and Theological Enterprise* (Grand Rapids: Eerdmans, 1984), ix.

17. McGrath, *T. F. Torrance*, 208.

18. McGrath, *T. F. Torrance*, 208, with reference to Torrance, "The Christian Doctrine of God," Auburn Lectures, 93.

approach, he adopted critical realism. He believed there was a right way to do Christian theology, and this was a *scientific* method, one which could be practiced in both science and theology—the latter he called "theological science." He admired Augustine for the symmetry of his theological form but disliked the extent to which neo-Platonism pervaded his thought; he owed a great deal to Karl Barth for the Trinitarian and incarnational ground, grammar, and thematic architectonic of his theology, and yet, he sought to move beyond Barth by working out more extensively "the scientific substructure of Christian dogmatics."[19]

Anselm and Barth were his primary theological influences in this regard, but Torrance, though not a scientist by training, spent twenty years studying science. He not only was (remarkably) awarded an honorary doctorate at Heriot-Watt University in Edinburgh but was compared by the awarding principal to Einstein.[20] He observed the scientific method of Einstein closely and noted the methodology of science as well as the levels and layers of meaning in science.[21] Sir Bernard Lovell, the works of Maxwell, and Michael Polanyi also had a significant impact on his thought and method. The gains to theology that this brings are summarized by Torrance in this way: "Without doubt the rehabilitation of a realist approach to knowledge which gives priority to the truth of being over truths of signification and statement opens the way for considerable clarification and simplification by making them point beyond themselves to a unifying ontological ground. This is bound to undermine a nominalist approach to knowledge."[22]

Thus, Torrance, as Achtemeier indicates, speaks firstly of a mutually beneficial conversation between theology and science, which is possible concerning formal methodological matters. This refers to the reality that the scientific method is employed in both disciplines. In other words, critical realism applies in both disciplines as the humble yet constructive way of gaining knowledge.[23] There is an undergirding assumption in both

---

19. Torrance, "My Interaction with Karl Barth," in *How Karl Barth Changed My Mind*, ed. D. K. McKim (Grand Rapids: Eerdmans, 1986), 55. A fuller account of the development of Torrance's methodology may be found in Habets, *Theology in Transposition*, 27–65.

20. For details of this event, see Habets, *Theology in Transposition*, 22.

21. Torrance, "The Stratification of Truth," in *Reality and Scientific Theology*, 131–59.

22. Torrance, "The Stratification of Truth," in *Reality and Scientific Theology*, 153.

23. For a fuller discussion of epistemological realism in Torrance's work, see Douglas F. Kelly, "The Realist Epistemology of Thomas F. Torrance," in *An Introduction to Torrance Theology*, 75–102.

disciplines that there must be some kind of correspondence between what is in the researcher's mind and what is being studied, between the models and patterns of the scientist's or theologian's mind and the actual reality under investigation (hence *realist*). Another way to say this, as indeed T. F. Torrance did, is that knowing follows being, epistemology follows ontology.[24] As a consequence, Douglas Kelly explains, "True rationality never seeks to impose a preconceived pattern on to the material it wishes to know. Instead, it humbly enquires of a given field of reality; it puts questions to it, and then—as Torrance so often says—it lets its questions be questioned."[25] The process of research will thus involve "purifying the active concepts that form the matrix of their encounter" as well as eliminating "distorting impositions of alien thought patterns that derive from outside sources."[26] In science, this involves the empirical process that moves from hypothesis, to carefully designed experiment, to evaluation, towards a thesis. Less obviously for some, in theology, this involves hearing the apostolic and ecclesial testimony concerning God's self-revelation in Christ. It also includes exegesis (as opposed to eisegesis) of the text of Scripture in light of its cultural-historical background, its literary genre, its grammatical meaning, and its rhetorical forms.

The need for clarification, already suggested above, has been and is necessary. For scientists who might balk at the idea of coming under the control of theology or even being associated with its epistemological method, it is clear that Torrance did not intend that there should be a hegemony of theology over the sciences. He acknowledged that each science had its own freedom for the development of its idiosyncratic procedures, analytical tools, thought structures, criteria, and language in the pursuit of its own subject within the natural order, without interference from theological science. Yet, Torrance, from a faith perspective, and grounded in a high Christology, has no doubt that whatever science discovers, it can never contradict first order, confessional theology. He also invites scientists as priests of God's good creation to reflect on what their discoveries reveal about the glory of Christ, inviting them evangelically into the response of worship and into the building of a theology that must include all reality, a theology that is encyclopedic. He

---

24. See Kelly, "The Realist Epistemology of Thomas F. Torrance," 76. He notes that this is discussed in Karl Barth in *Church Dogmatics* I/2, 5 and following.

25. Kelly, "The Realist Epistemology of Thomas F. Torrance," 76.

26. Achtemeier, "Natural Science and Christian Faith in the Thought of T. F. Torrance," 272.

invites the scientists to find the meaning of their work in the light of Christ, the Priest-King of the cosmos.

Theologians, for other reasons, might balk at the idea of crassly and uncritically employing the scientific method for discerning theological truth from divine revelation, be it general, special, or personal revelation. It is important to clarify that Torrance did not think methods from the natural sciences could be uncritically employed for the pursuit of the knowledge of the transcendent God. Furthermore, when he spoke of theology as a science, Torrance was using the term in a much broader sense than its sense in popular usage might convey. "Science," for Torrance, was conceived of as "an investigative discipline whose goal is to faithfully expound the intelligible structure of its own particular object."[27] This, for the natural sciences, is knowledge focused on the properties and behavior of the particular aspect of the natural order under consideration in that particular science, whereas for theology the focus "is upon God's self-disclosure in the history of Israel that culminates in the incarnation, life, death, and resurrection of Jesus of Nazareth"[28] and the meaning of reality derived from this orientation.

Scientific method means for theology that it, like natural science, involves a vigorous commitment to disciplined investigation, "as methodologically rigorous as the hard sciences."[29] It also involves a warranted belief that thought structures in the engraced human mind do mediate a true encounter with the reality of what is being encountered. The subject of inquiry in theology is principally the person and work of Christ as empirically encountered by the apostles and the church. This subject reveals the nature of the real God. Torrance's practice, following Barth, and over against Jürgen Moltmann, was to deny any idea that God's eternal being is constituted by his relations with creation or humanity in history. The revelation of the Son as Jesus of Nazareth was the revelation of the eternal Trinity in which the Son lived in coinherent relations with the Father and the Spirit. The noetic road to the immanent Trinity might be through the economic Trinity, or the revelation of the incarnate Word and the Spirit, but the ontic reality of the eternal being of God was necessary to the reliability of this economic revelation. There

---

27. Achtemeier, "Natural Science and Christian Faith in the Thought of T. F. Torrance," 271.

28. Achtemeier, "Natural Science and Christian Faith in the Thought of T. F. Torrance," 271.

29. Colyer, *How to Read T. F. Torrance*, 40.

could be no *meaning* to the incarnational revelation of God in Jesus Christ in the economic Trinity without its correspondence to the immanent Trinity.

Torrance railed on dualisms of a number of kinds, but none more so than cosmological dualism, which proposes a "separation between the reality or essence of something and the empirical sources of our knowledge about it— between substance and appearance."[30] This relates to what is "really real," and in this regard, Torrance was critical of the ancient Greek thought of both Aristotelian and Platonic or Neoplatonic sources, precisely because of his theology of the unconfused union of the divine and human natures of the incarnate Christ. Any philosophy that proposes that reality is in the heavenly or eternal realm of pure thought forms, and that concrete creation is itself not real, he saw as a denial of the goodness of God's creation and a confusion of God and creation. He was well aware that this philosophical orientation regarding creation explained the absence of science in the ancient Greeks precisely because they treated experimentation and the observation of concrete particulars as unimportant, preferring to speculate in a top-down manner, in an *a priori* rather than *a posteriori* way. Torrance knew that the ultimate theological reality of the Trinity was arrived at in an *a posteriori* way, as a response of the early church to the empirical reality that God had walked in their midst in the fully human person of Jesus Christ, who shared the divine essence and communion with the Father and the Spirit. As Achtemeier states, reflecting Torrance accurately, "The Nicene *homoousion*, which stands at the center of orthodox Christology, is the Church's emphatic declaration that the fullness of the divine being has become present and knowable within the realm of space and time in the historical, flesh-and-blood reality of Jesus Christ."[31]

In theology, this incarnational reality reflected in the term *homoousion* is vital for the *realism* piece in critical realism. This is at the level of divine revelation. The human reception of that revelation is, however, also necessary. The correspondence between objective reality and human knowing of it (in both theology and science), which defines the *realism* in critical realism, is assumed on the basis of another theologically foundational concept for Torrance. This is the principle of the intelligibility of revelation, be it general

30. Achtemeier, "Natural Science and Christian Faith in the Thought of T. F. Torrance," 271.

31. Achtemeier, "Natural Science and Christian Faith in the Thought of T. F. Torrance," 271.

or special, or to use a related term describing the capacity of the human recipient to perceive what is intelligible: perspicuity. The intelligibility of the creation to humanity finds its source ultimately in the Logos, the living Word who created all things in a manner that reflects wisdom and with an order that is discernible.

This does not mean that everything is simple. God who is the God of revelation is also the God of hiddenness. We are too feeble to endure the full light of the blazing glory of God. Just as the Son was here on earth as, to use Luther's term, the divine *incognito*, so, by analogy, theological and scientific findings are not always (or even mostly) found in facile ways. Jesus exhorts his followers to ask, seek, and knock, to persevere in prayer. The early church took almost four centuries to articulate its most crucial doctrines relating to the deity and humanity of Christ and the Trinity. Similarly, scientific knowledge is gained through painstaking work in the laboratory by researchers who can become dispirited. What's more, scientific discoveries often have an element of the serendipitous to them that confound any postulation of a directly proportionate relationship between hard work and success. This is what gives meaning to the descriptor *critical* in critical realism, as Torrance understood it. Torrance is not a logical positivist, nor a naïve realist. The correspondence between the human mind of the researcher and the reality they probe is not always direct and immediate. There is not a facile or always obvious correspondence between the empirical process and results of the investigation, on the one hand, and its reality, on the other. Some element of mystery remains, though mystery must not be conceived of as preventing further probing.

Torrance was significantly influenced by Michael Polanyi, a chemist and philosopher of science, in his understanding of epistemology, especially with respect to the tacit and personal nature of knowledge. Reality-mediating theories or doctrines both in science (e.g., Einstein's general relativity) and in theology (e.g., the Niceno-Constantinopolitan Trinity) are not facile, either in their discovery or in the straightforwardness of their correlation between empirical apprehension and theoretical construct. Torrance noticed that "creative leaps of cognition" were often involved in the crafting of theory and that there were tacit aspects to the comprehension of the deep structures of reality that were grasped intuitively, not just by formalized processes of rational inference. This did not imply an epistemological dualism for Torrance.

The mind of the knower and the object of knowledge were not separated by an unbridgeable gulf. The assumption that there is a bridge was based for Torrance in the presupposition of the goodness of God and in the reality of the incarnate Logos, who made and sustained the objective reality of creation. The Logos also mediates creation's accessibility, because he himself is intelligible and has made humans in his image to be capable of perceiving the intelligible in a perspicacious way.

Achtemeier has raised some objections to Torrance's claims to realist epistemology in theology and the natural sciences. He refers to the aforementioned "role of creative intuition and imaginative leaps of intellect"[32] which Torrance gained from the influence of Michael Polanyi and which seem to be in contradiction to the more passive posture suggested by critical realism. I suspect that there is very little tension here at all. Torrance would probably have seen active and passive aspects of the human encounter with reality as two aspects of the tacit personal encounter with whatever phenomenon is being considered. Leaps of intellect and intuition do not contradict evidence received; they are merely gifts that speed the discovery process. And they, like any other thoughts, have to be tested.

Achtemeier also speaks of recent research which has shown that "the universe changes in real and astounding ways when quantum systems are subjected to observation. ... The quantum mechanical universe appears to be one in which the mind of the knower 'presses back' upon reality in quite startling fashion."[33] He adds that "mind and universe are causally intertwined in odd ways that we are only beginning to understand."[34] What seems to be implied here is that human objectivity is even less reliable than is generally thought. In defense of Torrance, I am not sure that this really contradicts critical realism. It merely accentuates the *critical* nature of it. It may in fact reinforce it, if this causal intertwining holds.

Torrance did not argue merely for a nondualist view of knowledge and the cosmos. On the basis of a christological doctrine of creation, he argued for a nonmonist view of God and creation, and therefore of theology and science. In this aspect of his thought, Torrance owed a debt to renowned physicist and

---

32. Achtemeier, "Natural Science and Christian Faith in the Thought of T. F. Torrance," 296.

33. Achtemeier, "Natural Science and Christian Faith in the Thought of T. F. Torrance," 296–97.

34. Achtemeier, "Natural Science and Christian Faith in the Thought of T. F. Torrance," 297.

THEOLOGY AND SCIENCE IN TORRANCE

theologian John Philoponus (AD 490–570). Torrance eschewed Neoplatonic notions of material participation (*methexis*) of the creation in God, believing them to be harmful to both theology and science. With particular reference to theology, they were harmful in that they led to the limited description of God as an "Unmoved Mover," rather than the living God being capable of acting within creation (without being conditioned by creation or limited by it). Instead, Torrance proffered the view that creation was distinct from the Creator, and real and valuable in its own right as created, and at the same time, profoundly dependent upon the Creator Son under the life-giving influence of the Creator Holy Spirit. As such, the relational triune God, through the Son and the Spirit, is in a *koinōnia* (participational) relationship to the creation, which in turn permits the creation certain degrees of freedom to be and to become, participating in its own development. And this brings us to ontological matters.

BEING: COMMON MATERIAL INTERESTS OR ONTOLOGY—CHRIST THE SON OF THE FATHER

To recap, the assumption that underlies critical realism is that reality, or ontology, is truly reflected in the knower's knowing, or in epistemology. This refers to the divine being or attributes, in the case of theological science, and to created nature, in the case of the natural sciences. The assumption is that epistemology follows the ontology that undergirds it. As Habets notes, "The critical realism advocated by Torrance connects the knower and the known together in personal union, thus putting the knower (theologian) under a certain obligation to offer a rational account of that which exists independently of the knower (theology). By this means it is obvious that for Torrance and his scientific theology, as for Einstein and his natural science, epistemology follows ontology."[35]

The ontology to which Torrance was referring (and what is most relevant to the theology/science interface) specifically concerned the nature of creation in light of the nature of the triune God. The concern of the sciences is obviously the physical universe. Yet theological science expresses in various ways the nature of the physical universe in light of the God of creation, and it provides an explanation as to why the creation is intelligible and contingent.

---

35. Habets, *Theology in Transposition*, 56.

A christological orientation undergirds this also. Crucial to this union of theology and science has been the reality that God has chosen to make the physical universe the medium for the expression of his self-revelation and appropriated it "as the created medium of our knowledge of himself by entering our time and space as the man Jesus of Nazareth, who is fully (including spatio-temporally!) a human being without thereby ceasing to be God."[36]

One example of an ontological reality in theological science, which is the foundation of the assumption that epistemology follows ontology, is the goodness of the creation arising from the love of its triune Creator. Another, which flows from this goodness, is the intelligibility of God in his revelation and the contingent, engraced human intelligence given to receive it. Torrance, in fact, includes these concepts when he speaks of three ideas present in the church fathers around the notion of creation *ex nihilo*, all of which relate to the influence of theology on the sciences and all of which concern the underlying ontological realities of God discovered in the discipline of theology. These are expressed in *The Ground and Grammar of Theology*.[37] The first idea concerns the rational unity of the cosmos, grounded in the fact that the all-wise God, through the agency of the Son, is the Creator of all. Who God is *in se*—revealed through the economic revelation of the Son—ensures that there is one pervading *taxis*, or order, in the universe. This not only ensures that the universe does not exist in some kind of perverse ontological dualism but positively assures the seeker of truth that what they are discovering by way of empirical process corresponds to what really is.

The second idea is closely related, namely that the universe is intelligible or has a contingent rationality. Its rationality is grounded in the nature of the Creator, the Son. This involves the rejection of another dualism, the old Greek idea that the human mind was eternal and a participant (*methexis*) in the divine nature. Christian theology eschewed this dualism, "making the distinction between created and uncreated light and rationality that exists between God and humanity."[38] The human mind was a created, temporal entity and therefore not divine. This means that "God gives human

---

36. Achtemeier, "Natural Science and Christian Faith in the Thought of T. F. Torrance," 274.

37. Torrance, *The Ground and Grammar of Theology*, 48–50.

38. Habets, *Theology in Transposition*, 57.

intelligence its own (contingent) rationality,"[39] that is, a rationality that is real and yet derived from and dependent on the Creator, in a communion of persons, not a participation of substance. The fact that this given rationality is real makes both theology and science possible, and in a mutuality in this respect. It also influences the pursuit of knowledge toward humility and not arrogance.

The third patristic idea Torrance refers to introduces us to another ontological reality about creation and God. This is the contingent freedom of the universe, which is a corollary of the first two. This freedom is found first in the being of God. Torrance reflects the view of Athanasius that creation was a free act of the will of God. It is to be distinguished from the generation of the Son or the procession of the Spirit comes from within the being of the Father. The triune God did not need to create, as if to overcome some deficit, or under any necessity, but created in an overflow of divine love expressed in divine volition. What he created was distinct from himself, having its own particularity and degrees of freedom. The contingency of God in creating is reflected in the contingent nature of creation. The cosmos "depends from moment to moment upon the free grace of God in order to sustain it and its orderly operations," which "suggests an openness and capacity for novelty in the cosmic process which is reflective of the transcendent freedom of God."[40] Torrance expresses this well in *Ground and Grammar*:

> [God's] creation of the universe out of nothing, ... far from meaning that the universe is characterized by sheer necessity either in its relation to God or within itself, implies that it is given a contingent freedom of its own, grounded in the transcendent freedom of God and maintained through his free interaction with the universe.[41]

In a manner that speaks to the issue of whether participation of the creation in God is substantial or relational, Torrance adds,

> It was this doctrine of the freedom of the creation contingent upon the freedom of God which liberated Christian thought from the tyranny of the fate, necessity and determinism which for the pagan mind

---

39. Habets, *Theology in Transposition*, 57.

40. Achtemeier, "Natural Science and Christian Faith in the Thought of T. F. Torrance," 277.

41. Torrance, *Ground and Grammar*, 4.

was clamped down upon creaturely existence by the inexorably cyclic processes of a self-sufficient universe. Just as there is an *order* in the universe transcendentally grounded in God, so there is a *freedom* in the universe transcendentally grounded in the freedom of God.[42]

Torrance's view on one aspect of the ontology of God, namely divine sovereignty or providence, is of particular interest both theologically and scientifically, with implications for the theory of evolution, genetic mutations, and also in the quantum realm. For Torrance, the doctrine of providence, as it relates to the inner being of God, is christologically conceived. It is built on the manifestation of Jesus Christ—once again on the assumption that God's being and activity are not different from the being and activity of the Son, Jesus Christ. The sovereignty of God is not some "impersonal and deterministic brute force"[43] but is clothed in personal categories and at work "in creaturely littleness and human weakness."[44] In the cross of Christ, the power and providence of God as love are most clearly seen—a "total self-sacrifice supreme over sin and guilt, evil and death, over anything and everything that might separate us from God." Torrance "sees providence not as the perpetuation of the original act of creation, but as God conserving the creation in a *covenantal co-existence* with himself, preserving creation by interacting positively toward and within it, and caring for creation out of limitless grace by the Word and through the Spirit."[45] It is a "redemptive ruling over history" that brings the creation to its redemptive end in the outpouring of God's love for it. Thus, Torrance does not see providence as exercised from afar in a dualistic separation from the world. Rather, in Jesus Christ and by the Spirit,[46] God is "personally and directly present and active in creation, even

---

42. Thomas F. Torrance, *Divine and Contingent Order* (Edinburgh: T&T Clark, 1981), 4. (Italics mine.)

43. Colyer, *How to Read T. F. Torrance*, 165.

44. Thomas F. Torrance, *The Christian Doctrine of God: One Being Three Persons* (Edinburgh: T&T Clark, 1996), 221–22.

45. Colyer, *How to Read T. F. Torrance*, 165–66.

46. Significantly, Torrance speaks of the life-giving activity of the Spirit who is "able to sustain the creature in *open-ended* relation toward God without overwhelming or negating the reality and freedom of the creature." Colyer, *How to Read T. F. Torrance*, 217. The Spirit is, in Torrance's understanding, the agent of providence, wooing and influencing the creature (electron or human being) to its true *telos* in relation to God.

in its fallenness."[47] God does not deistically abandon creation but bears its suffering in incarnational co-suffering love.[48] God, says Torrance, acts freely in the world "in innumerable multivariable ways while being consistently true to his own nature as Holy Love and consistently true to his creation of the world with a contingent rational order of its own."[49] How this works out exactly in every case is an "incomprehensible mystery," just as creation *ex nihilo* is a mystery, comprehensible only to the extent of the revelation of the activity of God in Jesus Christ.[50]

The contingency of creation gives to it another ontological reality: the particularities of every created thing. The particularism of Duns Scotus especially[51] was crucial in the development of science.[52] Scientists must pay attention to particularity, to the "this-ness" of things. This is a specific aspect of ontology that determines epistemology, creating the sense of realism that scientists avow—that is, their sense that what science is discovering is actually there; it is real. The contingency of creation gave to a good creation degrees of freedom, including freedom to participate in its own development, in the *creatio continua*. The sustaining and sovereign rule of God the creator, in the Son and by the Spirit, is somehow compatible with this freedom of created matter, which is not to say that no mystery remains.[53] Suffice it to say, in

47. Colyer, *How to Read T. F. Torrance*, 166, reflecting Torrance, *The Christian Doctrine of God*, 221-22.

48. Torrance, *The Christian Doctrine of God*, 224.

49. Torrance, *The Christian Doctrine of God*, 222.

50. Torrance, *The Christian Doctrine of God*, 233.

51. Torrance was aware of the Franciscan tradition originating with St. Frances of Assisi himself, and Franciscan philosopher, St. Bonaventure (1217-1274), which offered a new kind of attention to the particulars of creation, as a seedbed for science. Their prodigy, Franciscan philosopher, Duns Scotus (1265-1308), a careful thinker, dubbed the "subtle doctor," offered a defense of the centrality of the will (voluntarism) in God's creation, and challenged Aquinas by suggesting that both creation and the incarnation transcend reason and are evidence of "irrational love," or its extravagance. Whatever we think of Scotus (univocity of being), he is to be credited with an awareness of the irreducible uniqueness and particularity of things, that is, the "this-ness" (*haeccitas*) of things that encouraged the pursuit of science (Scotus, *Ordinatio* II, d. 3, p. 1. q. 2, n. 48 [Scotus, (1950-), *Opera Omnia*, ed. C. Balic (Vatican City: Vatican Polyglot Press) 7:412-413; Paul Vincent Spade, *Five Texts on the Mediaeval Problem of Universals: Porphyry, Boethius, Abelard, Duns Scotus, Ockham* (Indianapolis and Cambridge: Hackett, 1994), 69]).

52. Lazar Puhalo, *The Evidence of Things Not Seen: Orthodox Christianity and Modern Physics*, 2nd ed. (Dewdney, BC: Synaxis Press, 2005), 14, 15.

53. Achtemeier challenges Torrance's assertions in *Divine and Contingent Order* that Einstein's theory of relativity does away with the deterministic nature of the universe inherent within a

the spirit of Karl Barth and Torrance, that quarks, electrons, and human persons are never freer and never more themselves than when they are in Christ, under the Spirit. They have freedom in his freedom, but they act as he acts in an asymmetric compatibilism of divine and human creative agency.

This area of Torrance's theology, the freedom of God and the contingent freedom of creation, also challenges the Aristotelian assumptions of medieval theology and the Greek notions of impassibility and immutability which resulted from the influence of Aristotle's Unmoved Mover on the God of the Scriptures. Habets's treatment of Torrance's discussion of this sums up his thought concisely:

> It is true that God is not moved by and is not changed by anything outside the divine being, and that God is not affected by anything or does not suffer from anything beyond the divine being. But this simply affirms the biblical fact that God is transcendent and the one who created *ex nihilo*. The Fathers did not mean that God does not move Godself or that God is incapable of imparting motion to what God has made. ... This is the God who was not always Creator but became Creator. This implies the notion that even in the life of God there is change. Nor was God eternally incarnate, for in Jesus Christ God became what God was not without ceasing to be what God was.[54]

Torrance drew on both Athanasius and Karl Barth in this aspect of his thought. The latter's assertions of the "being of God in God's act, and of the act of God in God's being, inseparably bound up with the transcendent freedom of God in God's love"[55] are central in Torrance's theological and scien-

---

Newtonian worldview. Achtemeier's objection is that Einstein's theory is in fact, still deterministic, in the sense that "the configuration of the relational space-time manifold evolves in rigidly defined patterns set by fixed and unchanging laws." Achtemeier, "Natural Science and Christian Faith in the Thought of T. F. Torrance," 295. Achtemeier concedes that his objection does not fatally compromise Torrance's general point that the overall "picture of the universe that modern science develops is *genuinely* nondeterministic and open when quantum mechanics, chaos theory, and developments in mathematical logic such as Gödel's theorem are added to the mix" (296). Achtemeier also affirms Torrance's claims with respect to our subjective "feel." Einstein's picture of the cosmos over against that of the Newtonian system in mathematics, for example, "has the 'feel' of a cognitive tool that provides entry into the mysteries of a universe that is deep and open, in stark contrast to the Newtonian cosmos that is determined and enclosed by a rigid framework of eternal mathematical structures clamped down upon it 'from above' " (296).

54. Habets, *Theology in Transposition*, 57.

55. Habets, *Theology in Transposition*, 58; see Torrance, *Theological Science*, 343.

tific accounts. There is much to reflect on in these statements. The biblical witness is consistent in its assertions that God is unchanging. Yet must we assume that these are references to character? This assertion, which challenges the scholastic notions of the Godhead, is grounded for Torrance in the incarnation, with its breathtaking implications. What is most important to note is that this area of discussion is a classic example of the ever-present influence of Christology in Torrance. He states that "patristic theology was tempted constantly by the thrust of Greek thought to change the concepts of impassibility and immutability in this direction, but it remained entrenched within the orbit of the Judeo-Christian doctrine of the living God who moves himself, who through his free love created the universe, imparting to its dynamic order, and who through the outgoing of his love moves outside of himself in the incarnation."[56]

In both creating and in becoming incarnate, we must reverently say that God *became* what he had not previously been. With Torrance we must surely be guided in our theology proper by Christology: the *factum* that the divine agent in creation was God the Son, and the *factum* that God, in the Son, became human for us. The fact that God always possessed the power to create, that creation was in the mind of God before it came into being, and that God the Son was *incarnandus*—that is, oriented toward becoming human in eternity past prior to the incarnation—invokes areas of philosophical[57] and theological[58] debate which we cannot entertain here.

---

56. Torrance, *The Ground and Grammar of Theology*, 65–66. In *The Christian Doctrine of God* (88–89), Torrance confirms that in his *ex nihilo* creation, God acted in an altogether new way, bringing into being entirely new events, for the creation of the world, *ex nihilo* is something new *even for God*.

57. The debate as to whether God is timeless or everlastingly temporal is evoked here, for one. Torrance took the temporalist position, though, as Mullins indicates, he "posits a distinction between the created time of the universe and the uncreated time of God," Ryan Mullins, "In Search of a Timeless God" (PhD thesis, University of St. Andrews, 2013), 38. See Torrance, *Theological and Natural Science* (Eugene, OR: Wipf & Stock, 2005), 50–51.

58. Torrance follows Karl Barth, who made much of God's act in eternally (or in eternity) electing to create the cosmos through agency of the Son and to have the Son enter creation and become human. What the act of God in electing the incarnation of the Son means exactly for the essence of the triune God *in se* is a hotly debated topic among Barth scholars, and principally, Bruce McCormack and George Hunsinger. For a summation of the controversy, see Phillip Cary, "Barth Wars: A Review of *Reading Barth with Charity*," *First Things* (April 2015): https://www.firstthings.com/article/2015/04/barth-wars. There is no doubt whatsoever that Torrance would reject McCormack's position flatly. There are plenty of statements in Torrance to back this up.

Most crucially what we can affirm by a *kata physic* approach to theology which functions in an *a posteriori* way, is that through the personal revelation of the Son, and by the Spirit, God is revealed to be, in himself, an eternal self-giving communion. He is a God who does not require creation but creates and redeems creation as an outflow of that life of loving communion. The creation as unnecessary, as extravagant, as requiring of individual attention in its particularity, as having contingent order and yet surprise, corresponds in all these ways to what science discovers it to be. But the contingent nature of God's freedom and the consequent contingent nature of the universe is that both theology and science defy an *a priori* approach to knowledge. It can only be discovered empirically.

For science, this is obvious. The Greeks could never discover science for they considered matter unworthy of study. Time does not permit discussion of how the presence of the Christian doctrine of creation in the medieval and Reformation periods fostered and prospered the discovery of science.[59] Theology also, in its core confessional nature, has been discovered by the church through its encounter with the incarnate Christ and the Holy Spirit—a firsthand encounter in the case of the apostles and then passed down and freshly experienced by the ecclesial community through the ages. Theological realism is at the heart of this experience and the crucial notion of the incarnation and the Trinitarian concept of *homoousios* were, according to Torrance, vital to it: "It is as our communion with God the Father through Christ and in the Spirit is founded in and shares in the inner Trinitarian consubstantial or *homoousial* communion of the Father, Son, and Holy Spirit, that the subjectively-given pole of conceptuality is constantly purified and refined under the searching light and quickening power of the objectively-given pole of divine revelation. Within that polarity Christian theology becomes what essentially is and ought always to be, *logike latreia*, rational worship of God."[60] Correspondingly, and in accordance with their own peculiar subject

59. See Achtemeier's discussion of "Overlapping Historical Development," in Achtemeier, "Natural Science and Christian Faith in the Thought of T. F. Torrance," 281–92. Achtemeier affirms with some reservations Torrance's view of the mutuality of the fields of theology and science with respect to the history of ideas, Achtemeier, "Natural Science and Christian Faith in the Thought of T. F. Torrance," 293–94.

60. Thomas F. Torrance, "Theological Realism," in *The Philosophical Frontiers of Christian Theology: Essays Presented to D. M. McKinnon*, ed. B. Hebblethwaite and S. Sutherland (Cambridge: Cambridge University Press, 1982), 193.

matter and techniques and levels, scientists in each area of study can also become participants in the rational priestly worship of God the Father and his Son by whom and through whom all things are made and in whom all priestliness is recapitulated through the work of the Holy Spirit.

Building on Einstein and Polanyi, Torrance considered hierarchical structures to be crucial for knowledge of being, or the ontology beneath the epistemology. For Einstein, the hierarchical structure which could be applied to each science consisted of the physical, the theoretical, and the meta-theoretical. Polanyi went further and proposed a hierarchy of sciences, with higher-level sciences having influence over those at a lower level, a principle which Torrance called "coherent integration from above."[61] This stood in contrast with the Newtonian, mechanistic reading of the lower levels up to the higher. Interestingly, in this regard, Einstein, Polanyi, and Torrance all reflected the methodological insights of Duns Scotus and Kurt Gödel.[62] Applying this to theology as the theological science, Torrance claimed for theology the highest level of knowing in light of its object of study, the triune God, and thus, in a modern era, recapitulated a defense of theology as the queen of the sciences.

This stratification, which reveals objective structures, or "the back-side of reality,"[63] within theological science itself entailed three categories or levels. First, there is the evangelical and doxological level, or "experiential apprehension" level, whose focal point is the encounter with Jesus Christ, both personally and in the church's worship and life, its *kerygma* and *didache*. This apprehension of the evangelical Trinity is a largely intuitive apprehension of God's self-revelation (an incipient theology[64]). It is the essential foundation for all theological reflection that will follow it. Second is the theological level in which the economic Trinity is encountered and explored. The heuristic device connecting the first and second levels is the *homoousion*. Third, there is the higher theological level, the ontological Trinity, which is, for Torrance, the decisive point for theological science, where the "objective structures

---

61. Habets, *Theology in Transposition*, 62.

62. Thomas F. Torrance, "Intuitive and Abstractive Knowledge: From Duns Scotus to Calvin," in *De Doctrina Duns Scoti, Congressus Scotisticus Internationalis: Studia Scholastico-Scotistica* 5, ed. C. Balic (Rome: Societas Internationalis Scotistica, 1968), 291–305, and Thomas F. Torrance, *Space, Time and Incarnation* (Edinburgh: T&T Clark, 2005), 86–90.

63. Torrance, "The Stratification of Truth," in *Reality and Scientific Theology*, 147.

64. Torrance, *The Christian Doctrine of God*, 89.

of reality" exist.[65] By means of what we know of the Father, Son, and Holy Spirit in the economy, Torrance states that "we seek to formulate in forms of thought and speech the hypostatic, *homoousial*, perichoretic relations in the eternal, dynamic Communion in loving and being loved of the three Divine Persons which God is."[66]

In sum, Torrance validated the need for a scientific approach to theology, one grounded in the revelation of Jesus Christ. Torrance was confident that such an approach would, by faith, uphold the first order confessional theology of the creeds. But Torrance also looked for every Christian to build an encyclopedic theology, rooted in first order theology but also formed by the discovery of reality in all the sciences, on the grounds that through Jesus Christ all things were made and through his vicarious life, death, resurrection, and ascension all things are being reconciled.

---

65. Torrance, *Reality and Scientific Theology*, 144–47.

66. Torrance, *The Christian Doctrine of God*, 109.

6

—

A COMPLEXLY RELATIONAL ACCOUNT OF THE *IMAGO DEI* IN TORRANCE'S VISION OF HUMANITY

Marc Cortez

INTRODUCTION

Despite the vast theological corpus produced over the course of his prolific career, few of Torrance's writings focused specifically on theological anthropology. This does not mean that he viewed anthropology as an unimportant doctrine, of course, since he routinely engaged various anthropological themes when dealing with topics like salvation, creation, and especially Christology. However, as Elmer Colyer points out, it does mean that "he has not given the same kind of sustained attention to this subject (at least in his published work) that he has to the broader contours of the doctrine of creation."[1] Consequently, Eric Flett notes that his theological anthropology lacks "the breadth and depth of engagement found in other more systematic treatments of this theme."[2]

---

1. Elmer M. Colyer, *How to Read T. F. Torrance: Understanding His Trinitarian and Scientific Theology* (Downers Grove, IL: InterVarsity Press, 2001), 173.

2. Eric G. Flett, "Priests of Creation, Mediators of Order: The Human Person as a Cultural Being in Thomas F. Torrance's Theological Anthropology," *Scottish Journal of Theology* 58 (2005): 162. Chris Woznicki argues that we should not be surprised by this given Torrance's argument that Reformed theology has always resisted viewing theological anthropology as "an independent article of faith," Christopher G. Woznicki, "Discerning Humanity in Christ: The Promise of Christology for Developing T. F. Torrance's Theological Anthropology" (PhD thesis, Pasadena, CA, Fuller Seminary, 2020), 3.

However, Torrance was well aware of the significance of anthropological concerns, noting, "At no point is theology more relevant today than in the issues it raises about our knowledge of man."[3] And one issue that Torrance did reflect on periodically throughout his career was the nature and significance of the *imago Dei*, which he viewed as central to a biblical account of humanity.[4] Torrance wrote extensively on the image in his early work, *Calvin's Doctrine of Man*.[5] Yet this work poses a number of interesting interpretive difficulties, most importantly for our purposes of discerning Torrance's own views in the midst of a work seeking to be a historical presentation of Calvin's perspectives. Fortunately, Torrance also lays out his views more clearly in two essays. The earlier essay, "The Word of God and the Nature of Man" was originally written in 1947 and then republished as part of a collection of essays in 1965.[6] As Myk Habets points out, "The republication of that article nearly twenty years later reflected its abiding relevance for Torrance."[7] A second essay, "The Goodness and Dignity of Man in the Christian Tradition," was published in 1988.[8] These two essays bookend four decades of theological reflection and contain much of what Torrance wanted to say about the *imago Dei*. Although he refers frequently to the image in his other writings, they largely recapitulate themes developed in these two essays. Consequently, we can develop a good sense of Torrance's overall doctrine of humanity, along with some of the more important concerns that might need to be addressed, by focusing our attention here.

We will begin with the christological and pneumatological aspects of Torrance's account since he presents those as fundamental to any adequate

---

3. Thomas F. Torrance, "The Word of God and the Nature of Man," in *Theology in Reconstruction* (Grand Rapids: Eerdmans, 1965), 99.

4. Torrance, "The Word of God and the Nature of Man," 102.

5. Thomas F. Torrance, *Calvin's Doctrine of Man* (Grand Rapids: Eerdmans, 1957). Jing Wei focuses extensively on this text in a dissertation on Torrance's anthropology, but in a way that often makes it difficult to know how we should identify Torrance's own position amid his historical analysis. Jing Wei, "Theological Anthropology of Thomas F. Torrance: A Critical and Comparative Exploration" (PhD thesis, The University of Edinburgh, Scotland, 2014).

6. Thomas F. Torrance, "The Word of God and the Nature of Man," in *Reformation Old and New*, ed. F. W. Camfield (London: Lutterworth, 1947), 121–41; Torrance, "The Word of God" (1965). All references in this essay will be to the 1965 publication.

7. Myk Habets, *Theosis in the Theology of Thomas Torrance* (London: Routledge, 2016), 28.

8. Thomas F. Torrance, "The Goodness and Dignity of Man in the Christian Tradition," *Modern Theology* 4 (1988): 309–22.

understanding of the human person. Then we will turn our attention to Torrance's particular account of the *imago Dei* itself, focusing on the extent to which Torrance incorporates relational, substantival, and functional perspectives into his view. In the final section we will address an apparent tension regarding whether we should say that the image of God was entirely lost at the fall before turning our attention to three issues that require further clarification or development if we want to pursue Torrance's vision of the *imago Dei* further. Ultimately, I will argue that Torrance offers a complexly relational vision of the *imago Dei*, but one on which some work remains to be done.

CHRISTOLOGY, PNEUMATOLOGY, AND THE KNOWLEDGE OF TRUE HUMANITY

The starting point for any discussion of humanity in Torrance's theology has to be the person and work of Christ. Torrance repeatedly emphasizes throughout his various writings that it is only in and through Jesus Christ that we can understand humanity fully. He finds this christocentric emphasis in Calvin's own anthropology, maintaining that humanity "must be understood exclusively from the Word made flesh."[9] And he clearly affirms it in his own anthropology: "It is in Jesus Christ, therefore, and in him alone, that the real truth of human nature is to be found," and thus it is only through Jesus that "we may now penetrate through all the distortion, depravity and degradation of humanity to the true nature of man hidden beneath it all."[10] This is how we can "discern what the basic structure of humanity is and ought to be."[11] Consequently, "There can be no question of trying to understand man out of himself, or from his relation to the world. He must be understood primarily from the Word made flesh."[12]

This christological starting point is secured for Torrance not only by Christ's true humanity but in and through his divine identity. "He is the one Man who is properly and completely in the image of God, but he is much

---

9. Torrance, *Calvin's Doctrine of Man*, 36.

10. Torrance, "The Goodness and Dignity of Man," 315.

11. Thomas F. Torrance, "The Soul and Person, in Theological Perspective," in *Religion, Reason and the Self*, ed. Stewart R. Sutherland and T. A. Roberts (Cardiff: University of Wales Press, 1989), 115.

12. Torrance, "The Word of God," 102.

more than that—he is the only One who is both the Image and the Reality of God, for in his incarnate Person God and Man, divine and human nature, are inseparably united."[13] Consequently, unlike all other humans who must receive their humanity from someone else, Jesus is the one who is not only fully human but who grounds the humanity of all others. "He is not only Man par excellence, Archetypal Man, but the one humanising Man, the fount from which all that is truly human is derived. ... For us really to be human, therefore, is to be in Christ."[14] Or, as he says with direct reference to the *imago Dei*, he is "the unique image-constituting Image of God," and it is therefore only by reference to him "that we must now think of human beings as created after the image of God."[15]

However, despite worries expressed in some quarters that this kind of christological concentration ultimately undermines the significance of the Spirit, Torrance repeatedly emphasizes the pneumatological shape of the human person as well. Following Karl Barth, Torrance maintains that "spirit" in the Bible refers not to some distinguishable "part" of a human person's being but denotes the basic relation between God and humanity established in and through the Spirit.[16] Although the Spirit sustains all created things, the Spirit is uniquely and intimately involved with human persons: "He is not only present to him upholding him from below in his bare contingent existence, but present to him in such an intimate way as to sustain him in his contingent openness to God and the address of his Word—that is what belongs to the created constitution of man as man, as what we call *homo sapiens*."[17] Indeed, all of the "endowments and virtues" of the human nature must be viewed as continual gifts of the Spirit, creating human creatures who can hear and respond to the God who creates them.[18] Consequently, the Spirit is "the ontological qualification ... of his whole creaturely being."[19]

For Torrance, this is the only theological framework within which we can arrive at a true understanding of the human person. Some might conclude

---

13. Torrance, "The Goodness and Dignity of Man," 317.

14. Torrance, "The Goodness and Dignity of Man," 318.

15. Torrance, "The Goodness and Dignity of Man," 317.

16. Torrance, "The Word of God," 103–4.

17. Torrance, "The Goodness and Dignity of Man," 310.

18. Torrance, "The Word of God," 106.

19. Torrance, "The Soul and Person," 110.

from this that such an approach must necessarily adopt an *exclusively* theological perspective on what it means to be human. After all, if we can only discern "the basic structure of humanity" through Jesus, and if this means that we cannot understand humanity "out of himself" or "from his relation to the world," what room could be left for disciplines like biology, psychology, or the neurosciences to make any meaningful contribution? At best it might seem that such approaches could offer only a little window dressing, some additional information layered onto an essentially theological picture of what it *really* means to be human. However, such a conclusion would be quite surprising given Torrance's famous appreciation for and engagement with the natural sciences throughout his theology. Consequently, we should expect to find here as well that Torrance values the contributions of these nontheological perspectives despite his robust commitment to a christologically grounded vision of humanity. Here, Torrance draws on the methodological commitments of Karl Barth, affirming the necessity of the sciences for understanding the phenomena of the human while still maintaining the centrality of theology for understanding the significance of that data:

> Theology is not concerned with the phenomena as such, but with the central relation of it all to God, and is a form of thinking that derives from God's Word and follows the movement of God's Word in its creative and redemptive operation—only incidentally, therefore, does it concern itself with the knowledge of phenomena as such, derived from empirical study alone. In the doctrine of man, for example, it is not concerned as theology with what medical science, with what physiology or chemistry, have to say about him, for it is concerned about the central relation of man to God which constitutes his reality as man, that is his being a child of God; but what it has to say here on the border of what empirical science discovers of "the phenomena of the human," as Barth speaks of it, does illuminate the world of man within which alone empirical science is pursued. That does not mean that theology can offer any information of the kind that is assimilable to the knowledge acquired by natural science or that is therefore of any use to it in its empirical activity, although it may serve to remind man of the limits and boundaries of his existence and of his knowledge, and help him to restrict his reflections within

the limits set by empirical approach to his object, that is, help him to retain strict objectivity as empirical science.[20]

Torrance fully affirms the value of nontheological inquiry into those aspects of human existence that are accessible through empirical analysis—in other words, the "phenomena" of the human. Nonetheless, such data is always limited by its scope of inquiry and can never arrive at the full knowledge of what it truly means to be human as revealed in the person and work of Jesus Christ.

Such a robustly christological vision of the *imago Dei* might also lead one to expect that Torrance's account of the image will focus largely on those New Testament texts that similarly define the image in christological terms (e.g., Rom 8:29; Col 1:15). However, Torrance offers two reasons for thinking that this would be a mistake. The first and most immediately apparent reason is the one that Torrance himself points out. The New Testament is thoroughly grounded in the Old Testament material such that any attempt to understand the former apart from a robust engagement with the latter would be fruitless. Consequently, Torrance affirms that "we must first give careful attention to the Hebraic understanding of man's creation and nature found in the Scriptures of the Old Testament" because "the New Testament revelation ... cannot be properly understood without due consideration of their presuppositions and roots."[21] This alone provides a strong foundation for affirming the necessity of close attention to the anthropology of the Old Testament. However, we should also appreciate the significance of another of Torrance's theological commitments: his conviction that creation is "proleptically conditioned by redemption."[22] For Torrance, since God created everything with an eye toward the redemption that he would achieve in and through Jesus Christ, we must recognize that the very fabric of creation has always been determined by the reality of redemption. In other words, as Myk Habets explains, "Christology actually conditions the creation in the first place, proleptically influencing its very reality. Our vision of creation must be here, as elsewhere,

---

20. Thomas F. Torrance, "Introduction," in *Theology and Church: Shorter Writings 1920–1928*, ed. Louise Pettibone Smith (London: SCM Press, 1962), 39–40.

21. Torrance, "The Goodness and Dignity of Man," 309.

22. See, for example, Thomas F. Torrance, *The Trinitarian Faith: The Evangelical Theology of the Ancient Catholic Faith*, 2nd ed., T&T Clark Cornerstones (London: Bloomsbury, 2016), 102. For a good discussion see Myk Habets, "How 'Creation Is Proleptically Conditioned by Redemption,'" *Colloquium* 41 (2009): 3–21.

a Christocentric one. Creation is not only *through* Christ, but also *for* Christ."[23] One implication of this is that Torrance could not countenance the possibility that a legitimate attempt to study creation, whether through the natural sciences or through Old Testament revelation, could ever be viewed as a non-christological endeavor. For both these reasons, then, Torrance's approach to the *imago Dei* consistently emphasized the importance of the relevant Old Testament texts for understanding the *imago Dei*.

A COMPLEXLY RELATIONAL
ACCOUNT OF THE *IMAGO DEI*

We can now address more directly the specific shape of Torrance's interpretation of the *imago Dei*. One way of doing so would be to try and locate Torrance's view in relation to other interpretations. According to one common taxonomy, views of the image can be characterized in terms of something human persons *are* (structural views), something that human persons *do* (functional views), or some way(s) in which humans are uniquely related to something else (relational views).[24] However, Torrance's view defies easy classification since his various discussions of the *imago Dei* contain elements that might suggest all three.

THE IMAGE AND ONTO-RELATIONAL PERSONHOOD

The relational interpretation enjoys strong support throughout Torrance's writings. In one of Torrance's clearest statements on the meaning of the image, he defines it straightforwardly as involving an essential relationality grounded primarily in our vertical relationship with God and secondarily in our horizontal relationships with one another.[25]

There can be no doubt that in the Bible the concept of the image of God does not have anything to do with the idea that man is constituted as a rational being. Rather does it have to do with the way in which the basic interhuman relations, called into existence by the Word and Spirit of God, is made to

---

23. Myk Habets, *Theology in Transposition: A Constructive Appraisal of T. F. Torrance* (Minneapolis: Fortress, 2013), 152.

24. Although many categorize views of the image in this way, you can see a brief explanation of these approaches in Marc Cortez, *Theological Anthropology: A Guide for the Perplexed* (New York: T&T Clark, 2010).

25. Torrance, "The Goodness and Dignity of Man," 311.

reflect in its creaturely difference a transcendent relation within God, and also to exhibit the basic covenant-partnership between God and mankind.[26]

Torrance emphasizes the primacy of the vertical by focusing on the idea that the *imago* is best understood as a form of "direct address."[27] We see this first in the word of creation itself, in which our creation *ex nihilo* reveals our absolute contingency and dependence as well as the fundamental significance of divine grace for human existence. However, this kind of contingent dependency is true of all created beings, and Torrance emphasizes as well that the act of creation involves a distinct form of divine address that summons humans into a particular relationship with their Creator:

> While this [contingency] applies to all created beings, physical and animal as well as human, it is distinctive of God's relation to the human creature through his Spirit that he is not only present to him upholding him from below in his bare contingent existence, but present to him in such an intimate way as to sustain him in his contingent openness to God and the address of his Word—that is what belongs to the created constitution of man as man, as what we call *homo sapiens*.[28]

However, Torrance does not focus exclusively on the vertical. Following the lead of Karl Barth, Torrance emphasizes the importance of the "male and female" in Genesis 1:27. This signals for Torrance the idea that human relationality has been created to serve as a creaturely echo of God's own eternal relationality.[29]

> It is not man or woman individually or as such that is said to be created after the image and likeness of God, but man as man and woman in their reciprocal and complementary relationship—that is, as man-and-woman in a unique analogical relation to God. The horizonal relation between them grounded in their vertical relation to God is a contingent reflection of God and represents a created correspondence to uncreated relations within God himself.[30]

---

26. Torrance, "The Goodness and Dignity of Man," 311–12.

27. Torrance, "The Goodness and Dignity of Man," 310.

28. Torrance, "The Goodness and Dignity of Man," 310.

29. Torrance, "The Goodness and Dignity of Man," 310.

30. Torrance, "The Goodness and Dignity of Man," 312.

The image thus qualifies as an instance of what Torrance famously refers to as an "onto-relation." Without spending too much time on this important and complex concept,[31] this is Torrance's way of referring to "relations so basic that they are inseparable from, and characteristic of, what realities *are*."[32] In other words, these relations are ontological in the sense that they comprise in some way the very essence of the entity in question. And this is precisely how Torrance views the Spirit-constituted relation that comprises the *imago Dei*. To be human *is* to stand in this particular relation.[33] Whether one does so faithfully or unfaithfully is a question that will need to be addressed below. Yet the relation remains. As Geordie Ziegler concludes, "In Torrance's thought, there is no such thing as the 'pure human'; there is only the human-in-communion-with-God or the human-alienated-from-God."[34] Consequently, the *imago Dei* in Torrance's theology is clearly a relational category from beginning to end.

THE IMAGE AND THE CAPACITY TO KNOW GOD

From the prior section it would seem clear that Torrance's view of the image qualifies as relational in a fairly robust sense. Indeed, like many who adopt this approach, Torrance has some rather harsh things to say about those traditional approaches that define the image in terms of some capacity intrinsic to human nature. "It is just here that a decisive break is made with the Aristotelian man of scholastic theology, in which the living, dynamic relation of man to God is translated into a substantival and logical relation."[35] Indeed, Torrance goes so far as to claim that "the very root motion of original sin" lay in attempting to claim the *imago* as "a natural possession" of human nature.[36] This is because such an approach seeks to ground human identity

---

31. For an interesting discussion of whether Torrance's onto-relational anthropology entails the kind of "relational ontology" affirmed by someone like John Zizioulas, see Woznicki, "Discerning Humanity in Christ," 118–37.

32. Colyer, *How to Read T. F. Torrance*, 55.

33. Elsewhere, Torrance explicitly uses onto-relational language to describe the nature of human personhood, see Torrance, "The Soul and Person."

34. Geordie W. Ziegler, *Trinitarian Grace and Participation: An Entry into the Theology of T. F. Torrance* (Minneapolis: Fortress, 2017), 153.

35. Torrance, "The Word of God," 102.

36. Torrance, "The Word of God," 106.

in its intrinsic capacities, rather than relying entirely on the divine-human relation to establish our significance.

However, Torrance also talks about the image in ways that make it sound more like he has a structural view of the image. Indeed, in "The Word of God and the Nature of Man," Torrance routinely emphasizes the significance of humanity's ability to hear, understand, and respond to the divine address as being a fundamental part of the *imago Dei*. "This means that unlike the other creatures of the world, man lives truly as man only in conscious and thankful relation to the grace of God, and in the consciousness of his own creaturehood."[37] Similarly, Torrance maintains that "man has been created an intelligent being in order to know God in such a way that in the act of knowing man is brought to re-live consciously, and in a qualitatively different fashion, the very movement of grace in which he is created and maintained in being."[38] This is what Torrance refers to as the "subjective" aspect of the *imago Dei*. The image is objectively grounded in God's gracious act of deciding to create humanity to be in loving, personal relationship with himself, but the image also involves a subjective aspect in which human persons hear, understand, and properly respond to the divine address. "And so the *imago dei* is the conscious but creaturely reflection in man of the Word and grace of God."[39]

We might be tempted to dismiss this as an early emphasis that was overcome in the more mature reflections of Torrance's later writings, yet this does not seem to be the case. Even in his later essay, Torrance emphasizes the importance of humanity's "capacity to respond as a rational subject and agent to himself."[40] And he concludes that essay with a brief reflection on how humanity's intellectual capacity is necessary for serving as the covenant-partner who responds with praise to "the marvellous rationality, symmetry, harmony and beauty" of God's amazing character. Consequently, it seems that an emphasis on humanity's intellectual capacity serves as a consistent motif in Torrance's understanding of the *imago Dei*. Thus, "to image the glory and grace of God belongs to his true nature as an intelligent being."[41]

37. Torrance, "The Word of God," 101.
38. Torrance, "The Word of God,"101.
39. Torrance, "The Word of God," 105.
40. Torrance, "The Goodness and Dignity of Man," 319.
41. Torrance, "The Word of God," 100.

Although the intellectual emphasis is more muted in this later essay, it still seems to be the case that Torrance relates our capacity for rationality directly to the *imago Dei* throughout.

Myk Habets concludes from all this that Torrance combines his strong emphasis on a relational view of the image with a rather traditional emphasis on the capacity for rationality. Torrance thus affirms "aspects of a substantive definition," but this must be viewed as offering only a partial definition given his relational interpretation of the image.[42] Eric Flett agrees, seeing both the relational and the substantival as working together in Torrance's view of the image. "For Torrance the image of God is both a noun and verb, it is both structure and reflection; it is both nature and calling."[43] Geordie Ziegler seems to have something similar in mind when he describes Torrance's view of the image as "multi-faceted."[44] However, such both/and interpretations leave unaddressed the question of how to reconcile this with Torrance's clear rejection of substantival views when criticizing earlier theologians. How exactly does this offer a "decisive break" with substantival views if it simply includes those views alongside a new element? Additionally, given Torrance's clear emphasis on the relational view, can it really be the case that he intends us to understand this relationality as simply one aspect of the *imago Dei*?

Chris Woznicki argues that we should view Torrance's position as *entirely* relational. On this account, "Torrance vigorously rejects substantial views," and we should understand the intellect to play only an instrumental role with respect to the image. "Intelligence or rationality plays a role in humans living as the image of God, yet the image itself does not consist in rationality or intelligence."[45] In other words, the distinction Woznicki seems to have in mind is that the image should be *defined* in entirely relational terms, but the intellect is a critical aspect of the *manner in which* human persons will live within the relationships marked out by the image. This allows Woznicki to maintain that the intellect is importantly related to the image without comprising (even a part of) the *imago Dei*.[46]

---

42. Habets, *Theosis in the Theology of Thomas Torrance*, 31.

43. Eric G. Flett, *Persons, Powers, and Pluralities: Toward a Trinitarian Theology of Culture* (Eugene, OR: Pickwick, 2011), 126.

44. Ziegler, *Trinitarian Grace and Participation*, 168.

45. Woznicki, "Discerning Humanity in Christ," 91.

46. Woznicki, "Discerning Humanity in Christ," 102.

While this approach has some attraction as a way of resolving the tension between Torrance's criticism and apparent affirmation of substantial views, certain aspects of Torrance's argument make this conclusion difficult to sustain. First, recall the distinction mentioned earlier between the objective and subjective aspects of the image, and note that Torrance talks about both as being legitimate *aspects of the image*. In other words, he does not refer to the subjective as describing something that is extrinsic to and merely instrumental for the image but as describing something properly as a part of the image itself. Additionally, when Torrance describes the Spirit's work of establishing the onto-relation that constitutes us as *imago Dei* creatures, he does not envision this as a bare relation apart from any substantial predicates. Instead, Torrance asserts that the Spirit establishes us to be particular kinds of creatures, which includes our particular capacities.[47] Finally, Torrance argues for human uniqueness in a way that makes this interpretation difficult to maintain. According to Torrance, all creatures enjoy the fundamental relation in which they stand in total dependence on divine grace for their existence at every moment. That relation "can be said of any creature, but the distinctive thing about man is that he was created in order to enjoy this relation in a conscious and intelligent fashion."[48] In other words, what distinguishes human persons with respect to the *imago Dei* is not "mere" relationality, but the distinct set of capacities that allows us to participate in and experience that relation in a distinct way. Consequently, our distinct capacities as human persons are so thoroughly integrated into Torrance's vision of the image that we have to consider them intrinsic to the meaning of the *imago Dei* itself.

Yet this does not mean that such affirmations are simply inconsistent with Torrance's critique of substantival views. It is important to note here that when Torrance expresses concerns about the traditional emphasis on a capacity like rationality, the concern is never with recognizing the importance of that capacity in itself. Instead, Torrance's real worry is with defining the image in terms of those intrinsic capacities *alone*, as though we could be

---

47. Torrance, "The Goodness and Dignity of Man," 310. Habets rightly points out as well that the idea of proleptic creation also suggests the significance of creaturely capacity, though I would differ on whether this means Torrance would say that the image is "incipiently" present in virtue of these capacities. See Habets, *Theosis in the Theology of Thomas Torrance*, 33.

48. Torrance, "The Word of God," 104.

images of God merely in virtue of possessing the relevant capacities. Instead, he is keen to emphasize that everything about the image depends on the primacy of divine action from beginning to end.

Man is a creature in total dependence of being, motion, and life, upon the gracious will of God. He is created out of nothing, and has neither origin nor being in himself, but is given being, and maintained in being, by the grace of God. In relation to God, therefore, man is only an image. That is to say, his life is absolutely reflexive of the action of God and can be lived only in a motion of continued reflection.[49]

However, nothing prevents Torrance from viewing our capacities as playing an intrinsic role in this absolute reflexivity. Indeed, Torrance argues that not only are the capacities of human nature themselves gifts of God but such capacities can only be used to reflect God's glory insofar as they are continually sustained and empowered through the work of the Spirit.[50] This is true even where Torrance sounds most critical of the substantive view. In one of his clearest statements he claims, "There can be no doubt that in the Bible the concept of the image of God does not have anything to do with the idea that man is constituted a rational being through sharing in the eternal reason let alone the essence of God."[51] We must notice here, though, that the worry he identifies is not with rationality itself but only with rationality when viewed as something that *in itself* establishes a relation to God through an *analogia entis*.[52]

Torrance's view of human capacities can thus be viewed as being just as relational as his account of the image itself. Yet this does not detract from the overall point of this section, which is that when properly understood within this relational framework, Torrance's view still makes the exercise of human capacities intrinsic to his definition of the *imago dei*.

The strength of Woznicki's interpretation, however, is that it emphasizes the centrality of relationality in a way that might be easy to miss with the partitive or multifaceted interpretations mentioned earlier. From what we have seen, though, it might be better to recognize that Torrance's view *is*

---

49. Torrance, "The Word of God," 102.

50. Torrance, "The Word of God," 104-5.

51. Torrance, "The Goodness and Dignity of Man," 311.

52. Torrance explicitly links his critique of a substantive view of the image to a Barthian critique of the *analogia entis* in Torrance, "The Word of God," 114-16.

multifaceted, in the sense that it contains (at least) relational and substantival aspects, but that the facets are not weighted equally. Or, even more accurately, we might say that the substantival aspect operates within an overall framework that is thoroughly relational. Ziegler cites Torrance as follows:

> Within the single thought of *imago dei* there is included a two-sided relation, but it is a relation which has only one essential motion and rhythm. There is the grace of God, and man's answer to that grace. Such an answer partakes of and subsists in the essential motion of grace—for even man's answer is the work of the Holy Spirit who through the Word forms the image anew in man, and forms his lips to acknowledge that he is a child of the Father. The *imago dei* is thus the conformity of an intelligent being to the will and Word of God.[53]

Such an interpretation grants the relational a kind of logical and theological primacy that better accords with Torrance's arguments, while still granting the substantival a place in his definition of the image.

THE IMAGE AND PRIESTLY MEDIATION

We can see that there are reasons for finding both relational and structural emphases in Torrance's view of the image. Yet we can also find strong support for what looks like a functional view of the image in Torrance's writings. According to Torrance, human persons have been called to serve a unique role in creation. Only humanity can serve as the "priest of creation,"[54] a phrase that suggests that human persons perform some function on behalf of the rest of creation, some task that nonhuman creatures are unable to perform on their own. Here Torrance most often emphasizes two ideas. First, humans alone are capable of rendering praise to the God who made all things *ex nihilo* and who draws all things toward their ultimate *telos* in himself. Although the whole earth is the theater of the glory of God, the universe itself cannot on its own provide any real knowledge of the God who created it, able only

---

53. Thomas F. Torrance, *Calvin's Doctrine of Man* (Eugene, OR: Wipf and Stock, 2001), 80, as cited by Ziegler pp. 161–62.

54. Torrance, "The Goodness and Dignity of Man," 322. For a good discussion of this, see Woznicki, "Discerning Humanity in Christ," 152–85.

to "*cry silently* for a transcendent agency in its explanation and understanding."[55] The critical function of the human person, then, is to serve as "the one constituent of the created universe through whom its rational structure and astonishing beauty may be brought to word in praise of the Creator."[56] In addition to serving as the mediator of praise, human persons were created with the intellectual abilities necessary to discern and bring forth "forms of order and beauty of which [creation] would not be capable otherwise."[57] Humanity has been called "to be a kind of midwife to creation, in assisting nature out of its divinely given abundance constantly to give birth to new forms of life and richer patterns of order."[58] This in turn promotes further praise as humanity comes to appreciate even more "the marvelous rationality, symmetry, harmony, and beauty of God's creation," giving expression to all of this wonder in "a glorious hymn to the Creator."[59] For Torrance, this explains humanity's unique location in the created order:

> From the perspective of theology man is clearly made the focal point in the interrelations between God and the universe. He is given a special place within the creation with a ruling and a priestly function to perform toward the rest of created reality. All lines of rationality and order, of purpose and fulfillment in the creation converge on him as man of God and man of science and depend on his destiny.[60]

We can clearly see that the idea of priestly mediation is central to Torrance's understanding of the human person. But how does he understand this vocation in relation to the *imago Dei*?

One possibility would be to try and explain this merely as another instance of Torrance's relationality, now adding a third relation (between humanity and the rest of creation) to the vertical (divine-human) and horizontal

---

55. Thomas F. Torrance, *Reality and Scientific Theology* (Eugene, OR: Wipf & Stock, 2001), 58. (Italics in original.)

56. Thomas F. Torrance, *The Christian Doctrine of God: One Being Three Persons*, 2nd ed., T&T Clark Cornerstones (Edinburgh: T&T Clark, 2016), 213.

57. Thomas F. Torrance, *Divine and Contingent Order* (Edinburgh: T&T Clark, 1998), 130.

58. Torrance, "The Goodness and Dignity of Man," 322.

59. Torrance, "The Goodness and Dignity of Man,"322. See also Thomas F. Torrance, "Man, Priest of Creation," in *The Ground and Grammar of Theology* (Charlottesville: University Press of Virginia, 1980), 1–14.

60. Torrance, *Divine and Contingent Order*, 129.

(human-human) relations described above. However, although the idea of mediation is inherently relational, the emphasis in Torrance's discussions is always on the functional aspect of mediation. This priestly role is something we are called to *do* in and for the rest of the created universe, which would suggest that if we were to view this as part of Torrance's understanding of the image, we would need to add a functional aspect alongside the relational and substantival. If we opted for this approach, we could draw from the argument developed in the last section and view this as an activity that is fully dependent on God's grace (maintaining the absolute reflexivity of the image) and that only operates within the framework of a proper relationship with God and others (maintaining the primacy of the relational aspect of the image).

Although I argued in the prior section that we have good reasons to include a substantival aspect to Torrance's view of the image, I think we need a different solution here. This is primarily because Torrance does not connect the image with the idea of priestly mediation in the way that we would expect if he thought the latter was intrinsic to the definition of the former. Instead, although he does mention the idea briefly at the end of "The Goodness and Dignity of Man in the Christian Tradition," it plays almost no role in explaining the nature of the image itself, and he makes no explicit use of the concept in his other extended discussions of the image. Similarly, although Torrance has several lengthy discussions of the idea that humans are the priests of creation, he does not draw on the *imago Dei* when doing so.[61] The fact that Torrance rarely brings these two ideas together with any real depth creates a significant interpretive hurdle for anyone wanting to argue that he thought of them as aspects of the same idea.

Here again, Woznicki suggests a different approach, maintaining that we should view this mediatorial function as something that is related to the image in some way without itself being an aspect of the image.[62] Although I was critical of such an approach in the prior section, Torrance's own discussions suggest that this might be the right solution here.

---

61. See, for example, Torrance, "Man, Priest of Creation"; Torrance, *Divine and Contingent Order*, 128–42.

62. Woznicki, "Discerning Humanity in Christ," 91.

THE IMAGE AND THE FALL

Now that we have surveyed the various aspects of Torrance's view of the image, we are in a position to consider the question of how the image has been affected by the fall. And here as well we face a challenging interpretive issue, one that Habets identifies as one of the primary tensions in Torrance's anthropology.[63] We will use Torrance's answer to this question as a way of probing whether Torrance's approach has any implications for whether we can and should view all humans as *imago Dei* beings.

Viewed from one perspective, Torrance clearly indicates that the image was completely lost at the fall. He bluntly states, "In himself, man has been utterly deprived of the *imago Dei* wherein his life consists."[64] For Torrance this follows from his argument that the image is ultimately grounded in humanity's covenant relationship with God and that it requires the reflective response of gratitude and praise. Since the fall shatters that covenant relationship and renders the human person incapable of offering the appropriate response, it would follow that we must view the image as completely obliterated by sin. This does not mean that Torrance thinks that the related capacities themselves have been removed or even damaged by the fall, only that in the condition of sin we are no longer able to use those capacities to offer the proper, image-bearing response. Nor does it entail that sin has severed all relationship between the Creator and his creatures, a severance that would result in our immediate annihilation given our continual dependence on God's grace to sustain our existence. Instead, "Total depravity does not entail on the Reformed view any ontological break in man's relation with God, but it does mean that the essential relation in which true human nature is grounded has been utterly perverted and turned into its opposite."[65] Consequently, the fall entails "the obliteration of the *imago Dei* in man."[66]

Nonetheless, Torrance affirms that there is an important sense in which we must say that the image *remains* despite the ravages of sin, even in those who are not yet reunited to God in and through Christ. In this sense, the image remains "no matter what happens" to the human person.[67] "In spite

---

63. Habets, *Theosis in the Theology of Thomas Torrance*, 32.
64. Torrance, "The Word of God," 106.
65. Torrance, "The Word of God," 107.
66. Torrance, "The Word of God," 108.
67. Torrance, "The Word of God," 105.

of all its depravity and distortion through sin, human nature is not, and cannot be, effaced or destroyed."[68] To understand how Torrance can maintain both that the image is completely lost and that the image remains, recall our earlier discussion of the objective and subjective aspects of Torrance's view. The objective aspect of the image refers to God's creational intention to draw humanity toward an eschatological *telos* and that intention is permanent and unchangeable. Consequently, there is a sense in which our status as image-bearers is permanent because it is secured by God's own intentions. The reason human nature cannot be "effaced or destroyed" is that "its ground and goal are lodged in God himself."[69] Here again we see Torrance's extrinsic view of the image at work. Insofar as "the ground and goal" of the image are "lodged in God himself," the only thing that could possibly obliterate the image entirely would be for God to change his own plans and purposes for humanity. Given that the truth of humanity is ultimately revealed in Christ, and given that this is precisely where we see how unshakably committed God is to the redemption and well-being of his people, we can be confident that the image can never be entirely removed in this sense. "That means that the *imago dei* was not dragged down by the Fall and made a prisoner of man's fallen nature ... but it continues to hang over man as a destiny which he can realize no longer, and as a judgment upon his actual state of perversity."[70]

However, since the subjective aspect of the image refers to our active participation in the image—the extent to which we adequately "mirror" God in creation—then we can say that the fall has completely obliterated the subjective aspect of the image. And notice that this holds for both the relational and the substantival aspects of Torrance's view. Torrance does not argue that the image endures because our relation to God endures. We have already seen that although he affirms a continued relationship, it is a relationship that has been perverted by sin into its opposite. And we have also seen that the mere Creator-creature relationship on its own cannot establish the *imago Dei* because it is a relation that holds for all creatures. Consequently, when Torrance emphasizes the obliteration of the image, he has in mind every

68. Torrance, "The Goodness and Dignity of Man," 314.
69. Torrance, "The Goodness and Dignity of Man,"314.
70. Torrance, "The Word of God," 107.

aspect of the image. Whatever remains, does so only in virtue of God's creation and eschatological intentions.

There is an important sense in which this holds true even for those who have been reunited to God in Christ through the Spirit. Since Jesus alone is the true image, he is the only one who truly expresses the praise and gratitude that are the proper response to the divine address. Consequently, to the extent that believers come to experience the *imago Dei*, it is only as they come to participate in Christ as a free expression of God's grace. Drawing from Calvin's sermon on Job, Torrance explains,

> It must be imputed by free grace. "Have we it through our own effort? Have we it by inheritance from our ancestors? No—but we have it by God's free gift through his own mere goodness." Thus, the original intention of God becomes event in man's existence only by the Word, and the *imago* is possessed only in faith and hope until we see Christ as he is and become like him. In Christ, therefore, we see the *imago Dei* to be the ground of our existence beyond our existence, but which becomes sacramental event here and now in the hearing of faith, as we are sealed with the Holy Spirit until the redemption of the purchased possession.[71]

Consequently, there is a very real sense in which, although all humans remain *imago Dei* creatures in the objective sense, Christ alone is the image of God in both the objective and subjective senses. Even believers only participate in the subjective reality of the image through the vicarious humanity of Christ.

THREE NEEDED DEVELOPMENTS

Torrance offers us a christological and pneumatological vision of the *imago Dei* in which human identity is objectively grounded in God's prior determination to call us into relation with himself and is subjectively realized in our own response of praise and gratitude. Although Torrance's presentation raises a number of questions that leave some room for interpretive debate, his view of the image is coherent, rich, and worth exploring further. However, there are at least three areas where significant weaknesses remain and need to be addressed.

---

71. Torrance, "The Word of God," 109.

First, despite Torrance's clear affirmation that our interpretation of the *imago Dei* needs to be rooted in the Old Testament texts in which we first encounter this concept, one looks in vain for any extended discussion or close analysis of those texts. Torrance frequently refers to themes and ideas developed from those texts, but he operates as though their meaning was either obvious or already well established. Yet Torrance was well aware of the interpretive history of these texts and long-standing disagreements on the nature of the *imago Dei*. Indeed, none of Torrance's extended discussions of the image shows any awareness of the extensive work done by Old Testament scholars or the importance of the ancient Near Eastern material that had come to dominate biblical scholarship in the first part of the twentieth century. If Torrance is correct and the Old Testament texts provide the necessary basis on which a christological interpretation of the *imago Dei* stands, then his own account must be judged lacking in this respect.

Second, although Torrance clearly assumes that the *imago Dei* is something that is limited just to human persons, it is not entirely clear why this would necessarily be the case given his own explanation of the image. Torrance assumes throughout his work that only human persons are capable of the kind of conscious intellectual work necessary to know God in his self-revelation and respond properly to that self-revelation with praise and gratitude. However, he neglects to consider possible counterexamples, the clearest of which would be the angels. They appear to have been created in fellowship with God, and they also seem to have the capacities necessary to respond with gratitude and praise. So why not follow the lead of someone like Aquinas and conclude that the angels too are made in the image of God?[72] Similarly, though somewhat more controversially, we might also argue that at least some of the more advanced animals (e.g., higher primates) have the

---

72. For a good discussion of this, see Celia Deane-Drummond, "God's Image and Likeness in Humans and Other Animals: Performative Soul-Making and Graced Nature," *Zygon* 47 (2012): 934–48. One could appeal here to Torrance's emphasis on male-female relationality as the creaturely analog to divine relationality. However, not only would I rather not get into a discussion about whether angels are sexually differentiated, but even if we affirmed that angels were not capable of imaging triune relationality in this way, such an objection would require arguing that male-female relationality is the *only possible* creaturely analog.

rudimentary capacities necessary to participate in a similar kind of personal fellowship with their Creator.[73]

Some might object here that this critique focuses too much on the substantival aspects of Torrance's account, downplaying his more fundamental emphasis on the unique divine-human relationship that grounds the *imago Dei*. However, recall that Torrance himself explains this unique relationship largely in terms of the ways in which human persons *participate* in this relationship. In other words, when dealing with questions about human uniqueness, Torrance routinely appeals to the unique cognitive and volitional capacities that allow human persons to enjoy fellowship with God in a way that is not true of other creatures.

Consequently, a better response to this worry would be to suggest that Torrance's account of human uniqueness would be better served by appealing to other aspects of his own argument, specifically the unique significance of the incarnation. If Jesus is the one who both reveals and grounds the truth about humanity, and if what we see in Jesus is God uniting himself to humanity in a way that is distinct from any other relation he bears with the rest of creation, then we have good grounds for maintaining human uniqueness with the respect to the *imago Dei* irrespective of whether any other creatures have similar capacities. This would still not require us to downplay the significance of those capacities entirely, but it would maintain that the capacities themselves should not be the theological basis of claims about what ultimately grounds human uniqueness.

Finally, it is difficult to hear Torrance's emphasis on the intellect, conscious thankfulness, and active fellowship without wondering about its implications for those human persons who are unable to participate in the ways he describes. As we have seen, Torrance emphasizes throughout his writings the importance of the inner, mental lives of human persons as necessary for proper participation in the *imago Dei*. And remember, for Torrance, *participating* in the image is not just an implication or correlation of the image, as though you could somehow *be* in the image of God without *participating* in the image. That is why Torrance can use such strong language when referring to the impact of sin on the image. It is not as though humans after the

---

73. We could also choose to investigate here what Torrance might have to say about intelligent extraterrestrials, but I will leave that for others to explore!

fall continued to be images of God despite the fact that they were no longer adequately participating in that reality. Instead, Torrance maintains that the image is completely obliterated except insofar as it remains in God's creational and eschatological intentions. If this is the case, it would seem that Torrance must offer a similar conclusion with respect to human persons who cannot participate in the image as he has described. Torrance's argument would seem to suggest that the image has been similarly obliterated in such people given that they cannot offer the necessary response. Torrance can still say that this person is *imago Dei* in the objective sense that their participation in the image remains God's creational and eschatological intention, but that does not seem to change the implication that all such human persons share the same obliterated-image status as those who are outside of Christ. Given our long history of downplaying the full humanity of persons with disabilities, many will question the wisdom of any view of the image that suggests that such persons do not participate fully in the *imago Dei*.

This issue is a little trickier to address than the prior two since Torrance himself does not deal with these kinds of questions in his essays on the *imago Dei*. From what we have already seen, though, one likely response would be to draw again on Torrance's distinction between the objective and subjective aspects of the image. We could claim here that what really matters about the image for affirming the full dignity and value of human persons, indeed for affirming human personhood itself, resides in the objective aspect of the image—God's faithful and permanent determination to create human persons for relationship with himself—thus grounding human identity in a way that transcends any possible infirmities experienced by particular human individuals. That this is likely what Torrance intended is strongly suggested by the way he argues in his later writings for the full personhood of the unborn.[74] However, this still entails that those with severe intellectual disabilities share the same obliterated-image status as non-Christians simply in virtue of their impairment. Ziegler points the way toward an alternative solution when he suggests that because the *imago Dei* is ultimately grounded in God's own activity, then it is something that "fundamentally is perceptible only by God himself."[75] Although this could be heard as referring only to

---

74. See, for example, Torrance, "The Soul and Person."
75. Ziegler, *Trinitarian Grace and Participation*, 165.

the objective aspect of the image, it could also suggest that even with respect to the inner life of human persons there is the possibility that some people actively participate in the *imago Dei* in a way that is not discernible by other people. Such an argument would obviously make it impossible to establish that they actually *are* participating in this way, but it would at least create the possibility of holding out hope that they do so. And we could pursue a third option by revising Torrance's account so that it aligns more with the interpretation suggested by Woznicki above, in which the substantive aspects are related to but not themselves a part of the *imago Dei*. As I have argued above, this would deviate somewhat from the account Torrance actually offers. Nonetheless, some might find such a Torrance-inspired reconstruction more attractive than either of the other two proposed solutions since it offers a more unqualified way of affirming the full image-bearing status of all human persons than the first option, and it does not require appealing to unobservable and unprovable claims about the inner lives of people like the second.

Regardless of what we think about these three possibilities, it seems most likely that a thoroughly Torrancean response to this question would need to draw from his robust emphasis on the vicarious humanity of Christ. While we do not have sufficient space remaining to unpack this concept fully, we have already seen that Torrance depicts Jesus alone as the one who truly images God such that even Christians only participate in the image proleptically. "In Christ, therefore, we see the *imago Dei* to be the ground of our existence beyond our existence, but which becomes sacramental event here and now in the hearing of faith, as we are sealed with the Holy Spirit until the redemption of the purchased possession."[76] Using such a framework, we might thus contend that persons with disabilities have precisely the same status with respect to the *imago Dei* as all of God's people: depending in faith on Christ's faithful participation on their behalf. Granted, this would require that we also revisit what Torrance means when he contends that we must receive this vicarious representation "in the hearing of faith," but that is a question for another essay.

---

76. Torrance, "The Word of God," 109.

7
—

BARTH, TORRANCE, AND EVANGELICALS

*Critiquing and Reinvigorating the Idea
of a "Personal Relationship with Jesus"*

Marty Folsom

A central tenet of evangelical practice is that one has a personal relationship with Jesus. This point raises some critical questions. What does it mean to engage in a personal relationship? Is God personal and available for personal relating? What is possible in discovering a meaningful, personal relationship with Jesus? Karl Barth and Thomas F. Torrance offer a horizon of hope for evangelical theology to rediscover the good news that makes the gospel deeply and biblically personal.[1]

While growing up, my parents held different philosophies: one focused on the life of the mind and the other of the heart. Neither parent fully met the need for understanding and engaging in personal relationships. When I became a committed seeker, I wrestled with learning how to practice quality personal relationships with other people and eventually with Jesus. I found promise in evangelical Christianity.[2] But I needed more. I found a way

---

1. In the *Biographical Dictionary of Evangelicals*, ed. Timothy Larsen (Downers Grove, IL: InterVarsity Press, 2003), Barth is missing, but Torrance is included; see Mark Husbands, "Thomas F. Torrance," 672–74, acknowledges their relationship.

2. I acknowledge that many forms of contemporary evangelicalism are in crisis when the personal is exchanged for the political. See James Davison Hunter, *To Change the World: The Irony, Tragedy, and Possibility of Christianity in Late Modern World* (Oxford: Oxford University Press, 2010).

forward in the thinking of Karl Barth and T. F. Torrance.[3] To properly engage theology and the Christian life, one must transcend beliefs in our heads or Christian practices that become habits. We need a change of mind called repentance. But our minds must be changed in personal engagement, grasped by God, to enter a personal, participative relationship.[4]

We should begin by investigating what it means to be "persons." From that insight, we may expand our discussion regarding our use of the term "relationship." If our understanding of persons is amiss, it will sabotage how we relate. As we turn an internal gaze to our thought-world, we miss essential connections with others. If I ask, "Who are you?" does your attention turn to reflection? That is the usual search for self, engaging with an inward focus.

If our understanding of relationships is mistaken, we will stay self-focused and miss the magic of real connection, intimacy, and deep friendship with others. Our task in this chapter will be to discern how the Trinitarian thinkers Barth and Torrance enrich the relational pursuits of evangelicals. The goal is to find greater relational depths with Jesus, and other humans, in authentic, fulfilling personal relationships.

Historically, evangelicals have pointed the way to a relational life with Jesus but have fallen short of a clear understanding for discernable reasons. The proposals of Barth and Torrance contribute to a more biblical, theological, and livable manner of personal relating.[5]

---

3. There is a long history of misreading Barth. He is portrayed as making the subjective human the center in a dialectical-paradoxical exposition of divine revelation. See Carl F. H. Henry, *Evangelicals at the Brink of Crisis* (Waco: Word, 1968), 13. Barth has since been shown to be faithfully Christ-centered in his thinking where the rational path of Henry has furthered the spread of rationalistic, individualistic Christianity: "His theology amounts to a rejection of personal revelation in favor of an absolute propositional revelation," Myk Habets, *Theology in Transposition* (Minneapolis: Fortress, 2013), 98. How we understand personal knowledge is central. Is it in engaging the other or through ideas in one's mind? Is evangelical Christianity about a relationship or a reasoned set of beliefs? According to Robert E. Webber, *The Younger Evangelicals* (Grand Rapids: Baker, 2002), 14, "Modern evangelicalism has identified with the Cartesian emphasis on reason and the empirical method."

4. The journal of the Thomas F. Torrance Theological Fellowship is called *Participatio*, in capturing the importance of this focus, https://tftorrance.org/journal/.

5. See Gary W. Deddo, *Karl Barth's Theology of Relations: Trinitarian, Christological, and Humans: Towards an Ethic of the Family* (New York: Peter Lang, 1999), and his article on the personal, "The Importance of the Personal in the Onto-relational Theology of Thomas F. Torrance," in *T&T Clark Handbook of Thomas F. Torrance*, ed. Paul D. Molnar and Myk Habets (London: Bloomsbury T&T Clark, 2020), 143–60.

I call myself an evangelical Christian. For me, that means participating in God's life with a loving commitment to the triune God revealed in Jesus, who is already committed to me. Consequently, I love my neighbor as an outworking of God's love and accept and love myself in the context of these relationships. I have spent four decades researching, teaching, writing, counseling, and speaking, discovering, and equipping others with the reality that understanding God and ourselves is all about relationships. I believe this is the way forward for the evangelical church as it seeks to live and share its good news. What is at stake is an authentic Christianity that is not captured by cultural conceptions and values.

WHAT IS THE IMPORTANCE OF PERSONAL RELATING TO AN EVANGELICAL?

When biblically and theologically attuned to God, the core meaning of being an evangelical is about a human relationship with God, based on God's initiative. Every discussion must begin with God, revealed in Jesus, and not our human hopes and ideals.[6]

To be evangelical is to *identify with good news* (*eu*, good; *angelic*, news or announcement). The content of this news is about the God-human relation. The core of this message is both given *by* Jesus Christ and is *about* who he is in acting to restore the God-human relation. Thus, John 3:16 is a central text affirming that God loves the world, sends Jesus, and calls for a responsive relation. The goal is life together. The gospel is about the actuality and possibility of a personal relationship.

Even further, this news is good as it enables an ongoing restored relationship with God. Jesus embodies this relationship by being God for us. He accomplishes this by also being fully human, taking on human form to fulfill the task of reconciling the relation. "God was in Christ, reconciling the world to himself," as 2 Corinthians 5:19 (NLT) affirms. God comes in person to restore a relationship. Our response entails a personal relation appropriate to what God has offered.[7]

---

6. Thomas F. Torrance, *The Ground and Grammar of Theology* (Belfast: Christian Journals Limited, 1980).

7. *Kata physin*, "according to the nature of the thing known." To know God is to focus on how God has made himself known in Jesus.

The Bible announces good news as the Word of God. The Bible is the text that facilitates the God-human relation. The Old Testament foreshadows and establishes God's commitment to embrace and engage humanity. The New Testament reveals the fulfillment of God's promise to act, revealed in Jesus and continued in the life of the church. The Bible facilitates a personal relationship between God and humans through its communicative connection. We are to search the Scriptures, not to find life in independence from God but to know Jesus personally (John 3:39), abiding in him (John 15:4), and loving others as we have been loved (John 13:34; 15:12).

Within the Bible, the central themes are about personal relationships. God takes on human form (incarnation) to demonstrate God's intent and personal involvement in restoring relations.[8] On the cross (atonement), Jesus removes what violates and alienates humanity from God.[9] This is key to the good news and is fulfilled in the resurrection that celebrates Jesus's ongoing life. He is *with* us to the end of the age (Matt 28:20) and *for* us as the Lord of our lives (Phil 2:10–11).

Jesus's good news is to be lived in the life of the church. We are evangelical by attending church to learn, through the Bible, to know this living God, to worship as an act of personal connection, and to build relationships with God's people as the body of Christ. We gather as an act of personal relating with God to be made into Jesus's body for a life of intimate relating (Heb 10:25). These affirmations are central yet interpreted in diverse forms. Involvement in the church for personal relationships with God and other humans is vital.

Finally, a personal response is critical in adopting the good news for one's own life.[10] This may be called coming to faith, making a commitment, deciding to follow Jesus, or identifying as a Christian. It is responsive and personal. We love because he first loved us. It is relational, implying an ongoing life together. This endeavor informs the life of devotion. Its formation process usually includes prayer as a daily relational connection, Bible study to hear

---

8. Thomas F. Torrance, *Incarnation: The Person and Life of Christ*, ed. by Robert. T. Walker (Downers Grove, IL and Milton Keynes: IVP and Paternoster, 2008).

9. Thomas F. Torrance, *Atonement: The Person and Work of Christ*, ed. by Robert. T. Walker (Downers Grove, IL and Milton Keynes: IVP and Paternoster, 2009).

10. Alister E. McGrath, *Evangelicalism and the Future of Christianity* (Downers Grove, IL: InterVarsity Press, 1995), 72, "At the heart of evangelical spiritualty lies the concept of a personally assimilated faith."

and grow with God, and participating in worship as a personal acting out of the importance of the relationship one has with Jesus.

To be an evangelical is to acknowledge the importance of a personal God who has acted for us and calls us to a personal relationship. Evangelicals contend that some form of a personal relationship with Jesus is indispensable and is expressed in some version of the points just discussed. The meaning of the gospel moves a person from ignorance and alienation. Conversion is a life-changing recentering relationship with Jesus in knowing God.[11] Despite setbacks on the journey, God calls us by grace to personal relationship and not to works. In theory, evangelicals trust the goodness of God to be the final word.

FINDING A BETTER WAY

Relationships are a mystery for which God alone has the mastery. Without God, humans do not have the resources to fulfill human relating. God uniquely provides a constructive understanding of how personal relationships work with God and neighbor and what this means for the self. Humans are slow to learn that we cannot be the masters of building our faith—we must heed the call to a relationship shaped by God.

God seeks restoration through participation in loving and meaningful relationships. Humans generally mess this up by pursuing their own benefits. Over the centuries, philosophers and theologians have encouraged humans to build their own destinies. Most people in the Western world avoid a life of intimacy in pursuit of security and self-control. This resistance leaves us alone with damaged or distant relationships and God becomes dismissed or downgraded to a servant at the beck and call of human desires. Few humans avoid the traps of desiring human success. But God's mastery is not completely absent, only neglected, resulting in the human failure in relationships.

Evangelicals have been sidetracked concerning understanding and living in personal relationships.[12] Too often, evangelicals have subverted

---

11. Timothy P. Weber, "Premillennialism and the Branches of Evangelicalism," in *The Variety of American Evangelicalism*, ed. Donald W. Dayton and Robert K. Johnson (Downers Grove, IL: InterVarsity Press, 1991), 14, "Evangelicalism is more than a point on the theological spectrum; it is a driving force, a dynamic bend on personal and corporate revival."

12. Case in point, Timothy Larsen, "Defining and Locating Evangelicalism," in *The Cambridge Companion to Evangelical Theology*, ed. Timothy Larsen and Daniel J. Treier (Cambridge: Cambridge University Press, 2007), 10–12, where the fifth point of being evangelical is one

Christianity, trading the truth of Jesus for the cultural seductions of esteem, power, influence, wealth, and prosperity.[13] Evangelicals preach to individual human needs but remain deaf to the divine wisdom of loving our neighbors. We want God in our life situations but not to be the protagonist of the story— we want to be the center. We want the Christian life to make us better people. Self-fulfillment rules the course of our lives, not a love of others. Stuck in our heads, we lose touch with God's heart and empathy for struggling humanity. Looking at the backs of heads in church becomes more than a metaphor in missing face-to-face encounters. What we need is knowing and being known by others. God fills our thoughts in our attempts to be informed Christians, but we neglect learning to hear the Great Shepherd's voice. We miss the essence of relationship building.

In our self-centered state, we judge others while nonjudgmentally affirming our own attempts to accumulate knowledge, hoping this is spiritual growth. We think of repentance as our change of mind in our beliefs and opinions. In actuality, it is a shift in orientation and an openness to be changed by the living God. But when we drift inwardly in our spiritual quest, we lose touch with reality. We cannot hope for intimacy in the seclusion of our minds. Knowing God as the God who comes to us is the better way. Knowing God through Jesus is the best way. The biblical call is to "fix our eyes on Jesus" (Heb 12:2 NIV).

In trying to appeal to the modern world, evangelicals split in several directions. Most commonly, an emphasis is placed on the rational when presenting the Christian faith[14] which makes being a Christian a matter of thinking and believing. Personal relating develops as theory without practice, as though one could believe in marriage but stay single in fear of its vulnerability. Living a good theory has merit in developing values that align with God's intent.

"who stresses the work of the Holy Spirit in the life of an individual to bring about conversion and an ongoing life of fellowship with God." The individual comes first and relationships come later. We can see this as problematic from the start—emphasizing separation, conversion, and sinful individuals that becomes a call to individual "activism."

13. Jacques Ellul, *The Subversion of Christianity* (Grand Rapids: Eerdmans, 1986).

14. Roger E. Olson, *Pocket History of Evangelical Theology* (Downers Grove, IL: InterVarsity Press, 2007) 102–3, states that Henry interpreted Barth as personal, historical, and dialogical and not rational, propositional, and cognitive. He saw Barth as leading to an anti-intellectual "flight from reason." Rational being becomes associated with the individual thinker. Relational being is conceived as personal and subjective. This split causes a great divide. We would do well to have thoughtful, passionate, interpersonal, Christ-centered theology to work with the whole.

However, thinking alone leads us to get stuck in our heads, replacing what is intended.

A Christianity focused on the internal will be profoundly awkward when relating to the God who loves in action. He wants connection. We want insight. The educational agendas of evangelical schools have attempted to be rationally competitive with the best of secular schools, providing a Christian form of understanding to convince the world about the wisdom of following Jesus. While rationality can be present in the relational, rationality can also exclude relationships as being too subjective. Thus, relationality can be seen as a fad, echoing the therapeutic, and consequently dismissed.[15] Ultimately, we prepare to face the world with an argument. Evangelical education may create those who can defend the faith and explain the contents of the Bible, but it does not develop great listeners or relationship builders, especially with potential converts or those deemed impossible to convert. Rational agendas do not translate well into relational connections.

However, other evangelicals have gone in the opposite direction from the rational. These evangelicals become emotionally driven in worship. The devotion of their hearts extends to being anti-intellectual. These Spirit-led evangelical denominations and nondenominations neglect developing thoughtful leadership. While trusting the gift of the Spirit to lead, human emotions easily take over the agenda. The neglected task is learning to engage the Spirit of Jesus humbly.

Likewise, some evangelicals want practical teaching and leading and pursue business and marketing strategies. They repeatedly repackage the Bible as a life-advice manual. Committed to the program, they resist developing a Christian intellect. They adopt strategies that measure success with numbers. The emotional power of success drives the mission. These approaches echo worldly models but are merely examples of human emotions employing human skills to achieve human outcomes of success. However, emotions, skills, and success are not the problematic issues. We need to focus on following the God who has come to us in Jesus and whom we follow by the Spirit.

---

15. Harold Kuhn, "Relationalism: Principle or Slogan?" *Christianity Today* (February 28, 1975): 49–50.

Rather than pursuing better theories or practice for the church based on human capacities, we need to discover what a restored relationship with the living God entails. The way forward is to thoughtfully engage the reality of God's coming in Jesus to shape our emotions and practices in a personal relationship. We must understand that theological science is not abstract or putting God under a microscope, but it is a careful pursuit in letting our relationship with God be entirely engaged in knowing Jesus.[16] We do not examine God as much as we allow all our ideas to be questioned, our language to be clarified, and our reality to be shaped by what God gives.[17] Rather than study the Bible, we must let it examine us by helping us know and hear the one who already loves us.

Discarding the theories and practices that are the fruit of human construction, Barth and Torrance bring something better. They call us to an attentive and clarifying openness to deeply know the God who speaks and invites us to respond in a life of intimacy. We know we are known and loved by Jesus, who demonstrates God's love for us. We acknowledge we are children of the Father as we cry out "Abba, dear Father" by God's Spirit (Gal 4:6; Rom 8:15). Who we are, not what we think or do, is central to our identity. We are who we are because of our transforming relationship with God, not just religious tradition or rational constructions.

Barth and Torrance begin with the God who speaks and makes all things known. Our relational life is lived in response to the call to love the divine persons and those around us. When we seek head knowledge or practices to please God instead of knowing and being known, we lose the intimacy that is the meaning of being in Christ by the Spirit, restored to the Father. We replace what God has offered with our projections that neglect what God has provided. We supplant God with our conceptions.

Much of what evangelicals pursue is a logical argument and a rational faith.[18] What we need is connection and participation in a life of hearing and

---

16. Thomas F. Torrance, *Theological Science* (Oxford: Oxford University Press, 1969).

17. Karl Barth, *Church Dogmatics*, ed. G. W. Bromiley and T. F. Torrance (Edinburgh: T&T Clark, 1932–1967). This set is a thorough working through the task of letting Jesus expose false theological assumptions so that the church may know and serve the living God in a manner appropriate to God's self-revelation.

18. This is evidenced by the popularity among evangelicals of apologetic works like Josh McDowell, *The New Evidence That Demands a Verdict: Evidence I & II Fully Updated in One Volume to Answer the Questions Challenging Christians in the 21st Century* (Nashville: Thomas Nelson, 1999),

acting in response to Jesus, knowing his Father through him by the work of the Holy Spirit. This connection means engaging a mystery through learning in a personal manner. It is appropriate to see a spouse or children as mysteries, growing with them and learning about them as they mature. The opposite is to take them for granted or to reduce the relationship to habits. God's mercies are new every day. Our responses and sharing of life should make room for the dynamics of growing together. This approach is not irrational; it is letting the reality of relationships shape our reasoning. Building on Macmurray's logic as used by Torrance, every revelation, action, or word of another shapes our reasoning as to who the other is and the reasoning of our own response.

It is not uncommon for marriages and faith commitments to lose mystery. Often, when we think we know the other, we have lost touch with their present reality, finding ourselves estranged and disconnected. Relating through day-by-day experiences is the best way to be personal. Otherwise, we fade from the relation into a life of independence.

God made us interdependent. Ordering our lives within the relation of interdependence is critical. If we begin with human capacities, we will fall tragically short of knowing God. A meaningful relationship is likely to develop if we learn to listen, respond, and engage in a life of discovery. That is where Barth and Torrance lead us.

SHEDDING THE OLD, EMBRACING THE NEW

Failure to understand what it means to be persons shatters our ability to develop personal relationships with God or other humans. The Bible reveals that God made us for relationships; it is not good for man or woman to be alone (Gen 2:18). The fall was a failure of connection. It is best to see that salvation implies reconciliation for relationship—by God. The history of humanity and the church reveals a life consistently resistant toward submitting to God and one another, leading to our age of independence. We must briefly survey where we are left in personal relating.

---

and Lee Strobel, *The Case for Christ: A Journalist's Personal Investigation of the Evidence for Jesus* (Grand Rapids: Zondervan, 1998).

THE EVANGELICAL UNDERSTANDING OF "PERSONS"

What has emerged culturally in our day regarding being a person? The American ideal of "we the people" has become "I the individual." If we ask, "What is a person?" we think primarily of an individual human with a brain. We may include their actions as well. One thinks and feels from a point distinct from other humans; we are persons separately, who may join others. Our sense of self is primarily based on experience. We observe and think about the world and our particular place in it. We think of ourselves as thinking selves.[19] We relate to other selves as embodied beings with brains, bumping against one another. Temporarily encountering each other, we then return to the cocoon of our minds. Yet, we do not know most others, feeling unknown by them ourselves. Once, society involved a web of relating, connected as family, community, and country. Now those connections are unraveling. We are on individual journeys.

The result of this cultural shift is that the evangelical gospel eventually becomes human-centered. Individualism, the pursuit of self alone, combines with the spirit of American free enterprise into rugged individualism. This shift has shaped transdenominational evangelicalism's distinctive institutions.[20] Each group serves the market of individuals on their particular quests to experience God. Gatherings become a collection of bodies who gain information and a spiritual experience but lack mutual knowing at most levels.

Today, evangelical Christians see themselves as individuals who once did not have a relationship with God but decided to follow Jesus. Subtly, this focuses the relationship on the human decision. A life of self-transformation follows. One is baptized as a sign of one's commitment. Communion is engaged as a sign of personal preparation to be proper and clean before God. Reading the Bible functions as an activity of personal (meaning individual) devotion. Lured into the cultural captivity of the Western commitment to individualism, where it is "all about me,"[21] the self becomes the center. The

---

19. This comes from Descartes's famous dictum, "I think, therefore I am." This Enlightenment way of thinking moves from listening to God toward the human confidence in rational thought without God.

20. George Marsden, *Reforming Fundamentalism: Fuller and the New Evangelicalism* (Grand Rapids: Eerdmans, 1987), 2.

21. Soong-Chan Rah, *The Next Evangelicalism: Freeing the Church from Western Cultural Captivity* (Downers Grove, IL: InterVarsity Press, 2001), 35.

gospel becomes human-centered.[22] The general call to be an evangelical is cast as a personal commitment to Christ.[23] Inadvertently, we become deaf to Christ and attentive to our next act of faith. Our faith becomes about us.

In presenting the Christian faith, evangelicals have described God, defined God's attributes, witnessed to God's acts, and attempted to give a rational case that this God is to be believed. Consider a classic evangelical theology like Millard Erickson's *Christian Theology*.[24] It presents the foundation of evangelicalism through a reasonable worldview that begins with the human coming to know God through argument, logic, and the experience of creation. The Bible is seen as a book to inform us about what God is like. Then, the human, especially with the problem of sin, is introduced. Theology follows an arrangement intended to appeal to issues of humans. God is presented as the solution to a problem, plus there is hope for earthly and eternal benefits—a future for our individual existence.

The person and work of Jesus are subsequently presented as the means of understanding our salvation (which is hotly debated as to what is our role, what *we* must do or acknowledge). The final stage of our existence is about what happens to us in the end. While God is undoubtedly discussed, the reasoning undergirding this evangelical theology leads to understanding God through divided subjects or beliefs centered on the human. "It seems reasonable to say that holding the beliefs that Jesus held and taught is part of what it means to be a Christian or follower of Christ ... that is the particular concern of Christian theology."[25] We try to believe what Jesus believed, instead of knowing him and through him knowing the Father in a personal relationship in the present.

This focus on an individual believing is the inward turn that has shaped the idea of the person in evangelical Christianity. This conception extends

---

22. Will Metzger, *Tell the Truth: The Whole Gospel to the Whole Person by the Whole People* (Downers Grove, IL: InterVarsity Press, 1981), 30–36. Even here, while unveiling the human-centeredness of most gospel presentations, the alternative "God-centered" approach begins with a "point of contact" in creation and a God who will save you. It is improved, but still makes faith a human decision as the personal submission of an individual.

23. The cover story of *Time*, "Back to that Oldtime Religion" (December 26, 1977): 53, states, "They believe in making a conscious personal commitment to Christ, a spiritual encounter, gradual or instantaneous, known as the born-again experience." There may be some change, but this is still at the center of evangelical belief.

24. Millard J. Erickson, *Christian Theology*, 1st ed. (Grand Rapids: Baker, 1987).

25. Erickson, *Christian Theology*, 20.

into the life of the church in shaping the individual, starting with conversion, through the process of discipleship, and persists into a life of service.

I fully admit that we do have a part in our journey with Christ. But if we think as individuals, we deflect from a relationship offered by the triune God. We become absorbed in the part we play.

NEW POSSIBILITIES FOR UNDERSTANDING "PERSONS"

Barth considered his theology to be evangelical.[26] His method concentrated on a theology informed by God as given in the person of Jesus. This required resisting the projection of human-informed ways of thinking onto God. For example, answering a question as simple as "what is love?" can be hijacked by human wish-fulfillment or experience. We do not naturally think from God's perspective or let Jesus inform the meaning of our terms. For Barth, a meaningful answer to "what is love?" could only correctly be answered by the source of love—the God who creates and fulfills love for creation in personal engagement. This answer occurs uniquely by hearing the living Word, Jesus, witnessed to in the written word, the Bible. Through the Bible, Jesus properly informs the preaching and practices of the church in response to God's speaking. In this way, personal relationships are made possible, becoming the goal of a more robust evangelical theology.

Discerning what we mean by a person must begin with Jesus. He is the only genuine person we may engage in understanding authentic personhood.[27] All others are fallen persons marred by sin. In Jesus, we find that a trustworthy person loves God, neighbor, and self as their primary mode of existing. Jesus is not just an individual who subsequently relates. He is always the Son of the Father, indivisibly associated with the Holy Spirit. As the last Adam, Jesus lives, dies, and rises again on behalf of all humanity (1 Cor 15:44–49). Jesus shows us that being a person is to exist in these constituting relationships. He makes us new persons as we are in him (2 Cor 5:17). Being a person is who we are in such relations, not as add-on connections in life. Relationships are essential to being a person.

---

26. Karl Barth, *Evangelical Theology: An Introduction* (Grand Rapids: Eerdmans, 1963).

27. Barth, *Church Dogmatics* IV/1, 92: "We cannot speak of the being of man except from the standpoint of the Christian and in the light of the particular being of man in Jesus Christ."

Jesus opens us to understand two other persons: his Father who sent him and the Spirit who comes to us in an ongoing relation. This one God exists in three persons. Each lives with the others and cannot be thought of as independent in any way. This is the triune God, personally relating with each other and us as community. This God manifests love that creates, reconciles, and restores human life with an eternal intention. The term *perichoresis* captures the internal life of mutual loving. Each makes room for the other and collaboratively, yet distinctively, acts personally as God, whose mission is to act, speak, and live the good news of divinely restored personal life.[28] This God made possible the renewing of personal life together. Our privilege is to live within the gift. This offering is the grace of God's presence, loving and sustaining us as persons "in Christ," meaning restoring us in relation and renewing us by the Spirit through the relation, not by our efforts. "Person" for Barth is Christ-centered, relational, and participative within the triune life.

The image of God is seen firstly in Jesus but also in the male-female structuring of humanity. This alignment is not merely husband and wife in relation but affirms that each gender has an other who is not like them but is made in correspondence with them.[29] Personal being is mutually interactive in the very structure of our relational being. Where sin focuses us on our separate selves, the gospel calls us to be restored in every dimension of our personal being together. This renewal is further manifested in the fruit of the Spirit, which is not internal emotions or attitudes but embodies the very character of transformed relations. Love is not just what we feel inside; it is a way of relating to another as we have been loved.

Barth opens the way for evangelicals to break free of individualized ideas of the person. He moves us beyond our inward-looking that focuses on humans growing as separated selves. Instead, we grow in the actuality of our knowing and being known by Jesus. We develop within the body of Christ and in our sharing in God's relation to all we engage. This transformation moves us from being-in-self to being-in-relation.

Torrance took Barth's Christ-centered thinking and developed it as a science. Science does not mean using empirical methods to study God.

---

28. Thomas F. Torrance, *The Christian Doctrine of God: One Being Three Persons* (Edinburgh: T&T Clark, 1996), 102.

29. Barth, *Church Dogmatics* III/2, 286–89.

Instead, he overcame the myth that science is impersonal; rather, science is best understood as the work of persons, knowing what *or who* is other than ourselves.[30] Thus, science engages and then reflects on the world of objects *and* persons.[31]

Torrance's use of discovery in his method restored proper scientific method as inquiry, rather than fitting knowledge into predetermined categories. Proper knowledge must be informed according to the particular nature of that which is to be studied.[32] Therefore, persons cannot be studied as impersonal objects alone. Admittedly, we do have material bodies, but we are personal beings as well. Looking at the physical alone is a half-truth. This conclusion deceives us regarding who we are and is worse when approaching God.

God cannot be understood as a person by looking at the physical world and reading in our interpretations what God might be like. God has spoken, embodied in the person of Christ. Therefore, we may know God personally. A way is open for relationship, but we must learn to listen. Good science attends to God's disclosure of reality, given in Jesus, and stays faithful to what is personally given.[33]

In the term onto-relations, Torrance captures the idea of being-in-relation.[34] This formulation means that neither the persons of the Trinity nor you and I are isolated selves; we are essentially related beings. We are relationally intertwined in our lives rather than existing like billiard balls that bump against one another. We live in a field of relationships, like a web. Our lives are interconnected so that each part exists in dynamic tension with the whole. Each point, where the lines meet, is our personal being. We are woven together into the web through our relationships with others. God exists that way from eternity but contingently makes us in like kind, in God's image. This manner of inter-existing is the dimension of the personal, the spiritual, and the relational. We are more than the sum of our physical existence.

---

30. Torrance, *Theological Science*, 9.

31. Thomas F. Torrance, *Reality and Scientific Theology* (Edinburgh: Scottish Academic Press, 1985), 26–27.

32. Thomas F. Torrance, *God and Rationality* (Oxford: Oxford University Press, 1971), 52–53.

33. Torrance, *The Christian Doctrine of God*, 82–83.

34. Torrance, *The Christian Doctrine of God*, 102.

The web is unity with particularity. In a web, when any point breaks, the web loses its integrity and collapses. Similarly, our human relationships are like the web that holds us together. This interweaving life includes our actions, conversations, promises, memories, and choices to be with specific others. Those are dynamic links. Some of these dynamics precede us (parents, family). Some are acquired along the way (friends, workmates). God has always existed, so the links to him are unboundedly permanent, extended from his existence. God made us, still loves us, and sustains us within the always existing field of his love. Our status as linked to him made personal relating possible. This one God exists as three persons. Through awakening to God's relational existence, we discover the source and meaning of the personal life into which we are drawn.

Once we see persons as essentially existing in relation, not merely as physical beings who subsequently intertwine, a new way is opened. We redirect from "What do I need to do *to become* personal with the other?"—that is the billiard ball trying to connect—to asking, "What do I do in my relationship *because* I am a person with them?" This approach engages the connections in our web of relations. The already existing relationships matter. The billiard ball model is self-focused: "What about me?" The web model is relationally focused: "How do we take what we have and grow together?" This transfer moves from "my performance" to "our relationship," opening the way for authentic personal relating with Jesus, who is God and human. He mediates our relation, bringing the life of God to us and bringing us into the embrace of God's life of love.[35] A personal relationship with Jesus adopts us into the intimate life of the triune God by his Spirit.

Torrance engages the triune God as one personal God existing in three indivisible persons. This personal God exists in a relationship of unity with particularity. Each person cannot exist without the other. Each is *involved* (unity) in the acting of the other. Each person acts in *distinctive ways* (particularity), affirming that they are not confused or conflated into an abstract unison, like a drop of water being absorbed into a glass of water. When we understand that we are essentially persons, our being in Christ provides a

---

35. Thomas F. Torrance, *The Mediation of Christ: Evangelical Theology and Scientific Culture*, 2nd ed. (Colorado Springs: Helmers & Howard Publishers, 1992).

call to let love shape our existing relations with others, enabling us to become more particularly who we are and grow because of that relationship.

The more we focus on ourselves, the more we deflate into the isolation of our solitary selves. The more we live in relationship, the more unique we become as persons, nurtured by the breath of the Spirit. To befriend many persons does not diminish our uniqueness; each person adds to our exceptionality.

Barth and Torrance were not particularly interested in developing a unique human personality, a term that points to a human, self-crafted effort to establish our individuality. These theologians were more interested in seeing that persons exist with a sense of self who cannot be without others and especially not without God as the source of all personal being.

In proper theology, the big reveal is that we have unknowingly been in a personal relationship with the triune God our whole lives. This God created us, surrounds us, loves us unconditionally, and is present every moment of our lives. He seeks to awaken us to his love, which is already provided. We transform as persons when we awaken to the reality of this already existing relation and are compelled to have our minds changed (repentance). We are born afresh, leaving behind the darkness and blindness of our ignorance. We come alive and live in light of the reality of our personal existence and not the illusion of our separateness and aloneness.[36]

This awakening is the work of the gospel. It restores our personal being away from fearing for our survival needs and the uncertainty of the future. It transforms us to see we are persons loved and accepted as beloved children. As we are pursued by God, knowing him allows us to see who we are as persons already embraced. This realization is like learning the sun, not the earth, is the center of our solar system. Things may appear as though the opposite is the case, but reality has won the day. With God, this is much closer to home; our very identity is transformed. We are more than a singular *Homo sapien*; we are children of God, who is ever-present to nurture us in love. This is good news!

For evangelicals, being a person has mainly been human-focused. The investigation of being fully human usually centers on what an individual may do to develop themselves, including "inviting Jesus" into our lives. However,

---

36. This idea fills the imagery of the Gospel of John.

God invites us into his divine act of redemption. Are there exceptions to this in evangelical understanding? Maybe, but once we examine the point of most gospel presentations, discipleship programs, worship service objectives, and more, we see that form of thinking impacts each individual's thoughts, feelings, and behaviors, undergirding every step of the task.

For Barth and Torrance, being a person is essentially explained through a Trinity-focused discovery process. They center on reasoning that attunes persons to the reality of God's personal being. Can they be misread? Absolutely, but the gospel agenda is clear—let God speak and let humans respond to this rich relationship for discipling, worshiping, and discovering who we are because of who God is for us and with us.

EVANGELICAL PROBLEMS WITH UNDERSTANDING "RELATIONSHIPS"

Evangelical Christians rightly value relationships. However, what this means is not always clear. If one understands a person as an autonomous self, then all relations will be acts of the self, attempting to engage the other. Inadvertently, this relationship focus defaults to *what the individual does*, entrenching relations in a billiard-ball world.

Beginning with the thinking self furthers individuality, as one's relation centers in their thoughts about the other, as if from the tower of the human mind, we focus on observing others. Relations become formed as thoughts about the others around us. The other becomes an object of observation and reflection. If the thoughts and feelings are good, the relationship is conceived as good, whereas uncertainty breeds fear and distrust. But any of these opinions in the mind miss the reality of personal connection.

Believing all is well, we may act with goodwill for the other. Our decision to act, and the action itself, becomes our part in what feels like a good relationship. However, this still is about the individual person. Our intent may or may not have our desired impact on the other. "My action" is not the same as "our loving interaction." What "I do" may rarely rise to what "we do" in relationship building. This inadequacy is especially true in parenting and marriage. It is also profoundly true with God. God is often assumed either to have acted long ago, leaving the rest to us, or God is watching us from a distance. When asked where Jesus is right now, many evangelicals will speak about heaven. Many people think of Jesus as an ancient model of what they should do now (what would Jesus do *if* he were here). Jesus is important but distant. Furthering the relationship appears to remain the work of the individual. What *we* do matters if the relationship is to survive.

What we do becomes the focus of growing the relationship. *We* pray; *we* are called to adore, confess, thank, and ask for what *we* need. *We* read the Bible to learn principles and precepts for the Christian life that *we* hope to live. *We* learn to rationally defend the faith and call others to decide to believe (hoping it forms a relationship). The spotlight is on *us*.

This lifestyle of autonomous self, pressing on to live for Jesus, easily becomes a solitary relationship. Jesus shows up when we think about him but is unknown most of the time. Beginning with a person as "self alone" ends up creating an impersonal relationship, meaning the other is an object of interest but they are not engaged in the mutuality of relating. We develop a Christian persona, a mask, so we fit into playing a part.[37] But we miss the depth of knowing and being known that reverberates from the Bible's witness to what Jesus intends.[38]

In our life of spiritual self-management, we develop categories and compartments. Our secular life is separate from our sacred activities. Also, we easily divide the world into "those who are loved by God" and "those who are the objects of God's disapproval." We have spaces where we act like Christians while keeping hidden parts of our thinking and behaving that we prefer to keep private. We cannot sense the partition and detachment this creates.

When our relationship with Jesus does not permeate our lifestyle, we may ask why we pursue, or neglect, our spiritual activities. What we are proud of easily takes on a performance character. We feel affirmed when we do well but judged with shame or guilt when we feel inadequate. But who is the judge? The average evangelical wants to live for Jesus but finds it a struggle. Sometimes, friends or church events feel relationally fulfilling. Still, life often feels like a lonely pilgrimage, without true intimacy of life with Jesus.

The non-Christians who share our space may easily become outsiders. We believe they have rejected God and consequently we find little to connect over. Loving our neighbor as ourselves can be challenging. Some neighbors

---

37. Barth, *Church Dogmatics* III/2, 82.

38. For example, 1 Corinthians 13:12 (NASB), "Now I know in part, but then I will know fully just as I also have been fully known."

seem like good Christians, but we see hypocrisy or immaturity in them; perhaps we divert our journey from them, lest they judge us. "Othering" in this sense is to diminish the other as incompatible with who we want them, and ourselves, to be. Even God's otherness becomes a problem. God seems absent, and we feel abandoned—like the relationship is up to us. The Father seems distant and angry. The Son is in heaven taking care of business. The Spirit is an intangible and unreachable presence.

Seeing persons as individuals sabotages our relationships with God, one another, and in the end, with a love of self as relational beings. Indwelling Christ's life, we may become initiators, active in friendships that demonstrate the presence of the living God in whom we find our true family.

NEW POSSIBILITIES FOR UNDERSTANDING "RELATIONSHIPS"

When we begin by seeing that a person is a being-in-relation, things change. God shows up in the person of Jesus. Jesus shows us what God is like and that the Father sent him to bring a new and sustaining relationship. We discover that, through Jesus, the Father is our Father as well. This status, as beloved sons and daughters, is our most essential identity. We are never alone or abandoned to be orphans in the world. Jesus promises to be with us always.[39] We are to focus on his presence, abiding in his love as he consistently is in us, in a loving and nourishing relationship that will never go away.[40] We are new creatures who were blind but now understand Jesus's personal presence. The Holy Spirit is sent to give us ears to hear the voice of the shepherd. We listen to the words of the Bible, and we hear that we are loved. As we listen, we feel the Spirit guiding us to live as those who have been loved genuinely and unconditionally and can responsively act like it.

For Barth and Torrance, God speaks. This is called revelation. It is not ideas that are revealed; it is the persons showing up in a personal encounter of self-giving. We are captured by grace that may shock or calm us, awakened in our encounter with the face of Jesus, who speaks to our hearts. This kind of connection only happens when we trust a friend and open up to them about who we are and who they are to us. We move from just talking about

---

39. Matthew 28:20 (NASB), "Behold, I am with you always, to the end of the age."

40. John 15:4 (NASB), "Abide in Me, and I in you. As the branch cannot bear fruit of itself, unless it abides in the vine, neither can you, unless you abide in Me."

our individual self to living in the mutuality of participating in a relationship with both fully involved. Jesus does not just reveal his Father as the king of the universe and creator of all things. He also brings us to his Father as the one who runs to meet his failed children with a crazy, restorative love.[41] Jesus opens our minds and emotions to what is already there so we may live in light of reality and not the illusions that clog our perceptions, such as a demanding God or a warped sense of personal failure.

In this Barth-and-Torrance mode of thinking about the God-human relation, we begin to know God as revealed in Jesus and discover we were known all along. Our task is not to do better at seeking God but to know the God who has always known us and acted to awaken and restore our personal life to know his personal presence. We are transformed by whom we go with, not by how well we perform in a spiritual quest. This new attentiveness does not mean we abandon prayer, Bible reading, and worship. We read with fresh eyes to understand the one to whom we are directed, rather than looking to see what we will get out of it.

The relationship develops through what Torrance calls "indwelling,"[42] referring to "participating in the active life of Jesus," by the Spirit, who is at work in us. Our part includes "a responsive, dynamic indwelling" within God's life.[43] Looking at words on this page, we focus on letters, words, sentences, and so on. But if we can look *through* the words to the reality they reflect—for example, "the best kiss I ever had"—we move past words to experience a meaningful relationship, at least for a few moments. We can also indwell the Bible's text. We discover grace coming from the Father's heart, expressed in the voice of the Son. The Spirit gives us ears to hear. Consequently, we will indwell the relationship that God has extended since eternity.[44] In this relational paradigm, we become good evangelical scientists in the field of the personal.

---

41. Luke 15:11-32. See also Thomas F. Torrance, *The Doctrine of Jesus Christ* (Eugene, OR: Wipf & Stock, 2002), 32, and Barth, *Church Dogmatics* IV/1, 395.

42. Torrance, *The Doctrine of Jesus Christ*, 49.

43. Thomas F. Torrance, *Reality and Evangelical Theology: The Realism of Christian Revelation* (Eugene, OR: Wipf & Stock 2003), 48.

44. Barth, *Church Dogmatics* II/2, 94, "The election of grace is the eternal beginning of all the ways and works of God in Jesus Christ."

Traditional science engages reality as a set of objects. In that mode, scientists exclude listening to persons as a valid scientific endeavor. But that exclusion is a choice we need not make. We cannot try to fit the object of our study, the infinite God and his world, into categories we already have. We need to listen afresh, letting reality inform our conclusions. This kind of relativity thinking was present in Einstein's methods. Newton saw the world through a lens that broke the world into parts. Each element was seen separately and impersonally. Einstein saw that everything is related to everything else. We need to understand everything with relativity in the fields of existence. This insight led to the world of modern, Einsteinian science. He did not work with relativism, where everyone has their own truth. No, relativity is simply an awareness that light, gravity, matter, and everything else must be understood as existing in a field where relations are at work. We must understand reality in its relationality, not in a fractured world of separate elements.

Barth and Torrance worked in the field of the personal. God is not a member of this field, but he created it and relates to it personally. To understand God and human persons, we cannot fit them into our pre-existing human reason and understanding. We may use categories of material, biological, spiritual, and personal in science, always allowing our knowledge to be adequately informed by the uniqueness of each person we come to understand.

The theological science of Barth and Torrance begins with the givenness of God in the person of Jesus. This givenness was witnessed to in the writings of the prophets and apostles in the Bible. As a scientific community called the church, we still listen and respond to what this living God said and says. We must learn to trust and correct our thinking to create a proper developing faith that corresponds with reality. We should develop confidence in other persons. We should learn to build trust as an authentic engagement with reality that establishes a personal relationship.

For Barth and Torrance, faith is science, a reasonable way of thinking when properly learning from and attuning to the object of study. The naturalistic scientist studies a silent world of things. The theological scientist explores the speaking world of God known in Christ. We may say this is a worshiping life sustained in the scientific community of the church, investigated every day with wonder and joy. This engagement informs our relationship with God, other humans, and the world God has made. Theological science does not exclude nature; it sees it within the scope of God's activity. This proper context gives meaning to all relating within it.

Having been found by the love of God, we see God's world and all other people from God's perspective. God's relation to it all informs our being, concerning God and how we love one another. Rather than seeing the other as a threat to self, we have a positive perspective on "othering" captured in the idea of "love one another as I have loved you" (John 13:34). A personal relationship is understood as created, restored, sustained, and nourished as we attune to the heart, voice, and living presence of God. This familiarity is not natural to us based on our own experiences. It is not common sense. Our natural experiences and common sense lack access to what God has given of himself in grace. Once we acknowledge that Jesus has come to provide us with access to his Father, friendship with himself, and the Spirit to understand who this God is and who we are in response, we have the possibility of a personal relationship with Jesus and his Father and the Holy Spirit.

CONCLUSION AND POSSIBILITIES

Evangelicalism's goal in desiring a personal relationship with Jesus is good, but by defaulting to an individualized understanding founded in Western thought, it has succumbed to a version of relating that sees the human as an agent separate from the other who is God. A more robust understanding opens humans to think about the nature of persons out of the heart and relating of God toward us.

Jesus does not have a wonderful plan for our life in any way separate from God. We are invited to share in the triune God's eternal relatedness. God persists with us to the end. Our relationships exist in the context of God's irreducible, interactive, mutually invested way of being together with us. If relationships are only ideas we believe in our heads, they become a philosophy. If they become a set of practices that operate externally as rules to guide us, they become a religion.

For the past forty years, my life has been one of learning all the ways humans try to create synthetic relationships with God, and there are many. But I have also tried to understand this personal God as the context of human life. This God made us. We are members of his family. We live in his presence. God made us to live in relationship and not in separation, isolation, or alienation. Many live in this sad state, even in the church. This heartbreak drives me forward to be more evangelical in the ways Barth and Torrance used the term, that is, compelled by God's good news in Jesus.

I searched long ago in evangelical churches to discover the possibilities yet to be found within Barth and Torrance. These men served the church by focusing on the logic of God revealed in the Logos of God, meaning Jesus. The Jesus of the Bible desires us to discover we are beloved by his Father. These theologians' evangelical signposts point in this personal direction for us.

Jesus lives in a relationship with all humanity. The future finds meaning in what already happened through him. The God of possibilities claimed us. The Father reached out to restore relationship. The Son reconciled the world to live in communion. The Spirit continues to give us breath and life, guiding and whispering that we are loved so we may act in response. We live as trustworthy persons within the gift personally offered to us. Good theology recognizes that a personal relationship with Jesus is not about us in the first place. A personal relationship with Jesus is about having our lives attuned to the heart of God revealed in Jesus, hearing his voice, and being joyfully obedient by his Spirit. Only this good-news gift can be evangelical and bring God's newness to our lives (Rom 2:4).

8

—

TORRANCE AND ATONEMENT

Christopher Woznicki

Among evangelicals, few doctrines have caused as much contention as the doctrine of atonement. The subject of contention has not been whether Christ has made atonement for sins; all agree that "Christ died for our sins in accordance with the Scriptures" (1 Cor 15:3b). Rather, disagreement has focused on the manner in which Christ's death accomplishes atonement and, more specifically, on the mechanism of penal substitutionary atonement (PSA). Questions like "Is PSA the correct model of atonement?" "Should PSA be the predominant model?" "Is PSA the foundational model?" and "Can the gospel be preached without PSA?" have dominated academic and pastoral discussions. Although these questions about PSA are of great importance, these types of questions have regrettably narrowed the discussion of atonement by evangelicals to a small subset of concerns.[1] Atonement is much richer than just penal substitution. As such, discussions about atonement ought to be much richer as well. As evangelicals, shouldn't we wish that our discussions reflect the beauty and breadth of this pillar of our faith? In this chapter, I argue that Thomas F. Torrance's doctrine of atonement can help evangelical theologians articulate richer and deeper accounts of atonement.

In making my argument about the usefulness of Torrance's doctrine of atonement for evangelicals, I begin by making an important distinction

---

1. A sad consequence of the narrowing down of atonement to merely PSA is that while evangelicals have made serious contributions to theology outside of the evangelical tradition in topics like Trinity, Christology, and theological anthropology, the same cannot be said about the doctrine of atonement. There are some exceptions though, see for example: Oliver D. Crisp, *Approaching Atonement: The Reconciling Work of Christ* (Downers Grove: IVP Academic, 2020), and Adonis Vidu, *Atonement, Law, and Justice: The Cross in Historical and Cultural Contexts* (Grand Rapids: Baker, 2014).

regarding atonement; I distinguish between atonement in a narrow sense and broad sense. With this distinction in place, I introduce two foundational convictions that underlie the structure of Torrance's doctrine of atonement, namely, that atonement is a mystery and that the doctrine of atonement should avoid the "Latin heresy." In the following sections, I give an overview of Torrance's doctrine of atonement, showing how the aforementioned convictions shape his account. I conclude by highlighting three areas where evangelicals ought to pay close attention to what Torrance had to say about atonement.

AT-ONE-MENT

What is atonement? Moral philosopher Linda Radzik writes that "atonement" is "the action of setting at one, or condition of being set at one, after discord or strife ... the etymology of 'atonement' is 'at-one-ment.' "[2] Eleonore Stump builds upon Radzik's explanation by highlighting its theological import. She explains, "'Atonement' is a word that was devised to express the idea that *at-one-ment* is a making one of things that were previously not one, namely, God and human beings."[3] Atonement on this construal is a broad concept. It refers to the at-one-ment of God and fallen human beings; on its own, the term does not provide a theory or model of how God and fallen human beings are set at one. Yet, despite the fact that atonement is a broad concept, in contemporary literature, atonement is "frequently taken narrowly to mean just making things right with God by means of Christ's crucifixion and death."[4]

Stump is not unique in noticing that there is a broad and narrow sense of atonement. Fred Sanders writes that "atonement" can be used specifically "to pick out the paschal work of Christ," in other words, Christ's death and resurrection.[5] Atonement can also be used in a broader sense, which not only includes the salvation accomplished by the incarnate Son but "also the application of that salvation to believers by the Holy Spirit."[6] Atonement, in the narrower sense described by Sanders, is the work of the triune God which

---

2. Linda Radzik, *Making Amends: Atonement in Morality, Law, and Politics* (Oxford: Oxford University Press, 2009), 6.

3. Eleonore Stump, *Atonement* (Oxford: Oxford University Press, 2018), 15.

4. Stump, *Atonement*, 7.

5. Fred Sanders, "Wesleyan View," in *Five Views on the Extent of Atonement*, ed. Adam Johnson (Grand Rapids: Zondervan, 2019), 157.

6. Sanders, "Wesleyan View," 157.

terminates upon the Son and has special reference to the cross. Atonement, in the broader sense, is a work of the triune God that describes the at-one-ment of God and fallen humans but which terminates upon the Son and the Holy Spirit.

The distinction highlighted by Stump and Sanders is important because, for the most part, contemporary evangelicals have limited the doctrine of atonement to one aspect of Christ's work, namely, the work of the cross. If evangelicals are keen on providing richer and deeper accounts of atonement, then we will need to expand our understanding of what we mean by atonement. In light of this, I suggest the following distinction:

Atonement Narrowly Conceived: The work of the triune God, mainly the work appropriated to Christ—especially his passion and death—that is part of setting fallen human beings at one with God.

Atonement Broadly Conceived: The entire work of the triune God—especially the work that is appropriated to Christ (i.e., his incarnation, life, death, resurrection, and ascension) and the Holy Spirit—that sets fallen human beings at one with God.

What Christ accomplishes on the cross is just one part of the at-one-ment between God and fallen human beings that is accomplished by the triune God. It is a crucial part of atonement, but it is not the entirety of atonement. By making the distinction between Atonement Narrowly Conceived and Atonement Broadly Conceived, I hope to highlight the fact that atonement is constituted by more than the cross. The accomplishment of at-one-ment between God and humans is a work of Christ that spans the entirety of his life; in an important sense, it is also a work of the Holy Spirit who actualizes the at-one-ment accomplished by Christ. Finally, although atonement is especially appropriated to the Son and to an extent to the Spirit, it is also a work of the Father—for the works of the triune God are undivided—as it is the Father who sends the Son to make at-one-ment.

TWO FOUNDATIONAL CONVICTIONS

Before describing Torrance's doctrine of atonement, it is necessary to describe two convictions that give rise to its structure: (1) atonement is a mystery, and (2) the Latin heresy obscures the nature of atonement.

ATONEMENT IS A MYSTERY

Torrance begins his Edinburgh lectures on atonement by stressing the importance of mystery when approaching the doctrine. As he describes the liturgy of the day of atonement in the Old Testament, he notes that the most important part of the act of atonement is done behind the veil, beyond human sight.[7] He explains, "That inner mystery God ordained to be completely veiled from human eyes: the innermost heart of atonement, its most solemn and awful part, was hidden from public view. It is ineffable."[8] This, Torrance believes, holds special significance for how we understand the atonement accomplished by Christ. Just as atonement in the Old Testament occurred behind the veil and beyond the sight of those for whom atonement was accomplished, Jesus enters behind the veil of God's immediate presence, acting as our high priest and mediator. As such, Christ's work was done "beyond the view of human kind—the nature of his work was unutterable."[9] This observation leads Torrance to believe that "the innermost mystery of atonement and intercession remains mystery: it cannot be spelled out, and it cannot be spied out."[10] Atonement is a mystery "more to be adored than expressed."[11]

That atonement is a mystery more to be adored than expressed does not mean that one cannot—or should not—speak of atonement. For Torrance, the mystery of atonement means that one cannot reason, *a priori*, to the fact of atonement in the death of Christ. If one were to be able to reason to atonement from *a priori* principles, then atonement would not actually be a mystery. If the doctrine of atonement cannot be built up from *a priori* principles, how then can one develop a doctrine of atonement? Torrance believes that one can only do so *a posteriori*; one must seek to understand atonement by unfolding its meaning from the way that God has revealed himself to us in salvation history.

The practical import of Torrance's emphasis on mystery is that he repudiates any logical or rational presuppositions that we may bring to the task of interpreting atonement. Rather, the presuppositions that we bring to

---

7. Thomas F. Torrance, *Atonement: The Person and Work of Christ*, ed. Robert T. Walker (Downers Grove, IL and Milton Keynes: IVP and Paternoster, 2009), 2.

8. Torrance, *Atonement*, 2.

9. Torrance, *Atonement*, 2.

10. Torrance, *Atonement*, 2.

11. Torrance, *Atonement*, 2.

atonement must be formed by God's revelation. Abstract principles of justice, punishment, metaphysics, forgiveness, and more, cannot form the basis for a doctrine of atonement, only those principles which are unfolded from God's self-revelation can be used to articulate an account of atonement. The second consequence of Torrance's emphasis on mystery is that Torrance downplays the usefulness of theories of atonement. Although the term "theory" is often used in atonement literature, it is often used imprecisely. A theory of atonement, according to Oliver Crisp, is an "explanation of what we should believe about what did, in fact, obtain in the case of his [Christ's] incarnation, life, death, and resurrection."[12] A theory of atonement is used to "offer a complete account of a given data set."[13] If this is what one means by theory, then it is clear that Torrance is not offering a "theory." As a mystery, atonement is ineffable; by definition, something that is ineffable cannot be comprehended by a "complete account of a given data set." If Torrance does not offer a theory of atonement, then what does he offer?

In *The Trinitarian Faith*, Torrance explains that when we ask what the precise nature of Christ's atoning work was, "we find Nicene theologians regularly falling back upon familiar biblical and liturgical terms like ransom, sacrifice, propitiation, expiation, reconciliation, to describe it, but always with a deep sense of awe before the inexpressible mystery of atonement through the blood of Christ."[14] What these terms reveal is that there is a "coherent pattern governed by an underlying unity in the Person and work of Christ."[15] Thus, there is room in Torrance's framework for adopting biblical and liturgical models of atonement to describe what Christ has done. These models can be put together as conjunctive statements. Once these statements are put together, we end up not with a theory of atonement but with a mysterian account of atonement.[16] That is, a coherent account, which makes use of biblical and liturgical models to describe the work of Christ but which is tempered by an understanding that atonement "remains something

---

12. Oliver D. Crisp, "Methodological Issues in Approaching the Atonement," in *T&T Clark Companion to Atonement*, ed. Adam Johnson (London: Bloomsbury, 2017), 329.

13. Crisp, "Methodological Issues," 329.

14. Thomas F. Torrance, *The Trinitarian Faith: The Evangelical Theology of the Ancient Catholic Church* (Edinburgh: T&T Clark, 1995), 168.

15. Torrance, *The Trinitarian Faith*, 168.

16. On "mysterianism" see Dale Tuggy, "Trinity," in *The Stanford Encyclopedia of Philosophy*, ed. Edward N. Zalta (Winter 2016 edition), http://plato.stanford.edu/entries/trinity/.

ultimately inconceivable and miraculous that we can never master and dominate and so express exactly in our own thought and speech."[17] As we will see below, Torrance's conviction that atonement is a mystery leads him to carefully examine various biblical models of atonement rather than offering a particular theory of atonement.

THE LATIN HERESY AND ATONEMENT

The second conviction that shapes Torrance's doctrine of atonement is that the "Latin heresy" has obscured the doctrine of atonement. According to Torrance, "in Western Christianity the atonement tends to be interested almost exclusively in terms of external forensic relations as a judicial transaction in the transference of penalty for sin from the sinner to the sin-bearer."[18] Torrance sees this way of understanding humanity's predicament and the solution as overly juridical. Furthermore, he sees the Western tradition as operating with an external rather than internal solution. Torrance deems this "gospel of external relations," where Christ's passion is understood in juridical terms as a transaction between Christ and the rest of humanity, the "Latin heresy."[19] In the Latin heresy, the incarnation becomes instrumental. It is a means rather than an end. Furthermore, the external understanding of the gospel does not address what Torrance thinks is one of humanity's major predicaments, namely alienation before God in both mind and will.

According to Torrance, the human mind is perverse. It is ignorant and requires labor to learn truth in a sin-darkened world.[20] It is subject to temptation.[21] It is diseased and stands in enmity and violence against God's reconciling love, turning God's truth into lies.[22] Not only is the mind in need of healing, the will stands in opposition to God's will and needs healing as well.[23]

---

17. Thomas F. Torrance, *Incarnation: The Person and Life of Christ*, ed. Robert T. Walker (Downers Grove, IL and Milton Keynes: IVP and Paternoster, 2008), 83. Torrance is referring to the mystery of incarnation, but given Torrance's understanding of the relationship between incarnation and atonement, the application of this quote is appropriate.

18. Thomas F. Torrance, *The Mediation of Christ* (Colorado Springs: Helmers & Howard, 1992), 40.

19. See Thomas F. Torrance, "Karl Barth and the Latin Heresy," *SJT* 39 (1986): 461–82.

20. Thomas F. Torrance, *Theology in Reconstruction* (Grand Rapids: Eerdmans, 1965), 13?

21. Torrance, *Incarnation*, 112.

22. Torrance, *The Mediation of Christ*, 39–40.

23. Torrance, *The Mediation of Christ*, 28.

If the human predicament were merely juridical, then it could be dealt with through a merely extrinsic solution. But Torrance is convinced that the human predicament is internal, and thus an external gospel is inadequate. If the fallen minds and wills of humans are to be healed, then God will have to take on the human mind and will and deal with it from the inside-out. Christ will have to assume human nature as it stands after the fall—with its fallen and depraved mind and will—because that which is not assumed is not healed—in other words, "what God has not taken up in Christ is not saved."[24] The internal solution will need to address the problem of the mind and will, problems that are ontological rather than merely forensic.

How does this bear upon the structure of Torrance's account of atonement? It reveals that Torrance attempts to avoid the Latin heresy—a gospel of external relations—at all costs. As Torrance explains, "the work of atoning salvation does *not* take place *outside* of Christ, as something external to him, but takes place *within* him, *within* the incarnate constitution of his Person as Mediator."[25] Elsewhere he says that "we must think of atoning reconciliation as accomplished *within* the incarnate constitution of the Mediator and not in some *external* transactional way between himself and mankind."[26] What this means is that it is impossible to articulate an account of atonement apart from an account of incarnation. The incarnation itself is redemptive; it "belongs to the inner heart of the atonement."[27] An account of atonement that does not give place to the incarnation as an atoning action will end up providing a merely moral or legal account of atonement and ignore the actual state of affairs between God and man. Such an account would not address the existential predicament of fallen human beings, and so a mere gospel of external relations—one built upon the Latin heresy—does not, in fact, promise good news. In the following section, we will see the role that the incarnation plays in Torrance's account of atonement as a "gospel of internal relations."

---

24. Torrance, *The Mediation of Christ*, 39.
25. Torrance, *The Trinitarian Faith*, 155 (italics in the original).
26. Torrance, "Karl Barth and the Latin Heresy," 475 (italics in the original).
27. Torrance, *The Trinitarian Faith*, 159.

INCARNATION AND TORRANCE'S
DOCTRINE OF ATONEMENT

"*Christ Jesus IS the atonement.*"[28] For Torrance, it is appropriate to describe Christ himself as the atonement because Christ does not simply make atonement; rather, atonement is made in Christ's person, not just his work. Torrance says,

> Atonement is something done ... within the ontological depths of the Incarnation, for *the assumption of the flesh by God in Jesus Christ is itself a redemptive act* and of the very essence of God's saving work. This takes place, not in some impersonal way, but in an intensely personal and intimate way within the incarnate Lord and his coexistence with us in our fallen suffering condition as sinners. *Incarnation is thus intrinsically atoning, and atonement is intrinsically incarnational.*[29]

The notion that atonement is intrinsically incarnational can be illustrated by examining the initial union and the continuous union of human and divine natures in Christ.

ATONEMENT AND THE INITIAL UNION OF
HUMAN AND DIVINE NATURES IN CHRIST

If Christ is to bring God and humans to a state of at-one-ment, Christ will need to redeem, heal, and sanctify human nature. To do this, Torrance believed, Christ had to assume human nature as it stood after the fall. Otherwise, that which is not assumed is not healed. Thus, Christ's assumption of fallen human nature is part of Christ's atoning work.

Recall that humanity suffers from ontological, not merely juridical, problems. Concerning the depraved human mind, Torrance says, "It is the alienated mind of man that God has laid hold of in Jesus Christ in order to redeem it and effect reconciliation deep within the rational center of human beings."[30] Concerning the will, Torrance says, "From within our alienation and in battle against our self will," Christ casts himself "in utter reliance upon God the

---

28. Torrance, *Atonement*, 94 (italics and capitalization in the original).

29. Thomas F. Torrance, "Dramatic Proclamation of the Gospel: Homily on the Passion of Melito of Sardis," in *Greek Orthodox Theological Review* 37 (1992): 155. (Italics in the original.)

30. Torrance, *The Mediation of Christ*, 39.

Father."[31] Christ prays, "Not my will (that is not the will of the alienated humanity which Jesus made his own), but thy will be done."[32] From within our own humanity, Christ offers "perfect filial obedience ... from within man's alienated life."[33] Torrance argues that to accomplish this kind of redemption, Christ needed to assume our fallen humanity.

For Torrance, the notion that a fallen human nature is assumed for the sake of at-one-ment between God and humanity is the logical entailment of the *non-assumptus* principle (i.e., what is not assumed is not healed). In a recent essay, however, Ian McFarland has challenged Torrance's use of the *non-assumptus* principle. He claims that to appeal to the principle as a ground for claiming that Christ had a fallen human nature is to misunderstand Gregory Nazianzen's famous maxim: "the unassumed is the unhealed."[34] He says that Gregory was concerned with the assumption of a *whole* human nature. If Christ did not have a human mind, then he had not assumed humanity in its fullness. McFarland argues that having a mind is an *essential* part of being human but having a fallen mind is merely a *contingent* part of being human. Thus, Gregory was concerned with the completeness (the essential parts) rather than the quality (the contingent aspects) of Jesus's humanity. This may be true of Gregory's concerns; still, it does not invalidate Torrance's use of the principle. Torrance appeals to the assumption of a fallen nature because he repudiates a gospel of external relations. Atonement has to be worked out from *within* Christ. In the case of humanity's corrupted mind and will, the healing of both features will have to occur *within* Christ or else they cannot truly be healed. To use a medical analogy, someone with malaria can only be healed of malaria if that person actually has malaria. Similarly, a fallen mind and will can only be healed if the person being healed actually has a fallen mind and will. Therefore, if fallen human nature is to be healed, then the one in whom the healing occurs must have a fallen human nature. Without Christ's assumption of a fallen human nature, human nature remains unhealed. Thus, "the whole man [in its essential and contingent properties] had to be assumed by Christ if the whole man is to

---

31. Torrance, *Atonement*, 117.

32. Torrance, *Atonement*, 118.

33. Torrance, *Atonement*, 118.

34. Ian McFarland, "Fallen or Unfallen? Christ's Human Nature and the Ontology of Human Sinfulness," *IJST* 10 (2008): 406.

be saved ... the unassumed is the unhealed ... what God has not taken up in Christ is not saved."[35]

Upon assuming fallen human nature, Christ sanctifies it. Thus, Torrance says, "in the very act of assuming our flesh, the Word sanctified it and hallowed it, for the assumption of our sinful flesh is itself atoning and sanctifying."[36] When the Son's divine nature is united to a fallen nature—or made at-one—the divine nature is not defiled by the fallen human nature. Rather, it sanctifies what has been marred and unites it again to the purity of God.[37] In *Theology in Reconstruction*, Torrance explains, "In his holy assumption of our unholy humanity, his purity wipes away our impurity, his holiness covers our corruption, his nature heals our nature."[38]

Summarizing Torrance's understanding of the role that the initial act of incarnation plays in atonement, we can say that he believes that in assuming a fallen human nature, the divine nature of the Son heals and sanctifies human nature. This act of at-one-ment between the divine nature and the fallen human nature has salvific effects that apply objectively to humanity. The healing union that is affected by the incarnation does not simply open up the possibility of sanctifying individuals' human nature. There is an objective sanctification of all those who possess a human nature in virtue of the Son's assumption of human nature.[39]

ATONEMENT AND THE CONTINUOUS UNION OF
HUMAN AND DIVINE NATURES IN CHRIST

The incarnation is a once-and-for-all at-one-ment act of God and man. The incarnation, however, is also a continuous union between God and man that is "carried all the way through our estranged state under bondage in freedom and triumph of the resurrection."[40] In treating the atoning role of Christ's

---

35. Torrance, *The Mediation of Christ*, 39.

36. Torrance, *Atonement*, 63.

37. Torrance, *Atonement*, 100.

38. Torrance, *Theology in Reconstruction*, 155–56.

39. See James Cassidy, "T. F. Torrance's Realistic Soteriological Objectivism and the Elimination of Dualisms: Union with Christ in Current Perspective," *Mid-America Journal of Theology* 19 (2008): 171, and Christopher Woznicki, "The One and the Many: The Metaphysics of Human Nature in T. F. Torrance's Doctrine of Atonement," *Journal of Reformed Theology* 12 (2018): 103–26.

40. Torrance, *Incarnation*, 96.

life, Torrance stresses that for atonement to occur in a way that does not fall prey to a gospel of external relations, it must occur *in* Christ over the whole course of his life from birth to death. In his consideration of the continuous union of divine and human nature in Christ, Torrance stresses that there are certain key moments in Christ's life that have special atoning significance for the rest of humanity. These key moments are grouped together under the notion of the "vicarious humanity of Christ."

What does Torrance mean by the "vicarious humanity of Christ"? Depending on the particular context of "vicarious," it can track with the concepts of "substitution," "representation," or "solidarity with."[41] Torrance's understanding of the concept, however, cannot be thought of as simply employing one or the other of these concepts of vicariousness. Torrance's understanding of the vicarious humanity of Christ includes both representative and substitutionary ideas. Kye Won Lee accurately explains Torrance's understanding of vicarious humanity and its relation to the gospel of external relations. He says, "If Christ acts for us only as our representative, then this would mean that Jesus is only our leader representing our act of response to God. If Jesus simply acts as a substitute in our place in an external-formal-forensic way, then his response would be 'an empty transaction over our heads' with no ontological relation to us."[42] How then should we define Torrance's doctrine of the vicarious humanity of Christ? Andrew Purves describes this doctrine by saying that Torrance "saw Christ's humanity not merely as exemplary but rather as through and through substitutionary, in which the covenant between God and humankind was entirely completed in him and by him for us."[43] Similarly, Christian Kettler explains that according to the doctrine of vicarious humanity, "Christ's humanity is not simply that which we imitated but is vicarious, on our behalf and in our place."[44] He elaborates upon this point, explaining that,

---

41. Donald Macleod, *Jesus Is Lord: Christology Yesterday and Today* (Fearn: Christian Focus, 2000), 133.

42. Kye Won Lee, *Living in Union with Christ: The Practical Theology of Thomas F. Torrance* (New York: Peter Lang, 2003), 163. Lee refers to Torrance, *The Mediation of Christ*, 79–98.

43. Andrew Purves, *Exploring Christology and Atonement: Conversations with John McLeod Campbell, H. R. Mackintosh, and T. F. Torrance* (Downers Grove, IL: InterVarsity Press Academic, 2015), 11.

44. Christian Kettler, *The God Who Rejoices: Joy, Despair, and the Vicarious Humanity of Christ* (Eugene, OR: Cascade Books, 2010), xv.

Jesus Christ is both the representative and substitute for my humanity. He represents my humanity before God the Father, having taken my humanity upon himself, bringing it back to God from the depths of sin and death. ... He is the substitute in my place, doing in my stead, what I am unable to do: live a life of perfect faithfulness to, obedience to, and trust in God. "Vicarious" at its heart means doing something for another in their stead, doing something that they are unable to do.[45]

The entirety of Christ's vicarious life is an atoning act, but there are several distinct moments in that act.[46] These key moments include (among others) Christ's baptism, repentance, adoration, praise, joy, suffering, confession, struggle with temptation, faith, obedience, faith, ministry, prayer, sanctification, death, and resurrection. To treat the atoning significance of each of these moments is beyond the scope of one chapter. However, I should highlight the atoning significance of several of these moments.

Consider Christ's baptism. Torrance says that "the truth of our baptism is lodged in Jesus Christ himself and all that he has done for us within the humanity he took from us and made his own, sharing to the full what we are that we may share to the full what he is."[47] Kevin Chiarot argues that "this understanding of the baptism of Jesus, and by implication, Christian baptism rests on the ontological foundation of the assumption of our fallen nature."[48] Chiarot's interpretation of the ontology of baptism is confirmed by Torrance's claim that baptism "was His identification in the body of his flesh with the whole mass of sin and death. By his Baptism He made Himself one with us all."[49]

Consider also Christ's vicarious acts of repentance and confession. Torrance states that Christ must be recognized as "acting in our place in all the basic acts of man's response to God: in faith and repentance, confession,

---

45. Christian Kettler, *The God Who Believes: Faith, Doubt, and the Vicarious Humanity of Christ* (Eugene, OR: Cascade Books, 2005), 6.

46. See the chapter titled, "The Atonement and Oneness of the Church" in Thomas F. Torrance, *Conflict and Agreement in the Church: Volume I Order and Disorder* (Eugene, OR: Wipf & Stock, 1996), 238–49.

47. Torrance, *The Trinitarian Faith*, 294.

48. Kevin Chiarot, *The Unassumed Is the Unhealed: The Humanity of Christ in the Christology of T. F. Torrance* (Eugene, OR: Pickwick, 2013), 175.

49. Torrance, *Conflict and Agreement in the Church*, 241.

penitence, sorrow, chastisement, and submission to divine judgement."[50] Elsewhere Torrance says that Christ "confesses our sin and submits perfectly to God, restoring mankind to oneness with God, both in regard to life and in regard to mind."[51] As an individual, Christ turns away from sin, bending back the wayward will of man into submission to the will of God. Christ also confesses humanity's propensity to sin, though Christ himself is not guilty of sin. Because Christ has performed these actions, humanity is said to have vicariously repented and confessed in Christ.

Consider also Christ's vicarious faith. Torrance explains that Christ takes "our place at every point where human beings act as human beings and are called to have faith in the Father."[52] Torrance is unambiguous about whom Christ's faith and obedience count for; Christ stands "in the place of Adam and all mankind," that is, he "stood in the gap created by man's rebellion and reconciled men and women to God by living the very life he lived in the perfection of obedience."[53] Thus, for Torrance, Christ's obedience has an atoning significance. Christ's obedience is actually ours. It does not stand external to us; instead, it is genuinely ours because of Christ's relationship to humanity. Christ has had faith as an individual; thus, humanity is said to have had faith vicariously in Christ.

Finally, consider Christ's death and resurrection. Torrance explains that "Christ's death for all mankind means that all men and women are already involved. ... Christ died for them when they were yet sinners, and in that he died, all died."[54] Christ's vicarious action on humanity's behalf also applies to the resurrection. According to Torrance, the resurrection is the sign that the union between the human and divine nature has held. At the cross, the union is almost destroyed, but at the resurrection, this union is permanently forged. Thus, after the death of Christ, human and divine natures are forever united in him. At-one-ment is accomplished by Christ for all human beings. Christ was baptized, repented, confessed, had faith, obeyed, died, and rose

---

50. Thomas F. Torrance, *Theology in Reconciliation: Essays towards Evangelical and Catholic Unity in East and West* (Grand Rapids: Eerdmans, 1976), 136.

51. Torrance, *Atonement*, 76.

52. Torrance, *The Mediation of Christ*, 82.

53. Torrance, *Incarnation*, 123.

54. Torrance, *Atonement*, 128. This, Torrance insists, does not entail universalism.

from the dead as an individual; his actions as an individual have an effect on all those who possess a human nature.[55]

SUMMARY

Myk Habets elegantly summarizes how atonement is accomplished through the once-and-for-all union of God and man in Christ, as well as the continuous union in Christ. He explains:

> The saving act of God in Christ was internal to the incarnate Son before it could be applied externally. ... Throughout the life of the incarnate Son the atoning exchange is made once and for all as human nature is taken up and given a place in God and thus grounded in his eternal unchangeable reality. ... In the incarnate person of the Son an ontological atonement has been perfectly accomplished—God and humanity have been reconciled once and for all.[56]

By assuming a fallen human nature, Christ sanctifies it, making at-one-ment between the divine nature and human nature. Moreover, Christ's entire life is one of atoning significance. What he does as an individual is done vicariously for the sake of all human beings. Christ's atoning work is not something that is external to him; rather, Christ's atoning work is done within Christ himself. Christ himself is the atonement; in Christ, God and humans are put at-one. For Torrance, any account of atonement in terms of external relations does not capture the heart of atonement. Failing to address how atonement has been accomplished *in Christ* would mean falling into the trap of the Latin heresy. In the next section, we will see how Torrance adopts biblical motifs and models of atonement to describe what Christ has done. We will note how these models can be put together as conjunctive statements to develop a mysterian account of atonement.

---

55. For an in-depth account of how Christ's vicarious humanity affects every human being and the metaphysics that underlie such an account see Woznicki, *The One and the Many*, 117–26.

56. Myk Habets, *Theosis in the Theology of Thomas Torrance* (Farnham: Ashgate, 2009), 56.

TORRANCE'S "NO-THEORY"
ACCOUNT OF ATONEMENT

Recall that a theory attempts to provide a complete account of a given data set. Given Torrance's emphasis on mystery, it is impossible for him to provide a theory of atonement in this technical sense of theory. But what about a model of atonement? A model "is a simplified account of complex data that is not the sober truth of the matter, but which is an approximation to the truth."[57] A model of atonement, thus, "attempts to represent in a simplified form something of the complexity of the saving work of Christ, which is beyond the complete explanation of any one account of the atonement."[58] There are good reasons for thinking that Torrance *could* develop a model of atonement. After all, a model emphasizes complexity and the approximation to truth; these features fit well with Torrance's emphasis on mystery. However, we should hesitate to say that Torrance provides a model of atonement since he does not attempt to provide *one* manner in which Christ's work provides atonement. The term "model" is still too comprehensive; it implies that all the data can fit neatly into one scheme.[59] Torrance is more comfortable speaking of atonement in terms of various biblical images and motifs rather than models of atonement. These various images can then be put side by side to reveal that they are held together by the union of God and man in Christ. Torrance explains:

> In seeking to unfold the meaning of the death of the Son, therefore, we must have recourse to putting together conjunctive statements based upon the inherent synthesis to be found in the person of the mediator and not in any logical or rational presuppositions which we bring to interpret what Christ has done for us.[60]

What are the images and motifs that, when put together, form Torrance's account of atonement?

---

57. Crisp, *Approaching Atonement*, 25.

58. Crisp, *Approaching Atonement*, 25.

59. This does not mean that advocates for models of atonement do not recognize the need for various models of atonement.

60. Torrance, *Atonement*, 4.

OLD TESTAMENT IMAGERY

The first set of images and motifs come from the Old Testament. Torrance is adamant about the permanent value of the structures of biblical thought and speech found in the Old Testament for theological reflection. He explains that the Old Testament provides "the New Testament revelation with the basic structures which it used in the articulation of the gospel."[61] These patterns and structures are transformed and imbued with new significance in Christ, nevertheless one cannot understand who Christ is and what he does apart from the Old Testament. Without the Old Testament, atonement remains an enigma; even his crucifixion would not be interpreted as an atoning sacrifice for sin.[62]

Three Hebrew word-groups dominate Torrance's discussion of the Old Testament atonement: *pdh, kpr,* and *g'l. Pdh* speaks of the "mighty act of God bringing deliverance from oppression, as in the redemption of Israel out of Egypt and the house of bondage, and from the power of death."[63] This aspect of redemption emphasizes that there is a high cost to be paid through the substitutionary life of one for another for the sake of setting someone free. *Kpr* has to do with "the expiatory form of the act of redemption, the sacrifice by which the barrier of sin and guilt between God and man is done away, and propitiation is effected between them."[64] Finally, *g'l* refers "to a concept of redemption out of destitution or bondage or forfeited rights undertaken by the advocacy of someone who is related to the person in need through kingship or some other bond of affinity or covenant love."[65] While each of these concepts of redemption remain distinct, they overlap with one another. For example, Torrance notes that all three concepts are used to speak of the redemption of Israel from Egypt. Additionally, they are used in Isaiah to speak of the suffering servant.[66]

The three Old Testament motifs are adopted and adapted to speak of Christ's work by the New Testament authors: "they are all taken for granted and are found woven together in the apostolic understanding and

---

61. Torrance, *The Mediation of Christ*, 18.
62. Torrance, *The Mediation of Christ*, 19.
63. Torrance, *The Trinitarian Faith*, 170.
64. Torrance, *The Trinitarian Faith*, 170.
65. Torrance, *The Trinitarian Faith*, 171.
66. Torrance, *The Trinitarian Faith*, 171.

presentation of the vicarious life and death of Christ." The concept represented by *pdh* describes Christ's work of overcoming the powers of darkness
and setting God's people free from the bondage of guilt and sin; it corresponds
to the dramatic aspect of atonement.[67] The concept of *kpr* is emphasized in
the New Testament by the notion that the ultimate ground for forgiveness
is God alone; it corresponds to the ritual-forensic aspect of atonement.[68] *G'l*
places a stress upon the nature of our redeemer and our kinship with him; it
stresses the ontological aspect of atonement.[69] These themes are also taken
up by the early church. Torrance explains that these concepts are found
in the history of the church, making their way into early Christian liturgy,
especially concerning the Eucharist, various theories of atonement, and the
Reformed notion of the *triplex munus*.[70]

JUSTIFICATION, REDEMPTION, RECONCILIATION

Another three word-groups dominate Torrance's discussion of atonement
in the New Testament. The first of these concerns justification. This aspect
of atonement emphasizes righteousness in terms of law and freedom from
bondage to the law. He argues that the adjectival form of the Hebrew word
for righteousness, *tsadiq*, primarily means "to be in the right with God," and
its causative form, *hitsdiq*, means "to put in the right with God."[71] In the New
Testament, *dikaiosynē* and its cognates carry a double meaning as well; they
can mean to judge or condemn in order to put right (justify or rectify), or
they can mean to deem right (justify as to declare right).[72] Torrance explains
that when God puts someone in the right, he reveals his own righteousness.
However, God's righteousness only comes to its fulfillment in human confession of God's righteousness or acknowledgment of it and obedience to it.
Justification, therefore, requires two agents: God, who justifies and reveals
his righteousness, and humanity, who acknowledges and confesses God's
righteousness. Justification, from the side of God and the side of humanity,
occurs in Christ. In Christ, humanity acknowledges its sinfulness. In Christ,

---

67. Torrance, *Atonement*, 53.

68. Torrance, *Atonement*, 53.

69. Torrance, *Atonement*, 53.

70. Torrance, *The Trinitarian Faith*, 172; Torrance, *Atonement*, 56, 59.

71. Torrance, *Atonement*, 100.

72. Torrance, *Atonement*, 101.

God judges humanity as sinful and puts it in the right, thereby revealing his own righteousness. At the same time, in his individual humanity, Christ offers up perfect obedience and faithfulness to God. Finally, in Christ, God deems humanity as being in the right. Thus, upon the cross, Jesus is the judge and the judged one upon the cross.

In addition to the forensic aspect of justification, Torrance speaks of atonement in relational terms as the act of recreating the bond of union between God and humanity—in other words, at-one-ment. This second aspect of atonement is reconciliation. Torrance argues that "reconciliation stresses the fact that God came down to our estate in order to assume fellowship with himself, to the effect that such a oneness between the sinner and God, that the sinner is exalted to share with God in his own divine life."[73] How does this happen? In Christ, in virtue of the hypostatic union, we have the turning of God to humanity and the turning of humanity to God. However, unlike other human beings, Christ "lives his life in perfect oneness [at-one-ment] with God, so achieving the reconciliation of God to humanity and of humanity to God."[74]

The final word group that Torrance focuses on is redemption. This word is a comprehensive term regarding salvation through justification, expiation, and reconciliation in Christ. It is eschatological and teleological. It is the consummation of God's redeeming purposes in the new creation. By looking at various Greek words related to redemption—e.g., *lutron, luo,* and *lutrosis*—he suggests that "redemption is the mighty act of God's grace delivering us out from the power of darkness and into the glorious liberty of the sons and daughters of God."[75] In Christ, humanity is redeemed from the power of darkness, the law, and the bondage of sin.

A NO-THEORY ACCOUNT OF ATONEMENT

The Edinburgh lectures provide a veritable biblical theology of atonement. By carefully examining Greek and Hebrew terms used in relation to atonement, as well as engaging Israel's history as narrated in Scripture, Torrance holds on to the manifold images and metaphors that are used to describe

---

73. Torrance, *Atonement,* 145.

74. Torrance, *Atonement,* 228.

75. Torrance, *Atonement,* 177.

atonement. Yet, one would be hard-pressed to find a theory or a model of atonement in these lectures. What emerges instead is a pattern that underlies these various images and motifs. The pattern, simply put, is that all we can say about atonement must be said in light of the hypostatic union: the at-one-ment of God and man in Christ. As Torrance explains, "The various aspects of atoning mediation ... reveal a coherent pattern governed by an underlying unity in the Person and work of Christ."[76] In other words, there is no theory of atonement. Christ just is the atonement.

ENRICHING EVANGELICAL ACCOUNTS OF ATONEMENT

How might Torrance's doctrine of atonement help stimulate evangelical theologians toward articulating richer and deeper accounts of atonement? I suggest three areas of Torrance's account that evangelical theologians ought to pay careful attention to.

THE ENTIRETY OF CHRIST'S LIFE HAS ATONING SIGNIFICANCE

"Without the cross, there would be no possibility of a company of forgiven, redeemed people joyfully celebrating their salvation."[77] The cross is of utmost importance to Christians; without it, there would be no Christians to speak of. Joel Green and Mark Baker state this point succinctly: "No cross, no Christianity."[78] Yet, despite the fact that Christ crucified is so central to the Christian faith, it is not the entirety of Christ's salvific work. Above I highlighted a distinction between Atonement Narrowly Conceived and Atonement Broadly Conceived. Evangelicals, in general, excel at speaking about atonement and the cross—that is, Atonement Narrowly Conceived. Donald Macleod's book, *Christ Crucified*, serves as a prime example of how Atonement Narrowly Conceived can overshadow Atonement Broadly Conceived. Toward the beginning of the book, Macleod offers the following caveat, "A word of caution is needed here, however. The centrality of the cross must not beguile us into ignoring a second striking feature of the story of the passion: the

---

76. Torrance, *The Trinitarian Faith*, 168.

77. Stephen R. Holmes, *The Wondrous Cross: Atonement and Penal Substitution in the Bible and History* (London: Paternoster, 2007), 1.

78. Mark Baker and Joel Green, *Recovering the Scandal of the Cross*, 2nd ed. (Downers Grove, IL: InterVarsity Press Academic, 2011), 19.

cross was but the climax of Jesus' sufferings. His whole life, from the cradle to the tomb was suffering."[79]

Even though Macleod offers this warning, he minimizes Christ's life to merely the suffering leading to the cross. Christ's life is simply a prelude—an important one, but a prelude nonetheless—to the cross. Macleod offers just one example of this trend among evangelical accounts of atonement. Crisp himself notes that "many Christians think that the life and ministry of Christ are preconditions for the atonement, not part of the atonement."[80] He compares the tendency to think of the work of Christ in terms of the performance of a stage actor. Some think that memorizing lines and rehearsals are merely preliminaries for the final performance. All the work that goes into performing on opening night is important, but it isn't part of the performance itself; it is a prerequisite to the actual performance. Likewise, Christ's birth, baptism, obedience, miracles, faith, prayers—among other moments in Christ's life—are not part of the performance of atonement; instead, they are prerequisites—albeit important ones—to the actual goal: the performance on the cross. Crisp, however, notes that this is not the only way to think of the life of a stage actor. He explains that "the disciplined formation and rehearsal taken together with the different professional performances are parts of one entire vocation, the vocation of acting."[81] Memorizing lines and rehearsing are just as essential to the part of acting as the performance itself. Likewise, we might want to say that birth, baptism, obedience, miracles, faith, prayers, and more, are part of the entire performance of atonement. Yes, the cross is the climax of that performance—without the cross, the performance would be incomplete—but the other parts constitute the performance as well.

A shift in thinking about Christ's life and work as a *prelude* to the performance versus thinking of his life and work as *part* of the performance would help evangelical theologians and pastors to put themselves in closer continuity with the early church. Irenaeus, for example, gave us his well-known doctrine of recapitulation in which Christ came to "recapitulate all things," becoming "a man amongst men, visible and palpable, in order to abolish

---

79. Donald Macleod, *Christ Crucified: Understanding the Atonement* (Downers Grove, IL: InterVarsity Press Academic, 2014), 16.

80. Crisp, *Approaching Atonement*, 19.

81. Crisp, *Approaching Atonement*, 19.

death, to demonstrate life, and to effect communion between God and man."[82] Similarly, Athanasius presents an account of Christ's work in which Christ's actions as an individual stand in the place of all other human beings, acting vicariously on our behalf.[83] The list of early church figures who think of the entirety of Christ's life—and not just the cross—as constituting at-one-ment between God and humans is long. James Payton notes this point saying, "The cross is always at the center of attention in patristic teaching about salvation. It is not the whole of salvation, of course: the incarnation, the last Adam, and the resurrection are closely interrelated with it. Even so, the cross is focal."[84]

Torrance's account of atonement, I suggest, is ripe for the picking when it comes to evangelicals who want to recover a broader account of Christ's atoning work. As we have seen, Torrance places a heavy emphasis on the fact that the incarnation has an at-one-ing effect.[85] According to Torrance, the once-and-for-all union of God and man in Christ that occurred at the moment of incarnation redeems, heals, and sanctifies human nature. Torrance's understanding of the incarnation's relation to atonement can help us to fulfill Gregory Nazianzen's injunction to "adore the birth by which you were loosed from the chains of your birth."[86] Additionally, Torrance's conception of the vicarious humanity of Christ can help us to fill out the meaning of Atonement Broadly Conceived, all the while emphasizing the importance of the cross as the place where divine judgment occurs.

THE MYSTERY OF ATONEMENT

Torrance's account of atonement can also help us recover the sense of mystery that ought to accompany thinking about this doctrine. A brief survey of recent books on atonement published by evangelical presses reveals that mystery does not have much place in an evangelical discussion of atonement. The term appears only once in the otherwise comprehensive book, *The Glory*

---

82. Irenaeus, *On the Apostolic Preaching*, trans. John Behr (Crestwood: St. Vladimir's Seminary Press, 1997), section 6.

83. Athanasius, *On the Incarnation*, trans. John Behr (Yonkers: St. Vladimir's Seminary Press, 2011), section 9.

84. James R. Payton Jr., *The Victory of the Cross: Salvation in Eastern Orthodoxy* (Downers Grove, IL: InterVarsity Press Academic, 2019), 89.

85. This put Torrance firmly in line with patristic teachings. See Payton, *The Victory of the Cross*, 77–78.

86. Gregory Nazianzen, *Oration* 38:17.

of the Atonement, and even then, it is only brought up to make a point of how much we can comprehend this mystery.[87] Mystery appears once in Oliver Crisp's, *Approaching Atonement*, where he notes that atonement is "one of the central *mysteries* of the Christian faith."[88] The term can be found seven times in the index of Joshua McNall's, *The Mosaic of Atonement*. But in those seven times, it refers to atonement twice, speaking of the mystery of the Trinity, and evil the other five times. When it does refer to atonement, McNall uses the term mystery to describe the puzzling nature of atonement once, and the other time he explains the role that mystery and mechanism ought to play in atonement theology.[89] McNall's belief that "mystery and mechanism must 'kiss' within atonement doctrine,'" is not frequently articulated by other evangelicals.[90] This should not be the case.

Evangelicals would do well to reread James I. Packer's classic essay, "What Did the Cross Achieve: The Logic of Penal Substitution." There Packer writes that mystery" should be foundational to how we approach atonement.[91] Like Torrance, who claimed that atonement is a mystery more to be adored than expressed, Packer worries that some Reformed theologians made atonement out to be "more like a conundrum than a confession of faith—more like a puzzle, we might say, than a gospel."[92] The methodological difference that mystery makes for articulating a doctrine of atonement, Packer explains, is significant. It means that all the parables, analogies, and images used in Scripture point to a reality, but that the models used to describe the reality of atonement are "like the nondescriptive models of the physical sciences," they "have an analogical character."[93] Packer summarizes his lengthy discussion of the role of mystery in atonement theology by saying, "If we bear in mind that all the knowledge we can have of atonement is of a mystery about which we can only think and speak by means of models, and which remains

87. Richard Gaffin, "Atonement in the Pauline Corpus," in *The Glory of the Atonement*, ed. Charles E. Hill and Frank A. James III (Downers Grove, IL: InterVarsity Press Academic, 2004), 155.

88. Crisp, *Approaching Atonement*, 10 (italics in original).

89. Joshua McNall, *The Mosaic of Atonement* (Grand Rapids: Zondervan, 2019), 83, 140.

90. McNall, *The Mosaic of Atonement*, 141.

91. A mystery, Packer explains, is "a reality distinct from us that in our very apprehending of it remains unfathomable to us," J. I. Packer and Mark Dever, *In My Place Condemned He Stood* (Wheaton, IL: Crossway, 2007), 57.

92. Packer and Dever, *In My Place Condemned He Stood*, 55.

93. Packer and Dever, *In My Place Condemned He Stood*, 62.

a mystery when all is said and done, it will keep us from rationalistic pitfalls and thus help our progress considerably."[94]

The rest of his essay articulates a model of PSA tempered by mystery. Thus, even with an emphasis on mystery, models and mechanisms can still have a place in atonement theology. Torrance, I argued earlier, does not give us a *theory* of atonement. Nevertheless, he shows us how various images from Scripture and history, when understood through the lens of the hypostatic union, allow us to present an account of atonement that is "confessional rather than explanatory."[95] Torrance, like Packer, can help evangelicals recover the doxological and methodological importance that mystery can have on the doctrine of atonement.

PENAL SUBSTITUTIONARY ATONEMENT

Torrance provides an account of atonement that captures the penal and substitutionary elements of atonement while rejecting versions of PSA that lend themselves to easy critique. Torrance explains that the priestly element of Christ's work "involves the notion of propitiation in which God turns away from his wrath to man in forgiveness and man is turned away from rebellion to draw near to God."[96] How is propitiation effected? Torrance says, "It is initiated and carried through by God, but by God from the side of God towards humanity and from the side of humanity towards God. God *himself* draws near—*he* propitiates himself."[97] This is done *in* Christ, in virtue of the fact that Christ is God and bears human nature itself. How does Christ accomplish this? By bearing the judgment that sin deserved. Torrance explains, "The wrath of God is removed only when his righteous will has punished sin and judged it" and that Christ takes "on himself the penalty due to all in death."[98] This is the penal element of atonement. Moreover, Torrance explains, Christ "took into himself and upon himself the righteous wrath of the divine love and freed us from receiving the stroke of the divine condemnation which we could not have endured, for under it we could only have been destroyed."[99]

---

94. Packer and Dever, *In My Place Condemned He Stood*, 64.

95. Purves, *Exploring Christology and Atonement*, 238.

96. Torrance, *Atonement*, 72.

97. Torrance, *Atonement*, 68.

98. Torrance, *Atonement*, 154; Torrance, *The Trinitarian Faith*, 157.

99. Torrance, *Atonement*, 154.

This is the substitutionary element of atonement. Torrance summarizes his understanding of something *like* PSA when he explains, "Christ bore in his physical existence and in the infliction of death on him the just judgment of God upon our sin."[100] Why then should we hesitate to say that Torrance affirms penal substitution as a model of atonement? The answer lies in how penal substitution has been historically conceived.

PSA theorists, for the most part, understand law as the fundamental reality of atonement.[101] Torrance's critique of this model is that it reduces the God-human relation to moral and legal relations, which are impersonal and external. Recall, Torrance emphasizes the personal and internal nature of atonement.[102] Because of this, atonement cannot involve an external penalty being transferred onto Christ, who acts as a substitute external to the ones whom he is making atonement for. Torrance's version of penal and substitutionary atonement has Christ stand as a substitute for humanity not because of a merely legal relation with humanity but because of an ontological bond with every human being. Moreover, a penalty is not imputed to Christ or transferred onto him. Rather, as the one who bears human nature itself and stands in ontological union with all human beings, he rightfully bears God's judgment for humanity's sins. Torrance's understanding of penal and substitutionary atonement deserves careful consideration from evangelicals who want to affirm penal substitution. It avoids the common objection against most models of penal substitution that guilt cannot be transferred.[103] However, it relies on an understanding of human nature in which Christ somehow bears the human nature of all humanity. This seems to imply an account of human nature where "humanity is essentially one—that there is a universal human nature in which individuals participate in."[104] For some, this metaphysical notion will be too exotic to seem plausible. Regardless of whether one is convinced by the metaphysics that underlie his account of atonement, the fact that Torrance provides a way to affirm penal and substitutionary

---

100. Torrance, *Atonement*, 69.

101. Stephen R. Holmes, "Penal Substitution," in *T&T Clark Companion to Atonement*, ed. Adam Johnson (London: Bloomsbury, 2017), 295.

102. James Denny, another Scottish theologian, makes a similar point. See, *The Atonement and the Modern Mind* (London: Hodder & Stoughton, 1911), 271.

103. See Crisp, *Approaching Atonement*, 109–11.

104. Benjamin Myers, "The Patristic Atonement Model," in *Locating Atonement*, ed. Oliver D. Crisp and Fred Sanders (Grand Rapids: Zondervan, 2015), 120.

elements of atonement while circumventing the guilt-transference objection shows that his account of atonement deserves further consideration.

CONCLUSION

My burden in this chapter has been to demonstrate that Torrance's doctrine of atonement can help stimulate evangelical theologians toward the articulation of richer and deeper accounts of atonement. Torrance, I have suggested, helps us to see how Christ's life—and not just his death—is atoning, that atonement is a mystery more to be adored than expressed, and that emphasizing the personal and internal aspects of penal substitution can help evangelicals avoid common objections against the doctrine. It should go without saying that evangelicals need not accept everything Torrance had to say about atonement. Still, I am convinced that engaging with him as a dialogue partner will enrich any attempt to spell out the good news of Christ's atoning work. This is something that every evangelical pastor and theologian should be eager to do.

9

—

TORRANCE AND CHRIST'S ASSUMPTION OF FALLEN HUMAN NATURE

Toward Clarification and Closure[1][*]

Jerome Van Kuiken

INTRODUCTION

A good barometer for a doctrine's interest to evangelicals is its coverage in the flagship American evangelical periodical *Christianity Today* (*CT*). The November 2019 issue of *CT* included an article on Christ's humanity by British evangelical theologian Oliver Crisp. The article allows that Christ may have had "a fallen human nature" while remaining sinless.[2] The very next month, *CT* published an online article in which Daniel Cameron, an adjunct professor at evangelical stronghold Moody Bible Institute, defended the same general position. Ironically, Cameron's article quotes an older essay of Crisp's in order to rebut it.[3] Crisp's older essay had opposed "the fallenness view"

---

1. [*] This is a revised and slightly altered version of "Sinless Savior in Fallen Flesh? Toward Clarifying and Closing the Debate," *Journal of the Evangelical Theological Society* 64 (2021): 327–40.

2. Oliver D. Crisp, "Tempted in Every Way? Making Sense of Jesus' Humanity in Light of Fleshly Temptations," *Christianity Today* (November 2019): 74.

3. Daniel J. Cameron, "What It Means that Jesus Was 'Without Sin,' " *Christianity Today*, December 5, 2019, https://www.christianitytoday.com/ct/2019/november-web-only/what-it -means-that-jesus-was-without-sin.html. Cameron quotes from Oliver D. Crisp, "Did Christ Have a *Fallen Human Nature?*," *IJST* 6 (2004): 270–88; repr. in his *Divinity and Humanity: The Incarnation Reconsidered* (Cambridge: Cambridge University Press, 2007), 90–117. See Daniel J. Cameron, *Flesh and Blood: A Dogmatic Sketch Concerning the Fallen Nature View of Christ's Human Nature* (Eugene, OR: Wipf & Stock, 2016) for a fuller rebuttal.

as compromising Christ's sinlessness. Now further study of the issue has led him to concede that fallenness and sinlessness need not be contraries in Christ's case.[4]

These two *CT* articles represent the popular-level tip of an iceberg in recent scholarship and debate on the question, "Did Christ become incarnate in a fallen or unfallen human nature?"[5] While Karl Barth is the most prominent name associated with the fallenness view, Thomas F. Torrance played a preeminent role in mediating Barth's view to English language Christian theology through coediting the English translation of Barth's *Church Dogmatics* and his own consistent advocacy of the fallenness view. My purpose in this essay is to address the concerns of Torrance's fellow evangelicals about the fallenness view, particularly as he articulated it, and then offer a way forward in the controversy.[6]

QUESTIONING FALLENNESS: SIX CONCERNS

For a summary of these concerns, I engage with the half-dozen objections to the fallenness view in Stephen Wellum's volume on Christology in Crossway's Foundations of Evangelical Theology series.[7] Wellum is my selected interlocutor for three reasons. First, he lays out the case against the fallenness view concisely yet comprehensively. Second, his volume may be fairly considered a contemporary standard for evangelical articulation of the classically

4. For a slightly earlier statement of Crisp's developing position, see Oliver D. Crisp, "On the Vicarious Humanity of Christ," *IJST* 21 (2019): 235–50.

5. The sources cited throughout this chapter merely sample the extensive scholarly literature on this issue. For a bibliography of the debate in 1991–2015, see E. Jerome Van Kuiken, *Christ's Humanity in Current and Ancient Controversy: Fallen or Not?* (London: Bloomsbury T&T Clark, 2017), 1–2nn1, 4–6. For additional contributions, see Crisp, "Vicarious Humanity," 236–37nn2–4; Christopher G. Woznicki, "'Begin at the Beginning': Method in Christological Anthropology and T. F. Torrance's Fallen Human Nature View," *Perichoresis* 19 (2021): 21–41, https://www.sciendo.com/article/10.2478/perc-2021-0009.

6. A further controversy may be whether Torrance ought to be classed as an evangelical since, e.g., he did not subscribe to a Warfieldian doctrine of biblical inerrancy. I concur with the Tyndale Fellowship, which includes Torrance in its publication, Robert T. Walker, "Thomas F. Torrance," in *British Evangelical Theologians of the Twentieth Century*, ed. Thomas A. Noble and Jason S. Sexton (London: Apollos, 2022), 197–219.

7. Stephen J. Wellum, *God the Son Incarnate: The Doctrine of Christ* (Wheaton, IL: Crossway, 2016), 232–35 (hereafter abbreviated as *GSI*). All but the third and fourth of these arguments (as enumerated below) reappear in Stephen J. Wellum, *The Person of Christ: An Introduction*, Short Studies in Systematic Theology (Wheaton, IL: Crossway, 2021), 159–61.

orthodox doctrine of Christ.[8] Third, Wellum is himself a bridge-builder between dispensationalism and covenant theology and so models in ecclesiology and eschatology what I hope to achieve in Christology.[9] So as not to strike an unhelpfully adversarial pose, I reframe Wellum's objections below as questions that may be legitimately put to the fallenness view. I also sequence them in reverse order of Wellum's presentation, beginning with theology and ending with Scripture. Since theological presuppositions tend to color one's reading of Scripture, these will be addressed first. To these questions we now turn.

1. *Does not the assumption of a fallen nature necessarily violate Christ's sinlessness?* As Wellum puts it, "A fallen incarnation *requires* that Christ is sinful or has the property of original sin."[10] The issue here is fundamentally one of definition. Consider the following distinctions:

1.   a. *Moral versus amoral effects of the fall.* While denying that Christ sinned or possessed the moral corruption of original sin brought on by the fall, orthodox theologians acknowledge that Christ suffered from the fall's amoral effects, such as grief, weariness, prolonged hunger, opposition by enemies and even neighbors and family members, desertion by friends, a sense of godforsakenness, and the emotional and physical agonies of dying.[11] Some who apply the language of "fallenness" to Christ use that term to refer to his being subject to these amoral effects even without sinning or possessing original sin. As Crisp writes in his *CT* article, "So perhaps Jesus can have a fallen human nature, provided we mean by that a human nature that feels the effects

---

8. Regarding these first two reasons, it is worth noting that Wellum's objections all appear in an earlier standard evangelical Christology, Donald Macleod's *The Person of Christ, Contours of Christian Theology* (Downers Grove, IL: InterVarsity Press, 1998), chap. 9, on which Wellum relies.

9. Notably in Peter J. Gentry and Stephen J. Wellum, *Kingdom through Covenant: A Biblical-Theological Understanding of the Covenants*, 2nd ed. (Wheaton, IL: Crossway, 2018).

10. Wellum, *GSI*, 235 (emphasis mine).

11. These effects are "amoral" in that they do not automatically signal the moral status of the one who suffers them (e.g., grief afflicts both the godless and the godly). Another term for them is "innocent infirmities."

of the fall—a bit like someone who may have flu-like symptoms even if she does not actually have the flu."[12]

2. b. *Assumption from versus assumption to.* The statement that "Christ assumed a fallen human nature" contains an ambiguity. It may refer to the condition *out of which* Christ assumed it or to the condition *into which* he assumed it. Although Torrance applies fallenness language to Christ's humanity, he also claims that the act of assumption was a sanctifying act that cleansed a formerly morally corrupt human nature, bringing it into a state of perfect holiness through union with the all-holy Savior. Torrance puts this claim succinctly and forcefully: "In the very act of taking our fallen Adamic nature the Son of God redeemed, renewed and sanctified it AT THE SAME TIME. ... The only human nature which our Lord HAD, therefore, was utterly pure and sinless."[13]

The pre-assumption impurity and sinfulness of the human nature that became Christ's may be thought of in two ways: first, if Christ's individual human nature is in view, then its corruption is only *logically*, not *chronologically* prior to its sanctifying assumption by the Word. That is, because his individual human nature is simultaneously conceived, assumed, and hallowed, we may make hypothetical but not temporal distinctions between these three aspects of the incarnation. Christ's humanity *would*

---

12. Crisp, "Tempted in Every Way," 74. Compare Crisp, *Divinity and Humanity*, 115–16. Here the key difference between his earlier and later views is not in substance but simply in terminology: the later Crisp is willing to apply the term "fallen" to Christ's innocent infirmities in a postlapsarian world.

13. Thomas F. Torrance, "Christ's Human Nature," *The Monthly Record of the Free Church of Scotland* (May 1984): 114 (capitalization his). Torrance is replying to editor Donald Macleod, "Did Christ Have a Fallen Human Nature?," *Monthly Record* (March 1984): 51–53. See also Thomas F. Torrance, *Incarnation: The Person and Life of Christ*, ed. Robert T. Walker (Downers Grove, IL and Milton Keynes: IVP and Paternoster, 2008), 61–64, 201, 231–32. This latter work and Thomas F. Torrance, *Atonement: The Person and Work of Christ*, ed. Robert T. Walker (Downers Grove, IL and Milton Keynes: IVP and Paternoster, 2009) together compose Torrance's Edinburgh Christology lectures, his most sustained, comprehensive treatment of the doctrine of Christ. In the interest of brevity, I shall draw heavily on these lectures in my coverage of Torrance's Christology. For additional support from other works of Torrance's, see the passages from Van Kuiken, *Christ's Humanity*, cited below.

have been sinful were it not sanctified by the hypostatic union.[14] Second, Torrance typically has in view how the incarnation relates to human nature in general.[15] From Genesis 3 onward, the Bible depicts humanity as corrupted by sin in every generation. It is this common, corrupt human nature that God the Son lays hold of in the incarnation and assumes into purifying union with himself, operating inseparably from the Holy Spirit's overshadowing of Mary.[16] The indivisible working of the creative Word and Spirit does not generate the Son's humanity *ex nihilo* but from Mary's own human substance, tainted as it is by the fall.[17] No prior immaculate conception of the virgin herself is necessary in order to shield Christ from original sin. On this understanding of Christ's sanctifying union with human nature, the statement, "Christ assumed a fallen human nature" carries the same implication as "Christ touched a leper"—in

---

14. Crisp, "Vicarious Humanity," 237–47, set forth this view without adopting it himself. (At this stage in the development of his thought, he still equated all fallenness with sinfulness.) See also R. Michael Allen, *The Christ's Faith: A Dogmatic Account* (London: T&T Clark, 2009), 130n105, who does adopt this view. More recently, he has come to recognize the same distinction between assumption "from (*a quo*)" and assumption "of and unto (*ad quem*)" that I have articulated above. See R. Michael Allen, "Christ," in Keith L. Johnson and David Lauber, eds., *T&T Clark Companion to the Doctrine of Sin* (London: Bloomsbury T&T Clark, 2016), 463. Allen still equates all fallenness with sinfulness, however.

15. Failure to account properly for this point leads to no end of confusion when reading Torrance. When he speaks of Christ's lifelong conflict with "our" depraved mind and perverse will and with the power of sin indwelling "our" flesh, Torrance does *not* mean that Christ's own human mind, will, and flesh were corrupted by sin throughout his earthly life; rather, he means that within the corporate mass of corrupt human nature, Christ's own personal humanity stands as a sanctified exception that conflicts with the sin infecting the rest of humanity. See Van Kuiken, *Christ's Humanity*, 31–42, esp. 38–40, which rebuts the faulty Torrance interpretation of, among others, Peter Cass, *Christ Condemned Sin in the Flesh: Thomas F. Torrance's Doctrine of Soteriology and Its Ecumenical Significance* (Saarbrücken, Germany: Dr. Müller, 2009); and Kevin Chiarot, *The Unassumed Is the Unhealed: The Humanity of Christ in the Theology of T. F. Torrance* (Eugene, OR: Pickwick, 2013).

16. Crisp, "Vicarious Humanity," 248–49, defends the consonance of the Son's sanctifying assumption of fallen human nature with the doctrine of inseparable operations. By contrast, Bello, "That Which Is Not Assumed," chap. 4, deploys a Thomistic account of inseparable operations to refute Barth's and Torrance's fallenness Christology. Unfortunately, Bello does not discuss Barth's and Torrance's own coverage of inseparable operations in chaps. 2 (Barth) and 3 (Torrance) of his volume, resulting in an apples-to-oranges comparison.

17. Wellum, *GSI*, 239 accepts that Christ is Adam's descendant while insisting that "the Holy Spirit created and sanctified the human nature that the Son assumed in his incarnation. And what God creates is very good—holy, pure, and uncorrupted." Torrance would concur.

both cases, rather than the Holy One being defiled, the defiled is made whole.[18]

The two sets of distinctions above may be combined in a complementary manner: Christ assumed his human nature from a humanity marked by both the moral and amoral effects of the fall. He sanctified it upon assumption so that within the hypostatic union it no longer had the moral effects of the fall and so was not "fallen" in the strongest sense. Still, it continued to be liable to the amoral effects of the fall until Christ's resurrection and so may be said to remain "fallen" in the weaker sense. Throughout his earthly life, at every stage of his human development, Christ had to preserve his perfect purity in the teeth of the temptation, weakness, ignorance, and suffering that are characteristic of fallen humanity, thus sanctifying that developmental stage. In this way his human nature could be fallen yet sinless.

2. If Christ's human nature was fallen, is not Nestorianism implied?[19] If Christ was sinless in person yet fallen in his human nature, then how are we to avoid a self-divided Savior whose holy, divine mind and will are locked in constant combat with a corrupt human mind and will? At best, such a scenario suggests a Romans 7–style split between the inner "I" who delights in God's law and the sin-dominated flesh that resists it. At worst, it suggests a Nestorian model of two independent persons or agents within a composite Christ. For an example of this implication, Wellum quotes nineteenth-century fallen-ness advocate Edward Irving.[20]

This charge has some validity when pressed against Irving. The Church of Scotland found him guilty of heresy and defrocked him for teaching "that in Christ there was the law of sin and death, which the law of the Spirit of life did ever prevail against ...; and that the thing spoken of in the holy Scriptures as holiness, is nothing else than the putting down of the law of sin and death in the members, by the law of the Spirit of life in the mind."[21] Irving's doc-

---

18. Torrance, *Atonement*, 440–41, draws this comparison.

19. Wellum, *GSI*, 235.

20. Wellum, *GSI*, 235n71.

21. This is his own summary of his view, as found in Edward Irving, *Christ's Holiness in Flesh, the Form, Fountain Head, and Assurance to Us of Holiness in Flesh* (Edinburgh: John Lindsay, 1831), 38–39. On 42–44, he notes and qualifies his habit of applying Romans 7:17 to Christ.

trine posits too sharp a divide between Christ's person and human nature, compromising his sinlessness with concupiscence.[22]

It is a mistake, however, to read Irving's idiosyncratic heterodoxy into other theologians' support for a fallenness view. For instance, while Barth cites Irving as a predecessor for his own fallenness Christology, it is only by way of secondhand, cursory acquaintance and without adopting the details of Irving's position.[23] Torrance early on critiques Irving while later citing him as a predecessor.[24]

Neither Barth nor Torrance portray Christ as perpetually suppressing corrupt desires, as Irving does. True, Barth claims that Christ "stepped into the heart of the inevitable conflict between the faithfulness of God and the unfaithfulness of man. He took this conflict into His own being. He bore it in Himself to the bitter end. He took part in it from both sides. He endured it from both sides."[25] But Barth immediately proceeds to deny that Christ was ever resistant to his Father.[26] Rather, he submitted to his Father's will that he, God the Son, associate with sinners, stand in solidarity with sinners, and endure punishment as a sinner, while also enduring the enmity of sinners against himself as the Holy One.[27] This, then, is the conflict that Christ bears in his theanthropic being: as human, he is the judged (by both God and humanity) while as God, he is the judge. Torrance concurs, taking a special interest in Christ's emotional and mental life within this conflict and the additional demonic opposition against him.[28] Barth's and Torrance's accounts avoid Irving's attribution to Christ's humanity of culpable impulses to sin.[29]

---

22. Michael Paget, "Christology and Original Sin: Charles Hodge and Edward Irving Compared," *Churchman* 121 (2007): 236–43; Van Kuiken, *Christ's Humanity*, 13–21, 156–57.

23. Barth briefly lists Irving along with several other nineteenth-century fallenness proponents in *Church Dogmatics* (*CD*) I/2, 154–55. On the significance (or rather, insignificance) of this fact for Barth's own position, see William Duncan Rankin, "Carnal Union with Christ in the Theology of T. F. Torrance" (PhD thesis, University of Edinburgh, 1997), 101, 249–57, esp. 249–50n50.

24. Rankin, "Carnal Union," 101–103 (incl. 103n235), 119; Andrew Walker, "The Angel of Regent Square," BBC Radio 4, December 1, 1984, 00:16:52–00:30:44. (Thanks to Richard McIntosh for calling my attention to this latter source.)

25. Barth, *CD* II/2, 397.

26. Barth, *CD* II/2, 397–98; see also *CD* IV/1, 269–71.

27. Barth, *CD* I/2, 152, 172; II/1, 152; III/2, 47–48; IV/1, 94–96, 165–66, 175, 216–24, 237, 239, 258, 552–53; IV/2, 92.

28. Torrance, *Incarnation*, 136–51, 231–56; Torrance, *Atonement*, 69–70, 75–167, 209–19, 437–47.

29. Van Kuiken, *Christ's Humanity*, 21–42, 161–63.

Theological progress depends on discerning not only the distinct use of terms between fallenness and unfallenness theologians but also the significant differences among fallenness theologians themselves.

3. *Does the patristic slogan "the unassumed is the unhealed" refer to Christ's* fallen *humanity or merely his full humanity?* To support his view of Christ's sanctifying assumption of a fallen human nature, Torrance appeals to Gregory Nazianzen's dictum Τὸ ... ἀπρόσληπτον, ἀθεράπευτον ("the unassumed is the unhealed"), sometimes abbreviated as the *non-assumptus*.[30] Wellum notes this appeal but disputes Torrance's interpretation. Nazianzen's statement comes from a letter in which he opposes Apollinarianism, the heresy that Christ did not assume a human mind. Wellum concludes, "At stake was whether Christ had a full human nature [i.e., mind as well as body], not whether that nature was fallen."[31]

This alternative interpretation of Nazianzen is correct in what it affirms but not in what it denies. The key question is, "*Why* did the Apollinarians deny that Christ took on a human mind?" Part of their concern was metaphysical coherence. A person with two minds, they believed, would be schizophrenic.[32] But the Apollinarians also had a soteriological rationale: they saw the human mind as the source of sin and so wished to preserve Christ's sinlessness by quarantining him from such a mind. Likewise, Apollinaris was alleged to hold that Christ brought his human body down from heaven—once again, in order to avoid any contamination by sinful flesh. Salvation, then, was a matter of our emulating an otherworldly role model.[33] Against the Apollinarian effort to maintain the Savior's sinlessness by buffering him from sinful human nature, the point of the *non-assumptus* is that it was precisely by his contact with human nature in its fullness *and* fallenness—mind and body, warts and all—that Christ could heal our nature from the inside out. Salvation came not by a splendid yet isolated exemplar but by one who, in

---

30. Gregory of Nazianzus, *Epistulae* 101.5 (PG 37:182c), quoted in Torrance, *Incarnation*, 62, 201, and *Atonement*, 441.

31. Wellum, *GSI*, 235.

32. Nazianzus, *Epistulae* 101.6–7.

33. (Pseudo[?]) Athanasius, *Contra Apollinarem*. 1.2, 7, 20; 2.1, 3, 6, 8, 11 (Jacques-Paul Migne, ed., *Patrologia Graeca* [Paris: Imprimerie Catholique, 1857–186] 26; see also Gregory Nyssen, *Antirrheticus adversus Apolinarium* (Werner Jaeger, *Gregorii Nysseni Opera* [Leiden: Brill, 1958] 3.1, 129–233).

Nazianzen's words, "was actually subject as a slave to flesh, to birth, and to our human experiences [πάθεσι]; for our liberation, held captive as we are by sin, he was subject to all that he saved."[34]

Nor was Nazianzen unique in this conviction. Athanasius interprets Philippians 2:7, with its language of Christ's "taking the form of a slave [δούλου]," as "putting on the enslavement [δουλωθεῖσαν] of the flesh to sin."[35] Yet rather than the Word being blemished by the flesh, he sanctified and freed it by assuming it.[36] Likewise, Nazianzen's Cappadocian colleague Gregory of Nyssa teaches, "But the apostolic word testifies that the Lord was *made into sin for our sake* [2 Cor 5:21] by being invested with our sinful nature."[37] Yet Nyssen also clearly asserts Christ's freedom from sinful deeds and desires.[38]

In commenting on John 1:14, Cyril of Alexandria echoes Nazianzen's dictum: "For what is not assumed, neither is saved [ὃ γὰρ μὴ προσείληπται, οὐδὲ σέσωσται]."[39] He describes the incarnation as "having the fallen body [τοῦ προσπεσόντος σώματος] united in an ineffable manner with the Word that endows all things with life."[40] Elsewhere he explains that "it was vital for the Word of God ... to make human flesh, subject to decay [ὑπενηνεγμένην τῇ φθορᾷ] and infected with sensuality [νοσήσασαν τὸ φιλήδονον] as it was, his own."[41] Given Cyril's status as the church father who first identified and

---

34. Gregory of Nazianzus, *Oration* 30.6 (Migne, *Patrologia Graeca* 36:109c); English Translation: Saint Gregory of Nazianzus, *On God and Christ: The Five Theological Orations and Two Letters to Cledonius*, trans. Frederick Williams and Lionel Wickham, Popular Patristics (Crestwood, NY: St Vladimir's Seminary Press, 2002), 97. On the significance of πάθος in Nazianzen's thought, see Christopher A. Beeley, *Gregory of Nazianzus on the Trinity and the Knowledge of God: In Your Light We Shall See Light*, Oxford Studies in Historical Theology (Oxford: Oxford University Press, 2008), ix–x.

35. Athanasius, *Or.* 1.43; Greek: William Bright, *The Orations of St. Athanasius Against the Arians* (Oxford: Clarendon, 1873; facsimile by Ann Arbor, MI: University Microfilms International, 1978), 45; ET mine.

36. Athanasius, *C. Ar.* 1:46–50; 2:47, 55–56, 61, 72; *Epict.* 4, 9.

37. Gregory of Nyssa, *Vit. Moys.* 2.33; ET: Gregory of Nyssa, *The Life of Moses*, trans. Abraham J. Malherbe and Everett Ferguson, The Classics of Western Spirituality (New York: Paulist, 1978), 62 (italics original).

38. See the evidence compiled by J. H. Srawley, "St Gregory of Nyssa on the Sinlessness of Christ," *JTS* 7.27 (1906): 434–41, as well as its assessment in Van Kuiken, *Christ's Humanity*, 118–22.

39. Cyril of Alexandria, *In Jo. Ev.*, John 1:14 (PG 74:89cd); ET mine.

40. Cyril of Alexandria, *In Jo. Ev.*, John 1:14 (PG 73:160c); ET Norman Russell, *Cyril of Alexandria*, The Early Church Fathers (London: Routledge, 2000), 105.

41. *First Letter to Succensus* 9 in Cyril of Alexandria, *Select Letters*, ed. and trans. Lionel R. Wickham, Oxford Early Christian Texts (Oxford: Clarendon, 1983), 78–79 (Greek on 78; ET on 79). As noted by T. A. Noble, *Holy Trinity: Holy People: The Theology of Christian Perfecting* (Eugene,

fiercely opposed Nestorianism as a heresy, it would be quite odd if Cyril himself were accused of Nestorianism over his teaching of a fallenness Christology!

In sum, there is patristic support for the view that Christ assumed human nature out of a fallen, even sinful state but sanctified it upon assumption so that it was thoroughly sinless through its union with him.[42] The church fathers who teach this view see it as vital for our salvation. Contemporary theologians will benefit by close, contextualized readings of these fathers of orthodoxy.

4. Does Christ need a fallen human nature in order to be truly tempted? and 5. Does Christ need a fallen human nature in order to be truly human?[43] These concerns may be addressed together. It is certainly the case that in the Genesis account, Adam and Eve were both truly, sinlessly human and subject to temptation prior to the fall.[44] It is also the case that the saints in glory are truly, sinlessly human yet presumably no longer liable to temptation. Strictly speaking, then, neither a fallen nor even a temptable condition is essential to being human. The real question is whether one's account of Christ's humanity fits with the particular stage in salvation history in which we find ourselves. Consider a counterfactual example: if Christ were to have become incarnate in first-century Judea but in a glorified human nature incapable of pain, death, or temptation, he still would have been technically human but likely

---

OR: Cascade, 2013), 191, the term φιλήδονον is literally "love of pleasure" and so, in context, refers to bodily pleasures generally. Wickham's translation "sensuality" might be mistaken as referring narrowly to sexual lust.

42. For an alternative interpretation of the church fathers, see Emmanuel Hatzidakis, *Jesus: Fallen? The Human Nature of Christ Examined from an Eastern Orthodox Perspective* (Clearwater, FL: Orthodox Witness, 2013). Hatzidakis's tome attempts to refute contemporary fallenness Christology but suffers from a superficial reading of the patristic evidence. His own view is essentially aphthartodocetic: Christ's humanity was so fully deified from conception onward that he was unable to experience temptation or even normal human development in any existentially meaningful sense, while his sufferings and death were apparently miraculous due to the natural impassibility and immutability of his flesh.

43. Wellum, *GSI*, 233–34.

44. The relationship of the early chapters of Genesis, the traditional doctrine of the fall, and current scientific accounts of human origins involves debates of its own. A recent primer is James B. Stump and Chad V. Meister, eds., *Original Sin and the Fall: Five Views*, Spectrum Multiview Books (Downers Grove, IL: InterVarsity Press Academic, 2020). My arguments should stand even if one were to view the original prelapsarian state as a purely symbolic, ahistorical ideal.

would have seemed inhuman to his afflicted Jewish compatriots. Indeed, christological views that approximate this hypothetical example (such as docetism, Eutychianism, and aphthartodocetism) were declared heresies by the early church. Our redemption depends on a redeemer who not only has all the proper ontological equipment (human mind, will, and body) but who has enough experiential solidarity with us to be effective as our representative before God.

Torrance's Edinburgh Christology lectures stress the agony Christ faced throughout his earthly life as he contended with temptation, disease, human and demonic opposition, and finally the godforsakenness of Golgotha.[45] Manifestly, Christ experienced all this in a fallen world and in solidarity with sinners, not in a paradisiac state isolated from the wicked and the wounded. Furthermore, Christ experienced all this not in a generic or *ex nihilo* or Platonically ideal human nature but in one assumed from the fall-stained line of Adam. Only in this way could he serve as a sinless yet sympathetic mediator. For these reasons, fallenness theologians like Torrance apply the term "fallen" to Christ's humanity.

On the other side of the debate, unfallenness theologians do not dispute the severity or non-Edenic environs or mediatorial significance of Christ's temptations, nor his lineage from sinners. When they deny that Christ was tempted or inherited a fallen state, they mean that his internal state was not one of personal guilt or moral corruption.[46] We have noted above how Torrance and Barth have concurred with this sentiment by denying that Christ struggled with sinful concupiscence during his earthly life. Yet Christ still suffered from the amoral effects of the fall. Proponents of the fallenness view take this fact as warrant for speaking of Christ's experience of a fallen

---

45. Torrance, *Incarnation*, 132–51, 231–56; Torrance, *Atonement*, 69–70, 75–167, 209–19, 437–47.

46. Wellum, *GSI*, 233: "Christ does not partake of the corrupted Adamic nature. Jesus [is] not 'in Adam' as we are, and thus he is not fallen. The New Testament acknowledges that Christ fully entered into the human condition, thus exposing himself to this fallen world." Crisp, *Divinity and Humanity*, 115–16: "Christ's sinless nature was affected by the Fall without actually being fallen" inasmuch as he "possessed the symptoms and effects of being sinful in terms of moral and physical weakness, without himself possessing the sinful human nature that gives rise to these effects." Macleod, *Person of Christ*, 229 (reformatted): Christ was in neither a fallen state nor a paradisiac state nor his presently glorified state but in a state of humiliation: "He was liable to all the miseries of this life; he was vulnerable to all its darker emotions; he was destined to lose communion with God; and he was mortal. But why? Not because he was fallen, but because, prompted by love, he freely chose to suffer with the fallen and, at last, to suffer *for* the fallen."

state. When they hear other theologians using the language of unfallenness to describe Christ's state amid temptation, it strikes them as rhetorically and conceptually relocating Christ to Eden and posting cherubim with a flaming sword to barricade him from solidarity with us.[47] Each side hears in the other's language innuendos that the other does not intend. Those in both the fallenness and unfallenness camps must listen carefully to one another, keeping in mind the slipperiness even of shared terms, so as to make theological headway.

6. *Does the Bible support fallenness Christology?* Wellum focuses on Paul's statements, interpreted in the same manner as Gregory Nazianzen's:

> Pauline expressions such as "born in the likeness of men" (Phil. 2:7), "being found in human form" (Phil. 2:8), and "in the likeness of sinful flesh" (Rom. 8:3) refer to our common human nature, not our corrupt human nature. ... The Pauline contrast between the first Adam and Christ as the last Adam makes sense only if Christ does not partake of the corrupted Adamic nature.[48]

In approaching these texts, the meaning of the word "likeness" (ὁμοίωμα) is a key consideration. Paul's line in Philippians 2:7 that Christ came "in the likeness of humans" (ἐν ὁμοιώματι ἀνθρώπων) could be taken to mean that Christ was only "human-like" rather than truly human. Such an interpretation would favor docetism. An orthodox understanding of "likeness" here is that it means a *concrete instantiation* of human nature, not a mere semblance of it. The same must be true of Paul's similarly worded claim in Romans 8:3 that Christ came "in the likeness of the flesh of sin" (ἐν ὁμοιώματι σαρκὸς ἁμαρτίας). To insist that "likeness" means "really alike" in Philippians 2:7 but only "somewhat alike" in Romans 8:3 is special pleading. According to Paul, Christ came in the concrete form of the flesh of sin.[49] But Paul does not stop there, and neither should we when making such a jarring claim.

---

47. E.g., Barth, *CD* I/2, 151–55, 189; Torrance, *Incarnation*, 212.

48. Wellum, *GSI*, 233.

49. As Wellum, *GSI*, 232, notes, this is the interpretation favored by C. E. B. Cranfield, *A Critical and Exegetical Commentary on the Epistle to the Romans*, 2 vols., 6th ed., International Critical Commentary (Edinburgh: T&T Clark, 1975), 379. See also Karl Barth, *The Epistle to the Romans*, trans. Edwyn C. Hoskyns (London: Oxford University Press, 1933), 277–82; Barth, *Epistle to the Philippians*, trans. James W. Leitch, 40th anniversary ed. (Louisville: Westminster John

Immediately Paul adds that Christ came in this manner precisely in order to condemn sin in the flesh so that the requirement of righteousness might be fulfilled in us (Rom 8:3–4). This passage in turn parallels 2 Corinthians 5:21, which says that the one who knew no sin was made sin on our behalf so that we might become righteousness in him. So too Galatians 3:13 teaches that Christ became a curse for the sake of our being freed from the curse of the law.[50] Like the church fathers who followed him, therefore, Paul sees his Lord as condescending to the human condition this side of the fall—but with the effect not of becoming corrupted by it but of rectifying it, condemning our sin by his perfect sinlessness and liberating us by his gracious power. In just this way, Christ is the last and greater Adam who more than makes right the first Adam's failure (Rom 5:12–21).

In addition to the Pauline material considered here, we also must glance at the Johannine material. Under our third point above, we found that Cyril of Alexandria read John 1:14 as recounting that Christ took a fallen body. This verse, "The Word became flesh," must be understood in light of the reference in John 1:12 to "the will of the flesh" that God sets aside in birthing his children. Similarly, 1 John 2:16 warns against "the lust of the flesh." For the Word to become flesh, then, is for Christ to assume not a neutral human nature but human nature in its willfulness and weakness. Yet just as Paul insists on Christ's perfect sinlessness, so too does the Johannine literature. Christ is the spotless lamb who bears away the world's sin (John 1:29), the sin-free Son who sets sin's slaves free (John 8:34–36, 46), and the pure one who destroys the devil's works and purifies his own people (1 John 1:7–2:2; 3:3–10). However tainted the human nature that Christ assumed, it became fully holy upon his assumption of it.[51] Just as the church holds together other paradoxes of Scripture like divine sovereignty yet human responsibility, the oneness yet threeness of God, and the deity yet humanity of Christ, so too must it hold together the fallenness yet sinlessness of Christ's flesh.

We have examined a half-dozen legitimate concerns raised by unfallenness proponents about the fallenness view of Christology. In each case we have found that these concerns may be eased by careful interpretation,

---

Knox, 2002), 63; Thomas F. Torrance, *The Doctrine of Jesus Christ* (Eugene, OR: Wipf & Stock, 2002), 109, 121, 123, 164; Torrance, *Incarnation*, 61, 63, 255.

50. Barth, *CD* I/2, 152–55; II/1, 397; IV/1, 165; Torrance, *Incarnation*, 61–62, 199, 255–56.

51. See Torrance, *Incarnation*, 61–65, echoing Barth, *CD* I/2, 151–59 on John 1:14.

whether of modern fallenness advocates like Torrance, the church fathers, or Scripture itself. Simultaneously we have nodded to the conceptual commonality buried beneath both sides' surface-level differences. The next section of this essay will stake out that common ground in more detail and offer a blueprint for building on it.

ENDING THE FALLING OUT: THREE PROPOSALS

Like the legendary land of Oz, the fallenness controversy has its share of straw men and tin ears. Each camp has suffered from caricature and in turn missed the nuances of the other's language and conceptuality. What follows are three measures to assist in resolving the conflict.

1. *Distance Irving.* Edward Irving is an endlessly fascinating figure in the history of Christian thought as a harbinger of modern Spirit Christology, Pentecostalism, pretribulational premillennialism, and fallenness Christology, all charged with the emotional power of his flamboyant rhetoric and life.[52] He is, however, a red herring in the current fallenness debate and an albatross around the necks of more recent fallenness theologians, whether hung there by themselves or their opponents. Rather than trying to rehabilitate him or appealing to him as a protomartyr for the cause, today's fallenness proponents would serve themselves better by following Torrance's early example and distancing themselves from Irving's heterodox stance.[53] Likewise, unfallenness advocates must avoid treating the views of mainstream fallenness

---

52. Several biographies of Irving have been published in the two centuries since his death, the most evenhanded of which is Tim Grass, *The Lord's Watchman*, Studies in Evangelical History and Thought (Milton Keynes: Paternoster, 2011). The others tend toward uncritical hagiography or heresiography.

53. Torrance, *Doctrine of Jesus Christ*, 122. Besides some of his biographers, attempted rehabilitators of Irving include the later Torrance in Walker, "Angel of Regent Square"; Colin Gunton, initially in Colin E. Gunton, "Two Dogmas Revisited: Edward Irving's Christology," *SJT* 41 (1988), 359–76 and often thereafter; Gunton's student Graham W. P. McFarlane, *Christ and the Spirit: The Doctrine of the Incarnation according to Edward Irving* (Carlisle, UK: Paternoster, 1996) and Graham W. P. McFarlane, ed., *Edward Irving: The Trinitarian Face of God*, The Devotional Library (Edinburgh: St. Andrew Press, 1996); James B. Torrance, "The Vicarious Humanity of Christ," in Thomas F. Torrance, ed., *The Incarnation: Ecumenical Studies in the Nicene-Constantinopolitan Creed A.D. 381* (Edinburgh: Handsel, 1981), 141; his student David W. Dorries, *Edward Irving's Incarnational Christology* (Fairfax, VA: Xulon, 2002); and Byung-Sun Lee, '*Christ's Sinful Flesh*': *Edward Irving's Christological Theology within the Context of His Life and Times* (Newcastle upon Tyne, UK: Cambridge Scholars Publishing, 2013).

theologians as warmed-over versions of Irving's doctrine.[54] He simply does not speak for them.

2. *Recognize conceptual commonality while tolerating terminological diversity.* Once Irving's idiosyncratic position is bracketed and we listen to what major representatives of both the fallenness and unfallenness camps *mean* (rather than simply what they *say*), a four-point conceptual consensus emerges:

a. *Human nature outside of Christ.* Both sides agree that human nature as we find it outside of the incarnate Christ exists under the scourge of original sin and all other effects of the fall. This was the condition of Jesus's forebears down to his mother Mary.

b. *Christ's conception.* Both sides concur that while Christ derived his human substance from his mother, that which he derived was cleansed, renewed, or created (*ex virgine*, not *ex nihilo*) so as to mark a decisive break with its morally corrupt condition outside of the hypostatic union.

c. *Christ's afflictions.* Both sides nevertheless affirm that Christ suffered the amoral effects of the fall throughout his earthly sojourn, culminating in his crucifixion.

d. *Christ's sinlessness.* Finally, both sides deny that Christ ever committed sin or experienced the culpability of corrupt concupiscence during his earthly life.[55]

---

54. Donald Macleod is an oft-repeated source of this fallacy. In his *Monthly Record* article, "Did Christ Have a Fallen Human Nature?," he lumped together Irving and Barth. After T. F. Torrance wrote a letter to the editor in rebuttal, Macleod included Torrance along with Barth and Irving as all holding a monolithic view. See, e.g., Donald Macleod, *The Person of Christ*, chap. 9 and *Jesus Is Lord: Christology Yesterday and Today* (Fearn, UK: Mentor, 2000), chap. 5. Macleod's material is cited uncritically by Wellum, *GSI*, 232–35; Allen, "Christ," 462n49; and Crisp, *Divinity and Humanity*, 93 (in light of the preceding material in Crisp and his citation from Macleod). Katherine Sonderegger has made the same error of lumping Irving and Barth in her *Systematic Theology Volume 1, The Doctrine of God* (Minneapolis: Fortress, 2015), 217. To his credit, Bello, "'That Which Is Not Assumed,'" 17, 86–87, acknowledges Barth's and Torrance's differences from Irving.

55. For documentation of this quadrilateral of consensus, see Van Kuiken, *Christ's Humanity*, chaps. 1–2 and pages 163–66.

Given these significant points of overlap, the question arises as to how much the fallenness debate is about matters of substance and how much is merely a quarrel over words. Even in the mid-twentieth century, Torrance's older contemporary Donald Baillie concluded that the conflict centered on the phrases "fallen human nature" and "assumption of human nature," but that it reduced to "an unnecessary and unreal theological dilemma."[56] If so, then the proper response by both sides may well be to hold firmly to the underlying common conceptuality while tolerating variant uses of the same terminology. Consider how the apostle Paul and James the Just apparently clash on whether justification is by faith apart from works or by faith plus works (Gal 3:6–14; Jas 2:14–26), yet agree at the conceptual level.[57] Recall that in the heat of the Arian controversy, Athanasius's *Tome to the Antiochenes* brokered an alliance between parties that used the term *hypostasis* in diverse ways because he discerned beneath the diversity a shared anti-Arian orthodoxy.[58] Perhaps a modern-day tome is overdue to unite fallenness and unfallenness parties against today's real christological heresies.

3. *Revise misleading terminology.* While toleration of differing uses of the same terminology is good, it prolongs a situation in which confusion over wording is a perennial risk. "Fallen" suggests "sinful and enslaved to depravity." "Unfallen" insinuates "still in Eden, isolated from the bulk of biblical history." Both terms are too static to capture well the change in human nature that occurred upon its union with God the Son. A better solution is for both camps to replace the troublesome terms with more precise and less theologically fraught language. During his earthly career, Christ's humanity was less prelapsarian or postlapsarian than *ex*-lapsarian. We may more accurately describe this dynamic reality by speaking of his human nature as "uprighted," "sanctified," "renewed," or "vicarious."[59] Perhaps the time is right to declare

---

56. Donald M. Baillie, *God Was in Christ* (New York: Charles Scribner's Sons, 1948), 17.

57. For a survey of the apparent contradiction between James and Paul and its solution, see P. H. Davids, "James and Paul," in Gerald F. Hawthorne, Ralph P. Martin, and Daniel G. Reid, eds., *Dictionary of Paul and His Letters* (Downers Grove, IL: InterVarsity Press, 1993), 457–61.

58. Athanasius, *Tome to the Antiochenes* 5–6; for context, see John Behr, *The Nicene Faith Part 1: True God of True God*, Formation of Christian Theology vol. 2 (Crestwood, NY: St. Vladimir's Seminary Press, 2004), 95–100.

59. The lattermost of these suggestions is Crisp's preferred term in his "Vicarious Humanity," 235–50.

a moratorium on the terms "fallen" and "unfallen" with respect to Christ's human nature.

CONCLUDING WITH A KISS: ONE FINAL PLEA

This essay has had two aims. First, it has sought to alleviate several characteristic concerns that evangelicals carry with regard to the claim by Torrance and others that Christ assumed a fallen human nature. Second, it has marked out a threefold path past the impasse of impassioned debate over this issue. I now conclude with a parable.

Faulkner prize–winning author and physician Richard Selzer tells of a young woman under his care whose cheek sustained an injury that left one side of her mouth permanently slack. Her husband visits her as she lies in her hospital bed. He surveys his bride's damaged face. Then he leans down to kiss her, carefully holding his own lips awry to conform to the distorted shape of hers. Awed by the husband's loving condescension, Dr. Selzer compares him with a Greek god manifesting as a man. But the good doctor's analogy is too timid. It is Christ's incarnation that the young man's action truly mimes.[60] God Most High has stooped in love, accommodating to our fallen state in order to unite with humanity in a holy kiss—the kiss of peace.

Let us as theologians follow suit, adjusting our argumentation and jargon so far as we can in order to accommodate one another's concerns. By so doing, our distinctions may yet share the kiss of peace.

---

60. Richard Selzer, *Mortal Lessons: Notes on the Art of Surgery*, Kindle ed. (New York: Houghton Mifflin Harcourt, 1987), locs. 415–32. I owe the tying of this tale to the incarnation to Dr. Matt Friedeman.

10

—

TORRANCE, THEOSIS, AND EVANGELICAL RECEPTION

Myk Habets

The doctrine of theosis (synonyms include deification and divinization), the teaching that a human can participate in the divine life in Christ and by the Spirit, became one of the most celebrated doctrines of the twentieth century. The twenty-first century is witnessing a further resurgence of interest in theosis across all the major Christian communions. It is rare to find a work on salvation, eschatology, or theological anthropology that does not make space for a discussion of theosis in some way. Evangelical reception of theosis has been mixed. Evangelicals were some of the first Western thinkers in contemporary theology to advocate for a doctrine of theosis, and many works of theology now feel the need to take a stance on the issue. Evangelicals display both acceptance and reticence over theosis. Those that accept theosis typically use it as a theme as opposed to a comprehensive doctrine, and in this way, pay lip service to it, allowing it to garnish their already established theology. Others reject theosis and repeat familiar, if lazy, caricatures of the doctrine as a way to dissuade its popularity. Thomas F. Torrance is one of the few Protestants to utilize a doctrine of theosis in an architectonic way. Torrance offers evangelicals resources for their own ressourcement of theosis. When fully understood, theosis acts as a powerful way to testify to the glory of God and the mystery of salvation.

EVANGELICAL RECEPTION OF THEOSIS

The Western reception of theosis is now established to the point where it is nonsense to say deification is an Eastern doctrine or the exclusive possession of Byzantine theology. It is firmly established that theosis is a biblical concept that is found throughout the New Testament and it is this fact that accounts for the unanimous Patristic reception of the concept. Theosis has been examined in Western thinkers throughout history, including Tertullian, Cyprian, Novatian, Hilary of Poitiers, Ambrose, Jerome, Augustine, Leo the Great, Boethius, and others in the early church.[1] Theosis was no less prevalent in Latin medieval Christianity, in figures as representative as John Scottus Eriugena[2] and Thomas Aquinas,[3] and it is found within Protestant Reformers and their successors, including Martin Luther,[4] John Calvin,[5] John and Charles Wesley,[6] Anglican divines such as Richard Hooker,[7] C. S. Lewis,[8]

---

1. Jared Ortiz, ed., *Deification in the Latin Patristic Tradition* (Washington, DC: The Catholic University of America Press, 2019).

2. Ernesto Sergio Mainoldi, "The Reception of the Greek Patristic Doctrine of Deification in the Medieval West: The Case of John Scottus Eriugena," in *Mystical Doctrines of Deification: Case Studies in the Christian Tradition*, ed. John Arblaster and Rob Frasen (London: Routledge, 2019), 60–71.

3. Anna N. Williams, *The Ground of Union: Deification in Aquinas and Palamas* (New York: Oxford University Press, 1999).

4. Carl E. Braaten and Robert W. Jenson, eds., *Union with Christ: The New Finnish Interpretation of Luther* (Grand Rapids: Eerdmans, 1998).

5. Carl Mosser, "The Greatest Possible Blessing: Calvin and Deification," *Scottish Journal of Theology* 55 (2002): 36–57.

6. Michael J. Christensen, "The Royal Way of Love: Deification in the Wesleyan Tradition," in *With All the Fullness of God: Engaging Deification Across Christian Traditions*, ed. Jared Ortiz (Lanham: Lexington Books/Fortress Academic, 2021), 177–201.

7. Arthur M. Allchin, *Participation in God: A Forgotten Strand in Anglican Tradition* (Wilton, CT: Morehouse-Barlow, 1988).

8. Myk Habets, "Mere Christianity for Mere Gods: Lewis on Theosis," in *A Myth Re-told: Re-encountering C. S. Lewis as Theologian*, ed. Martin Sutherland (Eugene, OR: Pickwick, 2014), 110–29.

as well as within Reformed theology,[9] Baptist theology,[10] Pentecostalism,[11] and many others.[12]

Contemporary evangelicalism is a beneficiary of doctrines of theosis that were taught by the early evangelical Anglicans, holiness teaching inherited from John Wesley, and the sung theology of deification found in the hymns of Charles Wesley,[13] popularized by C. S. Lewis and retrieved in our own day by evangelicals across the denominational spectrum. In 1994 several works by evangelicals were released, highlighting the doctrine of theosis. Daniel Clendenin, then visiting professor of Christian studies at Moscow State University, published an overview of Eastern Orthodox Christianity for evangelicals, published with Baker Books, and an essay on theosis in the *Journal of the Evangelical Theological Society*.[14] He followed these up in 1995 with an Eastern Orthodox reader, also with Baker Books.[15] For many evangelicals in North America, this might have been the first interaction they had with Eastern Orthodox theology and with the terms theosis, deification, and divinization.

Clendenin's work was meant to put Eastern Orthodoxy on the evangelical radar and to highlight how an esoteric sounding doctrine like theosis was biblical, traditional, and practical, even if it needed to be parsed in a Western mode and shorn of some of its Eastern mystical excesses. Clendenin illustrates how theosis and Western juridical notions of atonement are not antithetical but can be harmonized. Theosis is not pantheism; it is not teaching

---

9. Myk Habets, "Reforming Theōsis," in *Theōsis: Deification in Christian Theology*, ed. Stephen Finlan and Vladimir Kharlamov (Eugene, OR: Pickwick, 2006), 146–67.

10. Dongsun Cho, "Deification in the Baptist Tradition: Christification of the Human Nature through Adopted and Participatory Sonship without Becoming Another Christ," *Perichoresis: The Theological Journal of Emanuel University* 17 (2019): 51–73; and Myk Habets, "'As Far as Our Capacity Allows.' Deification in the Baptist Tradition," in Ortiz, ed., *With All the Fullness of God*, 155–76.

11. Edmund J. Rybarczyk, *Beyond Salvation: Eastern Orthodoxy and Classical Pentecostalism on Becoming Like Christ* (Carlisle: Paternoster, 2004).

12. Myk Habets, "Deification in Recent Anglican and Protestant Theology," in *Oxford Handbook of Deification*, ed. Andrew Hofer, Paul Gavrilyuk, and Matthew Levering (Oxford: Oxford University Press, forthcoming).

13. S. T. Kimbrough Jr., *Partakers of the Life Divine: Participation in the Divine Nature in the Writings of Charles Wesley* (Eugene, OR: Cascade Books, 2016).

14. Daniel B. Clendenin, "Partakers of Divinity: The Orthodox Doctrine of Theosis," *Journal of the Evangelical Theological Society* 37 (1994): 365–79; *Eastern Orthodox Christianity: A Western Perspective* (Grand Rapids: Baker, 1994).

15. Daniel B. Clendenin, ed., *Eastern Orthodox Theology: A Contemporary Reader* (Grand Rapids: Baker, 1995).

the absorption of humanity into God; it is not collapsing the creator-creature distinction; and it does not eradicate juridical notions of the atonement such as justification by grace through faith.[16] Clendenin concludes that East and West share a common Christian heritage, but within each, there is a difference in emphasis. Each tradition can learn from the other and, in that ecumenical exchange, be enhanced.

Following Clendenin's work, in 1997 the *Journal of the Evangelical Theological Society* published an essay by Daniel Rakestraw, then professor of theology at Bethel Theological Seminary, also recommending that "Evangelicals may receive considerable benefit from a clear understanding and judicious appropriation of the doctrine."[17] Rakestraw adopts Philip Edgcumbe Hughes's definition of theosis: "The reintegration of the divine image of man's creation through the sanctifying work of the Holy Spirit conforming the redeemed into the likeness of Christ, and also of the believer's transition from mortality to immortality so that he is enabled to participate in the eternal bliss and glory of the kingdom of God."[18] Rakestraw is, like Clendenin, clear to state that theosis implies no ontological change in humanity making it literally God and no ontological fusion with God, even if there is ontological participation in God. Like Clendenin, Rakestraw does not uncritically accept a doctrine of theosis. He raises several concerns such as its emphasis on the corporate nature of humanity over the individual, the emphasis on the sacraments as means of deification, and the overly ascetic forms theosis takes in the East. He concludes, however, by saying, "The strengths of theosis theology outweigh the weaknesses."[19]

Rakestraw sees several benefits to evangelicals retrieving a doctrine of theosis. First, it is biblical. Texts such as 1 Corinthians 2:16, 2 Corinthians 3:17–18, 2 Peter 1:4, Galatians 2:20, and so forth can be expounded with greater clarity by means of a doctrine of theosis. "The Pauline concept of our being 'in Christ' may take on new meaning as we realize more and more our genuine

16. Clendenin, "Partakers of Divinity," 373–74.

17. Robert V. Rakestraw, "Becoming Like God: An Evangelical Doctrine of Theosis," *Journal of the Evangelical Theological Society* 40 (1997): 257–69.

18. Rakestraw, "Becoming Like God," 261, citing P. E. Hughes, *The True Image* (Grand Rapids: Eerdmans, 1989), 281.

19. Rakestraw, "Becoming Like God," 267.

participation in the life and energies of God."[20] Second, the abundant life is held up as a real possibility for Christians in their present existence.

Rather than seeing our progressive sanctification as something done for us by God from outside, by God's acting upon our minds and wills from some external habitation, or as something we do from below as we pray to God above and seek to obey God here on earth, we may take a kind of quantum leap forward by understanding sanctification as the very life and energy of God in us.[21]

Third, while ambiguous on his final point, Rakestraw appeals to something like the architectonic function of theosis to help evangelical theology cohere.[22] Rakestraw concludes on a positive note, "The doctrine of divinisation merits the ongoing attention of Scripture scholars, theologians and pastors who desire to provide significant resources to Christians in their quest to become like God. For this is indeed why we were created."[23]

These initial forays into a doctrine of theosis were met with critique by some and acceptance by others. Since these first ventures in 1994, the language and concepts of theosis (deification/divinization) have flooded Western and evangelical theology. In 2007 Roger Olson commented on the renaissance of theosis in recent thought and noted its almost ubiquitous presence in Western theology: "It seems that almost every Protestant and Catholic theologian writing creatively and constructively in the last two or three decades has found it necessary to address the subject, and many are trying to incorporate it into their emerging theological visions. ... Most surprisingly, however, much of the contemporary discussion of deification is taking place in Protestant circles, including among evangelical Protestants."[24] Olson rightly points to evangelical advocates of theosis in Clark Pinnock,[25]

---

20. Rakestraw, "Becoming Like God," 268.
21. Rakestraw, "Becoming Like God," 269.
22. Rakestraw, "Becoming Like God," 269.
23. Rakestraw, "Becoming Like God," 269.
24. Roger E. Olson, "Deification in Contemporary Theology," *Theology Today* 64 (2007): 188.
25. Clark H. Pinnock, *Flame of Love: A Theology of the Holy Spirit* (Downers Grove, IL: InterVarsity Press, 1996).

Stanley Grenz,[26] and Veli-Matti Kärkkäinen.[27] An exhaustive update of this list would be enormous, but it is worth noting the adoption of theotic themes and theology in works of influence on evangelicals such as Michael Horton,[28] Robert Letham,[29] Oliver Crisp,[30] Ben Blackwell,[31] and Michael Gorman,[32] to name but a few.

Evangelicals who have interacted with a doctrine of theosis share some familiar concerns. Mark McInroy offers a clear summary of some of these concerns:

> Among critics, additional mischaracterizations tend to accompany the view of the doctrine as Eastern. Most prevalent is the perception of deification as an unchristian product of the Hellenization of Christianity. Also common is the notion that deification bridges the creator-creature distinction. Other critics worry that deification endorses an absorption of the human being into God that utterly dissolves that person's individuality. Most important for our purposes, many hold that deification proceeds according to a logic that fundamentally differs from that of justification, and these figures insist that the two doctrines cannot coexist in the same soteriological model.[33]

---

26. Stanley J. Grenz, *The Social God and the Relational Self: A Trinitarian Theology of the Imago Dei* (Louisville: Westminster John Knox, 2001).

27. Veli-Matti Kärkkäinen, *One with God: Salvation as Deification and Justification* (Collegeville, MN: Liturgical Press, 2004).

28. Michael Horton, *Covenant and Salvation: Union with Christ* (Louisville: Westminster John Knox, 2007), 181–215, 267–307.

29. Robert Letham, *Systematic Theology* (Wheaton: Crossway, 2019), 751–89.

30. Oliver D. Crisp, "Theosis and Participation," in *Being Saved: Explorations in Soteriology and Human Persons*, ed. S. Mark Hamilton, Marc Cortez, and Josh Farris (London: SCM Press, 2018), 85–101.

31. Ben C. Blackwell, *Christosis: Engaging Paul's Soteriology with His Patristic Interpreters* (Grand Rapids: Eerdmans, 2016).

32. Michael J. Gorman, *Inhabiting the Cruciform God: Kenosis, Justification, and Theosis in Paul's Narrative Soteriology* (Grand Rapids: Eerdmans, 2009); *Becoming the Gospel: Paul, Participation, and Mission* (Grand Rapids: Eerdmans, 2015); *Abide and Go: Missional Theosis in the Gospel of John* (Eugene, OR: Cascade Books, 2018).

33. Mark McInroy, "How Deification Became Eastern: German Idealism, Liberal Protestantism, and the Modern Misconstruction of the Doctrine," *Modern Theology* 37 (2021): 935n2. Clendenin offers his own list in *Eastern Orthodox Christianity*, 158–59.

Another evangelical, Baptist scholar Vladimir Kharlamov, outlines the concerns theosis raises amongst several influential evangelical Baptists. He points out

> several reservations that leading conservative Baptist theologians (Millard J. Erickson, Bruce A. Demarest, James Leo Garrett, and Kenneth Keathly) express toward implementing deification in Baptist theological discourse. The main concern among them is that Greek Patristic and Eastern Orthodox spirituality might present deification in terms of absorptive mysticism where a human person by being deified loses his/her identity and sort of dissolves into the divine.[34]

This is an often-leveled critique of theosis. It is, however, based on a fundamental misunderstanding.

> I would say, this is quite an ungrounded and made-up concern. Of course, there are forms of mysticism that have this understanding. I think what is at play here, if not simple unfamiliarity of abovementioned theologians with Christian mysticism, is some kind of semantic confusion when *Eastern* Orthodoxy and its mysticism gets confused with *Eastern* religions where we actually find the idea of absorption into the divine. ... In Christianity ... none of the Christian mystics would agree with this pantheistic understanding of human union with God. ... The Christian understanding of divinization is not the same as New Age spirituality as Erickson thinks. Following the same logic, one might ask what, for example, would prevent the idea of union with Christ (Erickson's preference for a substitute for deification) be interpreted in terms of absorptive mysticism?[35]

These critiques and concerns are significant and have tended to repel many evangelicals from embracing a doctrine of theosis. The work of Torrance presents one way in which these critiques might be answered and a Protestant doctrine of theosis compatible for evangelicals that can be recommended.

---

34. Vladimir Kharlamov, "Baptists and Theosis: Engagement, Constructive Approach, and Contribution," in *Baptist Sacramentalism*, ed. Anthony R. Cross and Philip E. Thompson, Studies in Baptist History and Thought vol. 4 (Eugene, OR: Pickwick, forthcoming), 24 (pages refer to the draft not the proof pages).

35. Kharlamov, "Baptists and Theosis," 24–25.

THOMAS F. TORRANCE AND THE RETRIEVAL
OF THEOSIS IN A PROTESTANT REGISTER

Notable Reformed-Orthodox dialogues resulted in a surprising discovery that the two communions had much in common in the area of theosis and sanctification. They both stressed the initiative of God, the need for grace, and the place of works as a response to both. This realization in the 1960s led to many Reformed theologians engaging in a theology of retrieval and looking to see what a Reformed doctrine of theosis might look like.[36] Thomas F. Torrance is the foremost figure in this regard. Torrance had a close association with Eastern theologians and Eastern Orthodoxy from early on in his academic career, forming close friendships with significant Orthodox figures such as Georges Florovsky, George Dragas, and others,[37] and eventually initiating and leading the Orthodox-Reformed International Dialogue sponsored by the Ecumenical Patriarchate and World Alliance of Reformed Churches (1979–2007).[38] Throughout these dialogues, the Reformed theologians realized that theosis does not threaten the creator-creature distinction; it does not collapse into a synergistic—meaning Pelagian—notion of works-righteousness; it is not a pantheistic (or panentheistic) absorption of humanity into the divine essence; it does not challenge or contradict the notion of forensic justification; it does not abrogate what Scripture teaches about justification or sanctification; and it does not counter the reality of being human in the kingdom of God.

Evangelical and Reformed theologian, Carl Mosser, has chronicled the journey of Reformed theology in its reception of theosis, highlighting how, from the beginning, major Reformers and their successors accepted theosis as a profoundly Christian doctrine. In the work of Calvin and other prominent Reformers, Mosser finds no contradiction between a doctrine of justification and a doctrine of theosis. "Justification pertains to the mechanics

---

36. This is chronicled in Carl Mosser, "Orthodox-Reformed Dialogue and the Ecumenical Recovery of Theosis," *The Ecumenical Review* 73 (2021): 131–51. See John McClelland, "Sailing to Byzantium," in *The New Man: An Orthodox and Reformed Dialogue*, ed. John Meyendorff and John McClelland (New Brunswick: Agora Books, 1973), 10–25.

37. See Matthew Baker, "Interview with George Dion Dragas Regarding T. F. Torrance," in *T. F. Torrance and Eastern Orthodoxy: Theology in Reconciliation*, ed. Matthew Baker and Todd Speidell (Eugene, OR: Wipf & Stock, 2015), 1–18; Matthew Baker, "The Correspondence between T. F. Torrance and Georges Florovsky (1950–1973)," *Particpatio* 4 (2013): 287–323.

38. Thomas F. Torrance, ed., *Theological Dialogue between Orthodox and Reformed Churches*, 2 vols. (Edinburgh: Scottish Academic Press, 1985, 1993).

of obtaining right standing before God, deification concerns the reception of divine life as the goal or telos of redemption. These concepts simply do different work within a full-orbed soteriology. That is why the Reformers did not hesitate to affirm both notions without the least bit of tension."[39] He concludes, "The Reformers we have surveyed show that one can affirm a full-orbed soteriology that is both forensic and transformational, Reformational and catholic."[40] In short, theosis was seen to be compatible with the staples of Reformed theology and, surprisingly, added to the richness of Reformed thought and life. These Reformed movements are mentioned because they mirror, in many respects, evangelical concerns more widely.

Looking at Torrance's teaching on theosis specifically, we find an affirmation of central evangelical convictions alongside a coherent account of theosis. Torrance writes:

> There are people who imagine that in eternity all personalities are swallowed up and lost in God, that all temporal distinctions, and all that is finite and individual, melt into the infinite. That may be the view of some heathen Nirvana, but it is certainly not the teaching of the Christian faith. … The Christian hope is fulfilled only in a new heaven and a new earth peopled with human beings living in holy and loving fellowship with God, with one another, and in harmony with the fullness of creation.[41]

The work of Christ is central to Torrance and evangelical theology. The Son, in Torrance's reading of Scripture, assumes human nature and lives a genuinely human life in relationship with God his Father through the Holy Spirit. This divine relationship enables Christ to be our savior, qualifies him for his reconciling ministry, and establishes his salvific connection with humanity. Ultimately, Christ must be seen as the personalizing person, the one in whom human persons are not simply justified but in whom we are remade and now live (2 Cor 5:17). Christ is the *arche* and *telos* of human existence, the one in whom humans are made (cf. Gen 1:26 with Col 1:15) and the one into

---

39. Carl Mosser, "Recovering the Reformation's Ecumenical Vision of Redemption as Deification and Beatific Vision," *Perichoresis: The Theological Journal of Emanuel University* 18 (2020): 19.

40. Mosser, "Recovering the Reformation's Ecumenical Vision," 19.

41. Thomas F. Torrance, *The Apocalypse Today* (Grand Rapids: Eerdmans, 1959), 176–77.

whom they will be transformed from glory to glory (2 Cor 3:18). By means of the incarnation, the Son becomes human to unite humanity and divinity together and achieve a deification of human nature. As the Father spoke of it, this wonderful exchange is the heart of a doctrine of theosis. The goal of humanity is worship, something Torrance defines as the gift of participating through the Spirit in the incarnate Son's communion with the Father. The locus of worship, and thus of theosis, is the church, the communion of saints created by the fellowship of the Holy Spirit. Throughout Torrance's doctrines of creation, anthropology, incarnation, reconciliation, and pneumato-ecclesiology, the concept of theosis plays a central and constitutive role in explaining a Christian theology of salvation.

The most concise definition of theosis Torrance uses is perhaps the following: "The lifting of [humans] up to partake of the living presence and saving acts of God the Creator and Redeemer."[42] Literally, *theosis* means "becoming god," and *theopoiesis* means "making divine" or "making into a god."[43] In English, theosis is typically translated as "divinization" or "deification." Theosis is a historic Christian doctrine and has never meant the fusion of divine and human, the loss of human nature, an absorption into deity, or the collapse of the distinction between the creator and the created.[44] This is illustrated in Torrance's plea, made in 1964 to the World Alliance of Reformed Churches. He calls for:

> [a] reconsideration ... of what the Greek fathers called *theosis*. ... *Theosis* was the term the Fathers used to emphasize the fact that through the Spirit we have to do with God in his utter sublimity, his sheer Godness or holiness; creatures though we are, men on earth, in the Spirit we are made to participate in saving acts that are abruptly and absolutely divine, election, adoption, regeneration or sanctification and we participate in them by grace alone. *Theosis* describes man's involvement in such a mighty act of God upon him that he is raised up to find the true centre of his existence not in himself but in Holy

---

42. Thomas F. Torrance, *Theology in Reconstruction* (Grand Rapids: Eerdmans, 1965), 244.

43. Geoffrey W. H. Lampe, *A Patristic Greek Lexicon* (Oxford: Clarendon, 1961), 649.

44. For a summary see Stephen Finlan and Vladimir Kharlamov, "Introduction," in *Theōsis: Deification in Christian Theology*, ed. Stephen Finlan and Vladimir Kharlamov (Eugene, OR: Pickwick, 2006), 1–8.

God, where he lives and moves and has his being in the uncreated but creative energy of the Holy Spirit. By *theosis* the Greek fathers wished to express the fact that in the new coming of the Holy Spirit we are up against God in the most absolute sense, God in his ultimate holiness or Godness.[45]

Torrance doubles down on this definition of salvation as theosis and argues that only a doctrine of theosis can combat particular emphases prevalent in our day which were already present in the 1960s, namely, the heretical teaching that there is a spark of the divine within each of us that needs to be released and the "emphasis of so many modern Protestants upon their own existential decisions or their own creative spirituality."[46] It is hard not to read this as a contemporary word for evangelicals! He continues:

Theosis is an attempt to express the staggering significance of Pentecost as the coming from on high, from outside of us and beyond us, of divine power, or rather as the coming of Almighty God, the Maker of heaven and earth, to dwell with sinful mortal man, and therefore as the emancipation of man from imprisonment in himself and the lifting of him up to partake of the living presence and saving acts of God the Creator and Redeemer.[47]

Further, in a declarative statement, we are told, "Jesus Christ is our worship, the essence of it and the whole of it, and we may worship God in Spirit and in Truth only as we are made partakers in his worship."[48]

Worship is the only mode appropriate to statements about the ends for which God created the world, including humanity. Torrance concludes, "Thus in our worship the Holy Spirit comes forth from God, uniting us to the response and obedience and faith and prayer of Jesus, and returns to God, raising us up in Jesus to participate in the worship of heaven and in the eternal communion of the Holy Trinity."[49]

---

45. Torrance, *Theology in Reconstruction*, 243.
46. Torrance, *Theology in Reconstruction*, 243.
47. Torrance, *Theology in Reconstruction*, 243–44.
48. Torrance, *Theology in Reconstruction*, 249.
49. Torrance, *Theology in Reconstruction*, 250.

As Word and Spirit cannot be separated, the work of Christ and the Spirit cannot be either. Christ is the savior, and the Spirit was at work within him to equip and enable him to be the Messiah. The same Christ and the same Spirit are now at work in the Christian, in the act of deifying transformation.

> It was through the power of the Spirit that Christ himself was born among us, lived his life of holy obedience and worship, gave himself in sacrifice for the sin of the world, rose again and ascended to the Father to be for ever the one offering and prayer that prevails for all mankind. It is through the power of the same Spirit who came down at Pentecost that we are united to Christ in his identification with us, and joined to him in his self-consecration and self-offering for us once and for all on earth and eternally prevalent in heaven. Jesus Christ who took our nature upon him has given to God an account for us, making atonement in our place, and in our name has yielded himself in sacrifice and worship and praise and thanksgiving to the Father. We have no other answer to the will of God, no other offering, no other response or worship, for without Christ we can do nothing.[50]

From the basis in worship and the twofold response of Christ and the Spirit— that is, Christ is the Word of God to humanity and the response of humanity to God—Torrance appeals to theosis first as a way to understand the work of Christ, and second, as a way to understand our human place and response. Christ takes to himself fallen human nature and redeems it, reconciles it, heals it, and restores it through his obedient life lived before the Father in the power of the Spirit. He dies for us and rises for our salvation, ascending to the right hand of the Father from which he reigns until his return to judge the living and the dead and make all things new. When fallen human creatures are regenerated by the Spirit, united to the incarnate Son, and brought before the Father, they are transformed, recreated, renewed, and restored in Christ.

> By coming into man the Holy Spirit opens him out for God. But at the very heart of this movement is the act of God in which he became man in order to take man's place, and give man a place within the

---

50. Torrance, *Theology in Reconstruction*, 248–49.

communion of the divine life. It is the act of the divine love taking the way of substitution, and opening up the way for a corresponding act on the part of man in which he renounces himself for God's sake that the divine love may have its way with him in self-less objectivity.[51]

In Christ, believers take on the character and attributes of Christ—they become Christlike. The transformation into Christlikeness is progressive and goes from glory to glory. Beginning now, our conformity to the image of Christ and the likeness of God continues for all eternity. At conversion, believers are given new natures and a new standing before God. At the resurrection, believers are given new bodies, immortal and glorious like the risen Christ's. And for eternity, believers are drawn further and further into a knowledge of the triune God and worship of him. Theosis is the declaration that salvation involves the forgiveness of sins by the work of Christ and so much more. Salvation is the stunning fact that believers are being made into the likeness of Christ, the perfect man, the incarnate Son of God, and in that recreation, believers participate in the mutual glorification of the triune persons in the Son full of the Spirit. No longer are we slaves, but we are now sons and daughters of God with the status, privilege, access, and relational intimacy of that familial reality.

As I have written elsewhere:

On more than one occasion Torrance argues against the idea of human nature being "deified," if by "deified" one means "made divine" in some *non-human* way. This is why he places so much stress on *theosis* understood through the Chalcedonian doctrine of the hypostatic union. Human nature is "reaffirmed and recreated in its essence as human nature, yet one in which the participant is really united to the Incarnate Son of God partaking in him in his own appropriate mode of the oneness of the Son and the Father and the Father and the Son, through the Holy Spirit."[52] This participation in the Divine life (*theosis*) is an eschatological mystery that Torrance is careful not to delve into inappropriately. *Theosis* begins now as we participate in

---

51. Torrance, *Theology in Reconstruction*, 138.

52. Citing Torrance, *Theology in Reconstruction*, 186.

the new creation through the Spirit; it is also "not yet" as we wait for the *Parousia* of the Lord when God in Christ will make all things new.

For Torrance the goal of *theosis* is not to become "God" or even, technically speaking, to become "gods." It is not the process of transcending the confines of human nature but the process and means by which the human can achieve true personhood. *Theosis* does not do away with our creatureliness; it fulfils it.[53]

The life of Christ effects a soteriological exchange whereby Christ takes what is ours (sin, mortality, etc.) and gives us what is his (sonship, immortality, etc.).[54] In the incarnation, the eternal Son takes to himself human nature and heals and redeems it; he deifies it, lifting it into the holy presence of the Father in the ascension. In Christ, atonement has been accomplished. On this basis, believers may be saved or deified, as they are united to the incarnate Son by the Holy Spirit. Torrance writes, "The ascension means the exaltation of man into the life of God and on to the throne of God. In the ascension the Son of Man, New Man in Christ, is given to partake of divine nature."[55] As a result, "through the Spirit Christ is nearer to us than we are to ourselves, and we who live and dwell on earth are yet made to sit with Christ 'in heavenly places,' partaking of the divine nature in him."[56]

As a summary statement of Torrance's theotic vision, it could be said,

> The result of *theopoiesis* is that Christ has totally redeemed, reconciled, cleansed, lifted, restored, and recreated human nature to what God had intended it to be in the first place.[57] The consummation of deified humanity is centered upon the summing up of all things in Christ, when he transforms us in the whole of our human nature. "When we see him we shall become like him, and when we become like him we shall see him with healed vision and recreated natures."[58]

---

53. Myk Habets, *Theosis in the Theology of Thomas F. Torrance* (Farnham: Ashgate, 2009), 44.

54. Thomas F. Torrance, *The Trinitarian Faith: The Evangelical Theology of the Ancient Catholic Church* (Edinburgh: T&T Clark, 1995), 182–83.

55. Thomas F. Torrance, *Space, Time and Resurrection* (Edinburgh: T&T Clark, 1998), 135.

56. Torrance, *Space, Time and Resurrection*, 135.

57. See Torrance, *Space, Time and Resurrection*, 139.

58. Habets, *Theosis in the Theology of Thomas F. Torrance*, 59, citing Torrance, *Space, Time and Resurrection*, 140.

Theosis is a doctrine that is utilized to express the reality of salvation in ways that cohere with our doctrines of creation, anthropology, ecclesiology, and eschatology. "God becomes human so that humans may become gods" is the patristic shorthand for theosis. Evangelicals, rightly, are hesitant to accept this language. Torrance is careful to nuance how we speak of theosis:

> The hypostatic union of the divine and human natures in Jesus preserves the human and creaturely being he took from us, and it is in and through our sharing in that human and creaturely being, sanctified and blessed with him, that we share in the life of God while remaining what we are made to be, humans and not Gods.[59]

Evangelicals are also hesitant to accept the idea that humans can be united with God so closely that they take on his likeness. And yet, that is precisely the heart of the gospel for Torrance (and the majority of the Christian faith!).

> The Holy Spirit interiorizes the knowledge of God within us, but He does this by actualizing within us God's own witness to Himself. The Holy Spirit is the eternal Communion of the Father and the Son and therefore when He is sent into our hearts by the Father in the name of the Son we are made partakers with the Son in His Communion with the Father and thus of God's own self-knowledge.[60]

Theosis expresses the core evangelical conviction that Christ is central to all of creation and the incarnation is the fulcrum point of history. In Christ, God has reconciled the world to himself and has taken our sin, alienation, and disobedience to himself and dealt with it once and for all in his perfect life and sacrificial death. In his resurrection and ascension, Christ exchanges his righteousness for our sin, and through the regenerating and sanctifying work of the Spirit, what is Christ's is now ours in a soteriological exchange. Believers receive in Christ sonship, immortality, and knowledge of, and participation in, the mutual glorification of the persons of the Holy Trinity. As far as our creaturely limits allow, believers become like Christ, like God.

The result, for Torrance, of articulating and adopting a doctrine of theosis is that a more relational form of Christianity is conceived in which believers

---

59. Torrance, *Space, Time and Resurrection*, 136.
60. Thomas F. Torrance, *God and Rationality* (London: Oxford University Press, 1971), 173–74.

join in intimate and fulfilling union with Christ, possessed by the Spirit, where they live out of the reality of being children of God. Church, sacraments, and good works all take their place within a context of worship, defined by James Torrance and clearly in agreement with Thomas Torrance's theology, as:

> the gift of participating through the Spirit in the incarnate Son's communion with the Father. It means participating in union with Christ, in what he has done for us once and for all, in his self-offering to the Father, in his life and death on the cross. It also means participating in what he is continuing to do for us in the presence of the Father and in his mission from the Father to the world. There is only one true Priest through whom and with whom we draw near to God our Father.[61]

True worship and the entire Christian life can be subsumed under the category of theosis. For these reasons and many more, Torrance sees theosis as a biblical, traditional, practical, and *evangelical* doctrine.

THE GOOD NEWS ABOUT THEOSIS

It will not come as a surprise to any informed reader that evangelicalism is at a crossroads. The post-fundamentalist, pietistic, modernistic message of twentieth-century evangelicalism served it well in a Western social context built on shared assumptions and values. The twenty-first century is not so kind to evangelicalism, and it finds itself having to change and adapt to a new, post-modern social context. The gospel remains the same, while the means to communicate it is always adapting. An increasing number of evangelicals see theosis as one means to proclaim the gospel of Jesus Christ in a new context in the hopes of gaining a fair hearing from unbelievers and developing a deeper, more intimate faith in believers.

Critical studies of evangelicalism abound, but solutions can also be found.[62] Carl Mosser believes a retrieval of theosis can add real value to the church. "Today mainline and evangelical Protestants alike tend to proclaim truncated, uninspiring, humdrum messages of salvation. The retrieval

---

61. James B. Torrance, *Worship, Community and the Triune God of Grace* (Downers Grove, IL: InterVarsity Press Academic, 1997), 9.

62. This is the thesis of Michael P. Gama, *Theosis: Patristic Remedy for Evangelical Yearning at the Close of the Modern Age* (Eugene, OR: Wipf & Stock, 2017).

of deification and the beatific vision is an opportunity to renew the message of God's lavish, whelming grace proclaimed by the church fathers and Reformers."[63] Mosser defines theosis as "what is presently true about the incarnate Son will be made true of the redeemed. Redemption in the fullest sense is simply for a human person to become everything Jesus presently is in his glorified, ascended, fully flourishing humanity enthroned at God's right hand."[64] To assuage evangelical suspicions that theosis is a turn to Eastern mysticism, he clarifies, "Affirming deification does not represent an undignified flight to the East but a journey back to the places in which the Reformed tradition was birthed."[65] It also pays practical dividends.

> Recovering the Reformation's ecumenical vision of redemption is worthwhile because paying greater attention to the telos of salvation helps orient the spiritual life, provides insight into God's redemptive purposes for humanity, and supplies resources for the contemporary theological task. Contemplation of God's promise to renovate our corrupt natures, give himself to be seen by us, and draw us into the divine life and love of the Trinity—to be by grace what Christ is by nature—renews hope and arouses praise.[66]

There are other reasons evangelicals should incorporate a doctrine of theosis into their theology. Rightly understood, a doctrine of deification does not reduce salvation to a moment in time, a crisis decision, or to the moment of justification. Instead, theosis is a way to highlight the coherence of justification and sanctification and, at the same time, keep eschatological transformation and the hope of glory squarely in view. The locus of theosis is the church, and this gives coherence to the faithful observance of the sacraments and of meeting together. Jesus is God by nature, and believers become gods by grace, reminding us that good works are not meritorious and that salvation is all of grace. Theosis cuts off any notion of idolatry—the idea that we can

---

63. Mosser, "Recovering the Reformation's Ecumenical Vision," 20.

64. Oliver D. Crisp, "Theosis and Participation," in *Being Saved: Explorations in Soteriology and Human Ontology*, ed. Marc Cortez, S. Mark Hamilton, and Joshua R. Farris (London: SCM Press, 2018), 87, citing Carl Mosser, "The Metaphysics of Union with God," unpublished paper, 4.

65. Carl Mosser, "The Gospel's End and Our Highest Good: Deification in the Reformed Tradition," in *With All the Fullness of God*, 101.

66. Mosser, "Recovering the Reformation's Ecumenical Vision," 21.

literally become God. Only in Christ and by the Spirit do believers find their true selves, crucified and risen, identified with Christ, and full of the Spirit. Theosis teaches human participation in God, not human replacement of God. To be deified is to remain a human creature, dependent on God, participating in the mutual glorification of the triune persons; it is to sit in heavenly places in Christ Jesus. While not an evangelical, Daniel Keating's words ring with evangelical truth: "The primary warrant, then, for Christian deification is that it ensures and enhances the full biblical revelation of our call: to become sons and daughters formed in the image of Christ; to be temples of the Holy Spirit and members of the household of God; to live in direct and eternal communion with the Father through the Son and in the Holy Spirit."[67]

Torrance's doctrine of theosis provides a model for the ways in which evangelical theology could incorporate a fuller, more biblically and theologically faithful account of the salvation available in Christ. "For by these He has granted to us His precious and magnificent promises, so that by them you may become partakers of the divine nature" (2 Pet 1:4 NASB).

---

67. Daniel A. Keating, *Deification and Grace* (Ave Maria, FL: Sapientia Press, 2007), 124.

11
—
THINKING AND ACTING IN CHRIST

Torrance on Spiritual Formation

Geordie W. Ziegler

Although it is widely recognized that Thomas F. Torrance was one of the most (if not the most) significant English-speaking theologians in the second half of the twentieth century, he is not typically considered a primary source when it comes to the subject of spiritual formation.[1] Few evangelical pastors and teachers are familiar with his name and fewer still among the spiritual formation guilds. This chapter seeks to address and change that, for the truth is, Torrance's theology provides the solid and dynamic, onto-relational and incarnational, Trinitarian grounding needed for the work of spiritual formation.[2]

---

1. Torrance is best known for his contributions to theological method, Trinitarian theology, ecumenical dialogue, and the relation between science and theology. However, undergirding and permeating all these themes lies his Christology, or "the doctrine of Grace," which as Torrance says, "must always be the centrum of a Christian dogmatic." See "Predestination in Christ," *Evangelical Quarterly* 13 (1941): 127-28. On the theme of Torrance's doctrine of grace, see my book *Trinitarian Grace and Participation: An Entry into the Theology of T. F. Torrance* (Minneapolis: Fortress Press, 2017).

2. I have written previously on this theme in the *Journal of Spiritual Formation and Soul Care*, "Is It Time for a Reformation of Spiritual Formation? Recovering Ontology" 11 (2018): 74-92.

BEGINNINGS: FROM MISSIONARY EVANGELIST
TO MISSIONARY THEOLOGIAN

Born and raised in China to missionary parents, Torrance approached his theological work with the mindset of a missionary and an evangelist.[3] In his teen years he assumed his mission field would be on Chinese soil, but as his studies at the University of Edinburgh progressed, Torrance's sense of calling began to simultaneously expand and narrow. His evangelistic calling would expand beyond the needs of inland China to a mission to "evangelize the foundations" of modern scientific culture.[4] Not unlike the demanding work of necessity undertaken by the early church, Torrance's missionary calling was one of reconstructing the foundations. This monumental undertaking would begin with the patristics, appreciate and critique the Reformers, and draw on modern thinkers with, of course, Karl Barth, as the most formative.[5] Yet this massive ressourcement and reconstruction also required a narrowing of his vocation to primarily work in and from Scottish soil. While his mission field literally was the church of Christ as a whole, the locus of his ministry, through ten years of pastoral work and over twenty-five years of teaching, would be the Church of Scotland.

This mix of callings would make Torrance an enigma to many, for he defies neat traditional boxes. He was an evangelist and missionary, yet a scholar's scholar and a theologian's theologian; a man of deep prayer and personal devotion, yet a fiery critic of ideas he deemed alien to the gospel;[6] a solidly

---

3. "Even as a professor of theology, I have always tried to be a missionary," The Thomas F. Torrance Manuscript Collection, Princeton Theological Seminary, Box 10.

4. I. John Hesselink, "A Pilgrimage in the School of Christ," *Reformed Review* 38 (1984): 60. Later, reflecting on the convictions which motivated his theological work, Torrance would write: "An evangelical theology is an evangelizing theology, for it is concerned with the winning and transforming of the human mind through conformity to the mind of Christ Jesus—not simply the minds of individual human beings but the mind of human society and culture in which individual human beings exist," Thomas F. Torrance, *Atonement: The Person and Work of Christ*, ed. Robert T. Walker (Downers Grove, IL and Milton Keynes: IVP and Paternoster, 2009), 444.

5. Torrance understood himself to be doing essentially the same kind of work as his mentor Karl Barth, whom he describes as "an evangelical theologian who spent his life in evangelizing the human reason," Torrance, *Atonement*, 442.

6. I once heard Bruce McCormack in St. Andrews, Scotland describe a time years earlier in which he ran into Torrance at Princeton. After exchanging a few brief pleasantries, and as they both were about to continue on their way, Torrance turned and said to McCormack, "You know, Bruce, I pray for you every day." Reflecting on that experience, McCormack was struck by the genuine spirituality of Torrance as a theologian who prays. *T. F. Torrance Lectures* (St. Andrews, Scotland, 2007).

Reformed theologian yet never bound to the abstract constraints of Reformed theology; a voice crying out for reform of the Church of Scotland, yet also of the Church of Rome, the Eastern Orthodox, and Protestant churches of all kinds (Anabaptists, Lutherans, Anglicans). To each and all Torrance's theme was constant: the call for a "Christological correction" that would establish the proper foundations for "a moral life that flows from grace"—a life in which the Father-Son relation is translated into the daily life of the children of God.[7]

While much of his work was focused on the academic, his work was also intended to speak to every man and woman. The proof of the fruitfulness of his colossal efforts is witnessed, not only in his prolific writings, but perhaps most significantly, in the hearts and minds of those who have been the beneficiaries of Torrance's theology. For those who have chosen to swim in the deep waters of his torrential springs, the fruit has been significant, and for a great many, life-changing. Through Torrance's labor of love, many have heard a profound and beautiful gospel-centered in the life and love of the Father, Son, and Spirit. I write as one of those whose life has been deeply impacted by Torrance's writings. As a theologian who has also spent nearly twenty years as a pastor of spiritual formation, I have found Torrance to be a bright and relentless voice, challenging me to a "repentant rethinking" of many aspects of the evangelical tradition in which I was formed. Because, like Torrance, my theological location continues to be broadly evangelical, throughout this chapter I will use the pronoun "we" when speaking of the tendencies of evangelicalism.

THE MODERN MALAISE OF EVANGELICALISM AND EVANGELICAL SPIRITUAL FORMATION

If Torrance's critique of spiritual formation within contemporary evangelicalism were to be boiled down to one phrase, it would be this: "It does not begin from a center in God." This diagnosis is extremely serious, for the doctrine of God is the most upstream dogma of all dogmatics. For Torrance, there is no distance between one's doctrine of God and the work of discipleship and

---

7. Thomas F. Torrance, "The Atonement: The Singularity of Christ and the Finality of the Cross: The Atonement and the Moral Order," in *Universalism and the Doctrine of Hell*, ed. Nigel de S. Cameron (Grand Rapids: Baker, 1993), 253; Thomas F. Torrance, *The Trinitarian Faith: The Evangelical Theology of the Ancient Catholic Church* (Edinburgh: T&T Clark, 1995), 160–61.

spiritual formation. We become like the one we worship. Torrance describes the essential work of the church when it comes to formation in this way:

> That transformation in our inner self in which we learn to think from a centre in God rather than from a centre in ourselves is the basic reorientation that takes place in the church of Jesus Christ. *Christian discipleship is the disciplined habit of thinking and acting in Christ*, for he is the one place where we may really worship God and believe in him as our Father.[8]

This is a striking definition of Christian formation, most notably in its emphasis on Jesus Christ *himself.* The "transformation" or "reorientation" of our inner selves, which we understand as discipleship or spiritual formation, Torrance describes as a "disciplined habit" that involves both "thinking and acting," and the locus of that thinking and acting is *in Christ.* For Torrance, there is nothing abstract or extrinsic about the Pauline phrase "in Christ." To think and act *in Christ* is not a euphemism for "knowing your position in Christ" or "imitating the character of Jesus." Torrance refuses such impersonal descriptions of Christian discipleship, and this is where Torrance's final clause stands out in its bold Trinitarian proclamation: "For *he is the one place* where we may really worship God and believe in him *as our Father.*"

We will have more to say on this later, but for now, we note that for Torrance, "life in Christ" is about a real and personal relation with the living, still incarnate Jesus, and with his Father who in and through Christ is also now our Father. This same Jesus has made us one with himself and sits at the Father's right hand whereby he includes us in his ongoing life of communion with the Father through the Holy Spirit. The gospel, according to Torrance, is that what was by nature "the closed circle of the inner life of God" which has now been "extended to include" or "made to overlap" with human life in and through Jesus.[9] "Human nature is now set within the Father-Son relationship of Christ."[10] Given this gospel, the task of spiritual formation, or rather, the ministry of the Spirit in and upon us, is to teach us to live from within that circle. Becoming the kind of people who actually "think and act

---

8. Torrance, *Atonement*, 376 (emphasis added).

9. Thomas F. Torrance, *Theology in Reconstruction* (Grand Rapids: Eerdmans, 1965), 241.

10. Thomas F. Torrance, *Space, Time and Resurrection* (Edinburgh: T&T Clark, 1998), 69.

in Christ" will require nothing less than the fundamental reorientation of our inner selves.

Torrance is quite serious when he speaks of the necessity of the renewal of our minds in light of the gospel: "Divine revelation conflicts sharply with the structure of our natural reason," which is twisted with an "ingrained mental alienation from God."[11] He likens the "agonizing experience" of muscular restructuring required of a concert pianist's hands to the "profound change in the mental structure of our innermost being" required of a "true theologian." Speaking to his students, Torrance writes, "As you let the truth of the gospel have its way with you, you will find the very shape and structure of your mind beginning to change. That is what the gospel is about, a *metanoia*, a radical repentant rethinking of everything before the face of Jesus Christ."[12]

Since our default is to think from a center in ourselves, guided by the logic of our own reason, we are bound to think of God in an "unworthy" way.[13] Reason is not neutral ground. It is "unregenerate and unbaptized." Making a decision of faith in Christ does not suddenly heal the problem. It simply puts us on the path:

> This transformation of the human mind and its renewal through assimilation to the mind of Christ is something that has to go on throughout the whole of our life—it is a never-ending discipleship in repentant rethinking as we take up the cross and follow Christ. That is why we cannot be theologians without incessant prayer.[14]

All of us are a product, to one degree or another, of our cultural location. This is even more the case when it comes to systems and structures, including church movements and theological traditions. Evangelicalism, as a child of the pragmatism and innovation of the Protestant work ethic, has exhibited an uncanny ability to utilize the tools of modern secular culture to produce large churches. One of the chief concerns which gave rise to the modern

---

11. Torrance, *Atonement*, 443.

12. Torrance, *Atonement*, 442–43. Torrance laments, "The great majority of Protestant and Roman Catholic theologians (and no doubt, clergy and lay people as well!) still operate, I am afraid, with an unregenerated and unbaptized reason, and thus avoid the agonsing experience of working out conformity to Christ in the ontological depths of their minds" (442).

13. Torrance notes Athanasius called this "irreligious way" of thinking *mythologia*. Torrance, *Atonement*, 446.

14. Torrance, *Atonement*, 446.

spiritual formation movement was a response to the pervasive superficiality and cheap grace proffered by televangelists and seeker-sensitive megachurches. The discrepancy between the number of converts versus disciples made it clear that churches were not necessarily making disciples, or "fully devoted followers." Richard Foster's 1978 book *Celebration of Discipline* called the church back to an emphasis on the concepts of character formation, holiness, and discipleship. In the 1990s, the movement gained momentum and spread through the writings and teachings of Dallas Willard. Discipleship could no longer be separated from conversion as Christians and churches were challenged to teach people how to live as Jesus lived, which Willard described as "inhabiting the kingdom of God." There is no doubt, as Gary Black Jr. points out in his book *The Theology of Dallas Willard*, that this served as a valuable corrective to the individualistic, corporate, and consumerist values of the Church Growth Movement that preceded it.[15]

Yet while the corrective has been and continues to be necessary, these endeavors have not been able to overcome the unholy fruit that continues to permeate contemporary church culture. Humanistic, tribalistic, and impersonal tendencies persist despite great investment of spiritual formation resources and energy. Before a world-wide pandemic exposed the ugly underbelly of our churches, perhaps we could have been excused for naively assuming formation into the image of Christ was happening to a larger degree than it in fact is. Today, Torrance's challenging words ring truer and more necessary than ever:

> Either you think from out of a mind centered in God through union with the mind of the Lord Jesus, or you think from out of a mind centered in yourself, alienated from God and inwardly hostile to the truth incarnate in the Lord Jesus, that is, in a way that is finally governed by the unregenerate and unbaptized reason.[16]

Such a transformation will require nothing less than "the agonizing experience of working out conformity to Christ in the ontological depths of their minds."[17]

---

15. Gary Black Jr., *The Theology of Dallas Willard: Discovering Protoevangelical Faith* (Eugene, OR: Pickwick, 2013).

16. Torrance, *Atonement*, 446.

17. Torrance, *Atonement*, 442.

THE THREE-LEGGED STOOL
OF SPIRITUAL FORMATION

The formative work of the Spirit in the life of a person involves the matura-
tion and integration of three primary movements. The first area has to do
with *the way we think*—with our theology and epistemology. Who is God?
What are human beings? How are we related? What kind of story are we
inhabiting? The second area has to do with *the way we live*. What rituals
and rhythms form us into the people of God? What relational and commu-
nal practices nurture our indwelling and abiding and experiencing God?
The third area has to do with *how we embody the character of Christ* in the
world through mission and service to others. What does faithfulness look
like Monday through Saturday? How do our inward and outward lives man-
ifest the fruit of the Spirit? How do we respond to trauma done to us or to
our neighbor?

All three of these areas need to be coordinated: theology, practice, and
character. Yet when examining the form spiritual formation takes in most
evangelical churches, nearly all the emphasis and energy is directed toward
the practices, followed by character, with the main concern being "how to."
The assumption seems to be that our theology—that is, the overarching story
that makes sense of and situates all else—is perfectly fine as is. The presump-
tion is that our doctrines do not need reexamining. In fact, to suggest the
possibility that parts of evangelical theology might need to be interrogated
and reformed is to risk rejection by the community.

REFORMED AND ALWAYS REFORMING?
THE NECESSITY OF INTERROGATING OUR FAITH

Integration of these three movements is necessary, and all three, in order
to remain faithful, require continual reforming. If we must prioritize one
over the others, the most upstream is our theology. If our theology is faulty
or anemic at points, if the story by which we make sense of our existence
in the world does not begin from a center in God, then we will be stuck in a
paradigm that does not fit reality.

It can be difficult and humbling for those (like Reformed evangelicals)
who originated by deconstructing faulty traditions to admit that their
attempts to faithfully reconstruct are also in need of some deconstructing.
Once we have created a box to secure those who are in and exclude those

who are out (whether the boundary markers restrict types of people, theological interpretations, ethical behaviors, political positions, etc. ... the list seems to keep growing), it can be difficult to change the shape or size of the box. More threatening still to do away with boxes altogether![18]

THE FAULT LINE—THE HUMANITY
OF THE RISEN CHRIST

Identifying the primary fault line that distinguishes Torrance's understanding of spiritual formation from that of classic evangelicalism is not difficult. Torrance names it himself: "In my view it is the main issue which divides all theologies and strikes them apart to the one side or to the other. *Are we to take the humanity of the risen Jesus seriously or not? Or are we to teach a Docetic view of the risen and ascended Jesus?*"[19] In brief, what Torrance is referring to is the nature of the relation between the creator and the creature. Torrance orders this relation by means of a thorough integration of several core christological doctrines: the hypostatic union, the vicarious humanity of Christ, the doctrine of the ascension, and what he calls "the *homoousion* of Grace." This set of fundamental theological tools represents a basic fault line that separates Torrance's theology from other theologies, and which, downstream, distinguishes a Torrance-inspired approach to spiritual formation from other theological approaches.

AN UNEXPECTED ALLY

While pursuing my doctorate, subsequently published as *Trinitarian Grace and Participation*, I began a regular rhythm of correspondence with my former seminary professor and mentor Eugene Peterson. Often, I would

---

18. This default defensive posture is evident in a recent online article: Joshua Ryan Butler, "4 Causes of Deconstruction," The Gospel Coalition, November 9, 2021, https://www.thegospelcoalition.org/article/4-causes-deconstruction/. Butler argues that "deconstruction is a symptom, not the root cause" and then goes on to offer four root causes. What is fascinating about the article is that at no point is the possibility entertained that some of our doctrinal formulations might themselves need reforming (reconstructing). The premise throughout is that deconstruction is unnecessary, for "we" already have and know the truth. The only problem is that "those people" do not know the truth we have been teaching.

19. Thomas F. Torrance, *Conflict and Agreement in the Church*, vol. 1 (London: Lutterworth, 1960), 98 (emphasis added). See Thomas F. Torrance, *Royal Priesthood* (Edinburgh: T&T Clark, 1993), 43. While Torrance is speaking in generalities, his analysis and critique is clearly relevant to evangelical theology.

send him chapters I was working on to see what he thought. During that time, I received around twenty-five letters from him. One letter in particular brought surprising clarity to my project and continues to direct my understanding of the church and formation. Peterson writes:

> In the American church there is virtually no ecclesiology, no body of Christ *humanity* to deal with, the humanity that is given to us through the mediation of Jesus' humanity. So the church is understood almost entirely in terms of its function, what we do for Jesus instead of what Jesus is doing for us. You and Torrance insist on something totally different, the church as ontological fact.[20]

It was his use of the phrase, "the church as ontological fact," that both captured my imagination and illuminated for me the crux of the issue. Peterson already saw what I was just beginning to discover through my study of Torrance. The church (and therefore each individual person) has an ontology rooted and grounded in the humanity of Christ which is far more significant than its function.

At the time of this letter, Peterson was drafting his book *Practice Resurrection: A Conversation on Growing Up in Christ*, which would be the capstone to his five-volume spiritual theology series. In his book, published the following year, Peterson elaborates:

> This way of understanding church is very, very American and very, very wrong. We can no more understand church functionally than we can understand Jesus functionally. ... An ontological understanding of church has to do with what it is, not what it does. And what it *is* is far wider, deeper, higher than anything it does, or anything we can take charge of or manipulate.[21]

"The ontological church," or what Peterson calls "the church in its Isness ... is previous to whatever we do or don't do. We do not create the church. It *is*. We enter and participate in what is given to us. ... There is more—far more—to the church than us. There is Father, Son, and Holy Spirit."[22]

---

20. Letter to Geordie Ziegler, March 7, 2009.

21. Peterson, *Practice Resurrection* (Grand Rapids: Eerdmans, 2010), 118–19.

22. Peterson, *Practice Resurrection*, 121.

Peterson, in his own language, is echoing the same fault line as Torrance: *"Are we to take the humanity of the risen Jesus seriously or not?"* To take the risen humanity of Jesus seriously is to recognize that Jesus Christ incarnate is the substance of the church's ontology, the ground of its being, the essence of its *Isness*. The Living Word of God, who spoke creation into existence, united himself to that creation and recreated it from within. Jesus *himself* is the new creation, and from his fullness he speaks the church into being.

From the dust of broken humanity, Jesus of Nazareth forged a new kind of humanity and established himself as its source and head.[23] When he ascended on high, he did not shed his humanity or leave it behind to corruption in the grave. For us and in our place, the God-man Jesus, perpetually presents himself *and us with him*, to the Father. Make no doubt about it, "human nature is now set within the Father-Son relationship of Christ."[24] The Father's desire is that what took place in Jesus of Nazareth through the Spirit would also take place in each of his siblings. What was by nature "the closed circle of the inner life of God" has now been "extended to include" or "made to overlap" with human life in and through the risen incarnate Jesus.[25]

Jesus Christ, the man, is the objective ontological ground of not only those in the church but of all human beings for all time. He is their Isness, such that their real life is hid with him in God. As such, the new humanity which he *is* commands the displacing, denying, and de-centering of all our alienating attempts to manufacture our own pseudo-ontological basis before God.

This fault line which Torrance identifies sets the trajectory for two contrasting frameworks for formation by the Spirit into the image of Christ. One paradigm is ontologically grounded in Christ; the other paradigm is functionally grounded in itself. For reasons which will become clear, I will call the former the "onto-relational participation paradigm" and the latter the "functional-separation paradigm." To demonstrate the significance of the differences between these two frameworks, we will briefly describe the ethos and fruit of the functional-separation paradigm before turning for

---

23. Torrance argues that the description of the church in the New Testament as the body of Christ is not metaphorical, but ontological. We are his body literally, for it is in his risen human existence that we live and move and have our being.

24. Torrance, *Space, Time and Resurrection*, 69. This fact is pointed to in the Pauline language of our adoption and constitution as joint heirs with Christ (Rom 8:14–17, 29; Eph 1:3–14; Gal 4:4–7).

25. Torrance, *Theology in Reconstruction*, 241.

the remainder of this chapter to the onto-relational-participation paradigm advocated by Torrance.

FUNCTIONAL-SEPARATION FORMATION

Dallas Willard has popularized a powerful metaphor related to the spiritual disciplines known as "training vs. trying."[26] Just as I could not run an entire marathon without training regardless of how hard I might try, so too, without the spiritual disciplines we are unable to reach our full potential even if we try very hard. Consistent with this metaphor, Willard defines spiritual exercises as activities in our own power that we engage in to enable us to do what we at present cannot do by direct effort.[27]

This simple principle has proven helpful to a great many people. "Trying hard to be like Jesus" is usually a recipe for frustration and exhaustion in the Christian life. After decades of trying hard, many admit defeat and give up trying at all. By contrast, the idea of spiritual training gives hope to the weary.

One of Willard's most prolific and popular disciples, John Ortberg, describes this as "the single most helpful principle I know regarding spiritual transformation." Reflecting upon his discovery of this principle years earlier while reading Willard's book, *The Spirit of the Disciplines*, Ortberg writes:

> I wish I could describe the hope I felt when I first came to understand this truth. ... For me, this truth brought light to the darkness. For the first time as an adult, I found the notion of following Jesus a real, concrete, tangible possibility. I could do it. Following Jesus simply means learning from him how to arrange my life around activities that enable me to live in the fruit of the Spirit.[28]

This makes sense to us for we can understand it in relation to any other sphere of life: athletics, music, health, fitness, learning a new language, and more. Why wouldn't Christian virtues be like all those other things? Why

---

26. Dallas Willard, *The Spirit of the Disciplines, Understanding How God Changes Lives* (San Francisco: HarperOne, 1999). I chose to use Willard as an example because of his popularity and influence in, at least, the North American context, and because I have great respect for him.

27. Dallas Willard, *The Great Omission* (San Francisco: HarperCollins, 2006).

28. John Ortberg, *The Life You've Always Wanted: Spiritual Disciplines for Ordinary People* (Grand Rapids: Zondervan, 2009), 47–48.

wouldn't we be able to train ourselves in the art of learning forgiveness, courage, or joy?

Ortberg notes a twofold danger, however, in that spiritual disciplines can induce guilt or become a burden. We feel guilty that we are not doing enough. We feel burdened by trying to do too much. Many believers find themselves schizophrenically consumed by both at the same time. Ortberg's solution to the burden of a performance orientation around spiritual disciplines is to remember that the point of it all is "growth in the ability to love God and people." He concludes:

> If we can do this [i.e., love God and people] without the practice of any particular spiritual disciplines, then we should by all means skip them. ... Spiritual disciplines are to life what calisthenics are to a game. Once the game starts, basketball players get no bonus points based on how many free throws they shot in practice. The only reason to practice them is to be able to make them in a game.[29]

The Solution Repeats the Problem

What do we find when we interrogate this approach with Torrance's question, "Does it take the humanity of the risen Jesus seriously or not?" If we reframe Torrance's question positively, we might ask, "What work or active role does the ascended incarnate Christ play in this description of the Christian life?" The answer to either question is: "He is not there, or if he is, he is certainly not the primary agent at work." For Torrance, this is a profoundly fundamental problem. Fundamental enough to be considered "the main issue which divides all theologies and strikes them apart to the one side or to the other."[30]

From Torrance's standpoint, the humanity of Christ is not simply a doctrine that sits quietly on the shelves of erudite philosophical theologians. Rather, it is the heart and center of the daily life of the Christian. Any description of any aspect of the Christian life must explicitly or implicitly integrate this if it is to be called by the name "Christian." If Torrance is right, dedicated spiritual training toward Christlikeness may not be as Christlike as it first appears.

---

29. Ortberg, *The Life You've Always Wanted*, 49–50.

30. Torrance, *Conflict and Agreement in the Church*, Vol. 1, 98. See *Royal Priesthood* (Edinburgh: T&T Clark, 1993), 43.

With regard to our discussion on the training versus trying metaphor, what are the implications of the absence of an active and relevant role for the risen Christ in his humanity? Due to space, we can only mention the main points. First, it is separate and independent: this paradigm understands the exercise of faith, obedience, and discipleship as the ways in which *we* respond to God. Absent a relevant role for the risen Lord, our response of faith is functionally unitarian. God does his part, and then we do ours. This framework and its accompanying language assume both a relational and an ontological distance between us and Christ, inevitably directing the focus of our attention back upon ourselves and the rightness of our responses.

Second, it is based on utilitarian means: to describe spiritual disciplines as training sessions implies that their value and purpose are purely utilitarian. These preparatory activities are not *themselves* a real participation in Christ; rather, they are a means toward acquiring grace in order to accomplish something else. Jesus himself is not needed here and now because *we* know what to do. *We* have a plan, and if *we* work on the plan, *we* will get the results *we* expect in the end. The personal activity of the Holy Spirit is impersonalized, commodified, and commandeered to serve our own personal self-construction project.[31]

Third, it has a performance orientation: most often Christlikeness is defined as imitating both the character and the actions of Jesus such that a "fully-devoted follower" of Christ will be a model of Christlike character, Christlike service, Christlike churchmanship, and more. However, when the standards of Christlikeness are highly correlated with devotional practices, service roles, and church involvement, it becomes easy (and natural) to regard the Christian life as a kind of project to be achieved through dedication, busyness, and detailed spiritual-growth plans. Whether the disciple is "training" or just "trying" makes no difference in the end because there is always more that could, or should, be done. God is sidelined while our activity takes center stage. His job is to help *us* with *our* project.

Fourth, it imitates a dead Jesus: in our striving to imitate or follow the example of Jesus (*imitatio Christi*), it is possible for Christ himself to be

---

31. The sin of Adam and Eve eating from the Tree of the Knowledge of Good and Evil seems to be relevant here. We were created for continuous fellowship with God, but we seek autonomy, at least in some areas of life.

rendered extraneous. We can follow the example of Jesus without follow-ing Jesus himself. A dead Jesus is much more predictable than a risen Jesus who is present and walks in our midst. Imitating an example does not require present-tense listening and attention.

Fifth, it can prioritize ideals, idols, and ideologies: when Christlikeness is defined by a set of morals and virtues lifted from the pages of Scripture, those morals and virtues can displace Christ himself as the goal. Rather than fixing our eyes on Jesus who is always with us, we fix our eyes on the pursuit of particular Christian virtues. Virtues become idols, taking our attention away from the one true living God. Over time, these ideals take on an idola-trous life of their own and morph into ideologies, while Jesus himself silently moves further and further from the center. We do not need Jesus when we have an ideology. History has demonstrated repeatedly how communities guided by idolatrous virtues are capable of doing very unchristlike things in the name of Christ.

Being Thrown Back Upon Ourselves

Each variation of the metaphor or concept above in its own way abandons grace by relating to the living Lord as if he were an inert and impersonal sub-ject matter. Each suggests that *we* are the center, the primary actor, toward which all else must refer. Each implicitly ignores, or actively resists, the personal summons of the living ascended Lord to hear his voice and obey him in faith.

Collectively, the loss of this Trinitarian dynamic creates a vacuum which the individual believer (or the church) must fill. Lacking a relevant contempo-rary role (beyond the bestowal of forgiveness) for the incarnate risen Christ to play, the life of faith and the work of ministry naturally falls upon the shoul-ders of the believer. The yoke of the functional-separation paradigm of spir-itual formation turns out to be a mix of activism, disassociation, and shame.

Absent the active mediation of Christ in his ascended humanity, the church inevitably is driven by an underlying current of activism. In the place of an absent Jesus, we substitute the frenetic activities of endless programmatic strategies, master plans, techniques, formulas, behavioral modifications, virtue ethics, and individualized spiritualities in an endless effort to justify ourselves and motivate ourselves to generate more iterations of renewal.

We can spend so much time and energy trying to do the things that would please God that we have no time left just to be with God. Our inner life can be so inundated by the outside inputs of external devotionals, books, podcasts, and Bible studies that we have no time to simply be present with the inner life we have worked so hard at creating. We can cultivate an interior life from which we remain disconnected.

The unintended effect of this paradigm is the promotion of shame. With the gifts of God standing on one side of the ledger and human effort standing on the other, creaturely activity can never be enough. Even though the promise of grace means one's eternal salvation is not in danger, the Christian life continues to be fraught with comparison, competition, performance, and self-justification. While God may not judge our meager offerings, we do; and we see very clearly how poorly we perform. The more conscientious the Christian, the more likely they will be anxious about their level of production. Turning to ourselves, we recommit and redouble our efforts to be "fully devoted" to Christ, all the while becoming increasingly devoted to a socially sanctified form of self-reliance. In the end, we potentially become less Christlike in our humanity than when we began.

Conclusion

The problem with the training versus trying metaphor is that it presents a false dichotomy. Neither one in fact adequately describes the life of the disciple. The whole project misses the mark, for even as the training or trying disciple seeks a center in God, they lead from a center in themselves. The fact is, Jesus does not call us to an ethic or virtuous ideal. He summons people to *himself* and calls them to remain present to himself. Yet, when the presupposition is some form of ontological separation, relational separation follows suit. Torrance advocates a different foundation: one based in union and communion that enacts itself relationally through participation.

From the brief analysis above we can begin to see why the humanity of the risen Christ is so important and so central to Torrance's theology. We can also see why Eugene Peterson, one of evangelicalism's most significant spiritual theology and formation guides, laments the absence of an ontological understanding of the church grounded in the mediation of Jesus's humanity.

ONTO-RELATIONAL PARTICIPATION PARADIGM

Having noted the fault line that separates Torrance's approach from the typical evangelical paradigm, which I have called functional-separation, the remainder of this chapter focuses on the onto-relational and participation dynamics revealed by Torrance's framework.

A Christological Ontology

This understanding of Christian existence begins with the insight that Jesus Christ alone establishes and reveals human nature. He is humanity as we all were intended to be—the true *imago Dei*. In the incarnation, Christ established an irreversible ontological relation with creation.[32] The humanity of every human being is mediated by the humanity of Christ.[33] Because of the resurrection and ascension of Jesus, Torrance asserts, "we are to think of the whole human race, and indeed of the whole creation, as in a profound sense already redeemed, resurrected, and consecrated for the glory and worship of God."[34] There are not two kinds of humans: those in the circle of the Triune life and those outside. To be a human creature is to be caught up in this onto-relational situation of participation in the Father, Son, and Spirit. As such, all of us have the same essential task: to become who we are in Christ. And the only way to do so is to learn from Jesus how to be human.

The life of Jesus reveals to us what it means to be a human person fully alive. He is the full and complete expression and enactment of receiving and returning love. In examining the dynamic nature of Jesus's human self, we discover what it means for us to be a human self and the reality behind all human personhood. In Jesus Christ "the eternal Son became man without overriding or diminishing the reality of the human person or hypostasis, but on the contrary, gave it real subsistence *in* himself. That is to say ... the human nature of Jesus was personalized or given *enhypostatic* reality in the

---

32. Thomas F. Torrance, *Theological Science* (London: Oxford University Press, 1969), 66–67. Irreversible refers to "one-directional" or by grace. This is a two-way relation which is established completely and freely from the side of God "out of pure grace."

33. Thomas F. Torrance, "Introduction," in *The School of Faith: The Catechisms of the Reformed Church*, ed. and trans. Thomas F. Torrance (London: The Camelot Press; New York: Harper & Brothers, 1959), cxiv. "The whole of creation is now put on a new basis with God, the basis of a Love that does not withhold itself but only overflows in pure unending Love. ... That applies to every man, whether he will or no. He owes his very being to Christ and belongs to Christ, and in that he belongs to Christ he has his being only from Him and in relation to Him."

34. Torrance, *Trinitarian Faith*, 183.

Person of the Son of God become man."[35] The union of God and man forged in the incarnate Son was a dynamic union, a hypostatic uniting established moment by moment, day by day, as the human Jesus aligned his will with the will of the Father. If Jesus Christ is the definition of humanity, then to be human is to be completely dependent upon God, to find our self out of ourselves in him. It is this relation between divinity and humanity in the hypostatic union that sets the terms within which human actions take place. This is the way of our participation in grace.[36]

Unlike Christ, we often contradict ourselves with sin and thereby contradict our humanity. However, when we live in alignment with the dynamic nature of our union with Jesus Christ that correspondence takes place in analogy to the dynamic movement of his life.

Inside Two Poles

One of Torrance's favorite passages was Galatians 2:20, in which Paul gives expression to the mystery of our existence: "I am crucified with Christ, nevertheless I live, yet not I. But Christ lives in me, and the life which I now live in the flesh, I live by the faith of the Son of God, who loved me and gave himself for me" (KJV).

Reflecting on this passage, Torrance writes, "Faith in Christ involves a polar relation between the faith of Christ and our faith, in which our faith is laid hold of, enveloped and upheld by his unswerving faithfulness."[37] Like the an- or enhypostasia, this "polar relation" involves a "primary pole" (the faithfulness of God in Christ "who lays hold of us and brings us into a living relation with himself") and a "secondary pole" (located within the embrace of the relation established in the primary pole) which is the response of the believer.

Our response (the secondary pole) is "an act of faith evoked by and sustained by the faithfulness of God" (the primary pole). In other words, our pole is not of ourselves but is a gift of God. The primary pole of the Christian

---

35. Torrance, The Christian Doctrine of God: One Being Three Persons (Edinburgh: T&T Clark, 1996), 230.

36. Torrance, Theology in Reconstruction, 114, 186.

37. Thomas F. Torrance, "Preaching Jesus Christ," in A Passion for Christ: The Vision that Ignites Ministry, ed. Jock Stein and Gerrit S. Dawson (Edinburgh: Handsel Press, 1999), 25.

life lies outside of ourselves.[38] The primary pole is the humanity of the risen Christ. Because he is truly human, we are human with him. And because he is God, we are with God in him. As there is no humanity apart from Christ, and there is also no human relation to God outside of that which is joined to Christ, Torrance describes Jesus Christ, *in his humanity*, as the significant "middle term" of divine-human relations.[39] The ascended incarnate Lord is the living objective basis for human participation in, and fellowship with, God.

In this case, the human response to God is never detached from Christ's response of perfect faithfulness to the Father for us. He is the primary pole in whom we respond as the secondary pole already embraced in him. Recalling Galatians 2:20, the life we live, we live on the wholly new basis of his faithfulness. This clarifies the movement of faith. For Torrance, "Faith is fundamentally a motion of receptivity to an objective ground beyond ourselves."[40] It involves a fundamental shift from thinking centered on the inward-turned and alienated self (the secondary pole) to thinking that is turned up and outward toward Christ (the primary pole) in whom one's life is hidden.[41]

SANCTIFICATION AS PERSONALIZATION

Grounded onto-relationally, spiritual formation within Torrance's framework is relentlessly personal and participatory. The humanity of the risen Christ secures the continuance and particularity of our humanity as we are trained by the Spirit to become finally and properly the human persons we are created to be in Christ.[42] In contrast to the dehumanizing consequences to human beings which take place when spiritual formation dehumanizes the risen Christ, the personalizing impact of Torrance's onto-relational

---

38. See Jerome Van Kuiken, "'Not I, but Christ'—Thomas F. Torrance on the Christian Life," in *T&T Clark Handbook of Thomas F. Torrance*, ed. Paul D. Molnar and Myk Habets (London: Bloomsbury, 2020), 243.

39. Thomas F. Torrance, *God and Rationality* (London: Oxford University Press, 1971), 145.

40. Ziegler, *Trinitarian Grace*, 280. "Active as never before, one lives in the passive voice, alert to be used, fearful of nothing, patient to stand and wait." Thomas Kelly, *The Sanctuary of the Soul: Selected Writings of Thomas Kelly* (Nashville: Upper Room, 1997), 26.

41. "That transformation in our inner self in which we learn to think from a centre in God rather than from a centre in ourselves is the basic reorientation that takes place in the church of Jesus Christ. Christian discipleship is the disciplined habit of thinking and acting *in Christ*," Torrance, *Atonement*, 376.

42. In Torrance's theology, "the movement within the salvation of men and women is from human being, a biological fact, to human person, a moral, theological fact." See Myk Habets, *Theosis in the Theology of Thomas Torrance* (Farnham: Ashgate, 2009), 55.

participatory theology effects considerable "healing and restoring and deep-ening [of] human personal being."[43] I conclude this chapter by highlighting five contrasts between these paradigms.

Participation (not separation): since Jesus himself has no autonomy from his relationship with the Father, Torrance's christological anthropology holds no legitimate place for autonomous human action. The Trinity is not a con-cept to believe in; they are a dynamic relationship we live inside. Christian existence does not take place in a unitarian context, but within a Trinitarian relation in which solitude is a group of four. Our life is ontologically and irre-vocably hidden with Christ in God.[44] The life we live, we live not as those who respond *to* Christ, as if we were separate and independent beings, but one in which we respond *inside* the faithfulness of his perfect response. Through the Spirit, we share in the Son's relation with the Father.

Constant *koinonia* (not dualist utilitarianism): given the objective onto-re-lational reality of our existence and given the way Jesus Christ fulfilled his divine vocation through relational fidelity to the Father, sanctification in the Christian life is reoriented from a moral category to an onto-relational one. The sanctified person is not morally perfect, but the one who faithfully faces God.[45] "Sanctification therefore takes place as we share in the *koinonia* of the Son with the Father through the Spirit."[46] Spiritual practices are not utilitar-ian means to accomplish something else. In Christ, ends do not justify means; rather, the ends *are* the means and the means *are* the ends. Every moment is a sacred *koinonia*, for every moment is mediated by the risen Christ who includes us in his human relationship with the Father.

Other-centered personalization (not self-focused performance): Torrance's onto-relational framework also pushes back against our default performance orientation at every point. The personalizing Spirit makes us personalized persons, by drawing us into genuine relations with the

---

43. Torrance, *Trinitarian Faith*, 230. See also, Torrance, *Conflict and Agreement in the Church*, Vol. 1, 98–99.

44. "We are with Jesus beside God, for we are gathered up in him and included in his own self-presentation to the Father," Torrance, *Space, Time and Resurrection*, 135–36.

45. Thomas F. Torrance, *Incarnation: The Person and Life of Christ*, ed. Robert T. Walker (Downers Grove, IL and Milton Keynes: IVP and Paternoster, 2008), 187. See Ziegler, *Trinitarian Grace*, chapter 4, "The Imago Dei and the 'Proleptic Self.'"

46. Ziegler, *Trinitarian Grace*, 264.

triune God and everything he has created.[47] The task of the disciple is to embrace Jesus's invitation by cultivating a shared identity and sharing in the mindset of Christ. Christ is the mediator and primary pole of our entire humanity, not just our spiritual life. As we learn to live within a shared identity, embracing our position at the secondary pole of our self, "personal forms of reflection are begotten in us as we are obedient to Him."[48] Because the primary active agent is the living, ascended incarnate Christ, the focus for believers is not inward, for we are drawn outward and upward into the praying and worshiping life of the Son.

Active learners (not imitators): Jesus invites all who would come to him to share in the relationship he has with his Father through the Spirit. Within this fully personal paradigm, we do not imitate a dead Jesus, but rather, participate in Christ here and now by the Spirit whom he sent to us. Jesus wants us to learn from him what it is like to be a child in the Father's kingdom. We let Jesus be our teacher as we walk with him and invite him into our minds and let him share his mind with us. As we learn to see what Jesus sees, we too will love as he loves. If we are to be formed into the image of Christ, we must take the "way of Christ's humanity,"[49] the same "basic soteriological inversion must be pushed through the whole region of the mind" until we are reschematized and inverted in "the whole of our mental system."[50] This is how our minds are converted and transformed. The New Testament calls this having "the mind of Christ."

Concrete persons in communion (not abstract ideals): spiritual formation is not defined by living up to a set of ideal virtues, nor by serving an abstract

---

47. Torrance, *The Christian Doctrine of God*, 160; and *God and Rationality*, 188. Eric Flett makes the point that in Torrance's description of the Christian life, "the terms personalization, humanization, and sanctification are nearly synonymous," Eric G. Flett, *Persons, Powers, and Pluralities: Toward a Trinitarian Theology of Culture* (Cambridge: James Clark, 2012), 40. Flett notes that Torrance tends to speak of the "work of the Spirit as 'sanctification' when referring to the created order in general, and as 'humanization' or 'personalization' when speaking of human creatures in particular," 44.

48. Torrance, *Theological Science*, 207.

49. See section "A Christological Ontology" above.

50. See Torrance, *Theology in Reconstruction*, 115–16 where he refers to Calvin, *Calvin's Commentaries*, Ed. the Calvin Translation Society, 22 vols. (Edinburgh, 1843–55) on Col 1:21 and *Institutes of the Christian Religion* (1559), Trans. F. L. Battles, Ed. J. T. McNeill, Library of Christian Classics 20–21 (Philadelphia: Westminster, 1960), 2.15.9. As a human, Christ had to work out his salvation and "beat his way forward by blows ... with strong cryings and tears," Torrance, *Incarnation*, 64 (Luke 2:52; Heb 5:7).

ideology, but by faithful fidelity to Christ himself. The central concern is the translation of the Father-Son relation in Christ into the daily life of the children of God.[51] The goal is that the way of our being (the way we live) might correspond to the truth of our being (in Christ). Real transformation of our inner being takes place inside the communion of the Father, Son, and Spirit. The *way* that the being of the disciple comes to align with the truth of the triune being is by participating with Jesus in the way he enacts his being with the Father in the Spirit. We only love like the God-who-loves by being in relational communion with that God such that we learn to love by being loved. We only become self-giving like the God-for-others by being in relational communion with that God such that we experience God as radically self-giving to us. Christlikeness is the fruit of *koinonia*.

CONCLUSION

In this chapter we have sought to demonstrate the important contribution and corrective that Torrance offers to evangelical spiritual formation. His mission was to evangelize the foundations by calling God's people, in all areas of life, to begin from a center in God rather than in ourselves. Such a radical repentant rethinking of all our ways is beyond us, yet there is a way forward if we can develop the disciplined habit of thinking and acting in Christ. Torrance argues that the primary fault line that divides all theologies is the significance of place given to the humanity of the risen Christ. We found an ally for Torrance within evangelicalism in Eugene Peterson who also laments the need for an ontological understanding of Christian existence.

In the light of Torrance's and Peterson's critiques, we considered the current state of spiritual formation within evangelicalism. As a test case, we chose a major theme (training vs. trying) from two of the most influential contemporary voices in the evangelical spiritual formation movement (Dallas Willard and John Ortberg). Our comparison revealed that Torrance's fault line does indeed divide, rather sharply, the evangelical functional-separation spiritual formation paradigm from Torrance's onto-relational participation paradigm of formation by the Spirit.

We noted several dehumanizing ramifications embedded in the functional-separation paradigm because of its lack of an active role for the humanity

---

51. Torrance, "Atonement and the Moral Order," 254.

of the risen Christ, namely, having the yoke thrown back upon ourselves. By contrast, we discovered the humanizing and personalizing impact of Torrance's onto-relational participation framework because of the active mediatorial role of Christ. To follow Jesus as his disciple is to take the way he took in his own humanity in which he received his personhood from his divine Sonship. For us to live in Christ is to live consciously within this same polar relation, in which we receive our life from him. As we learn to dwell inside our shared identity in Christ, the *koinonia* of the personalizing Spirit heals, restores, and deepens the personal part of our being.

Torrance is an evangelical theologian par excellence, who offers the church a way of being and living that is contemplative and dialogical, a way that calls her to vigilant attentiveness to Christ's real presence, and which ultimately transforms human beings into persons by lifting our hearts up and into the Lord. For Torrance, there is no Christian form of sanctification that is not also in Christ and therefore participatory. The next time we read a book or listen to a sermon, we may want to ask ourselves, "What work is the humanity of the risen Christ doing here?" If the answer is "nothing," we will do well to remind ourselves that our entire existence is a *koinonia* in the Son's *koinonia* with the Father in the Spirit.[52]

---

52. See Ziegler, *Trinitarian Participation*, 263–64.

12

—

"SEEKING LOVE, JUSTICE AND FREEDOM FOR ALL"

Using the Work of T. F. and J. B. Torrance
to Address Domestic and Family Violence[1]*

Jenny Richards

This chapter will outline the interdisciplinary contributions that the works of theologians Thomas F. Torrance and James B. Torrance[2] offer to Christians who are experiencing domestic and family violence, and the church leaders who support those working through trauma.[3] There are significant and beneficial commonalities in the theological method and teachings of both Torrance brothers which shed light on this issue. Both Torrances rejected dualism and embraced holism. They wrote harmoniously about covenant, and on the person and work of Jesus, and what these truths tell us about personhood, human relationships and dignity, mediation and reconciliation. All these concepts speak powerfully to the way in which the Father, Son, and Spirit view issues such as domestic and family violence, which fundamentally informs what a Christian response to those situations could look like for church workers and for people experiencing violence. The Torrances works

---

1. *James. B. Torrance, "The Ministry of Reconciliation Today: The Realism of Grace," in *Incarnational Ministry: The Presence of Christ in Church, Society, and Family; Essays in Honor of Ray S. Anderson*, ed. Christian Kettler and Todd Speidell (Colorado Springs: Helmers & Howard, 1990), 137.

2. To avoid confusion, future references will refer to "T. F." or "J.B." Torrance to distinguish the authors.

3. Thanks to my colleagues, associate professor Lorna Hallahan and Dr. Elise Ruthenbeck, for their perceptive and helpful comments on earlier drafts of this chapter.

can assist evangelical church leaders in explicitly addressing complex theological and pastoral issues that arise for Christians experiencing domestic and family violence, most notably in relation to their possible engagement with the justice system and broader questions of forgiveness and justice. Their theological works provide an ontologically grounded, nondualist framework from within which to conceptualize faith responses to domestic and family violence and a covenantal understanding of justice and the place of law and the justice system. J. B. Torrance's model of socio-political reconciliation,[4] developed in relation to South Africa and Northern Ireland, can also be adapted and drawn from in applying a holistic approach to the various theological teachings and relational issues relevant to addressing family violence pastorally and within a broader social framework.

There is less research on family violence against Christian women in Australia than there is in the US. Nonetheless, Australian research has shown that the occurrence of violence against Christian women is roughly equivalent to that against women outside of the church, and may in fact be somewhat higher, both for violence against Christian women and against Christian men.[5] Similar incident rates are indicated for the United States.[6] Considerable research has been undertaken for many years on pastoral responses to domestic and family violence against Christians. We know that theological beliefs can have varying functions: they can form a barrier to help-seeking; they can be used to justify violence;[7] or they can form part of a careful faith response to that violence.[8] It is clear both in Australia and in many other countries that faith leaders and faith communities have a central role to play in addressing the issue of domestic and family violence, due to the

---

4. J. B. Torrance, "The Ministry of Reconciliation Today," 130–39.

5. Ruth Powell and Miriam Pepper, *National Anglican Family Violence Research Report: for the Anglican Church of Australia*, NCLS Research Report (NCLS Research, 2021), 13.

6. Steve McMullin et al., "When Violence Hits the Religious Home: Raising Awareness About Domestic Violence in Seminaries and Among Religious Leaders," *Journal of Pastoral Care and Counseling* 69 (2015): 113.

7. Heidi Levitt and Kimberly Ware, "'Anything with Two Heads Is a Monster': Religious Leaders; Perspectives on Marital Equality and Domestic Violence," *Violence Against Women* 12 (2006): 1169; Lynne Baker, *Counselling Christian Women on How to Deal with Domestic Violence* (Bowen Hills: Australian Academic Press, 2010).

8. Baker, *Counselling Christian Women*; Elisabet Le Roux, *A Scoping Study on the Role of Faith Communities and Organisations in Prevention and Response to Sexual and Gender-Based Violence: Implications for Policy and Practice*, Unit for Religion and Development Research Stellenbosch University, South Africa Report (2015).

influence of a person's spiritual beliefs on their decision-making.[9] Christians are, understandably, strongly motivated to attempt to identify what their faith says about issues facing them and are more likely to choose a response to domestic and family violence that they believe is congruent with the tenets of their faith. For this reason, primary prevention that involves faith leaders is seen as best practice.[10] Nason-Clark notes, "Religious organizations and their leaders may be uniquely situated to alter, or at least challenge, attitudes that reinforce violence within the family."[11]

Despite this, tension consistently arises between a woman's desire to bring her faith to bear in her responses to the violence committed against her, and the need to attend to her own safety and well-being.[12] Studies demonstrate that these needs are commonly in conflict.[13] A ten-year American study by Zust and coauthors found that women were so influenced by faith in decision-making that they would resolve a conflict by remaining in abusive marriages, rather than compromise their faith.[14]

---

9. See, for example, Mandy Truong et al., *Faith Based Communities' Responses to Domestic and Family Violence*, CSRM working paper, no. 1 (Canberra: Australian National University, 2020); Beth Crisp, "Faith Communities as a Setting for the Prevention of Gender-Based Violence," in *Eliminating Gender-Based Violence*, ed. Ann Taket and Beth Crisp (London: Routledge, 2018), 124; Steve McMullin et al., "When Violence Hits the Religious Home," 113–14.

10. Leonie Westenberg, "When She Calls for Help: Domestic Violence in Christian Families," *Social Sciences* 6 (2017): 2, 6–7; Rene Drumm et al., "Clergy Training for Effective Response to Intimate Partner Violence Disclosure: Immediate and Long-Term Benefits," *Journal of Religion and Spirituality in Social Work: Social Thought* 37 (2018): 77; Shoshana Ringel and Juyoung Park, "Intimate Partner Violence in the Evangelical Community: Faith-Based Interventions and Implications for Practice," *Journal of Religion and Spirituality in Social Work: Social Thought* 27 (2008): 341.

11. Nancy Nason-Clark, *The Battered Wife: How Christians Confront Family Violence* (Louisville: Westminster John Knox Press, 1997).

12. Due to its gendered nature, current research on domestic and family violence against Christians predominantly involves violence by husbands against wives, which raises particular theological issues in circumstances where doctrines such as marital submission and male headship, and a wife's responsibility to look after the family (and by extension, ensure continuation of the marriage relationship) have been used to justify abuse, and to suggest that women should remain in dangerous relationships. In this chapter, research and theological teachings relevant to those issues will be discussed in terms of violence occurring from husbands to wives. However, theological teachings can also be twisted to justify abuse of husbands, and the gospel condemns domestic violence committed against husbands in no less certain terms.

13. Nancy Nason-Clark, "Christianity and the Experience of Domestic Violence: What Does Faith Have to Do with It?" *Social Work and Christianity* 36 (2009): 379, 382.

14. Barbara Zust et al., "10-year Study of Christian Church Support for Domestic Violence Victims: 2005-2015," *Journal of Interpersonal Violence* 00 (2018): 1.

Some Christian teachings and beliefs that can form barriers to help-seeking include those emphasizing the permanent and sacred nature of marriage (and its associated indissolubility) and teachings about male headship and female submission. These teachings are interpreted by abusive spouses as implying that wives are to obey husbands in everything.[15] This kind of teaching leaves women particularly vulnerable to marital rape.[16] These teachings intersect with beliefs that characterize domestic and family violence as a behavioral flaw or a spiritual problem, which should be resolved by prayer, and by having that prayerful response promoted as the appropriate response of a godly wife to the violence against her.[17] Research indicates that a conceptualization of domestic and family violence as a spiritual issue rather than a secular one, and the belief that forgiveness is inconsistent with police or justice system involvement, both form significant barriers to Christian women being able to access the protection of the justice system and seek safety from the violence they are experiencing.[18]

The holistic and ontologically grounded covenantal work of the Torrances is ideally placed to address both of these barriers. It can powerfully enable Christian women to engage with the justice system if they consider that an appropriate step[19] and, importantly, allow for the complex theological and pastoral issues to be carefully and comprehensively addressed. This is particularly relevant in ensuring that teachings about forgiveness not be considered in isolation or given primacy over teachings about justice, repentance, reparation, dignity, personhood, and worth. The gospel does not require justice to be forgone as an expression of faith, nor preclude involvement of

---

15. Maxine Davis, "The Intersection of Intimate Partner Violence Perpetration, Intervention, and Faith" (PhD thesis, Washington University, 2018).

16. Katie Edwards et al., "Rape Myths: History, Individual and Institutional-Level Presence, and Implications for Change," *Sex Roles* 65 (2011): 761.

17. Zust et al., "10-Year Study," 11; Truong et al., *Faith Based Communities Responses*, 6.

18. Excellent Chireshe, "Barriers to the Utilisation of Provisions of the Zimbabwean Family Violence Act among Abused Christian Women in Zimbabwe," *Journal of International Women's Studies* 16 (2015): 259; Tompson Makahamadze, Anthony Isacco, and Excellent Chireshe, "Examining the Perceptions of Zimbabwean Women about the Domestic Violence Act," *Journal of Interpersonal Violence* 27 (2012): 706.

19. It should be noted that justice system involvement is a choice which many people may not wish to pursue for a variety of reasons. The key here is simply to ensure that the justice system is not viewed as either outside of a faith response or as an "un-Christian" or "unforgiving" choice.

the justice system. In turn, this paves the way for greater freedom and restoration to occur.

THEOLOGICAL METHOD: HOLISM AND
ONTO-RELATIONAL FOUNDATIONS
FOR ADDRESSING VIOLENCE

The central way the work of T. F. Torrance is profoundly helpful in addressing issues relevant to domestic and family violence is his theological method: his realist epistemology, rejection of dualist frames of thinking, and his concept of onto-relations. The impact of T. F. Torrance's theological method on his understanding of the person and work of Christ, and his consequent understanding of human personhood and Christian discipleship, provide significant insight into the nuanced issues involved in addressing domestic and family violence.

T. F. Torrance applied a realist epistemology to all his work, not just his theology. This is unsurprising given that the bulk of his work was either on foundational theological methods and an exposition of the early church in that regard,[20] or on science, scientific method, and how science (particularly physics and metaphysics) and theology could mutually inform one another. T. F. Torrance's theological method is what informs his scientific method and approach to epistemology generally, rather than it being the other way around.[21] This is due to the centrality of his religious beliefs to his academic and pastoral careers and the fact that his Christian theological beliefs are prior to his scientific analysis. His realist epistemology has been described as "Christian realism,"[22] ostensibly because of this connection.

Methodologically speaking, T. F. Torrance's rejection of dualisms sits alongside his epistemology. It is central to his theological method and is highly relevant in approaching the issue of domestic and family violence. It

---

20. Thomas F. Torrance, *The Doctrine of Grace in the Apostolic Fathers* (Eugene, OR: Wipf & Stock, 1996), was written under the supervision of Karl Barth precisely on issues of epistemology and what the early church taught in relation to what belief in God as triune implies for an understanding of divine-human relations, the nature of a human being, and the ways in which human beings are to relate to one another and creation.

21. Elmer Colyer, *How to Read T. F. Torrance: Understanding His Trinitarian and Scientific Theology* (Eugene, OR: Wipf & Stock, 2007), 57n9.

22. Douglas Kelly, "The Realist Epistemology of Thomas F. Torrance," in *An Introduction to Torrance Theology: Discovering the Incarnate Saviour*, ed. Gerrit Dawson (London: T&T Clark, 2007), chapter 4.

influences not only the content of some teachings but also the way in which different teachings and faith issues interrelate and inform each other. T. F. Torrance applied his unitary framework to legal theory,[23] anthropology,[24] and to the question of violence in society.[25]

T. F. Torrance rejects the dualism between subject and object and God and the world which were embraced by Descartes and Newton.[26] He points to a need for a reconstruction of legal theory which has an ontological basis (which for T. F. Torrance means an onto-relational basis) and in which epistemology and ontology are integrated, rather than considered separately or dualistically.[27] Torrance defines onto-relation as "the kind of relation subsisting between things which is an essential constituent of their being, and without which they would not be what they are."[28] This concept of onto-relations reflects his realist epistemology:

> The natural unity of form and being, or the co-inherence of theoretical and empirical factors, which has come to light through the rigorous fidelity of natural science to the rational structures of the Universe to which we belong, is an epistemic feature that applies to the whole range of human knowledge at all its various levels. Hence *a transition from a dualist to a unitary basis with the realist integration of epistemology and ontology that this implies, is as imperative for us in law and in theology as it is in natural science.*[29]

He notes a disconnection caused by dualist thinking between morals and laws. This disconnection leads them to be abstracted from the broader context

---

23. Thomas F. Torrance, *Juridical Law and Physical Law: Toward a Realist Foundation for Human Law* (Eugene, OR: Wipf & Stock, 1997).

24. Thomas F. Torrance, "The Soul and Person, in Theological Perspective," in *Religion, Reason and the Self: Essays in Honour of Hywel D. Lewis*, ed. Stewart Sutherland and T. A. Roberts (Cardiff: University of Wales Press, 1989), 103–118; Benjamin Meyers, "The Stratification of Knowledge in the Thought of T. F. Torrance," *Scottish Journal of Theology* 61 (2005): 161–83.

25. Thomas F. Torrance, "Violence in Society Today: An Examination of the Destructive Forces Inherent in Modern Day Society," *Independent Broadcasting* 13 (1977): 15–18.

26. Colyer, *How to Read T. F. Torrance*, 325–26, citing particularly T. F. Torrance's work in *Transformation and Convergence in the Frame of Knowledge*, 6, on this point.

27. T. F. Torrance, *Juridical Law and Physical Law.*

28. Thomas F. Torrance, *Reality and Evangelical Theology: The Realism of Christian Revelation* (Eugene, OR: Wipf & Stock, 1982), 42–43.

29. T. F. Torrance, *Juridical Law and Physical Law*, 5 (emphasis added).

of society, thus limiting agency to violence-responses and excluding violence-prevention.[30] T. F. Torrance posits a unitary approach for morals and laws to enable them to "constitute the stable base not only for order but for freedom."[31]

T. F. Torrance's theological method, with its unitary approach and its onto-relational basis, has much to offer in the development of holistic faith responses to family violence. His work provides concepts of law and justice that have their ontological bases in the unity of the Father and the Son in the Spirit, making them profoundly relational and holistic in their content and outworking. This kind of non-dualist approach is fundamental. It allows for faith and justice system responses to cohere as each forming part of the work of God in responding to violence, rather than viewing a faith response as separate from and an alternative to the secular justice system. It also allows for the personhood of the victim/survivor and perpetrator to be more fully considered in developing responses, if all relevant teachings would be considered as an integrated whole, rather than disconnecting them from each other and giving an inappropriate emphasis. Importantly, from within an evangelical tradition, it would enable church workers to give content and meaning to forgiveness, grace, and the finished work of Christ in the lives of believers and for this to be done as a church body.

ONTO-RELATIONS, PERSONHOOD, AND A "CHRISTIAN" RESPONSE TO VIOLENCE

T. F. Torrance's theological method and his concept of onto-relations have profound implications for human personhood and relationships. Consequently, they are of crucial importance in both understanding the wrong of all forms of violence and providing a conceptual framework within which to approach the vast range of theological, personal, and pastoral issues that arise. For T. F., a realist approach requires returning again and again to the self-revelation of God in Jesus Christ as the incarnate Son of the Father, with all that this implies for what it means to be a human person made in the image of God. It is in Christ that God has personalized humanity, with such personalization

---

30. T. F. Torrance, "Violence in Society," 17.
31. T. F. Torrance, "Violence in Society," 17.

and relationality being constitutive of their reality.[32] Humanity is therefore understood as onto-relational, rather than primarily individual: "There is an inherent relatedness in human being which is a creaturely reflection of a transcendent relatedness in Divine Being. This is the personal or inter-personal structure of humanity in which there is imaged the ineffable personal relations of the Holy Trinity."[33] In Christ, human beings have been fitted for relationship with God and with one another, and are not to be regarded as isolated entities, but as persons-in-communion.[34] Our shared humanity in relation to Father, Son, and Spirit requires recognition of the other as likewise bearing the image of God. This is to be reflected in how we relate to one another. "Torrance maintains that within inter-human relations, the relations between persons also belong to what the persons really are."[35]

As our personhood and humanity are derived from Christ and bound up with him, this has ramifications for not only how we treat one another but what it means to be in communion with each other. Inasmuch as violence is caused by what "lies in the human heart that is turned selfishly in upon itself,"[36] marriage is intended to be a sacred refuge from all interpersonal violence. It is a relationship of unconditional love and self-giving, with mutual concern for the other. For T. F. Torrance, it is an "ordinance ... by which self-will is partially curbed and the individual self is made open to another in love."[37] It is an "ordinance of grace,"[38] not a sacrament.[39] The marriage relationship is not more important than the people in it. Moreover, Christians surrender to God, not to their spouse.[40]

Both T. F. and J. B. Torrances' works on the mediation of Christ, and our consequent participation in his vicarious humanity in covenant relationship

---

32. T. F. Torrance, "The Soul and Person," 114, citing A. Seth Pringle-Pattison, *The Idea of God in the Light of Recent Philosophy* (London: Oxford University Press, 1920), 291.

33. T. F. Torrance, "The Soul and Person," 109–10.

34. This is a recurrent phrase in much of his work. See also James B. Torrance, *Worship, Community and the Triune God of Grace* (Downers Grove, IL: InterVarsity Press, 1996), 152.

35. Geordie Ziegler, *Trinitarian Grace and Participation: An Entry into the Theology of T. F. Torrance* (Minneapolis: Fortress Press, 2017), 152.

36. T. F. Torrance, "Violence in Society," 17.

37. Thomas F. Torrance, "The Christian Doctrine of Marriage," *Theology: A Monthly Journal of Historic Christianity* 56 (1953): 162–67; 163.

38. T. F. Torrance, "The Christian Doctrine," 167.

39. T. F. Torrance, "The Christian Doctrine," 166.

40. T. F. Torrance, "The Christian Doctrine," 162.

with Christ, are relevant here.[41] A Christian man's wife is the person whom he is called to love the most. She is an image-bearer of the God he professes to love and serve. Jesus himself is in her, mediating his Sonship to her. She is participating in his life, as a beloved child of God. A wife cannot rightly be viewed as the one person that a man can get away with treating badly. The very idea of domestic and family violence is an anathema to the covenant love of God for humanity and especially the covenant of marriage. The word "violence" itself denotes something of the damage it does. Violence involves *violation* of one's personhood. A person who does violence to another, effectively denies the image of God in that person and the dignity of their personhood, in addition to doing violence to their own person and to their relationship by dishonoring them in that way. If a man does violence to his spouse, he also does violence to the marriage covenant itself and breaches its very foundation. Domestic and family violence, according to T. F. Torrance, is "a personal act against the person of God."[42] The gospel condemns all forms of domestic and family violence more comprehensively than any justice system ever could. This condemnation must be evident in our responses to it.

COVENANT VERSUS CONTRACT AND ITS RAMIFICATIONS FOR FORGIVENESS, REPENTANCE, AND JUSTICE

Perhaps the best-known aspect of J. B. Torrance's work is his view on the theological covenant. In much of his academic and pastoral work, J. B. Torrance distinguishes between a theological *covenant* and a legal *contract*. The conflation of covenant with contract lends itself to an erroneous contractual, legalistic understanding of theological covenant and, therefore, of the gospel itself.[43] J. B. Torrance's work on covenant and contract outlines an ontologically grounded theological understanding of covenant, with a basis

---

41. See, for example, Thomas F. Torrance, *The Mediation of Christ* (Edinburgh: T&T Clark, 1992); James B. Torrance, "Towards a Theology of Response," unpublished lecture notes (Fuller Theological Seminary).

42. Thomas F. Torrance, *Incarnation: The Person and Life of Christ*, ed. Robert T. Walker (Downers Grove, IL and Milton Keynes: IVP and Paternoster, 2008), 252, as noted in Ziegler, *Trinitarian Grace and Participation*, 175.

43. See James B. Torrance, "Covenant or Contract?: A Study of the Theological Background of Worship in Seventeenth Century Scotland," *Scottish Journal of Theology* 23 (1970): 51–76; J. B. Torrance, *Worship, Community and the Triune God of Grace*; James B. Torrance, "The Contribution of McLeod Campbell to Scottish Theology," *Scottish Journal of Theology* 26 (1973): 295.

in unconditional love. From this understanding come consequent relational obligations—such as forgiving one another and repenting from wrongs committed—which are also unconditional. Both J. B. Torrance and his son Alan Torrance have noted the doctrinal confusion that results from conflating the Hebrew word *Torah* with the Latin word *lex*.[44] There are crucial inconsistencies in meaning between the original Hebrew for covenant (*berith*) and equivalent words in Latin and in English. This conflation can be linked with the fact that the Latin word *foedus* means both covenant and contract.[45] I would add that this slippage is compounded within contemporary usage of "covenant" and "contract" because as a legal term there is no real difference in meaning between covenant and contract.

This shift in language has ramifications for how theological concepts are understood. In particular, it affects understanding the way in which God relates to humanity, and how people (notably husbands and wives) relate to each other, according to Christian teaching.[46] It can also affect our understandings of concepts such as forgiveness, repentance, and justice. It leads to conditional, uncertain, and legalistic understandings of those issues. As Alan Torrance notes, when juxtaposing the Hebrew word for righteousness (*tsedaqah*) with the Latin *iusticia* "the effect ... has been to translate thinking about God from essentially filial and koinonial categories into legal categories—from categories that are 'second personal' in character to impersonal, 'third person' modes of interpretation."[47]

Our understandings of those concepts can also become dualistic because by and large, contracts are dualist in both their structure and their operation. Contracts bring separate and equal parties together in a transactional and legalistic relationship. Further compounding and perhaps reflecting this,

---

44. Alan J. Torrance, "Forgiveness and Christian Character: Reconciliation, Exemplarism and the Shape of Moral Theology," *Studies in Christian Ethics* 30 (2017): 301–2.

45. J. B. Torrance, "Covenant or Contract?" 62; Alan J. Torrance, "Forgiveness and Christian Character."

46. J. B. Torrance, "Covenant or Contract?" 52–56, 62. See also discussion in Alan J. Torrance and Michael Banner, eds., *The Doctrine of God and Theological Ethics* (London: T&T Clark, 2006), 172–74; Todd Speidell, ed., *Trinity and Transformation: J. B. Torrance's Vision of Worship, Mission and Society* (Eugene, OR: Wipf & Stock, 2016); Alexandra S. Radcliff, *The Claim of Humanity in Christ* (Downers Grove, IL: InterVarsity Press, 2016); Myk Habets, "'To Err is Human, to Forgive is Divine': The Ontological Foundations of Forgiveness," in *The Art of Forgiveness*, ed. Philip Halstead and Myk Habets (Lanham: Lexington Books/Fortress Academic, 2018), 3–16.

47. Alan J. Torrance, "Forgiveness and Christian Character," 303.

the nature versus grace model seen in federal theology separates law from grace, rather than incorporating an understanding of law that is covenantal and redemptive in its operation.[48] Instead, J. B. Torrance insisted on what is effectively a thoroughly onto-relational concept of theological covenant and focused on what it tells us about the heart and motivation of the Trinity and the effectiveness of the reconciling person and work of Christ as mediator through his vicarious humanity.[49] For these reasons, while not doing so explicitly, in rejecting a contractual view of God, J. B. Torrance implicitly shared T. F. Torrance's rejection of dualism in our understanding of God or of God and human relations in covenant.[50] Theological covenants are profoundly ontologically grounded.

J. B. Torrance speaks of covenant as "a promise binding two people or two parties to love one another unconditionally."[51] This means that covenant is inherently relational. It is not based on or motivated by either law or self-interest. In these terms, then, a covenant is the *opposite* of a contract, which is entirely conditional and based in law, not in love. Further, a contract presupposes two previously separate individuals who are only connected by this abstracted legal agreement between them. This is in sharp contrast to a theological covenant, which is onto-relationally grounded, because "love and communion belong to the basic equation of personhood."[52] In Scripture, marriage is the most frequent example of the two-sided covenants that exist between individuals.[53] These covenants involve obligations for both parties, which are open-ended obligations of love, rather than contractual and performative.

---

48. See James B. Torrance, "Nature-Grace Model of Federal Theology," unpublished lecture notes; "Covenant or Contract," 67–68.

49. J. B. Torrance, "Towards a Theology of Response."

50. Although he does not refer to it as a dualism, because of his rejection of the Contract God, J. B. Torrance does reject the separation or dichotomy between nature and grace that is a feature of federal theology. See, for example, "Covenant or Contract," 67–68, where he notes that this would constitute a "departure from the great emphasis of the Reformation that nothing is prior to grace." Newtonian and Cartesian dualism between subject and object are precisely what we see in the requirement of a contract for the two parties to be equal and independent.

51. J. B. Torrance, "Covenant or Contract?" 54.

52. Ziegler, *Trinitarian Grace and Participation*, 159.

53. Note that marriage also has a secular legal meaning and is thus often understood as a contractual relationship. It can be so, but that is not the Christian understanding of marriage that Torrance is positing.

A covenantal understanding is grounded in unconditional love and emphasizes the person and work of Christ; whereas a contractual, dualist understanding is grounded in legalistic, abstracted, performative actions of our own which try to condition God into loving us, or at best into continuing to accept us—an outworking of legal repentance. In a contractual understanding, our actions in response to the love of God are given equal weight to the work of Jesus, in contrast to our response being wrapped up in the vicarious humanity of Christ.[54] A covenantal understanding of the gospel recognizes the finished work of Christ as sufficient to both establish and maintain the Christian's identity as a child of God and to fulfill the obligations of the relationship. Both T. F. Torrance and J. B. Torrance emphasize this understanding of covenantal response, using Calvin's concept of "evangelical repentance" as distinct from "legal repentance." The former understands forgiveness as being extended from God on the basis of grace, and therefore prior to any repentance occurring, rather than forgiveness being conditional, grounded in an individual meeting certain "legal" requirements such as repenting in order to somehow "earn" the forgiveness and love of God.[55] Christians' response to God's self-revelation in Christ is one of evangelical, not legal, repentance and living out of divine love. This frees Christians to fully acknowledge not only God's love, but their own wrongs, and address those appropriately. As Ziegler notes, T. F. "Torrance is ... championing ... a new motivation for obedience, which is not driven by self-justification but grounded upon a filial relation with the Father established in Christ ... [one that is] 'ruled by the indicatives of God's love rather than externally governed by the imperatives of the law.'"[56]

An approach to forgiveness that does not move from an ontological basis can descend into something legalistic and devoid of personhood.[57] Correspondingly, so can our approach to domestic and family violence responses. A failure to ground forgiveness ontologically risks its abstraction

---

54. See, for example, J. B. Torrance, "Towards a Theology of Response," 2.

55. This doctrine of forgiveness was a key part of Calvin's teaching and a point of departure from church doctrine during the Reformation. See Andrew B. Torrance, "John Calvin and James Torrance's Evangelical Vision of Repentance," in Speidell, *Trinity and Transformation*, 134–56.

56. Ziegler, *Trinitarian Grace and Participation*, 181–82, quoting Thomas F. Torrance, *The Trinitarian Faith: the Evangelical Theology of the Ancient Catholic Church* (Edinburgh: T&T CLark, 1995), 253.

57. See Habets, "To Err Is Human," 3.

from its relational basis, thus distorting it into a demanded response, disconnected from its location in the love and forgiveness of the Father and devoid of its life-affirming and restorative content.[58] This understanding of forgiveness is profoundly important in relation to domestic and family violence. The gospel emphasizes freedom and restoration, not forgiveness in an abstract sense. Divine forgiveness is part of the way in which restoration and freedom are accomplished for humanity through Christ. Forgiveness in human relationships, then, has a necessary and important part to play in living out the gospel,[59] but that is not the goal itself. It is one part of the way love is lived out, or what J. B. Torrance refers to in a covenantal context as "love in action." Crucially, the other part of love in action within a covenant is the response to forgiveness: unconditional repentance, in which wrongs are freely admitted, justice is committed to, and reparations are made.[60]

J. B. Torrance's work on covenant has been applied to questions of theological ethics and to foundations for human relationships, particularly in developing a relational framework which does not focus on conditional obligations.[61] This is due to the nature of covenants involving unconditional love. It requires the relationship to be one in which there is no room for the behavior of the parties to be dependent on anything done by the other person, such as only extending someone forgiveness if they apologize or take certain actions.

Based on this model, individuals who relate in a covenant relationship to each other would extend forgiveness irrespective of whether the other person had first repented.[62] Importantly, this does not obviate the need for the other person to unconditionally repent and make reparations for wrongs done. Instead, those obligations make up the content of what an unconditional, loving response to right that wrong would look like in practical terms. "A covenantal relationship for James Torrance is a relationship grounded in love for the other and hence one that is unconditional, permanent, and

---

58. Habets, "To Err Is Human," 7.

59. See Alan J. Torrance, "Forgiveness and Christian Character," 307–8.

60. J. B. Torrance, "The Ministry of Reconciliation Today," 137.

61. Alan J. Torrance and Banner, *The Doctrine of God*, 172–74; Alan J. Torrance, "Introduction," in Speidell, *Trinity and Transformation*, 13–14.

62. J. B. Torrance, "Covenant or Contract?" 57–62; Alan J. Torrance, "Introduction," in Speidell, *Trinity and Transformation*, 13–14.

irrevocable. ... It *lasts as long as the love of the loving covenantal actor lasts.* ... And the relationship is consequently characterized by complete loyalty and unswerving fidelity."[63] A man who commits any form of violence against his wife has broken his marriage covenant, his commitment to love her unconditionally, irrevocably, and in complete loyalty and unswerving fidelity. His response to his sin against his wife must be one of unconditional repentance, which includes a commitment to his wife's restoration and safety.

It is this aspect of J. B. Torrance's work on covenant and forgiveness and how those are incorporated into a model of reconciliation that is most relevant to questions of what a Christian response to family violence might look like and, particularly, what scope exists within that faith-based response to include the involvement of the justice system. This is crucial for ensuring that a Christian response to domestic and family violence operates covenantally and not contractually. Having a transactional/contractual perspective for how a covenantal relationship is to be lived out can be harmful. If the obligation to forgive someone unconditionally is abstracted from its ontological basis and applied transactionally, we risk a wife essentially being told that the main word of the gospel in response to the violence against her is a legalistic requirement that she forgive, rather than a condemnation of the violence against her and an affirmation of who she is—and who she remains—in Jesus despite the violent actions of another. Instead, ontologically grounded forgiveness flows out of the finished work of Christ and the violated person's identity as a human being created in the image of God, in service to her restoration and her vindication. It *promotes* justice, rather than obviating the need for justice.[64] Sin and evil are dealt with relationally, in and through the person of Christ. In this way, they do not have to be minimized, justified, or explained away. They can be acknowledged, faced, and carefully dealt with by the perpetrator, to bring restoration to both parties. Neither divine nor human forgiveness operates in a way that exempts us from the social or legal consequences of our wrongdoing. However, knowing

---

63. Douglas Campbell, "Covenant or Contract in the Interpretation of Paul," *Participatio: The Online Journal of the T. F. Torrance Theological Fellowship* 3 (2014): 182–200; 187–188 (emphasis added).

64. See discussion in Alan J. Torrance, "Forgiveness and Christian Character," 310–11, citing Miroslav Volf, *Exclusion and Embrace: A Theological Exploration of Identity, Otherness, and Reconciliation* (Nashville: Abingdon Press, 1996), 123.

that we are forgiven may enable us to accept those consequences and do the work required to face ourselves, make amends, and ultimately participate in our own restoration.

PRACTICAL APPLICATION:
J. B. TORRANCE'S MODEL OF HOLISTIC,
COVENANTAL RECONCILIATION

One outworking of J. B. Torrance's work on theological covenant involved developing a model of reconciliation that outlines implications of covenantal relating for church leaders and individual Christians. These implications center on a covenantal understanding of personal, social, and ministry obligations. He developed the model to assist churches in their efforts toward reconciliation in both Northern Ireland and South Africa.[65] While there are important differences to bear in mind, this model sheds important light on theological concepts that also address domestic and family violence, both in its faith-community contexts and in the potential involvement of the justice system.

J. B. Torrance's model takes a holistic, ontologically grounded understanding of covenant as its basis. He sets out a composite definition of reconciliation, involving love, justice, and freedom, which operate interdependently: "There can be genuine reconciliation in society only when injustice is brought into the open and dealt with. Likewise, there can be no true justice without freedom. Love, justice and freedom are the anatomy of true reconciliation, and are mutually dependent."[66]

Forgiveness does not have its own place in this model. It is one part of the expression of love. This is also where repentance sits, with both forgiveness and repentance operating covenantally and thus unconditionally. They operate in tandem so that the extension of forgiveness to the perpetrator requires unconditional repentance and reparation as the loving response: "Such forgiveness unconditionally demands repentance and *must be received in repentance* if there is to be genuine reconciliation, and such reconciliation

---

65. James B. Torrance, "Reconciliation, Sectarianism and Civil Religion in South Africa and Northern Ireland," unpublished paper. This paper was used as part of his course materials and notes for various speaking engagements in both countries. See also J. B. Torrance, "The Ministry of Reconciliation Today," 130–39.

66. J. B. Torrance, "The Realism of Grace," 136.

will doubtless require reparation. ... Repentance is the necessary response to forgiveness, not its 'condition.' "[67]

Repentance, and particularly a preparedness to provide reparation, are part of justice, and it follows that the provision of justice is the responsibility of the perpetrator. It is not for the wronged party to have to carry the burden of enacting justice. Instead, the perpetrator should commit to seeing that justice is done as part of their commitment to making the situation right. J. B. Torrance's key point is that justice, love, and freedom need to be held together, and this is achieved as evangelical churches consider all aspects of the gospel together and move away from considering our vested interests. Where this does not occur, demands for justice can themselves become disconnected from the gospel.[68] He does not see a Christian, covenantal, loving response as requiring that justice be forgone in order for either love or forgiveness to be extended. Instead, as he notes when quoting from a document prepared in relation to the ending of apartheid, "love without justice is sentimentality."[69]

Justice, for J. B. Torrance, involves the response of the individual to their own wrongdoing and the response of the church to its wounded members' cries for justice.[70] He notes that a correct response in all of these interrelated areas enables the church's "ministry of reconciliation," which involves contributing to the restoration of both parties. On a practical level, this cannot occur for the perpetrator unless they are prepared to receive forgiveness and respond in unconditional repentance. A man who denies or minimizes his violence is unable to be reconciled to his wife, even if she wants reconciliation. However, because unconditional forgiveness operates in tandem with unconditional repentance, yet is not conditional upon it, the wife's restoration, freedom, and vindication are not dependent on the husband's acknowledgment of his violence or his repentance of it.

This is due to the key practical element which J. B. Torrance identifies in relation to the connection between forgiveness, repentance, and reconciliation: forgiveness must be received by the perpetrator in repentance if reconciliation is to occur. This model of justice, forgiveness, and freedom

---

67. J. B. Torrance, "The Realism of Grace," 137.
68. J. B. Torrance, "The Realism of Grace," 136–37.
69. J. B. Torrance, "The Realism of Grace," 136.
70. J. B. Torrance, "The Realism of Grace," 137.

all occurring together and being interdependent provides a practical way to navigate a common feature of domestic and family violence—that is, when an abusive spouse denies or minimizes their violence. In the context of domestic and family violence, an unrepentant abusive spouse remains a profoundly dangerous one. Any form of domestic and family violence, including emotional abuse, financial abuse, spiritual abuse, sexual abuse, and coercive control,[71] are deep-seated issues of power and control that require individual counseling by professionals (not anger-management or couple counseling) before safety can be restored to a relationship. This model provides a crucial circuit breaker, as questions of safety and the continuation of the marriage relationship are kept distinct from the question of how forgiveness can occur and how justice can be provided. Reconciliation does not have to be conflated with the perpetuation of the marriage. It can involve separate restoration of the individuals. Even where both parties are in a position to extend forgiveness and to receive forgiveness in repentance and make reparations, it may nonetheless not be safe, possible, or simply desirable for a marital relationship to resume, and such an outcome is not "un-Christian."

This model also provides guidance for pastoral issues that arise in evangelical churches. When unconditional forgiveness is necessarily connected to unconditional repentance, and both of those are viewed as equally placed and operating in tandem rather than disconnected, there is space for church workers to ask what that unconditional repentance and reparation might look like on the part of any individual perpetrator. A repentant husband should be willing to accept all of the consequences of his conduct, including any consequent fracturing of the marriage, police involvement, a protection order, or criminal charges, as being something that falls to him to submit to as part of providing reparation. There may, in time, be a way forward in relation to their marriage, but that would be a matter for them to decide and must not be prescribed (and still less demanded), just as forgiveness itself dare not be demanded.

---

71. Emotional abuse and coercive control are significant issues in Christian marriages; see Shane Sharp, "Resisting Religious Coercive Control," *Violence Against Women* 20 (2014): 1407.

Instead, in this model the wife can more readily be restored, and her capacity to forgive is part of the humanity that is given back to her by the gospel.[72] Forgiveness, when improperly emphasized, cripples the church's ministry of reconciliation by presenting an incomplete parody that perpetuates and amplifies harm and injustice. The church must not have a vested interest in any particular outcome. It must, instead, remain committed to the restoration of the full humanity of both parties: something that a shallow parody of forgiveness profoundly denies. The safety, personhood, and dignity of the victim/survivor should be the paramount concern of an evangelical church community, as they hear the cries of the oppressed and respond to them.[73] The church finds more space in this model to fulfill its mandate to prioritize the needs of the victim for restoration and protection (rather than the perpetrator's need for forgiveness), because it is the *perpetrator's* responsibility to ensure that her needs are prioritized as part of his unconditional repentance and his commitment to seeing justice done.

While developed for sociopolitical application in response to racial and religious harms in Northern Ireland and South Africa, this model has the potential to be applied in personal relationships involving violence also. In particular, it can address the concerns of justice system involvement being inconsistent with forgiveness, as this model would see the submission of a perpetrator to the justice system as required of them as part of their commitment to make reparations and entirely consistent with a faith response. It is also a holistic model that does not abstract some doctrines from others. Nor does it predetermine what reconciliation might look like in any given situation. It would not require a wife to return to live in a violent, dangerous household. Neither would it leave room for a husband to "presume upon [his wife's] forgiveness where he is not willing to see justice done."[74] It provides a strong doctrinal basis from which to hold perpetrators to account, without discounting the love of God for them. It enables covenant love to be extended, rather than sentimentality. This model, combined with the Torrances' other works on interrelated doctrines, provides a comprehensive framework that would enable a wife to engage with all relevant faith issues and come into

---

72. See J. B. Torrance, "The Realism of Grace," 137; and Alan J. Torrance, "Forgiveness and Christian Character," 308–11.

73. J. B. Torrance, "The Realism of Grace," 137.

74. J. B. Torrance, "The Realism of Grace," 137.

dialogue with the justice system because her responsibilities and well-being would not be dependent on any particular response or acknowledgment being made by her husband. The same would be true for Christian leaders seeking to provide pastoral support.

CONCLUSION: SEEKING LOVE, JUSTICE, AND FREEDOM FOR ALL

The holistic, onto-relational framework utilized by the Torrances radically impacts our understanding of justice and the law itself. T. F. Torrance cautioned in no uncertain terms against allowing dualisms to impact our interpretation of how or why God interacts with humanity, just as J. B. Torrance cautioned against both a contractual view of God and consequent legalism being imported into the gospel due to language slippage. These cautions are two sides of the same coin, as contracts are dualist in their nature and their operation. Wherever legal and theological terms are misconstrued, disaster is sure to follow both doctrinally and pastorally. The works of T. F. and J. B. Torrance indicate key areas where this has occurred and ways in which to remedy it. Dualist and contractual understandings radically alter our understandings of not only forgiveness and repentance but also reconciliation, justice, and law. Necessarily, then, they also affect our understanding of the relative place of the justice system in responding to domestic and family violence. Justice is *not* synonymous with vengeance or punishment either in a legal sense *or* in a Christian sense. Reducing our understanding of justice to mean that someone is vengefully being sent to jail does a disservice to the reality of the nuances within the justice system, which includes consideration of forgiveness, contrition, concepts such as rehabilitation, and the relationships involved in domestic and family violence as part of sentencing processes. Likewise, it belies the fullness of the gospel message which incorporates justice for victims/survivors.

In an ontologically grounded, holistic, covenantal understanding of the gospel, grace insists on both justice and restoration and provides a place from within which to address common misconceptions that arise from either misunderstanding the place and operation of the justice system, or from a shallow or abstracted understanding of various teachings. These misunderstandings lead readily to minimization, viewing abuse as merely an emotional/anger issue, a marriage dispute, or even just a sin rather than also a crime.[75] This can obstruct the development of a space for the perpetrator to face the extent of their brokenness and the call of God to make full reparation and ensure justice is done. The Christian response to domestic and family violence extends beyond the responsibility of an abuse victim/survivor to forgive. A man who has committed domestic and family violence has an obligation to respond to his own violence as a Christian. Especially as a party in a marriage covenant, he has obligations to the one whom he has harmed, including an obligation to see justice done for her. If his breach of the marriage covenant amounts to a crime, he could have an obligation to submit to the justice system process and plead guilty in order to spare his wife the ordeal of a trial and in order to vindicate her and contribute to the restoration of the dignity that his violence has denied her. In covenant marriage, a husband's call is to grow in Christ and into ever more Christlike behavior as he loves his wife unconditionally, and it is appropriate for the church to be active in encouraging him to take responsibility for doing this, because, for T. F. Torrance, a Christian marriage is to be lived out within the life of the church community, rather than regarded as private.[76]

It is clear that justice is not an alternative or lesser response to forgiveness. It is not an un-Christian response, and a person's safety does not have to be sacrificed for the sake of performative forgiveness that honors no one. Instead, justice, forgiveness, repentance, and the dignity and worth of all people are to be central in the Christian approach to violence.

The horrific reality of domestic and family violence within Christian relationships poses theological, personal, pastoral, and legal challenges for people experiencing it and for their church communities. The works of the Torrances provide a holistic, onto-relational foundation from which these issues can be accommodated in a way that allows for Christian responses to address and incorporate legal issues and the justice system rather than sitting outside of it, and it paves the way for dignity and hope to be expressed with pastoral responses emphasizing and prioritizing the safety, dignity, and personhood of the victim/survivor.

---

75. Definitions vary among jurisdictions, however most forms of domestic and family violence amount to criminal offenses, and all of them enable protection orders to be sought.

76. T. F. Torrance, "Marriage," 166.

The unconditional and relational understandings of law and justice seen in the concept of covenant and an onto-relational grounding give us a broader relational understanding for law from a faith point of view that is closer to the justice system than we might previously have thought. Along with love and freedom, justice should be viewed as *central* to personal reconciliation— whether the relationship itself is reconciled or not. In turn, this approach enables the covenant love, justice, and freedom inherent in the gospel to be more fully expressed by churches, more fully experienced by those women and men who endure domestic and family violence at the hands of their spouses, and more fully demonstrated to the wider community in witness to the unconditional love of the Father, Son, and Spirit.

13
—

TOWARD A TRINITARIAN THEOLOGY OF WORK

Peter K. W. McGhee

INTRODUCTION

In his fascinating book, *The Pleasures and Sorrows of Work*, philosopher Alain de Botton offers the following quote:

> Most of us stand poised at the edge of brilliance, haunted by the knowledge of our proximity, yet still demonstrably on the wrong side of the line, our dealings with reality undermined by a range of minor yet critical psychological flaws (a little too much optimism, an unprocessed rebelliousness, a fatal impatience or sentimentality). We are like an exquisite high-speed aircraft which for lack of a tiny part is left stranded beside the runway, rendered slower than a tractor or a bicycle.[1]

This quote could describe Christian reflections on work. Much of this writing captures various aspects of Christian thought and practice about work but a "part" is often missing. For instance, some authors focus on vocation, for others, work has a kingdom focus, and yet for others still, the emphasis is on work as liberation from oppression.[2] However, what is *prima facie* absent is a comprehensive Trinitarian theology of human work.

---

1. Alain de Botton, *The Pleasures and Sorrows of Work* (London: Hamish Hamilton, 2009), 127.

2. See, for example, Leland Ryken, *Work and Leisure in a Christian Perspective* (Eugene, OR: Wipf & Stock, 2002); Ben Witherington III, *Work: A Kingdom Perspective on Labor* (Grand Rapids:

Certainly, many authors employ aspects of the Trinity in their writings. For instance, Paul Marshall claims Scripture is authoritative about human work and supports the Spirit's role in connecting our labor and God's creative work.[3] Other writers have compared the Trinity with various aspects of human work. Douglas Meeks, for example, argues "that each person of the Trinity engages in distinctive personal work: The Father creates, the Son redeems, and the Spirit creates anew."[4] By extension, Meeks argues the Trinity criticizes all economic systems that exclude people from work that gives them distinctive meaning and value (e.g., sweatshop labor). Meeks also notes the Trinity "engages in cooperative and equalitarian work." The whole community of Father, Son, and Spirit contribute their labors to creation, redemption, and new creation without elevating any one person of the Trinity above the others.[5] Again, extending this idea to the human realm Meeks claims the Trinity condemns all forms of economics that alienates and/or dominates workers and that promotes a class structure (e.g., capitalism). Finally, Meeks describes the Trinity as self-giving love; the divine persons work together for the life of the triune community.[6] This last point implies that all ideological systems that dehumanize individuals, as opposed to embracing their uniqueness, are invalid (e.g., Marxism).

Another author in this field is Dorothy Sayers. While not primarily a theologian, her astute writings on work are based on a Trinitarian framework.[7] Similar to Meeks, Sayers describes how the Trinity is shown in the structure of human beings and their work. Given humans are made in the image of God whose first act in Scripture was to create, Sayers develops an analogy between God's Trinitarian act of creation (the Father equates with creative idea, the Son equates with creative energy, and the Spirit equates with creative power) and the action of human working, using the creative artist as a

---

Eerdmans, 2011); and James R. Cochrane and Gerald West, eds., *The Three-fold Cord: Theology, Work and Labour* (Hilton, SA: Cluster Publications, 1991).

3. Paul Marshall, "Vocation, Work and Jobs," in *Labour of Love: Essays on Work*, ed. Paul Marshall (Toronto: Wedge Publishing Foundation, 1980), 1–19.

4. M. Douglas Meeks, *God the Economist* (Minneapolis: Fortress Press, 1989), 132.

5. Meeks, *God the Economist*, 133.

6. Meeks, *God the Economist*, 134.

7. See Dorothy L. Sayers, *The Mind of the Maker* (London: Metheun, 1941) for the best explanation of this.

metaphor.[8] From this analogy, Sayers deduces that the human experience of work mirrors the nature and relationships of the triune persons, which means their mystery is both observable and demonstrable.

While better than piecemeal applications of the Trinity, the issue of comparative approaches like that of Meeks and Sayers, is their social Trinitarian nature. Social Trinitarianism, an idea whose widespread currency came from the works of Jürgen Moltmann and John Zizioulas, is characterized by a three-personal God, a relational ontology, a historical reorientation, and a practical relevance.[9] While several of these criteria are useful for understanding the Trinity's nature, others pose challenges to a proper Trinitarian theology of work. For instance, Karen Kilby argues social Trinitarianism is projectionist, in that it projects analogies drawn from inter-human relationships back into the Trinity in order to make this concept practical.[10] This is what Sayers is doing with her analogy of human artists and God's triune creativity. Another criticism comes from Carl Mosser, who claims social Trinitarianism "collapses the distinction between the economy of salvation narrated by the text [Scripture] and the life of God in himself."[11] Again, Meeks reflects this error with his analysis comparing the triune God's inner nature with the problems of economic systems.

What is needed for a Trinitarian theology of work is a framework that supports the three-personal and relational ontology of God, without reducing his immanent nature to the economy of salvation and without analogizing away his inherent otherness. Unfortunately, much of the theology of work literature is neither Trinitarian nor evangelical in the fullest sense. It often starts with creation as opposed to God's triune grace. It does not incorporate human work seriously or fully as part of God's triune atonement of that same creation and, in doing this, risks divorcing our labors from Jesus Christ's incarnation and the Holy Spirit's work. Finally, it often has a legalistic tone

---

8. Dorothy L. Sayers, "The Image of God," in Sayers, *The Whimsical Christian* (New York: Macmillan, 1978), 113.

9. Gijsbert van den Brink, "Social Trinitarianism: A Discussion of Some Recent Theological Criticisms," *International Journal of Systematic Theology* 16 (2014): 333–36.

10. Karen Kilby, "Perichoresis and Projection: Problems with Social Doctrines of the Trinity," *New Blackfriars 81* (2000): 442.

11. Carl Mosser, "Fully Social Trinitarianism," in *Philosophical and Theological Essays on the Trinity*, ed. Thomas McCall and Michael C. Rae (Oxford: Oxford University Press, 2009), 147.

in that we work to prove God's soteriological favor toward us.[12] This redirects our labor away from Christ and to ourselves, which is a notable limitation of vocational approaches.[13] Consequently, this chapter offers an evangelical Trinitarian theology of work—a theology that is sourced in God's being, revealed through Jesus Christ who "has acted in your place in the whole range of your human life and activity [including work],"[14] and transformed and glorified it back to God by the Spirit. While under no illusion of providing a full exposition, this chapter uses the Trinitarian theology of Thomas F. Torrance as an exploratory way forward. Torrance is known as the "theologian of the Trinity"[15] for emphasizing the Trinity as the central doctrine of Christianity and for conceptualizing how the Trinity engages with the world and vice versa. Therefore, it seems proper to apply his ideas to one of our most common earthly activities—working—and recommend this to contemporary evangelicals.

The chapter outline is as follows. The first section presents a brief history of the theology of work, with an emphasis on Protestant understandings. The second section introduces Torrance's critical realism, which forms the basis for his Trinitarian theology. This will then be applied to work via Torrance's notion of the social coefficient and his view of humans as priests of creation. The third and fourth sections offer implications of this Trinitarian approach to working for evangelical consideration.

THEOLOGIES OF WORK

There is no doubt the Bible is about God's work. From Genesis through Revelation, we see God's efforts to achieve his purposes. There is also no doubt the Bible requires humans to work. In Genesis 2:15 God entrusts *adam* (humans) with his creation in a manner that contributes to human flourishing (see, e.g., Lev 19:9-10; 25:10; Amos 5:11). Later, the New Jerusalem as seen in the vision of Zechariah 8:10-12 "does not offer freedom from work, but

---

12. This was adapted from Myk Habets and Bobby Grow, "Introduction," in *Evangelical Calvinism: Essays Resourcing the Continuing Reformation of the Church*, ed. Myk Habets and Bobby Grow (Eugene, OR: Pickwick, 2012), 12.

13. Witherington, *Work: A Kingdom Perspective on Labor*, 23-25.

14. Thomas F. Torrance, *The Mediation of Christ*, 2nd ed. (Colorado Springs: Helmers & Howards, 1992), 103.

15. See Paul D. Molnar, *Thomas F. Torrance: Theologian of the Trinity* (Farnham: Ashgate, 2009), 31-72 for a thorough discussion of why Torrance has this label.

freedom in work."[16] Similar themes occur in the New Testament where Jesus emphasizes the value of work, while criticizing those who exploit others (see, e.g., Matt 20:1–16; Luke 6:24–25; 11:46–47). Many of Paul's letters reference work as a necessary part of successful human living (see, e.g., Eph 4:28; 1 Thess 4:11; 2 Thess 3:10). Work, unfortunately, is also cursed (Gen 3:19). As Jensen notes, "Almost as soon as God entrusts human persons with tilling the soil, they experience work as backbreaking toil. Expulsion from the Garden results in a lifetime of hard work."[17] The past centuries have not lessened this curse. Today many experience work as exploitation and alienation. Whether it be children in sweatshops, production workers locked into manufacturing drudgery, or managers enslaved to efficiency and profit, work is not as it should be.

Early Christian thinkers did not develop a systematic theology of work. Instead, they focused on labor's effects on individual character. As Miroslav Volf writes, the role of work was "to muzzle the evil and disobedient flesh."[18] One classic text in this vein is *The Rule of St. Benedict* which exhorts believers to work and regulate their hours each day so as to avoid idleness.[19] Along similar lines, William of St. Thierry claimed, "The greatest evil which can befall the mind is unemployed leisure." He believed work "should always leave something in the mind that will contribute to the soul's advancement."[20] Perhaps it was not until Thomas Aquinas that work gained serious theological attention. However, Aquinas, like his predecessors, also viewed work as a necessary evil to enable the good contemplation of God—only labor that molded the soul and led to meditation contributed to human flourishing.[21]

Responding to the Catholic claim that only monastic work was spiritual, the Protestant Reformers argued that every Christian had both a spiritual

---

16. David R. Jensen, *Responsive Labor: A Theology of Work* (Louisville: Westminster John Knox Press, 2006), 24.

17. Jensen, *Responsive Labor*, 27–28.

18. Miroslav Volf, *Work in the Spirit: Toward a Theology of Work* (Eugene, OR: Wipf & Stock, 2001), 72.

19. Jensen, *Responsive Labor*, 31.

20. Jensen, *Responsive Labor*, 31.

21. Volf, *Work in the Spirit*, 70. Interestingly, Karl Barth shares this idea. He claimed that Scripture provides no positive imperative to work, while it does have a command to rest. For Barth, we are called to Christ's work and away from secular labors. See Karl Barth, *Church Dogmatics III/4: The Doctrine of Creation*, ed. T. F. Torrance and Geoffrey W. Bromiley (Edinburgh: T&T Clark, 1961), 472.

call and a worldly call.[22] The spiritual was the internal call of God on the individual. The worldly call was about serving God through one's work. Of these Protestant views, two are worth noting. Martin Luther particularly disliked monasticism which, in his opinion, conceived vocation too narrowly along with his belief that monasteries lived off the work of others.[23] In response to this, Luther argued that the contemplative life goes together with the mundane aspects of ordinary work. Jensen cites one of Luther's favorite examples of this: "When a father goes ahead and washes diapers or performs some other mean task for a child ... God, with all his angels and creatures, is smiling—not because that father is washing diapers, but because he is doing so in Christian faith."[24] Consequently, all work, regardless of its stature, is a vocation. John Calvin, another Reformer, developed Luther's ideas such that all human actions, not just work, were included. For Calvin, lowly occupations were also part of God's calling: "No task will be so sordid and base, provided you obey your calling in it, that it will not shine and be reckoned very precious in God's sight."[25] It was not that work had any more value than anything else humans did, it was the fact that God called us to work which made it spiritual. While both Luther and Calvin emphasized a worldly vocation, Luther's focus was on loving service to God through our labors, whereas Calvin emphasized vocation as essential to a properly structured human life that contributes to God's redemptive plan for transforming the world.[26]

These ideas were further elaborated by Puritan thinkers in the sixteenth and seventeenth centuries, and they were the first to systematically develop the difference between the general (or internal) call and the particular (or external) call, while also trying "to steer a middle path between the extremes of the idler and the workaholic."[27] Ryken quotes the words of Adam to Eve in

22. R. Paul Stevens, *The Other Six Days* (Grand Rapids: Eerdmans, 2000), 75. Given the evangelical focus of this chapter, there is a deliberate emphasis on Protestant views of work. Readers interested in modern Catholic perspectives of work should read Darrell Cosden, *A Theology of Work* (Eugene, OR: Wipf & Stock, 2004), 19–35.

23. Jensen, *Responsive Labor*, 34.

24. Martin Luther, "The Estate of Marriage," in *Works*, vol. 45 cited in Jensen, *Responsive Labor*, 34.

25. John Calvin, *Institutes of the Christian Religion*, 3.10.6 cited in Jensen, *Responsive Labor*, 35.

26. Ian Hart, "The Teaching of Luther and Calvin about Ordinary Work: 2 John Calvin (1509–64)," in *Evangelical Quarterly* 67 (1995): 135.

27. Ryken, *Work and Leisure in Christian Perspective*, 35.

Milton's epic poem *Paradise Lost* as a good example of the Puritan work ethic: "Man hath his daily work of body or mind appointed, which declares his dignity, and the regard of Heaven on all his ways."[28] Ironically, the Puritans, in condemning greed and materialism, while at the same time promoting thrift and industriousness, contributed significantly to their own economic development. Consequently, several commentators have noted that Reformation ideas about vocation,[29] blended with Puritan thinking and Lockean rights, paved the way for modern-day capitalism and its associated challenges.[30] Protestant denominations mostly continued this Puritan understanding until the twentieth century when vocation took a more protological focus, meaning "the initial creation is [seen as] the theological and ethical starting point for reflection on work."[31] Even Karl Barth, despite being critical of natural theology, offered up a view that used the Sabbath, which is within the creation motif, as the paradigmatic starting point for work: "Can we understand the working day, the day of labour in relationship to our fellow-men, or any of its commands, before we have understood the holy day?"[32]

While the vocational perspective has been the most widespread theological approach to work until recently, it is not without problems. First, it is "indifferent toward alienation in work."[33] Since it is not the inherent value of the work itself that defines a vocation but rather that God gives us the work for his purposes, all work, no matter how dehumanizing, could be vocational. Second, the notion of vocation harbors a dangerous ambiguity. There is a tendency, particularly within Luther's *vacatio externa* and his *vacatio spiritualis*, of conflating these two ideas such that the secular supersedes the spiritual

---

28. Ryken, *Work and Leisure in Christian Perspective*, 35.

29. Especially that of John Calvin who "articulated a work ethic that strongly encouraged the development of Geneva's enterprise culture" as opposed to Luther whose "economic thought was hostile to any form of capitalism, which largely reflects his unfamiliarity with the sophisticated world of finance then emerging in the public life of the cities," both cited in Alister E. McGrath, "Calvin and the Christian Calling," *First Things* 94 (June/July 1999): 31–35.

30. See, for example, Max Weber, *The Protestant Work Ethic and the Spirit of Capitalism*, 2nd ed. (London: George Allen & Unwin, 1976); Richard H. Tawney, *Religion and the Rise of Capitalism* (1926; repr., London: Penguin, 1964); and Robert N. Bellah, *Habits of Heart: Individualism and Commitment in American Life* (Berkley: University of California Press, 1985).

31. Cosden, *A Theology of Work*, 42.

32. Barth, *Church Dogmatics* III/4, 51.

33. Volf, *Work in the Spirit*, 107.

call.[34] Third, when we combine points one and two above, there is a risk that vocation is used ideologically thereby ennobling dehumanizing work or, worse still, work that breaks God's commandments.[35] Finally, vocational work is not suited for modern living where people change jobs frequently or have more than one job. The idea an individual should "toil in accordance with his powers and in keeping with his calling. ... You should have a happy spirit and an active body, but in such a way that you abide in *your assigned place*"[36] betrays a static view of the social order.

In addition to these criticisms, the vocational view has a pseudo-soteriological effect in that it provides individuals with false assurance: "I am doing God's work through my calling." Interestingly, with the rise of industrialization and the demise of Christianity (in the West at least), work itself has become a religion. Most people find their self-worth and salvation not in their spiritual calling but in their career and their material accomplishments, and indeed this is how Western society often measures people's value today.[37]

In response to such criticism, several thinkers have moved away from the notion of vocation, although this idea still haunts their writings. Contextual models, for example, understand work in relationship to political, economic, racial, or gender oppression using notions like freedom and frameworks like liberation theology to address points of conflict. Suffice it to say, several of these approaches are not Trinitarian.[38] Others, like Jürgen Moltmann, David Jensen, and Miroslav Volf combine an interest in context with a non-vocational focus on aspects of God's triune nature. Moltmann, for instance, is suspicious of instrumental approaches to work because of their inherent alienation. He claims joy, freedom, and play are essential parts of working and that work can be made meaningful.[39] He does this by focusing on the-

34. Volf, *Work in the Spirit*, 107.

35. Volf, *Work in the Spirit*, 108.

36. Martin Luther, "Notes on Ecclesiastes," in *Works*, vol. 15 cited in Jensen, *Responsive Labor*, 35.

37. See Tim Kasser, "Materialistic Value Orientation," in *The Palgrave Handbook of Spirituality and Business*, ed. L. Bouckaert and L. Zsolnai (Houndsmill, Basingstoke: Palgrave Macmillan, 2011), 204–11 for a discussion of this.

38. Cosden, *A Theology of Work*, 43. A good example of this is Dorothee Söelle (with Shirley A. Cloyes), *To Work and To Love: A Theology of Creation* (Philadelphia: Fortress Press, 1984).

39. Jürgen Moltmann, *On Human Dignity, Political Theology, and Ethics* (Philadelphia: Fortress Press, 1984), 41–42.

ology proper, and especially on the idea that God is a worker, leading to his main premise that human work should reflect God's work in creation. When it does this, human work becomes significant because it participates via Christ's work on the cross in God's redemptive plan for creation.[40] It can also be enjoyable because the creativity involved in working echoes God's own playful ingenuity.

David Jensen, similar to Moltmann, argues God's nature includes working, and given we are made in his image, then work must be part of being human and "that a theology of work, properly framed, begins by describing God's work for us."[41] Understanding God as a worker allows Jensen to uphold the intrinsic value of labor: "God gives the world all that it needs and works to distribute goods to all creation. The divine life shares with others in giving that spills out for the life of the world."[42] Consequently, we should work in a way that reflects God's divine labor. Jensen does apply a Trinitarian lens to work, but like Meeks and Sayers, he uses God's triune life as a model of the moral and practical norms by which work can be judged.[43] He further argues that if our work is reflective of God's work, then Christianity's task is the redemption of work from its corrupted state. The best way to do this, Jensen states, is via equitable opportunity for all in the capitalist system. For example, "A society that envisioned full employment and the full utilization of persons' gifts would provide opportunities for vocational training, further education, and transportation to work for those who need it."[44]

Miroslav Volf's theology of work has a strong pneumatological emphasis. Starting with the notion of new creation, Volf argues that human work, via the power of the Spirit, contributes to God's future eschatological transformation.[45] The Spirit does this by gifting Christians (see Gal 5:22–23) with the ability to emulate the values of God's new creation in their work. This means all Christians have the same calling through the Spirit, and his gifts guide Christians to structure work according to God's ultimate purposes. It also means that "good work" (see 1 Cor 3:12–15) can be evaluated since it reflects

---

40. Moltmann, *On Human Dignity*, 42.

41. Jensen, *Responsive Labor*, 44.

42. Jensen, *Responsive Labor*, 7.

43. Jensen, *Responsive Labor*, 49–66.

44. Jensen, *Responsive Labor*, 60

45. Volf, *Work in the Spirit*, 81.

spiritual values and cooperates with God's plan.[46] Work which alienates us from God, his creation, and each other, work that dehumanizes, demeans, and destroys is ultimately worthless because it has no value in God's future kingdom. As Volf notes, work is not ideological; it is a spiritual partnership "with God on the project of the new creation."[47]

While each of these theologies offers a new lens by which to view work, none are entirely Trinitarian. Rather they emphasize either theocentric, Christocentric, or pneumacentric aspects, and where they are Trinitarian, it is a flattened approach that tends to view the Trinity "as a society on which human society can be modelled."[48] What is required is a fuller theology of work that does for the whole Trinity what Volf initiated regarding the Spirit. This chapter aims to begin this process by developing a theology of work using Thomas F. Torrance's Trinitarian framework because, as Gunton has noted, "the only satisfactory account of the relation between the Creator and the creation is a trinitarian one."[49]

TORRANCE'S TRINITARIAN FRAMEWORK

Natural theology argues for an understanding of God's purposes without recourse to special revelation. According to Christian tradition, *existentia* is conditional on the prior *essentia* of God (see Gen 1:1).[50] Moreover, according to McGrath, this "is a created correspondence—that is to say, that the reality of God is rendered in the created order, including humanity at its apex" (see Gen 1:26-27).[51] Consequently, it follows, using a critical-realist approach,[52] that our experiences of reality offer us insights into God's nature.

---

46. Volf, *Work in the Spirit*, 91.

47. Volf, *Work in the Spirit*, 116.

48. Richard Bauckham, *The Theology of Jürgen Moltmann* (London: T&T Clark, 1995), 179.

49. Colin E. Gunton, *Christ and Creation* (Bletchley: Paternoster, 1992), 75.

50. Alister E. McGrath, *Reality* (Grand Rapids: Eerdmans, 2002), 227.

51. McGrath, *Reality*, 227.

52. Critical realism is a philosophical methodology that argues for the existence of objective reality independent of the human mind, while also claiming humans can know this reality albeit through social lenses. Critical realism stratifies knowledge into three distinct, but dependent, levels: the real (objective reality), the actual (causal outcomes/events of objective reality), and the empirical (human experience of these outcomes). Human experiences of outcomes/events infer underlying structures open to study using methods pertinent to the nature of the objective reality under investigation. If the object studied is God, then theology is the best method for doing this. Within theological circles, this idea has been adapted to "designate a style of realism which is sensitive to the historically situated and personally involved character of theological

As McGrath notes, this is not an independently obvious truth but a truth based on the prior truth of God's creation. Such a stratified understanding allows us to argue that every level of human inquiry and every type of human activity "addresses itself to God their creator who is revealed through them."[53] However, by itself this natural theology is limited in providing full access to God, for as Habets attests, "God cannot be known 'behind his back' as Torrance phrases it, nor can we know God without his willing himself to be known."[54] Only God can fully reveal God, not the works of God alone. This necessitates the incarnation and Pentecost.

For Torrance, this means "the Trinity is the ultimate ground of theological knowledge of God, the basic grammar of theology."[55] Torrance states the Trinity is known from our "evangelical (from the Father, through the Son, and by the Spirit) and doxological (in the Spirit, through the Son, and to the Father) participation in the gospel," which means that there is no conflict between true theology and true doxology.[56] This knowledge is only possible because of Jesus Christ's incarnation and mediation on humanity's behalf and because the Holy Spirit joins us to Christ who is *homoousios* with the Father such that "He lifts us up into the inner communion of [God's] divine Being."[57] Indeed, without God becoming incarnate in Jesus Christ within our space and time, we would not be able to articulate or understand the doctrine of the Trinity.

Torrance rejects dualism, which for him "distorts the revelation and mediation of God in Jesus Christ."[58] Instead he defends a theological explanation of the Trinity, which reflects the three-tiered critical-realist structure of

---

knowledge, while resolutely declining to let go of the ideals of truth, objectivity, and rationality" in McGrath, *Reality*, 195.

53. McGrath, *Reality*, 227.

54. Myk Habets, *Theosis in the Theology of Thomas Torrance* (Farnham: Ashgate, 2009), 95.

55. Thomas F. Torrance, *The Ground and Grammar of Theology* (Edinburgh: T&T Clark, 1980), 158–59.

56. Elmer M. Colyer, *How to Read T. F. Torrance: Understanding His Trinitarian and Scientific Theology* (Eugene, OR: Wipf & Stock, 2001), 287.

57. Torrance, *The Ground and Grammar of Theology*, 154.

58. Tapio Luoma, *Incarnation and Physics: Natural Science in the Theology of Thomas F. Torrance* (New York: Oxford University Press, 2002), 87.

human knowledge and the systems of reality found in the natural sciences.[59] Described this way, the evangelical Trinity is a "stratified structure compris-ing several coordinate levels concerned with God as he is in himself, with the incarnation of his self-revelation in Jesus Christ, and with our receiving and articulating of that revelation."[60] If we turn this around, then the following doxological description is also applicable:

> A stratified structure arising from the ground of our evangelical experience, knowledge and worship of God in the life of the Church, deriving from the historical revelation of God as Father, Son and Holy Spirit mediated to us in the incarnate life and work of Jesus Christ, and directed to the transcendent mystery of God the Father, the Son and the Holy Spirit as he is in his one eternal Being.[61]

Before moving forward with this, three points must be raised. First, this understanding of the Trinity is an *a posteriori* reconstruction of how we interact with God. If it is cut off from the saving grace of the gospel, it become meaningless.[62] Second, the triune God is a personal being and inter-acts with us in a personalizing manner, which "entails the transformation of our minds and our lives so that we respond in a fully personal manner in faith, worship, obedience, and love in the Spirit through the Son to the Father."[63] As Colyer notes, we must think of these levels and any movement between them as personal and redemptive; this is not simply a knowledge exercise. Finally, all three levels are mutually correlated; the lower levels are not less important since the evangelical Trinity cannot be independent of the doxological Trinity. As McGrath notes, "A failure to recognize the mutual interconnectedness of these levels can lead to theological reflection

---

59. Torrance argues that "the stratified structure of scientific knowledge usually comprises three levels of thought coordinated with one another: the primary or basic level, which is the level of our ordinary day-to-day experience, and the loosely organised natural cognitions it involves [i.e., the empirical]; the secondary level of scientific theory with its search for rigorous logical unity of empirical and conceptual factors [i.e., consistent measurable outcomes/events]; and the tertiary level where we develop a more refined and higher logical unity with a minimum of refined concepts or relations [i.e., a better understanding of objective reality]" in Thomas F. Torrance, *The Christian Doctrine of God* (Edinburgh: T&T Clark, 2001), 84.

60. Torrance, *The Christian Doctrine of God*, 83.

61. Torrance, *The Christian Doctrine of God*, 83.

62. Colyer, *How to Read T. F. Torrance*, 292.

63. Colyer, *How to Read T. F. Torrance*, 293.

being divorced from Christian experience ... or from its proper ontological foundations."[64]

Our first strata of Trinitarian understanding, Torrance calls "doxological."[65] At this level, we experience Jesus and his gospel through the Spirit to understand that Christ is our Savior and Lord. This, in turn, causes us to respond with belief, worship, and obedience.[66] Torrance notes that this is not a private experience but instead is to be shared in the life of the church. As we do this, our lives "begin to take on the imprint of the evangelical Trinity."[67] As we grow in this Trinitarian reality, it prepares us for the second strata of engagement, the theological. This means shifting from the "level of 'experiential apprehension' of God and discerning the structures which lie within it."[68] This moves our awareness of the Trinity to that of the economic (i.e., how the Father, Son, and Spirit interact and how they relate to the world). The third, and final strata, the higher theological level, "involves moving from a level of economic trinitarian relations to what God is ontically in Himself."[69] This last movement indicates how God reveals himself to us through Christ and the Spirit and reflects who he is in himself. This means our worship, faith, and obedience to God are founded in the very being of God.

For Torrance, these three stratified levels are how the triune God reveals himself to us and how we, in turn, come to know him. If we start with the doxological level (i.e., our faith, worship, and obedience to him), then as already noted, the primary place we develop these is in the church. If we do this through Christ and in the Spirit, then we gradually formulate theological knowledge of God. This understanding is not just epistemic but personal, relational, and sanctifying. While the church plays a key purpose in Torrance's framework, other social contexts likewise improve theological understanding of the Trinity and its relevance for those contexts. Eric Flett makes a similar point:

---

64. McGrath, *Reality*, 237.

65. Torrance, *The Christian Doctrine of God*, 88.

66. Colyer, *How to Read T. F. Torrance*, 293.

67. Colyer, *How to Read T. F. Torrance*, 294.

68. Torrance, *The Christian Doctrine of God*, 91.

69. Torrance, *The Christian Doctrine of God*, 93. This, of course, does not mean that we understand the Trinity fully. There is a mystery to the eternal God that is unfathomable to finite beings.

It is my belief that Torrance's work contains a wealth of material for the development of a trinitarian theology of culture, specifically in his conception of the nature and dynamics of "social coefficients of knowledge," which in turn are grounded in his understanding of God as triune, creation as contingent, and human persons as stewards created in the image of God.[70]

With this thought in mind, the rest of this chapter will endeavor to explore work as a social context in which Christians learn about and enact their knowledge of the triune God of Jesus Christ.

TOWARD A TRINITARIAN UNDERSTANDING OF WORK

Torrance uses a unique term for the social reality where we enact these learnings about the triune God: the *social coefficient of knowledge*, which Flett describes as:

> the social embodiment of a knowing relation. ... The social coefficient receives from, responds to, and reflects the character of the objective reality it stands in relation to. ... It serves as a subjective and social lens through which persons are enabled to participate in a knowing relation with realities that are external to them, and to be modified by those realities in an appropriate manner. ... The consequence is a dynamic social reality that enables, sustains, and reflects the knowing relation that is central to it.[71]

In Torrance's work, the only social coefficients are Israel and the church, but, in principle, many other contexts, such as the modern organization, could be labeled similarly.[72]

---

70. Eric G. Flett, "Priests of Creation, Mediators of Order: The Human Person as Cultural Being in Thomas F. Torrance's Theological Anthropology," *Scottish Journal of Theology* 58 (2005): 61, 182.

71. Eric G. Flett, *Persons, Powers, and Pluralities: Toward a Trinitarian Theology of Culture* (Eugene, OR: Pickwick, 2011), 142.

72. Myk Habets applies this to classrooms in "'Will This Be in the Exam?' The Social Coefficient of Knowledge in the Theological Classroom," in *Theological Formation for Christian Missions: A Festschrift for Ian Walter Payne*, ed. Roji Thomas George and Aruthuckal Varughese John (Bangalore: SAIACS Press, 2019), 121–32.

Flett states that "social coefficients are formed around 'knowing relations,' which for Torrance, are composed of an objective and subjective pole."[73] This means that in every social reality there is a real object that can be known as well as a subject who does the knowing. As a critical realist, Torrance argues the object exists apart from the subject's knowledge of it, even though that knowledge can interact with the object to create a new knowing relation. In other words, the object, the subject, and the relationship between them "act together to form particular social coefficients."[74] Of importance here is the notion that the relation between the object and subject must be "properly ordered" such that in coming to know the object, the subject is transformed and the social reality is reflective of both object and subject.[75] The relationship between the object and the subject is not just functional, rather it is a moral relation. In other words, if that relationship is unhealthy, the social reality (i.e., work) will be unhealthy and distorted.[76]

When Torrance refers to the objective world, he means both the divine and created reality that exists apart from our knowledge of it. Inbuilt within these realities is a particular design and purpose and "these must be understood and respected if both humans and non-humans are to realize their true ends."[77] For this to happen, the subject "must allow the object to dictate the means by which it is known, and to make sure that there is congruence between the means of obtaining knowledge and the knowledge to be obtained. ... The means used must be appropriate to the end pursued."[78] If we unpack this idea further, then our knowledge of God, and his inbuilt design within the created order (the objects), should dictate how we (the subject) operate in our workplaces (the social reality), and should transform our work behavior to be in line with this knowledge. Instead of dehumanizing work practices, such as with sweatshop labor or using destructive environmental actions, we might act in ways that respect the *imago Dei* in our employees while looking to minimize waste and harm in nature. However, such behavior is unlikely for the reasons explained below.

73. Flett, *Persons, Powers, and Pluralities*, 150.
74. Flett, *Persons, Powers, and Pluralities*, 150.
75. Flett, *Persons, Powers, and Pluralities*, 151.
76. Flett, *Persons, Powers, and Pluralities*.
77. Flett, *Persons, Powers, and Pluralities*, 155
78. Flett, *Persons, Powers, and Pluralities*, 155.

For Torrance, human beings are onto-relational. This means that we are "constituted as a personal being through relation to God, and to others, and to the world. ... To be constituted in such a way requires that the person be open to that which is beyond him or herself."[79] In other words, the subject constantly interacts with the real objects (e.g., God, creation, other people) of their thinking to create new social realities that are incomplete in themselves. In Torrance's view, this capacity forms the basis for expressing the image of God and for proper human stewardship of creation.[80] The danger here is that as much as an individual is open to the world, the world also influences and determines how an individual acts. Many Christians, for example, feel called to work in certain industries or roles but often their ministry inclinations are overridden by the need for security, status, and wealth. To avoid this, Torrance argues, "It is only through a divine Trinity who admits us to communion with Himself in his own transcendence that we can be consistently and persistently personal, with the kind of freedom, openness, and transcendent reference which we need both to develop our own personal and social culture."[81] In other words, social realities such as work are incomplete in themselves. No matter how hard we try to improve the underlying structures and daily operations of "work" and all that this requires, we will never be able to achieve that end unless we formulate our thinking and any consequent action with reference to the Trinity. If we try to redeem work within the fallen created order alone, our efforts are doomed to fail.

Healthy social realities orient individuals away from their own subjectivity and toward the object that defines their social life. They have a series of symbols, structures, and rituals that "have a semantic intentionality that constantly refers individuals beyond themselves to the intelligible ground of reality where the true locus of meaning exists."[82] However, because social realities like economies and business form through historic interactions, they can become institutionalized and take on a life of their own. For instance, the ideology of free market capitalism underpinning much of modern work practice is a product of ideas combining Lockean rights, Hume's subjectivity,

---

79. Flett, *Persons, Powers, and Pluralities*, 165.

80. Flett, *Persons, Powers, and Pluralities*.

81. Thomas F. Torrance, *Reality and Scientific Theology* (Edinburgh: Scottish Academic, 1985), 196.

82. Flett, *Persons, Powers, and Pluralities*, 167.

Adam Smith's economics, social Darwinism, anti-communism, and individual expressivism to mention but a few.[83] Very few people understand this history and its limitations, and as such thoughtlessly accept the view that markets should make political and social decisions, that government should play little role in the market with business being given increased autonomy, that the influence of unions should be curtailed, that workers should be given much less rather than more social protection, that morality has a limited role to play in economic decision-making, that the individual is more important than the community, and that gross inequality is a natural and necessary outworking of market economics. If social realities like the economy and business are not congruent with divine and contingent order, then a change in human knowing and normative acting must take place.

Fortunately, as Torrance notes, the personal transcendent ground of the contingent order (i.e., the Trinity) "acts creatively upon us, not to reproduce itself in our formalizing activities, but to call them, as it were, into contrapuntal sequences and patterns of an open texture through which it can reverberate or resound in the human spirit."[84] How does the Trinity do this? Via the Archimedean point of Jesus Christ. Because economies and work are part of the created order and are susceptible to social determinism, we need something or someone beyond our reality that enables us to understand the true meaning, purpose, and *telos* of these. Without Jesus Christ, we lose a transcendent reference point by which to judge social realities like economies and work. Instead of being *imago Dei*, we become *Homo Economicus* (Economic Man) fixated on maximizing self-interest and economic growth.[85] Such thinking ensures we become alienated from our labor, from our community, and from the environment.

Take a business like Coca-Cola as an example. Their drive for efficiency can mean workers in the developing world are unable to gain the full benefits of their labor.[86] Moreover, their management's need to meet profit goals

---

83. Sumantra Ghoshal, "Bad Management Theories Are Destroying Good Management Practices," *Academy of Management Learning & Education* 4 (2005): 75–91.

84. Torrance, *Reality and Scientific Theology*, 99.

85. See Amartya Sen, *On Ethics and Economics* (New York: Basil Blackwell, 1987) for a discussion of *Homo Economicus*.

86. See Amanda Ciafone, *Counter-Cola: A Multinational History of the Global Corporation* (Berkeley: University of California Press, 2019), 184–226 for an example of Coke's use of cheap labor in Columbia.

can encourage public relations campaigns that target the vulnerable[87] while also externalizing social harms (e.g., health costs) to the wider community.[88] Finally, activities such as Coca-Cola's appropriation of water in India can contribute to wider social (e.g., effluents from Coke's operations damaged crops and made villagers ill) and environmental damage (e.g., they significantly depleted groundwater supplies).[89] Without the triune God of Jesus Christ "who admits us to communion with himself in his own transcendence,"[90] we dehumanize as well as depersonalize our relationship with the world and move away from God's *transformatio mundi* for creation.

Through the efforts of Christ, our work is brought into partnership with God. However, knowing this is not enough, we must have "a movement of personal response and commitment in worship, obedience, and love in which the transformation of our mind or a spiritual reorganization of our consciousness of God [in relationship to our work] takes place."[91] This is only achievable by the agency of the Holy Spirit who empowers our labor toward the true end of creation. Without the Spirit to transform our praxis, our work risks becoming an Archimedean point and therefore is "lost since there is no further living contact with the reality the coefficient refers to or that formed and nourished it. ... The social coefficient is then free to determine and construct its own meaning and *telos* unbounded by the constraints of reality."[92]

This raises two questions: first, why does human labor contribute to the divine *telos*? And second, how does human labor do this? Again, Flett is helpful in answering the first of these questions. Citing Torrance, "Since God has purposely created and formed [humans] for partnership and fellowship with himself, there is no genuine reciprocity between them without the inclusion of a distinctly anthropomorphic ingredient," Flett argues that "God welcomes

87. Benjamin Wood, Gary Ruskin, and Gary Sacks, "Targeting Children and Their Mothers, Building Allies and Marginalizing Opposition: An Analysis of Two Coca-Cola Public Relations Requests for Proposals," *International Journal of Environmental Research and Public Health* 17 (2020): 12.

88. Jerry Kopf, Joel Carnevale, and Damon Chambers, "Globalism, Capitalism, and Negative Externalities: Anecdotes of Bad Behavior," *Journal of Global Business Issues* 7 (2013): 45–46.

89. Georgina Drew, "Coca-Cola and the Moral Economy of Rural Development in India, South Asia," *Journal of South Asian Studies* 44 (2021): 477–97.

90. Torrance, *Reality and Scientific* Theology, 114.

91. Torrance, *The Christian Doctrine of God*, 88.

92. Flett, *Persons, Powers, and Pluralities*, 204.

and desires anthropomorphic/subjective elements in the mediation of his revelation."[93] In other words, work that has been redeemed by the Spirit to be an act of worship, obedience, and love is embraced by the triune God. At the same time, he remains transcendent over it, as an essential part of his *transformatio mundi*. This leads us to the second question of how our finite, contingent labor could contribute to God's divine *telos*. Torrance succinctly answers this with: "Jesus Christ is our human response to God."[94] In citing Galatians 2:19-20, Torrance argues that we have been united with the vicarious humanity of Jesus Christ, which means our imperfect faith (and our corresponding imperfect worship, obedience, and love) is adopted by Jesus Christ and becomes his perfect faith (and his corresponding perfect worship, obedience, and love). As Kettler notes, this involves "all human responses [including our work] to God, which even though they are Christ's are still our responses."[95] This union of Christ, states Kettler, is founded on the idea that Christ is our mediator and priest. As mediator, he reconciles us to God. As priest, Christ "takes upon himself our prayers and worship, to appear before the holiness of the Father, something we are unable to do."[96] These actions personalize and humanize us such that our *imago Dei* is gradually redeemed and transformed.

In summary, if we go back to Torrance's stratified understanding of the Trinity, then we can say that "good" work and a "flourishing" economy, as part of the created order, are social realities that must be ultimately grounded in God the Father, mediated to us through the Son's incarnation, and continuously transformed and empowered as worship, obedience, and love back to God by the Holy Spirit and through the vicarious humanity of Jesus Christ. Moreover, we can say that Christian human agency in the workplace is enabled by the mediation and priesthood of Christ such that Christians now have a calling not in the traditional sense, but as priests of creation. The triune God of Jesus Christ revealed what good work is, and we now are

---

93. Thomas F. Torrance, "The Christian Apprehension of God the Father," in *Speaking the Christian God: The Holy Trinity and the Challenge of Feminism*, ed. Alvin F. Kimel (Grand Rapids: Eerdmans, 1992), 128 cited in Flett, *Persons, Powers, and Pluralities*, 207.

94. Torrance, *The Mediation of Christ*, 80.

95. Christian D. Kettler, "Jesus Christ Is Our Human Response to God," in *T&T Clark Handbook of Thomas F. Torrance*, ed. Paul D. Molnar and Myk Habets (London: Bloomsbury T&T Clark, 2020), 212.

96. Kettler, "Jesus Christ Is Our Human Response to God."

tasked with imaging our good work back to God. Without social realities like economies, organizations, and work, it would not be possible for humanity to fulfill our true calling,[97] which implies we could not participate in the triune God's divine plan for creation.

This is not social Trinitarianism because we are not abandoning the economic/immanent distinction nor are we saying that the interior relations of the Trinity are equal to, or analogous with, human social realities such as economies, organizations, and work. Rather, we are saying "what God is 'toward us' and 'in the midst of us' he really is in *himself*,"[98] which means that if we want to know what good work is, then we must start with the grace, faith, and revelation that come from the triune God of Jesus Christ and not from our own self-knowledge, and we must recognize that it is God who is conditioning our work and not us who is conditioning his. Our main "job" as Christians, if you like, is to "stand as an embodied witness [in our workplaces] of the glory and eternal purpose of God."[99]

IMPLICATIONS FOR WORKING

According to Alexander Schmemann:

> The first, and basic definition of man is that he is the priest. He stands in the center of the world and unifies it in acts of blessing God, of both receiving the world from God and offering it to God—and by filling the world with his Eucharist, he transforms his life, the one that he receives from the world, into life in God, into communion with him.[100]

As *imago Dei*, human beings occupy a special position on the border of the physical and the spiritual, and therefore, they have the function and privilege of assisting "creation as a whole to realise and evidence its rational

---

97. Flett, "Priests of Creation, Mediators of Order," 171.

98. Thomas F. Torrance, *The Trinitarian Faith* (Edinburgh: T&T Clark, 1997), 130 (emphasis in original in bold). According to Thomas Noble, Torrance could provide a solution to the "ongoing debate between social trinitarians and those emphasizing the unity of God" because he is doing something quite different, as cited in Jason Radcliff, "T. F. Torrance in the light of Stephen Holmes's Critique of Contemporary Trinitarian Thought," *Evangelical Quarterly* 86 (2014): 36.

99. Flett, "Priests of Creation, Mediators of Order," 176.

100. Alexander Schmemann, *For the Life of the World: Sacraments and Orthodoxy*, 2nd ed. (Crestwood, NY: St Vladimir's Seminary Press, 1973), 15.

order and beauty and thus express God."[101] Since work is an essential part of this process, what might be the implications of this for our daily lives? If we think of Christian work as acts of worship and obedience, then it can only be fully understood as participating in Jesus Christ's continuing ministry. Therefore, whatever these implications are, they must present back to the triune God of Jesus Christ as a reflection of his self-revelation to us—they must be concerned with the things that he is concerned with. This clearly excludes certain things, while still leaving us with a broad canvas on which to paint our working lives.

If we start with the excluded things, then any work that mars the *imago Dei* and does not contribute to God's *telos* for creation is to be avoided, as is any work that cooperates with powers that scheme against God's plan. An example may be helpful here. In April 2013, a garment building in Bangladesh, the Rana Plaza, collapsed killing over 1,000 workers and injuring more than 2,500. Only five months earlier, 112 workers were killed when the Tazreen garment factory, also in Bangladesh, caught on fire. These incidents, among the worst ever, highlighted the working conditions in the fashion sector in Bangladesh. Workers, "mostly women and young girls, are exposed every day to an unsafe work environment with a high incidence of work-related accidents and deaths, as well as occupational diseases."[102]

In addition to this, the garments from these factories are often fast fashion—items that are produced and priced cheaply to copy the latest catwalk style and then pumped through stores to maximize on current trends, after which they are quickly dumped by consumers as new styles emerge. As a result of this accelerated process, fast fashion has become the second biggest polluter in the world after the oil industry.[103] What drives these exploitative and destructive practices? At one level, the answer is simple: the desire of these companies to maximize returns for themselves and for their

---

101. Habets, *Theosis in the Theology of Thomas Torrance*, 45.

102. The International Labor Organization, *The Rana Plaza Accident and Its Aftermath*, https://www.ilo.org/global/topics/geip/WCMS_614394/lang--en/index.htm.

103. James Conca, "Making Climate Change Fashionable—The Garment Industry Takes on Global Warming," *Forbes*, December 3, 2015, https://www.forbes.com/sites/james-conca/2015/12/03/making-climate-change-fashionable-the-garment-industry-takes-on-glob-al-warming/?sh=2d61acd79e41.

shareholders in an industry that is worth over three trillion dollars and constitutes more than 2 percent of the world's gross domestic product.[104]

At risk of overstating the obvious, the treatment of garment workers in Bangladesh violates the human status as *imago Dei,* not only of the workers but also of the managers who approve, and the shareholders who benefit from, such inhumane conditions. At the same time, the garment industry significantly damages God's creation through the exhaustion of nonrenewable resources, the production of greenhouse gases, and the use of immense amounts of water and energy for the purpose of making as much money as possible. Such behaviors do not respect the inherent dignity and contingent necessity that come from being onto-relational persons, and they lead us to serve the things and powers of this world that divert our worship, obedience, and love from God.

Work as a ministry of participation with the triune God means being a priest of creation who stewards the world to bring praise to its creator. Another way of putting this is to view humans as the light of the world (see Matt 5:14) or indeed all the cosmos (see Rom 8:19). Practically speaking, this involves actions like caring for the least well-off, implementing fair labor practices, developing business systems that are sustainable, and working in ways that glorify God and respect the environment and humanity. Again, an example from the fashion industry may help. Freeset (now restructured as Joyya) is an evangelical Christian social enterprise operating mostly in India and set up in 2001 with a specific focus on combating extreme poverty and human trafficking in the Sonagachi red-light district of Kolkata. As Rob Kilpatrick and Edwina Pio note, Freeset was "a 'just' business, where justice for all is the outcome—justice for the client, the worker, the investor and the environment has its basis in shalom, a Biblical concept of complete social well-being and peace."[105] As an organization, Freeset believed all persons, irrespective of their condition, are "entitled to respect and a voice in their own affairs and future. No one is to be categorized as 'other' and thus stigmatized and discriminated against."[106] They achieved this by providing economic opportunity for sex workers via the manufacture and distribution of

---

104. Conca, "Making Climate Change Fashionable."

105. Rob Kilpatrick and Edwina Pio, "I Want to Touch the Sky: How an Enterprise Challenges Stigma for Sex-workers," *Equality, Diversity, and Inclusion* 32 (2013): 278.

106. Kilpatrick and Pio, "I Want to Touch the Sky," 283.

fair-trade bags and apparel. At a more practical level, this involved actions such as a living wage, flexible work hours that revolve around family needs, childcare, health and retirement benefits, financial literacy, and interest-free loans. Freeset also stewarded the environment by using organic and sustainable raw materials, water-based inks, and supply-chain transparency.[107] Notably, there is a stark contrast between Freeset and the garment companies in the Rana Plaza disaster. Instead of seeing people as disposable assets, this just enterprise worked to "overcome the eroding power of stigma and economic marginalization for those who have been rendered silent by circumstance, culture and collusion."[108]

A Christian's labor is not about imaging the dominant economic ideology, nor is it about having a high degree of personal witness, piety, giving, or neighborliness, which, for many evangelicals, work seems to boil down to.[109] Instead, Christians are tasked with imaging God in themselves and others back to God. Their true calling is to free creation from its slavery to sin and, by doing so, conform their work "with the way it has been ordered by the Father and redeemed by the Son."[110]

IMPLICATIONS FOR EVANGELICALISM

Bebbington's famous evangelical quadrilateral has four distinctive criteria: conversionism, biblicism, crucicentrism, and activism (e.g., the abolition and temperance movements).[111] However, there is evidence that during the 1970s and 1980s, traditional evangelicals (especially in North America) increasingly interpreted social reform to be necessary for such issues as abortion, sexual immorality, family values, and immigration rather than concerns like economic inequality, gender disparity, and environmental degradation.[112]

---

107. This information was retrieved on October 11, 2021, from https://freesetglobal.com/.

108. Kilpatrick and Pio, "I Want to Touch the Sky," 286.

109. Shirley J. Roels, "The Business Ethics of Evangelicals," *Business Ethics Quarterly* 7 (1997): 115. Although this article is older, in my experience these notions still underpin much of Christian thinking about work.

110. Flett, "Priests of Creation, Mediators of Order," 178.

111. David W. Bebbington, *Evangelicalism in Modern Britain: A History From the 1730s to the 1980s* (London: Unwin Hyman, 1989), 128.

112. See, e.g., Clyde Wilcox, "Evangelicals and the Moral Majority," *Journal for the Scientific Study of Religion* 28 (1989): 400-414; Steven Brint and Seth Abrutyn, "Who's Right About the Right? Comparing Competing Explanations of the Link Between White Evangelicals and Conservative Politics in the United States," *Journal for the Scientific Study of Religion* 49 (2010): 328-50; David R.

Similarly, in the work context, most late-twentieth-century evangelicals differentiated themselves from the cultural mainstream. They often focused on personal lives and individual salvation, supported a free-market system, and demonstrated little interest in the broader economic, environmental, and political dimensions of society.[113] These shifts, especially in North America, contributed to idiosyncrasies like the "moral majority," "which became synonymous with evangelicalism for many" and "the election of Donald Trump, who garnered the support of 81 percent of self-identified white evangelicals."[114]

While an evangelical left has existed since the 1970s,[115] increasing numbers of contemporary evangelicals are becoming interested in the wider social and environmental issues that stem from how we engage with, and work in, the world. For instance, Sabrina Danielsen's content analysis of evangelical magazines over a twenty-five-year period, found that consideration of environmental issues increased.[116] A similar shift has happened regarding social justice issues with secular journalists like Nicholas Kristof of the *New York Times* and Lisa Miller of *Newsweek* writing that "evangelicals have become the newest internationalists" in fighting things such as global slavery, AIDS, and human rights abuses around the world and that "some Christians, exhausted by divisive wedge politics, are going back to the Bible and embracing a wider-ranging agenda, one that emphasizes reaching out to the poor and disenfranchised."[117] When embedded in the work context, this new approach means addressing economic injustice and disparity as well as questioning the role of a system that pursues profit above all else. It also

---

Swartz, *Moral Minority: The Evangelical Left in an Age of Conservatism* (Philadelphia: University of Philadelphia Press, 2012); and Jonathan Malloy, "Political Opportunity Structures, Evangelical Christians and Morality Politics in Canada, Australia, and New Zealand," *Australian Journal of Political Science* 52 (2017): 402–18.

113. Jennifer M. Buck, "Evangelicals and a Theological Response to Globalization: A Commentary on Particularized Issues," *Theology Today* 78 (2021): 90.

114. Jessica Joustra, "What Is an Evangelical? Examining the Politics, History, and Theology of a Contested Label," *The Review of Faith & International Affairs* 17 (2019): 7, 16.

115. Swartz, *Moral Minority*, 178, 181.

116. Sabrina Danielsen, "Fracturing Over Creation Care? Shifting Environmental Beliefs Among Evangelicals, 1984–2010," *Journal for the Scientific Study of Religion* 52 (2013): 199.

117. Nicholas D. Kristof, "Following God Abroad," *New York Times*, May 21, 2002, https://www.nytimes.com/2002/05/21/opinion/following-god-abroad.html, and Lisa Miller, "An Evangelical Identity Crisis," *Newsweek*, December 11, 2006, https://www.newsweek.com/evangelical-identity-crisis-106601.

involves balancing economic progress with a theological understanding of human beings as agents in, and stewards of, God's creation.

While this shift in focus has been welcomed by some, others have construed it as a split within, or even something antithetical to, evangelicalism.[118] This division between the "right" and "left" wings of evangelicalism often becomes political, but perhaps the conflict stems from deeper theological misunderstandings about the nature of God, human beings, creation, and their interaction. This is where Torrance may be of help. The aspect of Torrance's thinking that is germane here is his rejection of dualism. God is not cosmologically separated from "this world of empirical actuality in space and time."[119] While he is not conditioned by it, God personally interacts with the world via redemptive "self-revelation in Israel, in the incarnation of Jesus Christ, and in the outpouring of the Spirit at Pentecost."[120] How God has revealed himself to us is how he is in himself. Therefore, his being desires the redemption of the world and all its economic, social, and environmental dimensions. The idea that work should only revolve around the individual and their personal calling counteracts this broader understanding and feeds the narrative of the sacred versus the secular.

Torrance also rejects the idea that an epistemological disjunction exists between humans (the knowing subject) and the reality of the created order and of God (the known object).[121] The nature of creation, and of God, are such that human beings can successfully interact with them if they respond in a manner appropriate to the object's self-revelation. This means that our work should reflect its grounding in the Trinity, and if Jesus Christ mediates that grounding, then how our work responds to him determines the social and material worlds we indwell. When our work participates, individually and collectively, in Jesus's continuing ministry of worship, obedience, and love, then we are doing "good work." Gary Deddo supplies an example of this participation by using the feeding of the five thousand in Mark 6:30–44. In this passage, Jesus participates in his Father's work (see John 5:19) and then brings his disciples in as part of this labor. He did not need the disciples, but

118. Danielsen, "Fracturing Over Creation Care?" 198.

119. Torrance, *The Trinitarian Faith*, 47.

120. Colyer, *How to Read T. F. Torrance*, 59.

121. Colyer, *How to Read T. F. Torrance*, 59.

he "found a wonderful way for them to participate in this humble exhibition of the divine compassion of his heavenly Father. ... The disciples got to be involved in the very thing Jesus (and his father) were doing."[122] This implies that work that copies the Son, work that reconciles human economies to his Father, is the standard by which all work should be judged, not on whether it is legal, protects natural and negative rights, maximizes profit, or enhances economic prosperity.[123]

Finally, as onto-relational persons made in the image of Christ, we are contingent, first, on creation and then ultimately on the triune God of Jesus Christ. When we work in ways that ignore or reject this, then not only is our labor corrupt, but we eventually work against God's redemptive plan for all of creation. Several negative outcomes of such behavior were indicated throughout this chapter. When we work with creation to emulate its divine order, then we become a form of embodied worship that participates in God's *transformatio mundi*.[124] This participation gives meaning and purpose to our labor, which becomes more than just working hard, being honest, sharing the gospel, and supporting family values (although all these are important activities). Instead, our mundane labors, bonded to Jesus Christ's humanity and enabled by the Spirt, contribute to God's eschatological *transformatio mundi*, thereby giving "legitimate forms of work intrinsic value while investing it with ultimate meaning via its relation, indirectly through sanctification and directly through what humans create, to the new creation."[125] Using Torrance's Trinitarian framework as the basis for our understanding offers a view of work that is so much more than what evangelicals typically envision it to be.

---

122. Gary W. Deddo, "Our Participation in Christ's Continuing Ministry," in *An Introduction to Torrance Theology*, ed. Gerrit S. Dawson (London: T&T Clark, 2007), 148–49.

123. See Milton Friedman's seminal work *Capitalism and Freedom*, 40th anniversary edition (Chicago: University of Chicago Press, 2002) for his argument that free-market capitalism is the best system for ensuring human flourishing.

124. See how Torrance does this work in relation to juridical law in Thomas F. Torrance, *Juridical Law and Physical Law: Toward a Realist Foundation for Human Law* (Eugene, OR: Wipf & Stock, 1997).

125. Peter McGhee and Myk Habets, "Priests of Creation and Mediators of Order: Taking God to Work," in *Faith and Work: Christian Perspective, Research, and Insights into the Movement*, ed. Tim Ewest (Charlotte, NC: IAP, 2018), 83.

14

—

TORRANCE AND GLOBAL EVANGELICALISM

Some Potential Generative Exchanges with
Contemporary Indian Evangelical Theology

Stavan Narendra John

Thomas F. Torrance was a decorated theologian, but he considered himself "a missionary at heart" and viewed his "theological work as a form of missionary activity."[1] In light of such a firm conviction, it is surprising that there are few studies that investigate Torrance's theology from a missional and global theology perspective.[2] The *Global Dictionary of Theology* consults Torrance's works in relation to the following themes: Barthianism, heaven, scientific theology, space, and the Trinity, specifically the Filioque Controversy.[3] These references highlight Torrance's global appeal on dogmatic themes, but interestingly in an article on the theology of mission, there is no mention

---

1. Thomas F. Torrance, "Thomas Torrance Responds," in *The Promise of Trinitarian Theology: Theologians in Dialogue with T. F. Torrance*, ed. Elmer M. Colyer (Lanham: Rowman & Littlefield Publishers, 2001), 304.

2. Two notable exceptions are: Caroline G. Seed, Daniel Lioy, and Rikus Fick, "Thomas F. Torrance: Theology and Mission in Practice," *In die Skriflig* 50 (2016): 1-10; and Joseph H. Sherrard, *T. F. Torrance as Missional Theologian: The Ascended Christ and the Ministry of the Church* (Downers Grove, IL: InterVarsity Press, 2021), especially 1-10, 217-28.

3. See the following articles in *Global Dictionary of Theology*, ed. William A. Dryness and Veli-Matti Kärkkäinen (Downers Grove, IL: InterVarsity Press, 2008; repr., Bangalore: Omega Book World, 2019): Roland Chia, "Barthianism," 104-5; Daniel G. Reid, "Heaven," 371; Alister E. McGrath, "Scientific Theology," 800-801; Chun Ho Park, "Space," 845-47; and Robert Letham, "Trinity, Triune God," 904.

of Torrance's theological contributions to missional discourse.[4] It would be unfair to fault a dictionary article for failing to mention this, especially since Torrance's scholarship does not adequately explore the integral role missions plays in his theology.[5] If future works are to highlight Torrance's contribution to mission theology, one must insist with Joseph Sherrard that "Torrance's extensive and wide-ranging theological corpus presents a coherent and comprehensive missional theology," where the stress is on providing a *"theological* account," not one that focuses on "sociology and [a] cultural analysis" of mission theology.[6]

With respect to global theology, many theologians from the majority world church are engaging with Torrance's theology.[7] Within these works, the focus is invariably on expounding the richness and depth of Torrance's literary output, with very little dialogue with contextual theological themes.[8] The future of Torrance scholarship from the majority world context promises to highlight resonances that are more context-specific.[9] This article anticipates in-depth studies that bring Torrance into dialogue with contextual

---

4. See Charles E. Van Engen, "Mission, Theology of," in Dryness and Kärkkäinen, *Global Dictionary of Theology*, 550–62.

5. See Seed, Lioy, and Fick, "Thomas F. Torrance: Theology and Mission in Practice," 1, "The missional nature of much of Torrance's dogmatic and biblical theology has largely remained unexplored"; Sherrard, *T. F. Torrance as Missional Theologian*, 6, "Few [Torrance] studies have drawn attention to the extent to which Torrance presents a comprehensive vision of the church, its missional nature, and its service and ministry to the world."

6. Sherrard, *T. F. Torrance as Missional Theologian*, 7.

7. A few recent monographs from majority world scholars include: Hakbong Kim, *Person, Personhood, and the Humanity of Christ: Christocentric Anthropology and Ethics in Thomas F. Torrance* (Eugene, OR: Pickwick, 2021); Dick O. Eugenio, *Communion with the Triune God: The Trinitarian Soteriology of T. F. Torrance* (Eugene, OR: Pickwick, 2014); and Titus Chung, *Thomas Torrance's Mediations and Revelation* (Farnham: Ashgate, 2011).

8. Kim, in his conclusion, acknowledges that his study was intentionally limited to critically engaging with Torrance's theological anthropology and ethics. Kim suggests that one way to constructively develop his work would be to bring Torrance, a representative of "western thought," into dialogue with "Confucianism's … eastern thought" vis-à-vis their respective anthropologies and conceptions of ethics. The result of such an exchange would be mutually enriching, Kim believes. For more, see Kim, *Person, Personhood, and the Humanity of Christ*, 185.

9. Two works that anticipate further contextual interactions with Torrance's works are by Vhumani Magezi and Christopher Magezi: "Christ Also Ours in Africa: A Consideration of Torrance's Incarnational, Christological Model as Nexus for Christ's Identification with African Christians," *Verbum et Ecclesia* 38 (2017): 1–12; and "Healing and Coping with Life within Challenges of Spiritual Insecurity: Juxtaposed Consideration of Christ's Sinlessness and African Ancestors in Pastoral Guidance," *Hervormde Teologiese Studies* 73 (2017): 1–12.

theological concerns by highlighting some potential generative exchanges between Torrance and contemporary Indian evangelical theology.

TORRANCE'S THEOLOGICAL
FOOTPRINT IN INDIA

Torrance never visited India, nor did he write extensively on any topics specifically related to Indian theological concerns. Therefore, as an Indian evangelical Christian, it would be easy to dismiss him as irrelevant. However, two factors prevent one from coming to such a conclusion. First, Torrance was a Scottish theologian, a tradition that is no stranger to India. Brian Stanley in his article, "The Theology of the Scottish Protestant Missionary Movement," seeks to distill the theological legacy of Scottish Protestant missionaries in the nineteenth and twentieth centuries. He begins his pursuit by insisting that Scottish missionaries played a "disproportionately large" role within the "British Protestant overseas missionary enterprise."[10] Stanley substantiates his claim by highlighting the indelible impact Scottish missionaries left in countries such as Egypt and China and in continents such as Africa and South America.[11] Torrance may not have had a direct connection to India, but the Protestant Scottish theological tradition he represents has had an enormous impact in India that arguably continues today through the educational institutions they left behind.[12]

Joshua Kalapati documents the legacy of the educational initiatives of Scottish missionaries in the nineteenth century and the early part of the

---

10. Brian Stanley, "The Theology of the Scottish Protestant Missionary Movement," in *The History of Scottish Theology, Volume III: The Long Twentieth Century*, ed. David Fergusson and Mark W. Elliot (Oxford: Oxford University Press, 2019), 51.

11. Stanley, "The Theology of the Scottish Protestant Missionary Movement," 51–52.

12. See Joshua Kalapati, "The Scottish Educational Mission in India: An Appraisal," in *Breaking Barriers and Building Bridges: An Appraisal of the Missionary Legacy in India*, ed. Joshua Kalapati, Daniel Jeyaraj, and Gabriel Merigala (Chennai: Mylapore Institute for Indigenous Studies/Inter Church Services Association, 2016), 141. Kalapati avers that the educational initiatives begun by Scottish missionaries, for example the "Scottish Church College in Kolkata, Wilson College in Mumbai and Madras Christian College in Chennai," bequeathed to India an "enduring legacy" of shaping students within their institutions who would go on to serve the country in a variety of capacities. Kalapati believes these "illustrious alumni" serve as a testament of "God's providence for modern India." Madras Christian College alone lists alumni ranging from the former President of India, Sarvepalli Radhakrishnan, to former CEO of PepsiCo, Indra K. Nooyi, to renowned theologians such as Pandipeddi Chenchiah. For more, see https://mcc.edu.in/distinguished-alumni/.

twentieth century.[13] His assessment is mostly positive and includes public reforms against "social evils and superstitions"; investment in the education of "the Hindu elite, who later played a major role in nation-building," through evangelistic initiatives that sparked and welcomed "the Indian renaissance movement and the regeneration of Hinduism"; and finally, through training leaders such as V. S. Azariah, K. T. Paul, Chenchiah, Chakkarai, D. G. Moses, Paul D. Devanandan, and Rajaiah D. Paul they bequeathed a legacy of strong leaders who would serve the Indian church.[14] Kalapati highlights certain negative aspects of this relationship through a recollection from V.S. Azariah and an observation from Stephen Neill. V. S. Azariah remembers certain interpersonal issues between missionaries and native church leaders, wherein instead of "friendship" what he received from some missionaries was "condescending love."[15] Stephen Neill, Kalapati notes, observes it was common for Scottish missionaries (and all missionaries in general at that time) to think of conversion as leading someone to the "Christian faith" and "to the European ways and European habits of dressing."[16] Irrespective of these negative aspects, Kalapati concludes his observations on a hopeful note: "The educational mission of the Scottish missionaries in Madras Presidency was an ennobling saga of sacrifice and a story of success."[17] Torrance is relevant for Indian theology in general because of the Scottish theological legacy he represents.

Second, Indian evangelical Christians should not dismiss Torrance, even though he did not have a personal connection to India, because he was able to impact many parts of the world through the students whom he taught and mentored. Stanley points out that the contribution of Scottish theology to missions in the nineteenth and twentieth centuries must also include all those Scottish leaders who remained in their home country but trained others

---

13. Joshua Kalapati, "The Early Educational Mission of the Scottish Missionaries in Madras Presidency: Its Social Implications," *Scottish Bulletin of Evangelical Theology* 16 (1998): 140–55.

14. Kalapati, "The Early Educational Mission of the Scottish Missionaries," 153–54.

15. Kalapati, "The Early Educational Mission of the Scottish Missionaries," 155n51, where he notes the words are from V.S. Azariah, "The Problem of Co-operation Between Foreign and Native Workers," in *History and Records of the Conference Together with Addresses Delivered at the Evening Meetings* (Edinburgh: Oliphant, Anderson, & Ferrier, 1910), 306–315.

16. Kalapati, "The Early Educational Mission of the Scottish Missionaries," 155n52, refers to Stephen Neill, *A History of Christianity in India (1707–1858)* (Cambridge: Cambridge University Press, 1985), 321.

17. Kalapati, "The Early Educational Mission of the Scottish Missionaries," 155.

"by their personal example, preaching, writing, or mentoring ... theological students for missionary service."[18] Stanley lists eminent figures such as David Bogue "who trained some 70 per cent of the London Missionary Society's Indian missionaries before 1826," and others such as Thomas Chalmers, John Love, Annie Hunter Small, and David S. Cairns, all of whom had a significant role in training others for missionary work, even if they themselves were based in Britain.[19] Torrance rightfully deserves a place alongside the eminent Scottish personalities listed above, as many missionaries trained under him while he taught at New College in the University of Edinburgh. In relation to India, one missionary he trained in particular stands out: Robin Boyd, an Irish missionary to India.[20]

Torrance, along with John McIntyre, supervised Boyd's PhD thesis entitled "The Place of Dogmatic Theology in the Indian Church," subsequently abridged and published as An Introduction to Indian Christian Theology.[21] Siga Arles notes the significance of Boyd's contribution, among other eminent works by Indians, to the growth of theologies and missiologies that were indigenous in nature when he comments: "His Introduction to Indian Christian Theology (1969) has become the standard textbook at the B.Th. and B.D. levels for the course in Indian Christian theology."[22] Arles correctly describes Boyd's work as a survey of "the earliest contributors and then moving on to consider the early, middle, and later pioneers of Indian indigenous theology."[23] Therefore, while it may be too much to claim that Boyd's great legacy to the Indian church is due to the influence of Torrance (and McIntyre), one can at least highlight the ongoing relevance of Torrance for Indian theology in general because of the role he played in encouraging and guiding a study that continues to be formative for generations of Indian seminary students.[24] Any

---

18. Stanley, "The Theology of the Scottish Protestant Missionary Movement," 52.

19. Stanley, "The Theology of the Scottish Protestant Missionary Movement," 52.

20. Robin Boyd served as a missionary in Gujarat, India, from 1954–1974. See Robin H. S. Boyd, "My Pilgrimage in Mission," International Bulletin of Mission Research 40 (2016): 267–79.

21. Boyd, "My Pilgrimage in Mission," 268. His published thesis is Robin H. S. Boyd, An Introduction to Indian Christian Theology (Madras: Christian Literature Society, 1969; repr., Delhi: ISPCK, 2014).

22. Siga Arles, "The State of Mission Studies in India: An Overview and Assessment of Publications and Publishing," International Bulletin of Missionary Research 34 (2010): 157.

23. Arles, "The State of Mission Studies in India," 156.

24. Kirsteen Kim describes Boyd's An Introduction to Indian Christian Theology as his "best-known monograph" in the Indian context. Kim goes on to explain that Boyd's focus on

reflection of the significance of Torrance's theology for India must therefore begin with Robin Boyd.

In what follows, the focus will be on the following theologians who have directly and indirectly interacted with Torrance with specifically Indian theological concerns. First, Robin Boyd on Indian theological reception history; second, Ajit Prasadam on theological pedagogy; and finally, Steven Tsoukalas on comparative theology. These three representative areas will shed light on the kind of theological reception Torrance has received with respect to Indian theology.

ROBIN BOYD ON TORRANCE AND INDIAN THEOLOGICAL RECEPTION HISTORY

Robin Boyd and Torrance had many biographical commonalities. Boyd, like Torrance, was born in a missionary family; both his parents served in Gujarat State, India,[25] whereas Torrance's parents served in Chengdu, China. Both Torrance and Boyd did part of their theological studies at the University of Edinburgh; they also volunteered to serve in the British Army during the same time period in the Second World War (1943–1945)—Torrance as a chaplain and Boyd as a cryptographer.[26] Torrance and Boyd also shared an enduring passion for missions—China[27] for Torrance and India[28] for Boyd—

---

theologizing for the Indian church by focusing on the Indian theological reception history was "the first in the field," Kirsteen Kim, "Review of Robin Boyd, *Beyond Captivity: Explorations in Indian Christian History and Theology,*" *Studies in World Christianity* 22 (2016): 174.

25. See Boyd, "My Pilgrimage in Mission," 265, where he mentions that his father served in Gujarat for a total of thirteen years, and his mother for a total of ten years.

26. See Alister E. McGrath, *Thomas F. Torrance: An Intellectual Biography* (London: T&T Clark, 1999), 69–77; Boyd, "My Pilgrimage in Mission," 266.

27. See Seed, Lioy, and Fick, "Thomas F. Torrance: Theology and Mission in Practice," where the authors argue that Torrance's missionary heartbeat for China was "lifelong" (9) not just something that characterized his early and later life.

28. See Robin Boyd, *Beyond Captivity: Explorations in Indian Christian History and Theology* (Bangalore: Centre for Contemporary Christianity, 2014), xx, where Boyd, after a lifetime of Christian ministry in various capacities, writes, "All my writing has had the underlying theme of Mission—God's Mission. And the last fifteen years or so have seen me becoming once more focussed on India—to my great delight and profit."

church unity,[29] pastoral ministry,[30] preaching,[31] and theological writing.[32] However, it was, perhaps, their common appreciation for Karl Barth that allowed their paths to cross.

Boyd, as did Torrance, had the privilege of studying with Karl Barth for a short period of time; his impact on his life was so great that he even paid tribute to him after he passed away in a *Guardian* newspaper article in Bangalore.[33] In his article, Boyd fondly remembers that he studied under Barth "in Basel in 1953-54 while Barth was lecturing every day on what was later to appear in print as *Church Dogmatics* IV/2, *The Doctrine of Reconciliation.*"[34] Barth asked him one question in particular, Boyd recalls, that remained with him throughout his theological career.[35] Later in life, Boyd provides more context and explains the significance of Barth's question:

---

29. See Thomas F. Torrance, *Theology in Reconciliation: Essays Toward Evangelical and Catholic Unity in East and West* (Eugene, OR: Wipf & Stock, 1996), 9, where his Trinitarian theological convictions that grounded a lifetime of ecumenical pursuits are made clear: "Yet the more deeply we press into the material centre of the Church's faith in Christ and in the Holy Trinity, the greater is the pressure disposing us to reach agreement with one another." See also Boyd, *Beyond Captivity*, 231, where he believes that the ecumenical efforts of the Indian church serve as a model for the global church: "Although the debate on Christian unity may not sound particularly 'Indian,' it in fact is so, since the work of Christian unity has made more progress in India than anywhere else. This is an important contribution of India to the world Church," Boyd, "Early Impulses of Indian Christian Theology (1) Some Unfinished Business" In *Beyond Captiviy*, 230-41.

30. See McGrath, *Thomas F. Torrance*, 59-84, for an account of Torrance's decade in pastoral ministry, which includes two years of service as a chaplain for the British Army during World War II; see "My Pilgrimage in Mission," for an account of Boyd's four years of service with the Church of North India (1970-1974), and thirteen years of service with two different churches in Australia (1974-1980; 1987-1994).

31. See Myk Habets, "*Theologia Is Eusebia*: Thomas F. Torrance's Church Homiletics," in *T&T Clark Handbook of Thomas F. Torrance*, ed. Paul D. Molnar and Myk Habets (London: T&T Clark, 2020), 259-76, for an overview of Torrance's theology of preaching, which Habets argues is "immensely and attractively readable and accessible" (259) in comparison to a common stereotype of his more academic works that are considered too complex. See Boyd, *Beyond Captivity*, xxiv, where Boyd emphasizes his love for preaching: "For me personally, preaching has always been an essential part of my ministry—perhaps indeed the most essential part."

32. See McGrath, *Thomas F. Torrance*, xi, who notes that before and after retirement Torrance produced a total of 610 works of theology. Boyd's works do not compare to Torrance in volume, but arguably, his work on Indian Christian Theology continues to be generative for Indian theologians. For a compilation of several writings across his lifetime of ministry, see Boyd, *Beyond Captivity*.

33. Boyd, "Karl Barth, 1886-1968: a *Shishya's* Tribute," *Guardian*, January 1969. For more, see Boyd, *Beyond Captivity*, 129-32.

34. Boyd, *Beyond Captivity*, 129. Torrance's interactions with Barth during his doctoral studies were in 1937-1938. For more, see McGrath, *Thomas F. Torrance*, 42-46.

35. See Boyd, *Beyond Captivity*, 131.

At one of those late night sessions with a few students, which Barth so much enjoyed, and knowing that I was about to leave for India, he asked me, "Are these big books of mine going to mean anything in India?" Sadly, I never gave him a proper answer in his lifetime; yet in a way, all that I ever wrote about Indian Christian theology was an attempt to answer that question.[36]

Boyd, without a doubt, chose his PhD topic in 1959 during his first furlough from India with Barth's question as a motivating factor: "Feeling it was time to take up Barth's challenge, I took as my subject 'the place of dogmatic theology in the Indian Church.' "[37] While Boyd does not mention why he chose to study under Torrance, arguably, it was because of his high regard for him as a scholar of Barth.[38]

In his thesis, "The Place of Dogmatic Theology in the Indian Church," Boyd remembers that he was initially unsure about what direction to take, but eventually decided it was better to learn from the existing Indian theological reception history rather than impose his own theology.[39] Boyd writes, "Fortunately I decided that rather than starting from my own conception of dogmatics I had better find out what sort of theology Indian theologians had in fact written."[40] Boyd describes his PhD writing phase, which took him seven years, as "a wonderful journey of discovery."[41] The end result was a massive seven hundred pages of doctoral work, but this length was not an issue with his supervisors, recalls Boyd, because he "was able to persuade ... [them] that it was important that the material should *all* be included, so as to

36. Boyd, "Early Impulses of Indian Christian Theology." For more, see Boyd, *Beyond Captivity*, 218.

37. Boyd, *Beyond Captivity*, 218. The full title was: "The Place of Dogmatics in the Indian Church: A Study of the Development of Indian Christian Theology and an Assessment of its Significance."

38. While this comment is more in the realm of conjecture, it is pertinent to note that Boyd praises Torrance's book on Barth's early theology: "This is a very useful and illuminating introduction to the early Barth by one who is himself the leading British exponent of Barthian theology." For more, see Boyd, "Review of T. F. Torrance, *Karl Barth: an Introduction to his Early Theology, 1910–1931*," Biblical Theology 16 (1966), which can be found in Boyd, *Beyond Captivity*, 96–102.

39. Boyd, *Beyond Captivity*, 218.

40. Boyd, *Beyond Captivity*, 218.

41. Boyd, *Beyond Captivity*, 218–19.

make sure that the information was available to other researchers."[42] Within the study, Boyd briefly interacts with and appropriates Torrance's theological methodology, and it is this aspect in particular that may shed light on the relevance of Torrance for contemporary Indian evangelical theology.[43]

In the latter part of his study, in a section entitled "The Place of Dogmatic Theology in the Indian Church," Boyd acknowledges Torrance as a formative theological guide on the subject of dogmatics: "I am indebted to Prof. T. F. Torrance for his explanation of the meaning of dogmatics, and for much of the material in this section."[44] Within this section Boyd distinguishes between "dogma" and "dogmatics" by noting how the former is based on the views of "external authorities," while the latter originates "in accordance with its own interior principles."[45] Indians have rarely encountered a dogmatic approach to theology, notes Boyd; what they have mostly encountered is "dogma," which they have strongly resisted, he explains, citing Hindu apologist Dr. Radhakrishnan and Christian theologian Chenchiah as examples.[46] He adds, "The profound grappling with Truth which true dogmatic theology demands is surely not alien to the Indian tradition."[47]

In the same section of his work, Boyd highlights five main points regarding doing dogmatic theology in the Indian church, which I summarize below:

1. Existing Indian theologies function like "the Prolegomena to an Indian Dogmatics," because they focus on important desiderata that will be required in a more "complete Church Dogmatics."[48]

2. Dogmatic theologies will have to take the prevailing Hindu disinclination toward excessive creedal imposition in mind by having only "minimal 'official' dogmatic theology" and a maximal allowance for a diversity of secondary views, all the while

---

42. Boyd, *Beyond Captivity*, 219 (emphasis original).

43. See Robert H. S. Boyd, "The Place of Dogmatic Theology in the Indian Church: A Study of the Development of Indian Christian Theology and an Assessment of its Significance" (PhD thesis, University of Edinburgh, 1966), 677–87.

44. Boyd, "The Place of Dogmatic Theology in the Indian Church," 677n1.

45. Boyd, "The Place of Dogmatic Theology in the Indian Church," 677.

46. Boyd, "The Place of Dogmatic Theology in the Indian Church," 678.

47. Boyd, "The Place of Dogmatic Theology in the Indian Church," 678.

48. Boyd, "The Place of Dogmatic Theology in the Indian Church," 680.

encouraging each one to stay true "to the inner content and logic of the faith."[49]

3. Creedal formulations from the West will have an enduring value for the Indian church but they cannot function in a "permanent" capacity: "the Indian Church must in time develop its own confessions" in order to better communicate essential Christian truths "into [Indian] regional languages."[50]

4. Theological trailblazers, rather than systematicians, adept at contextualizing the Christian message for India, are the need of the hour: "India's immediate need is not so much for an Aquinas or a Calvin, but for men like Clement and Origen, men of adventurous mind and vivid imagination, preachers like Sundar Singh who can convince men's minds in their own language and win their hearts."[51]

5. The global church will be edified by a theological dogmatics from the Indian church, written by "Indian Christian theologians," because only they "have grown up in and are thoroughly familiar with the Hindu environment and ways of thought, but who have found the object of their search in the Christ who has sought and found them."[52]

In light of Boyd's views, what can one learn about his perspective on the relevance of a theologian such as Torrance for the Indian church and her theology? Boyd does not answer this question directly, but a clue about how he would answer comes from his assessment of Karl Barth's relevance for India.

---

49. Boyd, "The Place of Dogmatic Theology in the Indian Church," 680–82. On page 682, Boyd correctly explains: "Hinduism abounds in 'dogmatic theology,' i.e. systematic statements about beliefs, but does not normally give any kind of official sanction, though in any particular school the weight of tradition comes very close to such sanction."

50. Boyd, "The Place of Dogmatic Theology in the Indian Church," 682–84. Interestingly, on page 683 Boyd notes that "Nicaea and Chalcedon and Augsburg and Westminster will not cease to be of significance, but their language will not be that recited in village Churches," thereby underscoring the lasting theological value of the creeds and confessions, but also prioritizing the need for "an Indian Confession of the Faith" for the church in India.

51. Boyd, "The Place of Dogmatic Theology in the Indian Church," 685.

52. Boyd, "The Place of Dogmatic Theology in the Indian Church," 686.

It seems unlikely indeed that the Indian Church will ever make a very deep study of "all these big thick books," full as they are, not merely of universal and timeless Biblical insights, but also of the accumulated theological lore of the Western Church. ... The place of Barth in the Indian Church, is perhaps not so much that of a Protestant *doctor angelicus*, but rather, in his own favourite figure, that of a signpost, pointing the way to a *new* theology, the most exciting and truly new theology which has emerged since Chalcedon, and pointing out that the road to that theology lies only through Scripture, Christology and the Church.[53]

One can infer from Boyd's views about Barth that Torrance will be relevant for his method of theology, rather than for the specific content of his theology. In other words, while his theology may never become a normative theological resource for the Indian church, how he did his theology will have enduring value.

The prescient value of Boyd's comments on Karl Barth will require a separate study,[54] and it is perhaps too early to assess whether a similar kind of evaluation can be made about Torrance's theology with respect to the Indian theological reception of his oeuvre.[55] However, Boyd's views vis-à-vis Indian theological reception history has the tacit (if not explicit) approval of Torrance (since he was one of his supervisors) and potentially sheds light on how Torrance's theology can better engage with theologies that are driven by more context-specific concerns in the majority world. Furthermore, Torrance's dogmatic theological approach highlights the relevance of his theological methodology for contexts such as India, and it may be a useful insight for those working on bringing Torrance into dialogue with contextual theological interlocutors in the future. Boyd's interactions with Torrance in his PhD thesis can be an illuminating resource for such projects.

---

53. Boyd, *Beyond Captivity*, 101–2.

54. An unpublished and provisional working document of master and PhD theses from select theological seminaries in India shows that many Indian theologians have interacted with Barth's theology from as early as 1968 in relation to topics such as religion, death, comparative theology, justification, natural theology, biblical exegesis, the doctrine of Scripture, the image of God, and the doctrine of predestination. See Yesan Sellan and Chacko Chacko, "A Directory of Theses and Dissertations in Indian Theological Libraries: 2010," unpublished report.

55. There are not enough works on Torrance by Indian theologians to make a proper assessment about whether Indian theologians find his method more important than his content.

AJIT A. PRASADAM ON TORRANCE
AND THEOLOGICAL PEDAGOGY

In his 2005 Princeton Theological Seminary doctoral study, Ajit Prasadam briefly uses Torrance's theology, among other works, to help construct a theological pedagogy that he believes will effectively counter manifestations of the caste system in the church.[56] In his own words, he seeks to "show ways in which, through Christian education, the caste system can be transformed in the minds of the people, beginning with school age children, and thus result in the structural changes in the church."[57] He draws from social, political, religious, and educational interlocutors in order to make a case for the construction of a curriculum that will move "beyond conscientization toward a full transformation of oppressed persons and oppressive structures."[58] He finds Torrance particularly helpful because of his stress on "epistemology" vis-à-vis both "science and theology" and the concrete particulars of Jesus that attest to his full divinity and his genuine humanity.[59] Both these aspects, Prasadam notes, have "implications for personhood and humanity, and the meaning of community, characterized by *koinonia*, which reflects *perichoresis* in the Trinity."[60] He sheds further light on the meaning of both points in an analytical section that focuses on, among other things, showing how these theological insights apply in real life.[61]

While it is not always clear whether Prasadam is crediting Torrance for his application-oriented insights, since he is drawing among other resources from Torrance's theology in the section,[62] one can be reasonably confident about the following. Prasadam wishes to convey that Torrance's views on

---

56. Ajit A. Prasadam, "Beyond Conscientization: James E. Loder's Transformational Model for Christian Education in the Indian Context and Beyond" (PhD thesis, Princeton Theological Seminary, 2005), 363–89.

57. Prasadam, "Beyond Conscientization," 35.

58. Prasadam, "Beyond Conscientization," 334. By "conscientization," he means "the process of raising one's critical consciousness about social, economical, and political reality and the formulation of action against the oppressive elements of reality." See Prasadam, "Beyond Conscientization," 28n56. Here, Prasadam refers to Paulo Freire, *Pedagogy of the Oppressed*, trans. Myra Berjman Ramos (New York: The Seabury Press, 1998), 19, as the source of his definition of the term.

59. Prasadam, "Beyond Conscientization," 378.

60. Prasadam, "Beyond Conscientization," 378.

61. Prasadam, "Beyond Conscientization," 383–84, 387.

62. See Prasadam, "Beyond Conscientization," 389n14, where Prasadam acknowledges, "In the development of this section I am indebted to Torrance, *The Mediation of Christ*."

epistemology in relation to theology and science can serve as a helpful resource to undercut a dualism in scientific and anthropological studies that fosters racism.[63] In an earlier section, he clearly explains the force and relevance of this point for India: "The subject-object dualism influenced ethnographic studies of the 19th century in India, which led to racial categorization of castes. Thus, a discussion of epistemology is important to the project of humanization of humanity."[64] Prasadam also wants to underscore that Christology and the Trinity testify to a "relational thinking that calls for the dismantling of all hierarchical ordering whether in the caste system or patriarchy as a sub-unit in the caste system."[65] He highlights the need for social interactions in the world to reflect the Trinity: "When reality is perceived as relationality then social reality needs to be ordered to show Trinitarian relations."[66] Within such a model, Prasadam believes, there is no room for the caste system to operate.[67]

Prasadam's interaction with Torrance is mostly positive, but he does indicate that Torrance's theology in comparison to that of Indian theologian M. M. Thomas does not sufficiently address ethical and contextual topics, such as a "theology on pluralism, systematic issues like racism, casteism, and poverty."[68] He goes on to clarify that one can find resources from other theological loci within Torrance to address such issues, for instance, "from his discussions of sin and evil."[69] While contemporary Torrancean theologians are addressing the subject of ethics in his theology,[70] Prasadam flags additional topics that resonate with important global theological concerns which will be important to address in future works on Torrance's theological ethics. In all, Prasadam's interaction with Torrance is brief but indicates the potential fecundity of Torrance's theological insights for a variety of issues that he himself may not

---

63. Prasadam, "Beyond Conscientization," 387.

64. Prasadam, "Beyond Conscientization," 366.

65. Prasadam, "Beyond Conscientization," 384.

66. Prasadam, "Beyond Conscientization," 384.

67. Prasadam, "Beyond Conscientization," 384.

68. Prasadam, "Beyond Conscientization," 386.

69. Prasadam, "Beyond Conscientization," 386.

70. For a recent exploration on how Torrance's theology addresses ethics, see: Todd H. Speidell: *Fully Human in Christ: The Incarnation as the End of Christian Ethics* (Eugene, OR: Wipf & Stock, 2016); and "The Soteriological Suspension of the Ethical in the Theology of T. F. Torrance," *Participatio* 5 (2015): 56–90.

have directly addressed in his theology, which in this case is how to uproot the caste system from the church; he also raises areas for further consideration in Torrance's theology, especially related to ethics and other religions.

STEVEN TSOUKALAS ON TORRANCE AND COMPARATIVE THEOLOGY

Comparative theologian Steven Tsoukalas in an article entitled *"Theōsis*: A Comparative Study of T. F. Torrance and Rāmānuja," critically appropriates Myk Habets's methodology of studying Torrance's understanding of theosis in his brief engagement with the same concept in the works of the great Hindu theologian Rāmānuja (c. 1017–1137).[71] Specifically, Tsoukalas follows Habets's way of discerning a theology of theosis in Torrance from the many implicit indicators to it in his entire theological corpus.[72] With regard to Rāmānuja, Tsoukalas writes, "Though the words themselves were likely unknown to Rāmānuja, through his works one can see a *notion of theōsis.*"[73] Therefore, just as Habets "deploy[s] creative imagination in a manner that is tested and controlled by Torrance's own concerns"[74] in order to construct a theology of theosis from his oeuvre, Tsoukalas does the same with Rāmānuja.[75] Tsoukalas calls his comparative study of Torrance and Rāmānuja's respective understandings of theosis "an imaginative conversation."[76] In order to truly appreciate his work, one must first recognize how his methodological convictions lead to keen insights about both theologians.

Methodologically, Tsoukalas focuses on interpreting their positions from within their own theological frameworks.[77] Therefore, for Torrance, convictions such as: "the Triune God as wholly other than creation, *creatio ex nihilo*,

---

71. Steven Tsoukalas, "Theōsis: A Comparative Study of T. F. Torrance and Rāmānuja," *Journal of Hindu-Christian Studies* 30 (2017): 53–61.

72. Tsoukalas, "Theōsis," 58n1, where he refers to and is drawing insights from Myk Habets, *Theosis in the Theology of Thomas Torrance* (New York: Routledge, 2016), 2. Habets's book was originally published by Ashgate in 2009.

73. Tsoukalas, "Theōsis," 53 (emphasis in original).

74. Tsoukalas, "Theōsis," 58n1, quotes from Habets, *Theosis in the Theology of Thomas Torrance*, 2.

75. Tsoukalas, "Theōsis," 58n1.

76. Tsoukalas, "Theōsis," 53.

77. See Steven Tsoukalas, *Kṛṣṇa and Christ: Body-Divine Relation in the Thought of Śaṅkara, Rāmānuja, and Classical Christian Orthodoxy* (Eugene, OR: Wipf & Stock, 2006), for a monograph where he puts his methodology into practice.

creation (including souls) as finite and dependent upon God, creation (including souls after the fall one day being reconciled to God" are foundational.[78] This leads to an interpretation of theosis in Torrance wherein "there is no ontological transformation [of human beings] into the divine essence," but nevertheless "an ontological transformation of believers' *humanity*."[79] In other words, while human beings will never become divine, they will become the human beings they were "intended to be."[80] For Rāmānuja, Tsoukalas explains, the overarching theological worldview is that of:

> viśiṣṭādvaita (qualified non-dualism). Rāmānuja's God is Lord Viṣṇu-Nārāyaṇa, who is personal, non-dual, and all. The Lord is ultimate reality. Yet, the Lord as ultimate reality/all is "qualified" (viśiṣṭa) by bheda (difference) — there is bheda between Viṣṇu-Nārāyaṇa, the universe, and ātman-s (souls). Further, the universe and ātman-s are the body of the Lord, are real, and are ontologically equal with the Lord.[81]

In other words, according to Tsoukalas, Rāmānuja contends that there is a distinction between God and everything else (universe, souls), but all that exists other than God is within the being of God.[82] Within such a view, therefore, theosis entails: "partaking of and participating in the divine nature ... in part because they share originated ontological oneness with the Lord."[83] In light of reading their theologies within their own frameworks, Tsoukalas goes on to identify interesting similarities and dissimilarities in their views of theosis.

---

78. Tsoukalas, "Theōsis," 54.

79. Tsoukalas, "Theōsis," 54.

80. Tsoukalas, "Theōsis," 54, correctly describes Torrance's views of theosis as becoming " 'truly human,' " but when he explains what Torrance's view means he seems to suggest that the *telos* for humankind is to become like the pre-fallen Adam and Eve: "The incarnation of the Son, occurring within the life of the Trinity, undergirds the sanctifying ontological and functional transformation of humanity toward fulfillment of what Eden was intended to be." Since Tsoukalas's work is brief, it is unfair to critique him on this point, but perhaps, he could have highlighted how, according to some interpretations of Torrance's theology, the eschatological existence for humankind is one where "even more is gained in Christ than was lost in Adam. ... an even higher order than the condition that was lost in the Fall" will be obtained at the eschaton. See Habets, *Theosis in the Theology of Thomas Torrance*, 30–31.

81. Tsoukalas, "Theōsis," 55.

82. Tsoukalas, "Theōsis," 55.

83. Tsoukalas, "Theōsis," 55.

Tsoukalas discerns at least eight similarities between Torrance's and Rāmānuja's views on theōsis, but according to him it is important to note that these are notional similarities, and when explored deeper significant differences emerge.[84] Space will not permit an exploration of all these eight points, but two should suffice to highlight where they agree and where they may part ways.

First, incarnation/*avatāra*: Tsoukalas notices how both theologians share a worldview that is conducive to God becoming incarnate; "With Kṛṣṇa as *avatāra* (descent [of God in human form]), Rāmānuja's ontology lends to a 'god-man' doctrine."[85] Such a view, Tsoukalas explains, "is a type of hypostatic union notionally similar to Christ's" because it contains an affirmation of the reality of "the material universe" and the reality of Kṛṣṇa's humanity.[86] However, Tsoukalas insists that the meaning of this incarnation differs drastically for each theologian.[87] For Torrance, avers Tsoukalas, the incarnation is an affirmation of a genuine identification with humanity because "Torrance posits Christ's humanity *ex nihilo* (by way of Adam and Eve)"; whereas for Rāmānuja, Kṛṣṇa "does not identify with humanity," because his humanity is formed out of God's being.[88] The contrast can be illumined further through the use of the category of *homoousios*: "Kṛṣṇa as *avatāra* is *homoousios* with Viṣṇu-Nārāyaṇa, but there is no subject-object *homoousion*," since both the personal identity and the material of the human ontology are divine.[89] While Tsoukalas does not make the contrast with Torrance explicit on this point, one can deduce from what he states that, for Torrance, Christ is both *homoousios* with God and with human beings.[90]

Second, humanity: Tsoukalas believes that Torrance's theology can affirm a doctrine of humanity that continues into the eschaton, in contrast to Rāmānuja; but he avers that "in a profoundly Hindu sense," one can perceive a "truly human" theology for the present life in Rāmānuja's theology.[91] In

---

84. Tsoukalas, "Theōsis," 55.

85. Tsoukalas, "Theōsis," 56.

86. Tsoukalas, "Theōsis," 56.

87. Tsoukalas, "Theōsis," 56.

88. Tsoukalas, "Theōsis," 56.

89. Tsoukalas, "Theōsis," 56.

90. See Thomas F. Torrance, *Incarnation: The Person and Life of Christ*, ed. Robert T. Walker (Downers Grove, IL and Milton Keynes: IVP and Paternoster, 2008), 203.

91. Tsoukalas, "Theōsis," 57–58.

matters of eschatology, Tsoukalas observes that Torrance's Christian "linear view of a single-occurring history" versus Rāmānuja's Hindu "samsāric yugic cycles [which] occur eternally" allow "no consummating event for material humanity in order to bring it fully to what it was intended to be" in Rāmānuja's theology, whereas it does in Torrance's.[92] Furthermore, Tsoukalas explains that eschatological embodiment and distinctive human identity are important for Torrance, whereas it is not for Rāmānuja because of the latter's "notion of the liberated *ātman*."[93] These eschatological differences notwithstanding, Tsoukalas asserts that within a Hindu framework Rāmānuja's theology of humanity preserves the belief in being "truly human" for the present life because "to be truly human is to fulfill one's *dharma* (duty [according to caste]) in both the vertical and the horizontal in the real ... world and in participation with the divine."[94] In providing such an interpretation, Tsoukalas is reading each theologian within their own respective frameworks.

Tsoukalas's brief work on Torrance's and Rāmānuja's understanding of theosis is a demonstration of his other more substantial works in comparative theology where he "labors intensely to understand" other theologies "through the reading of texts."[95] Tsoukalas's method is also practiced by Indian evangelical scholars of Hinduism and as such provides a helpful model for interreligious discourse.[96] While more can be said about Tsoukalas's work, it is important to notice the generative potential of Torrance's theology in a variety of discourses, including comparative theology. Future works on Torrance's theology vis-à-vis global theology can find in Tsoukalas (and in his use of Habets's work) a helpful model for fruitful interaction with themes and religious figures from the majority-world contexts.

---

92. Tsoukalas, "Theōsis," 58.

93. Tsoukalas, "Theōsis," 58.

94. Tsoukalas, "Theōsis," 58.

95. Tsoukalas, *Kṛṣṇa and Christ*, 3.

96. See John Arun Kumar, "Towards an Integral Theology in Interreligious Context: A Comparative Study of Theologies of a Christian and an Advaitin," in *Theological Formation for Christian Missions: A Festschrift for Ian Walter Payne*, ed. Roji Thomas George and Aruthuckal Varughese John (Bangalore: SAIACS Press, 2019), 133–55.

CONCLUSION

I have suggested some generative possibilities for a dialogue between Torrance and contemporary Indian evangelical theologies. While Torrance did not interact specifically with Indian theological concerns, he remains relevant for the Indian context because of his relation to the Scottish Protestant theological tradition that continues to impact India through its educational institutions, his indirect imprint he left on Indian theology because of his theological mentoring, and the fecundity of the theological themes he addressed not least since it has found conversation partners (in India and others writing about Indian theology) who find it useful in addressing and dialoguing with a diverse array of subjects, ranging from ethics to comparative theology. The future of Torrance scholarship from the majority-world context promises to highlight a host of other themes that will benefit from Torrance's insights and speak into areas within his own theology in helpful and constructive ways. As evangelicalism expands, pushing ever into new contexts and territories, it too will have to take up the task of global, comparative, and contextual theology. Torrance's work is already proving itself a worthy forerunner in this regard.

SELECT BIBLIOGRAPHY

—

Primary Sources[1]

Torrance, T. F. "Athanasius: A Reassessment of His Theology." *Abba Salama* 5 (1974): 171–87.

Torrance, T. F. *Atonement: The Person and Work of Christ*. Edited by Robert T. Walker. Milton Keynes: Paternoster; Downers Grove, IL: IVP Academic, 2009.

Torrance, T. F. *Calvin's Doctrine of Man*. London: Lutterworth, 1949.

Torrance, T. F. *Christian Theology and Scientific Culture*. New York: Oxford University Press, 1981.

Torrance, T. F. "Comments." Pages 302–3 in *The Sciences and Theology in the Twentieth Century*. Edited by A. R. Peacocke. London: Oriel Press, 1981.

Torrance, T. F. *Conflict and Agreement in the Church: Volume One: Order and Disorder*. London: Lutterworth, 1959.

Torrance, T. F. *Conflict and Agreement in the Church: Volume Two: The Ministry and the Sacraments of the Gospel*. London: Lutterworth, 1960.

Torrance, T. F. "Crisis in the Kirk." Pages 13–23 in *St Andrews Rock*. Edited by S. Lamont. London: Bellew, 1992.

Torrance, T. F. "Dialogue – Grace and Sacraments: The Roman Doctrine of Grace from the Point of View of Reformed Theology." Pages 46–77 in P. F. Fransen, *Intelligent Theology*. Vol 3. London: Darton, Longman & Todd, 1969.

Torrance, T. F. "Divine and Contingent Order." Pages 81–97 in *The Sciences and Theology in the Twentieth Century*. Edited by A. R. Peacocke. London: Oriel Press, 1981.

Torrance, T. F. *Divine and Contingent Order*. New York: Oxford University Press, 1981. Reprint, Edinburgh: T&T Clark, 1998.

Torrance, T. F. *Divine Meaning: Studies in Patristic Hermeneutics*. Edinburgh: T&T Clark, 1995.

---

1. The most complete bibliography of T. F. Torrance's works can be found on the website of the Thomas F. Torrance Theological Fellowship: https://tftorrance.org/bibliographies.

Torrance, T. F. "Doctrinal Consensus on Holy Communion: The Arnoldshain Theses." *Scottish Journal of Theology* 15 (1962): 1–35.

Torrance, T. F. "Einstein and God." *Reflections 1*, Princeton: Center for Theological Inquiry (Spring 1998): 2–15.

Torrance, T. F. "Foreword." Pages ix–xii in G. Del Re, *The Cosmic Dance: Science Discovers the Mysterious Harmony of the Universe*. Philadelphia: Templeton Foundation Press, 1999.

Torrance, T. F. "From John Knox to John McLeod Campbell: A Reading of Scottish Theology." Pages 1–28 in *Disruption to Diversity: Edinburgh Divinity 1846–1996*. Edited by D. F. Wright and G. D. Badcock. Edinburgh: T&T Clark, 1996.

Torrance, T. F. *God and Rationality*. London: Oxford University Press, 1971. Reprint, Eugene, OR: Wipf & Stock, 1997.

Torrance, T. F. "Hugh Ross Mackintosh: Theologian of the Cross." *Scottish Bulletin of Evangelical Theology* 5 (1987): 160–73.

Torrance, T. F. "Incarnation and Atonement: Theosis and Henosis in the Light of Modern Scientific Rejection of Dualism." *Society of Ordained Scientists*, Bulletin No. 7, Edgeware, Middlesex (Spring 1992): 8–20.

Torrance, T. F. *Incarnation: The Person and Life of Christ*. Edited by Robert T. Walker. Milton Keynes: Paternoster; Downers Grove, IL: IVP Academic, 2008.

Torrance, T. F. "Interview with Professor Thomas F. Torrance." Pages 42–54 in *Different Gospels*. Edited by Andrew Walker. London: Hodder & Stoughton, 1988.

Torrance, T. F. "Introduction." Pages ix–xxvii in *Theological Dialogue Between Orthodox and Reformed Churches*. Vol 1. Edited by T. F. Torrance. Edinburgh: Scottish Academic Press, 1985.

Torrance, T. F., ed. "Introduction." Pages ix–xxiv in *Theological Dialogue Between Orthodox and Reformed Churches*. Vol 2. Edinburgh: Scottish Academic Press, 1993.

Torrance, T. F. "Introduction." Pages xi–xxii in *The Incarnation: Ecumenical Studies in the Nicene-Constantinopolitan Creed A. D. 381*. Edited by T. F. Torrance. Edinburgh: Handsel Press, 1981.

Torrance, T. F. "Introduction to Karl Barth." Pages 7–54 in *Theology and Church, Shorter Writings 1920–1928*. London: SCM, 1962.

Torrance, T. F. "Intuitive and Abstractive Knowledge: From Duns Scotus to Calvin." Pages 291–305 in *De Doctrina Ioannis Duns Scoti. Congressus Scotisticus Internationalis. Studia Scholastico-Scotistica 5*. Edited by C. Balic. Rome: Societas Internationalis Scotistica, 1968.

Torrance, T. F. "John Philoponos of Alexandria, Sixth Century Christian Physicist."
    Pages 261–65 in *Texts and Studies*. Vol 2. London: Thyateira House, 1983.

Torrance, T. F. *Juridical Law and Physical Law: Toward a Realist Foundation for Human
    Law*. Edinburgh: Scottish Academic Press, 1982. Reprint, Eugene, OR: Wipf
    & Stock, 1997.

Torrance, T. F. "Karl Barth and Patristic Theology." Pages 215–39 in *Theology Beyond
    Christendom: Essays on the Centenary of the Birth of Karl Barth May 10, 1986*.
    Edited by J. Thompson. Allison Park, PA: Pickwick, 1986.

Torrance, T. F. "Karl Barth and the Latin Heresy." *Scottish Journal of Theology*, 39/4
    (1986): 461–82.

Torrance, T. F. *Karl Barth: An Introduction to His Early Theology 1910–1931*. Reprint,
    Edinburgh: T&T Clark, 2000.

Torrance, T. F. *Karl Barth: Biblical and Evangelical Theologian*. Edinburgh: T&T Clark,
    1990.

Torrance, T. F. *Kingdom and Church: A Study in the Theology of the Reformation*.
    Edinburgh: Oliver & Boyd, 1956.

Torrance, T. F. "Memoranda on Orthodox/Reformed Relations." Pages 3–18 in
    Theological Dialogue Between Orthodox and Reformed Churches. Vol 1. Edited
    by T. F. Torrance. Edinburgh: Scottish Academic Press, 1985.

Torrance, T. F. "My Interaction with Karl Barth." Pages 52–64 in *How Karl Barth
    Changed My Mind*. Edited by D. K. McKim. Grand Rapids: Eerdmans, 1986.

Torrance, T. F. "Newton, Einstein and Scientific Theology." *Religious Studies* 8 (1971):
    233–50.

Torrance, T. F. "Phusikos Kai Theologikos Logos, St Paul and Athenagoras at
    Athens." *Scottish Journal of Theology* 41 (1988): 11–26.

Torrance, T. F. "Preaching Jesus Christ." Pages 23–32 in *A Passion for Christ: Vision
    that Ignites Ministry*. Edited by G. Dawson and J. Stein. Edinburgh: The
    Handsel Press, 1999.

Torrance, T. F. *Preaching Christ Today*. Grand Rapids: Eerdmans, 1994.

Torrance, T. F. "Predestination in Christ." *Evangelical Quarterly* 13 (1941): 108–41.

Torrance, T. F. *Reality and Evangelical Theology*. Philadelphia: Westminster Press,
    1982. Reprint, Downers Grove, IL: InterVarsity Press, 1999.

Torrance, T. F. *Reality and Scientific Theology*. Edinburgh: Scottish Academic Press,
    1985.

Torrance, T. F. "Realism and Openness in Scientific Inquiry." *Zygon* 23/2 (June 1988):
    159–69.

Torrance, T. F. "Review of B. B. Warfield, The Inspiration and Authority of the Bible." *Scottish Journal of Theology* 7 (1954): 104–8.

Torrance, T. F. "Review of E. D. Willis, *Calvin's Catholic Christology*." *Scottish Journal of Theology* 23 (1970): 92–94.

Torrance, T. F. "Review of Leanne Van Dyk, *The Desire of Divine Love: John McLeod Campbell's Doctrine of the Atonement*." *Scottish Journal of Theology* 49/1 (1996): 125–27.

Torrance, T. F. *Royal Priesthood: A Theology of Ordained Ministry*. 2nd ed. London: Continuum T&T Clark, 1993.

Torrance, T. F. *Royal Priesthood: Scottish Journal of Theology: Occasional Papers* No. 3. Edinburgh: Oliver and Boyd, 1955.

Torrance, T. F. *Scottish Theology from John Knox to John McLeod Campbell*. Edinburgh: T&T Clark, 1996.

Torrance, T. F. *Space, Time and Incarnation*. Edinburgh: T&T Clark, 1997.

Torrance, T. F. *Space, Time and Resurrection*. Edinburgh: T&T Clark, 1998.

Torrance, T. F. "spiritus Creator." In *Le Traité sur le Saint-Espirit de Saint Basile*. Edited by L. Visher. Taizé: Presses de Taizé, 1969. Reprint: *Verbum Caro* 23 (1969): 63–85.

Torrance, T. F. "The Atonement and the Oneness of the Church." *Scottish Journal of Theology* 7/3 (1954): 245–69.

Torrance, T. F. "The Atonement: The Singularity of Christ and the Finality of the Cross; The Atonement and the Moral Order." Pages 225–56 in *Universalism and the Doctrine of Hell*. Edited by N. M de S. Cameron. Carlisle: Paternoster, 1992; Grand Rapids: Baker, 1992.

Torrance, T. F. "The Atoning Obedience of Christ." *Moravian Theological Seminary Bulletin* (Fall 1959): 65–81.

Torrance, T. F. *The Being and Nature of the Unborn Child*. Edinburgh: Handsel Press for the Scottish Order of Christian Unity, 2000.

Torrance, T. F. *The Biblical Doctrine of Baptism*. Edinburgh: The Saint Andrew Press, 1958.

Torrance. T. F. "The Doctrine of the Holy Trinity According to St. Athanasius." *Anglican Theological Review* 71 (Fall 1989): 395–405.

Torrance, T. F. "The Christ Who Loves Me." Pages 9–20 in *A Passion for Christ: Vision that Ignites Ministry*. Edited by G. Dawson and J. Stein. Edinburgh: The Handsel Press, 1999.

Torrance, T. F. *The Christian Doctrine of God: One Being Three Persons*. Edinburgh: T&T Clark, 1996.

Torrance, T. F. "The Christian Apprehension of God the Father." Pages 120-43 in *Speaking the Christian God: The Holy Trinity and the Challenge of Feminism*. Edited by A. F. Kimel, Grand Rapids: Eerdmans, 1992.

Torrance, T. F. *The Christian Frame of Mind: Order and Openness in Theology and Natural Science*. Edinburgh: Handsel Press, 1985.

Torrance, T. F. "The Concept of Order in Theology and Science." *The Princeton Seminary Bulletin* 5/2 (1984): 130-39. [Previously published in *The Month*, Second New Series 16 (1983): 401-4.

Torrance, T. F. "The Deposit of Faith." *Scottish Journal of Theology* 36/1 (1983): 1-28.

Torrance, T. F. "The Distinctive Character of the Reformed Tradition." Pages 2-15 in *Incarnational Ministry: Essays in Honor of Ray S. Anderson*. Edited by C. D. Kettler and T. H. Speidell. Colorado Springs: Helmers and Howard, 1990.

Torrance, T. F. *The Doctrine of Grace in the Apostolic Fathers*. Thesis for Basel University. Edinburgh: Oliver and Boyd, 1948.

Torrance, T. F. *The Doctrine of Jesus Christ: Auburn Lectures 1938-39*. Eugene, OR: Wipf & Stock, 2002.

Torrance, T. F. "The Doctrine of Order." *Church Quarterly Review* 160 (1959): 21-36. [ET of "La doctrine de l"ordre." *Revue d'Histoire et de Philosophie Religieuses* 38 (1958): 129-42.]

Torrance, T. F. "The Framework of Belief." Pages 1-27 in *Belief in Science and in Christian Life: The Relevance of Michael Polanyi's Thought for Christian Faith and Life*. Edited by T. F. Torrance. Edinburgh: Handsel, 1980.

Torrance, T. F. "The Goodness and Dignity of Man in the Christian Tradition." *Modern Theology* 4/4 (1988): 309-22.

Torrance, T. F. *The Ground and Grammar of Theology*. Charlottesville: University of Virginia Press, 1980. Edinburgh: T&T Clark, 2001.

Torrance, T. F. *The Hermeneutics of John Calvin*. Monograph Supplements to the Scottish Journal of Theology. Edinburgh: Scottish Academic Press, 1988.

Torrance, T. F., ed. *The Incarnation: Ecumenical Studies in the Nicene-Constantinopolitan Creed A. D. 381*. Edinburgh: Handsel Press, 1981.

Torrance, T. F. *The Mediation of Christ*. New enlarged edition. Edinburgh: T&T Clark, 1992.

Torrance, T. F. *The Ministry of Women*. Edinburgh: Handsel, 1992.

Torrance, T. F. "The Ministry of Women." Pages 269–84 in *The Call to Serve: Biblical and Theological Perspectives on Ministry in Honour of Bishop Penny Jamieson.* Edited by D. A. Campbell. Sheffield: Academic Press, 1996.

Torrance, T. F. "The Place of Michael Polanyi in the Modern Philosophy of Science." *Ethics in Science and Medicine* 7 (1980): 57–95.

Torrance, T. F. "The Place of the Humanity of Christ in the Sacramental Life of the Church." *Church Service Society Annual* 26 (1956): 3–10.

Torrance, T. F. "The Problem of Natural Theology in the Thought of Karl Barth." *Religious Studies* 6 (1970): 121–35.

Torrance, T. F. "The Reconciliation of Mind: A Theological Meditation upon the Teaching of St. Paul." Pages 196–204 in *Theology in the Service of the Church: Essays in Honor of Thomas W. Gillespie.* Edited by W. M. Alston. Grand Rapids: Eerdmans, 2000.

Torrance, T. F. "The Relation of the Incarnation to Space in Nicene Theology." Pages 43–73 in *The Ecumenical World of Orthodox Civilisation. III. Russia and Orthodoxy: Essays in Honor of Georges Florovsky.* Edited by A. Blane. The Hague: Mouton, 1973.

Torrance, T. F. "The Relevance of Orthodoxy." Pages 9–19 in *The Relevancy of Orthodoxy.* Edited by J. B. Logan. Stirling: The Drummond Press, 1970.

Torrance, T. F. *The School of Faith: The Catechisms of the Reformed Church.* London: James Clarke, 1959.

Torrance, T. F. *The Soul and Person of the Unborn Child.* Edinburgh: Handsel Press for the Scottish Order of Christian Unity, 1999.

Torrance, T. F. "The Soul and Person in Theological Perspective." Pages 103–18 in *Religion, Reason, and the Self: Essays in Honour of Hywel D. Lewis.* Edited by S. R. Sutherland and T. A. Roberts. Cardiff: University of Wales Press, 1989.

Torrance, T. F. "'The Substance of the Faith': A Clarification of the Concept in the Church of Scotland." *Scottish Journal of Theology* 36/3 (1983): 327–38.

Torrance, T. F. "The Transcendental Role of Wisdom in Science." Pages 131–49 in *Facets of Faith and Science: Vol 1: Historiography and Modes of Interaction.* Edited by J. van der Meer. Lanham, MD: University Press of America, 1996.

Torrance, T. F. *The Trinitarian Faith: The Evangelical Theology of the Ancient Catholic Church.* 1988. Edinburgh: T&T Clark, 1995.

Torrance, T. F. "The Trinitarian Foundation and Character of Faith and of Authority in the Church." Pages 79–120 in *Theological Dialogue Between Orthodox and Reformed Churches.* Vol 1. Edited by T. F. Torrance. Edinburgh:

Scottish Academic Press, 1985.

Torrance, T. F. "The Triunity of God in the Nicene Theology of the Fourth Century."
   Pages 3–37 in *Theological Dialogue Between Orthodox and Reformed Churches.*
   Vol 2. Edited by T. F. Torrance, Edinburgh: Scottish Academic Press, 1993.

Torrance, T. F. *The Uniqueness of Divine Revelation and the Authority of the Scriptures.*
   Edinburgh: Rutherford House, 1995.

Torrance, T. F. *Theological and Natural Science.* Eugene, OR: Wipf & Stock, 2002.

Torrance, T. F., ed. *Theological Dialogue Between Orthodox and Reformed Churches.* Vol
   1. Edinburgh: Scottish Academic Press, 1985.

Torrance, T. F., ed. *Theological Dialogue Between Orthodox and Reformed Churches.* Vol
   2. Edinburgh: Scottish Academic Press, 1993.

Torrance, T. F. *Theology in Reconciliation: Essays Towards Evangelical and Catholic
   Unity in East and West.* London: Geoffrey Chapman, 1975. Reprint, Eugene,
   OR: Wipf & Stock, 1997.

Torrance, T. F. *Theology in Reconstruction.* Grand Rapids: Eerdmans, 1965.

Torrance, T. F. "Theological Realism." Pages 169–96 in *The Philosophical Frontiers
   of Christian Theology: Essays Presented to D. M. MacKinnon.* Edited by B.
   Hebblethwaite and S. Sutherland. Cambridge: Cambridge University Press,
   1982.

Torrance, T. F. *Theological Science.* London: Oxford University Press, 1969. Reprint,
   Edinburgh: T&T Clark, 1996.

Torrance, T. F. "Thomas Torrance Responds." Pages 303–40 in *The Promise of
   Trinitarian Theology: Theologians in Dialogue with T.F. Torrance.* Edited by E.
   M. Colyer. Lanham, MD: Rowman & Littlefield, 2001.

Torrance, T. F. *Transformation and Convergence in the Frame of Knowledge:
   Explorations in the Interrelations of Scientific and Theological Enterprise.*
   Grand Rapids: Eerdmans, 1984.

Torrance, T. F. *Trinitarian Perspectives: Toward Doctrinal Agreement.* Edinburgh: T&T
   Clark, 1994.

Torrance, T. F. "Truth and Authority: Theses on Truth." *Irish Theological Quarterly*
   39 (1972): 215–42.

Torrance, T. F. "Ultimate Beliefs and the Scientific Revolution." *Cross Currents* 30
   (1980): 129–49.

Torrance, T. F. "Ultimate and Penultimate Beliefs in Science." Pages 151–76 in *Facets
   of Faith and Science: Vol 1: Historiography and Modes of Interaction.* Edited by J.
   van der Meer. Lanham, MD: University Press of America, 1996.

Torrance, T. F. "Universalism or Election?" *Scottish Journal of theology* 2 (1949): 310–18.

Torrance, T. F. *When Christ Comes and Comes Again.* London: Hodder and Stoughton, 1957.

Torrance, T. F. *Word of the Gospel.* Christian Journals, 1984.

Torrance, T. F. et al. "Working Paper on the Holy Trinity." Pages 109–21 in *Theological Dialogue Between Orthodox and Reformed Churches.* Vol 2. Edited by T. F. Torrance, Edinburgh: Scottish Academic Press, 1993.

Select Secondary Sources

Achtemeier, P. M. "Natural Science and Christian Faith in the Thought of T. F. Torrance." Pages 269–302 in *The Promise of Trinitarian Theology: Theologians in Dialogue with T. F. Torrance.* Edited by E. M. Colyer. Lanham, MD: Rowman & Littlefield, 2001.

Achtemeier, P. M. "The Truth of Tradition: Critical Realism in the Thought of Alasdair MacIntyre and T. F. Torrance." *Scottish Journal of Theology* 47/3 (1996): 355–74.

Achtner, W. *Physik, Mystik und Christentum: eine Darstellung und Diskussion der natèurlichen Theologie bei T. F. Torrance.* Frankfurt am Main: P. Lang, 1991.

Anderson, R. S. "Reading T. F. Torrance as a Practical Theologian." Pages 161–83 in *The Promise of Trinitarian Theology: Theologians in Dialogue with T. F. Torrance.* Edited by E. M. Colyer. Lanham, MD: Rowman & Littlefield, 2001.

Anderson, R. S. "Real Presence Hermeneutics: Reflections on Wainwright, Thielicke, and Torrance." *Theological Students Fellowship Bulletin* 6/2 (1982): 5–7.

Anderson, R. S. *Historical Transcendence and the Reality of God: A Christological Critique.* Grand Rapids: Eerdmans, 1975.

Apczynski, J. V. "Torrance on Polanyi and Polanyi on God: Comments on Weightman's Criticisms—A Review Essay." *Tradition & Discovery: The Polanyi Society Periodical* 24/1 (1997–1998): 32–34.

Avis, P. *Christians in Communion.* London: Geoffrey Chapman Mowbray, 1990.

Bauman, M. *Roundtable: Conversations with European Theologians.* Grand Rapids: Baker, 1990.

Burgess, A. *The Ascension in Karl Barth.* London: Ashgate, 2004.

Chiarot, Kevin. *The Unassumed Is the Unhealed: The Humanity of Christ in the Christology of T. F. Torrance.* Eugene, OR: Pickwick, 2013.

Clayton, P. *Explanation from Physics to Theology*. New Haven & London: Yale University Press, 1989.

Colyer, E. M. "A Scientific Theological Method." Pages 205-237 in *The Promise of Trinitarian Theology: Theologians in Dialogue with T.F. Torrance*. Edited by E. M. Colyer. Lanham, MD: Rowman & Littlefield, 2001.

Colyer, E. M. *How To Read T. F. Torrance: Understanding his Trinitarian and Scientific Theology*. Downers Grove, IL: InterVarsity Press, 2001.

Colyer, E. M. *The Nature of Doctrine in T.F. Torrance's Theology*. Eugene, OR: Wipf & Stock, 2001.

Colyer, E. M., ed. *The Promise of Trinitarian Theology: Theologians in Dialogue with T. F. Torrance*. Lanham, MD: Rowman & Littlefield, 2001.

Colyer, E. M. "Thomas F. Torrance." Pages 460-67 in *A New Handbook of Christian Theologians*. Edited by D. W. Musser and J. L. Price. Nashville: Abingdon, 1996.

Colyer, E. M. "Thomas F. Torrance on the Holy Spirit." *Word and World* 23/2 (Spring 2003): 160-67.

Comstock, W. R. "Book Review: The Ground and Grammar of Theology." *Journal of the American Academy of Religion* 52 (1984): 190-91.

Dawson, G., and Stein, J., eds. *A Passion for Christ: Vision that Ignites Ministry*. Edinburgh: The Handsel Press, 1999.

Deddo, G. W. "The Holy Spirit in T.F. Torrance's Theology." Pages 81-114 in *The Promise of Trinitarian Theology: Theologians in Dialogue with T. F. Torrance*. Edited by E. M. Colyer. Lanham, MD: Rowman & Littlefield, 2001.

Del Colle, R. "'Person' and 'Being' in John Zizioulas' Trinitarian Theology: Conversations with Thomas F. Torrance and Thomas Aquinas." *Scottish Journal of Theology* 54/1 (2001): 70-86.

Dragas, G. D. "Professor T. F. Torrance on his 80th Birthday." *Church and Theology* (Athens) 12 (1993): 566-76.

Dragas, D. G. "The Significance for the Church of T. F. Torrance's Election as Moderator of the General Assembly of the Church of Scotland." *Ekklesiastikos Pharos* 58 (1976): 214-26.

Edwards. D. L. *The British Churches to the Future*. London: SCM Press 1973.

Flett, E. G. "Priests of Creation, Mediators of Order: The Human Person as a Cultural Being in T. F. Torrance's Theological Anthropology." *Scottish Journal of Theology* 58/2 (2005): 161-83.

Ford, D. F. "Review of T. F. Torrance, The Trinitarian Faith: The Evangelical Theology of the Ancient Catholic Church." *Scottish Journal of Theology* 43/2 (1990): 263–67.

Ford, D. F. "Review of Thomas F. Torrance, *Reality and Scientific Theology*." *Scottish Journal of Theology* 41/2 (July 1988): 273–80.

Fransen, P. F. "Dialogue—Grace and Sacraments: Reflections on the Conditions and Possibility of an Ecumenical Dialogue." Pages 78–100 in *Intelligent Theology*. Vol 3. London: Darton, Longman & Todd, 1969.

Grenz, S. J. *Rediscovering the Triune God: The Trinity in Contemporary Theology*. Minneapolis: Fortress, 2004.

Gunton, C. "Being and Person: T. F. Torrance's Doctrine of God." Pages 115–37 in *The Promise of Trinitarian Theology: Theologians in Dialogue with T.F. Torrance*. Edited by E. M. Colyer. Lanham, MD: Rowman & Littlefield, 2001.

Guthridge, J. *The Christology of T. F. Torrance: Revelation and Reconciliation in Christ*. Excerpta ex dissertation ad Lauream. Melbourne: Pontificia Universitas Gregoriana, 1967.

Habets, M., Paul D. Molnar. *T&T Clark Handbook of Thomas F. Torrance*. London: Bloomsbury T&T Clark, 2020.

Habets, M. "'The Essence of Evangelical Theology.' Critical Introduction to Thomas F. Torrance, *The Trinitarian Faith: The Evangelical Theology of the Ancient Catholic Church*." Pages vii–xxxii in Thomas F. Torrance, *The Trinitarian Faith: The Evangelical Theology of the Ancient Catholic Church* Cornerstones Series. London: T&T Clark, 2016.

Habets, M. "The Fallen Humanity of Christ. A Pneumatological Clarification of the Theology of Thomas F. Torrance." *Participatio* 5 (2015): 18–44.

Habets, M. *Theology in Transposition: A Constructive Appraisal of T. F. Torrance*. Minneapolis: Fortress, 2013.

Habets, M. "Theological Interpretation of Scripture in Sermonic Mode: The Case of T. F. Torrance." Pages 43–69 in *Ears that Hear: Explorations in Theological Interpretation of the Bible*. Edited by Joel Green and Tim Meadowcroft. Sheffield: Sheffield Phoenix, 2013.

Habets, M. *Theosis in the Theology of Thomas Torrance*. Ashgate New Critical Thinking in Religion, Theology and Biblical Studies. Farnham: Ashgate, 2009.

Habets, M. "The Doctrine of Election in Evangelical Calvinism: T. F. Torrance as a Case Study." *Irish Theological Quarterly* 73, no. 3-4 (2008): 334–54.

Hardy, D. W. "Theology and Natural Science." Pages 647-68 in *The Modern Theologians*. Edited by D. W. Hardy. Oxford: Blackwell, 1997.

Hardy, D. W. "Thomas F. Torrance." Pages 71-91 in *The Modern Theologians: An Introduction*. Vol 1. Edited by D. F. Ford. Oxford: Blackwell, 1989.

Harvey, N. P. "Frames of Reference for the Resurrection [Pannenberg and Torrance]." *Scottish Journal of Theology* 42/3 (1989): 335-39.

Hebblethwaite, B. "T. F. Torrance: An Intellectual Biography, A Review." *Scottish Journal of Theology* 53/2 (2000): 239-242.

Heltzel, P. "Thomas Torrance." In *Dictionary of Modern Western Theology*. http://people.bu.edu/wwildman/WeirdWildWeb/courses/mwt/dictionary/mwt_themes785.

Henry, C. F. H. *God, Revelation and Authority*. Vol 3. Waco, TX: Word, 1980.

Heron, A. I. C. "T. F. Torrance In Relation to Reformed Theology." Pages 31-49 in *The Promise of Trinitarian Theology: Theologians in Dialogue with T.F. Torrance*. Edited by E. M. Colyer. Lanham, MD: Rowman & Littlefield, 2001.

Heron, A. I. C. *A Century of Protestant Theology*. Philadelphia: Westminster, 1980.

Hesselink, I. J. "A Pilgrimage in the School of Christ—An Interview with T. F. Torrance." *Reformed Review* 38/1 (1984): 49-64.

Hunsinger, G. "The Dimension of Depth: Thomas F. Torrance on the Sacraments of Baptism and the Lord's Supper." *Scottish Journal of Theology* 54/2 (2001): 155-76.

Hunsinger, G. "The Dimension of Depth: Thomas F. Torrance on the Sacraments." Pages 139-60 in *The Promise of Trinitarian Theology: Theologians in Dialogue with T.F. Torrance*. Edited by E. Colyer. Lanham, MD: Rowman & Littlefield, 2001.

Hunsinger, G. *Disruptive Grace: Studies in the Theology of Karl Barth*. Grand Rapids: Eerdmans, 2000.

Kaiser, C. B. "Humanity in an Intelligible Cosmos." Pages 239-67 in *The Promise of Trinitarian Theology: Theologians in Dialogue with T. F. Torrance*. Edited by E. Colyer. Lanham, MD: Rowman & Littlefield, 2001.

Kang, Phee Seng. "The Epistemological Significance of Ὁμοοσὺν in the Theology of Thomas F. Torrance." *Scottish Journal of Theology* 45/3 (1992): 341-66.

Kernohan, R. D. "Tom Torrance: The Man and the Reputation." *Life and Work* 32/5 (May 1976): 14-16.

Kettler, C. D. *The Vicarious Humanity of Christ and the Reality of Salvation*. Lanham, MD: University Press of America, 1991.

Klinefelter, D. S. "God and Rationality: A Critique of the Theology of Thomas F. Torrance." *Journal of Religion* 53 (1973): 117–35.

Kruger, C. B. "The Doctrine of the Knowledge of God in the Theology of T.F. Torrance: Sharing in the Son's Communion with the Father in the Spirit." *Scottish Journal of Theology* 43/3 (1990): 366–89.

Langford, T. A. "T. F. Torrance's *Theological Science*: A Reaction." *Scottish Journal of Theology* 25/2 (May 1972): 155–70.

Lee, K. W. *Living in Union With Christ: The Practical Theology of Thomas F. Torrance.* Issues in Systematic Theology. Vol 11. New York; Bern: Lang, 2003.

Louth, A. "Science and Mystery." Pages 45–72 in *Discerning the Mystery: An Essay on the Nature of Theology.* Oxford: Clarendon, 1983.

Luoma, T. *Incarnation and Physics: Natural Science in the Theology of Thomas F. Torrance.* An American Academy of Religion Book. New York: Oxford University Press, 2002.

McCall, T. "Ronald Thiemann, Thomas Torrance and Epistemological Doctrines of Revelation." *International Journal of Systematic Theology* 6/2 (April 2004): 148–68.

McGrath, A. E. "Profile: Thomas F. Torrance." *Epworth Review* 27/3 (2000): 10–15.

McGrath, A. E. *T. F. Torrance: An Intellectual Biography.* Edinburgh: T&T Clark, 1999.

McKenna, J. "Review of Thomas Torrance's *Theological and Natural Science.*" Metanexus: The online Forum on Religion and Science. https://metanexus.net/.

McKinney, R. W. A., ed. *Creation, Christ and Culture: Studies in Honour of T. F. Torrance.* Edinburgh: T&T Clark, 1976.

Macleod, D. "Dr. T. F. Torrance and Scottish Theology: A Review Article [*Scottish Theology from John Knox to John McLeod Campbell*, 1996]." *Evangelical Quarterly* 72/1 (Jan 2000): 57–72.

Macleod, D. *Jesus is Lord: Christology Yesterday and Today.* Great Britain: Mentor, 2000.

Macleod, D. *The Person of Christ.* Contours of Christian Theology. Leicester: Inter-Varsity Press, 1998.

Macleod, D. "Christology." Pages 172–77 in *Dictionary of Scottish History and Theology.* Edited by D. F. Wright, D. C. Lachman, and D. E. Meek. Edinburgh: T&T Clark, 1993.

McPake, J. L. "The Reception of the Theology of Karl Barth in Scotland [diss. abstract, Edinburgh, 1994]." *Tyndale Bulletin* 47/1 (May 1996): 181–84.

Marley, A. G. *T. F. Torrance: The Rejection of Dualism*. Vol 4. Nutshell Series. Edinburgh: Handsel Press, 1992.

Martin, R. K. *The Incarnate Ground of Christian Faith: Toward a Christian Theological Epistemology for the Educational Ministry of the Church*. Lanham, MD: University Press of America, 1998.

Mascall, E. L. *Theology and the Gospel of Christ: An Essay in Reorientation*. London: SPCK, 1977.

Molnar, P. D. *Freedom, Necessity, and the Knowledge of God in Conversation with Karl Barth and Thomas F. Torrance*. London: T&T Clark, 2022.

Molnar, P. D. "Incarnation, Resurrection and the Doctrine of the Trinity: A Comparison of Thomas F. Torrance and Roger Haight." *International Journal of Systematic Theology* 5/2, (2003): 147–67.

Molnar, P. D. *Divine Freedom and the Doctrine of the Immanent Trinity: in Dialogue with Karl Barth and Contemporary Theology*. London: T&T Clark, 2002.

Molnar, P. D. "God's Self-communication in Christ: A Comparison of Thomas F. Torrance and Karl Rahner." *Scottish Journal of Theology* 50/3 (1997): 288–20.

Morrison, J. D. "Heidegger, Correspondence Truth and the Realist Theology of Thomas Forsyth Torrance." *Evangelical Quarterly* 69/2 (1997): 139–55.

Morrison, J. D. *Knowledge of the Self-Revealing God in the Thought of Thomas Forsyth Torrance*. Vol 2. Issues in Systematic Theology. New York: Lang, 1997.

Morrison, J. D. "Thomas Forsyth Torrance's Critique of Evangelical (Protestant) Orthodoxy." *Evangelical Quarterly* 67/1 (1995): 53–69.

Muller, R. A. "The Barth Legacy: New Athanasius or Origen Redivivus? A Response to T. F. Torrance." *Thomist* 54 (1990): 673–04.

Neidhardt, W. J. "Thomas F. Torrance's Integration of Judeo-Christian Theology and Natural Science: Some Key Themes." *Perspectives on Science and Christian Faith* 41/2 (1989): 87–98.

Newell, R. "Torrance, Thomas Forsyth." Pages 549–51 in *Dictionary of Historical Theology*. Edited by T. Hart. Grand Rapids: Eerdmans, 2000.

Norris, F. W. "Mathematics, Physics and Religion: A Need for Candor and Rigor." *Scottish Journal of Theology* 37/1 (March 1984): 457–70.

O"Donoghue, N. D. "Creation and Participation." Pages 135–48 in *Creation, Christ and Culture: Studies in Honour of T. F. Torrance*. Edited by R. W. A. McKinney. Edinburgh: T&T Clark, 1976.

Palma, R. J. "Torrance, Thomas F." *Encyclopedia of the Reformed Faith*. Louisville: Westminster John Knox, 1983.

Palma, R. J. "Thomas F. Torrance's Reformed Theology." *Reformed Review* 38/1 (Autumn 1984): 2–46.

Peters, T. "Theology Through Philosophy." Pages 252–85 in *The Modern Theologians*. Edited by D.W. Hardy. Oxford: Blackwell, 1997.

Polkinghorne, J. C. "Review of T. F. Torrance, *Reality and Scientific Theology*." *Journal of Theological Studies* 37/2 (1986): 679–82.

Pratz, G. "The Relationship Between Incarnation and Atonement in the Theology of Thomas F. Torrance." *Journal for Christian Theological Research*, 3/2 (1998). http://apu.edu/~CTRF/articles/1998_articles/pratz.html.

Prosch, H. *Michael Polanyi*. New York: State University of New York, 1986.

Purves, A. "The Christology of Thomas F. Torrance." Pages 51–80 in *The Promise of Trinitarian Theology: Theologians in Dialogue with T.F. Torrance*. Edited by E. M. Colyer. Lanham, MD: Rowman & Littlefield, 2001.

Redding, G. *Prayer and the Priesthood of Christ in the Reformed Tradition*. Edinburgh: T&T Clark, 2003.

Rehnman, S. "Barthian Epigoni: Thomas F. Torrance's Barth-Reception." *Westminster Theological Journal* 60/2 (Fall 1998): 271–96.

Richardson, K. A. "Revelation, Scripture, and Mystical Apprehension of Divine Knowledge." Pages 185–203 in *The Promise of Trinitarian Theology: Theologians in Dialogue with T.F. Torrance*. Edited by E. M. Colyer. Lanham, MD: Rowman & Littlefield, 2001.

Richardson, K. A. "The Contemporary Renewal of Trinitarian Theology: Possibilities of Convergence in the Doctrine of God." Pages 183–92, 289–91 in *The Nature of Confession*. Edited by T. R. Phillips and D. L. Ockholm. Downers Grove, IL: InterVarsity Press, 1996.

Ritchie, B. *T. F. Torrance in Recollection and Reappraisal*. Eugene, OR: Wipf & Stock, 2021.

Rodd, C. S. "The Most Significant Theologian [T. F. Torrance: An Intellectual Biography, by A. E. McGrath, 1999; review essay]." *Expository Times* 111/7 (April 2000): 252.

Schubert, F. D. "Thomas F. Torrance: The Case for a Theological Science." *Encounter* 45/2 (Spring 1984): 123–37.

Shepherd, V. "Thomas F Torrance and the *Homoousion* of the Holy Spirit." A paper delivered at the annual meeting of the Thomas Torrance Theological Fellowship (November 17, 2006). http://www.tftorrance.org/meetings/Homoousion-of-the-Holy-Spirit.pdf.

Sherrard, J. H. *T. F. Torrance as Missional Theologian: The Ascended Christ and the Ministry of the Church.* Downers Grove, IL: IVP Academic, 2021.

Shuster, M. "What is Truth: An Exploration of Thomas F. Torrance's Epistemology." *Studia Biblica et Theologica* 3 (1973): 50-56.

Siemens, D. F. "Two Problems with Torrance [reply to W. J. Neidhardt, 41 (1989): 87-98]." *Perspectives on Science and Christian Faith* 43/2 (1991): 112-13.

Smail, T. A. "Review of *the Mediation of Christ*, by Thomas F. Torrance." *Scottish Journal of theology* 38 (1985): 241-44.

Spjuth, R. *Creation, Contingency and Divine Presence: In the Theologies of Thomas F. Torrance and Eberhard Jüngel.* Lund: Lund University Press, 1995.

Thiemann, R. *Revelation and Theology: The Gospel as Narrated Promise.* Notre Dame: University of Notre Dame Press, 1985.

Torrance, D. W. "Thomas Forsyth Torrance: Minister of the Gospel, Pastor, and Evangelical Theologian." Pages 1-30 in *The Promise of Trinitarian Theology: Theologians in Dialogue with T. F. Torrance.* Edited by E. M. Colyer. Lanham, MD: Rowman & Littlefield, 2001.

Torrance, I. R. "A Bibliography of the Writings of Thomas F Torrance 1941-1989." *Scottish Journal of Theology* 43/2 (1990): 225-62.

Van Kuiken, E. Jerome. *Christ's Humanity in Current and Ancient Controversy: Fallen or Not?* London: T&T Clark, 2017.

Walker, R. T. "Thomas F. Torrance." Pages 197-219 in *British Evangelical Theologians of the Twentieth Century: An Enduring Legacy.* Edited by Thomas A. Noble and Jason S. Sexton. London: Apollos, 2022.

Weightman, C. "Polanyi and Mathematics, Torrance and Philosophy of Science: A Response to Apczynski's Review." *Tradition & Discovery: The Polanyi Society Periodical* 24/1 (1997-1998): 35-38.

Weightman, C. *Theology in a Polanyian Universe: The Theology of Thomas Torrance.* New York: Lang, 1994.

Wigley, S. D. "Karl Barth on St. Anselm: The Influence of Anselm's 'Theological Scheme' on T. F. Torrance and Eberhard Jüngel." *Scottish Journal of Theology* 46/1 (1993): 79-97.

Woznicki, C. *T. F. Torrance's Christological Anthropology: Discerning Humanity in Christ.* Routledge New Critical Thinking in Religion, Theology and Biblical Studies. London: Routledge, 2022.

Yeung, J. H-K. *Being and Knowing: An Examination of T. F. Torrance's Christological Science.* Jian Dao Dissertation Series 3. Theology and Culture 1. Hong Kong: China Alliance Press, 1996.

SUBJECT INDEX

—

NAME INDEX

—

SCRIPTURE INDEX

—

Old Testament

New Testament

STUDIES IN HISTORICAL
& SYSTEMATIC THEOLOGY

Studies in Historical and Systematic Theology is a peer-
reviewed series of contemporary monographs exploring
key figures, themes, and issues in historical and systematic
theology from an evangelical perspective.

—

Learn more at LexhamPress.com/SHST